For Franck Vimelli,
who is in the heritage
of Roman law and
civilization,
with the friendship
of
Giuseppe F. _____

The New Map of the World

The New Map of the World

THE POETIC PHILOSOPHY
OF GIAMBATTISTA VICO

Giuseppe Mazzotta

PRINCETON UNIVERSITY PRESS

PRINCETON, NEW JERSEY

Copyright © 1999 by Princeton University Press
Published by Princeton University Press, 41 William Street,
Princeton, New Jersey 08540
In the United Kingdom: Princeton University Press,
Chichester, West Sussex

Library of Congress Cataloging-in-Publication Data

Mazzotta, Giuseppe, 1942–
The new map of the world : the poetic philosophy of Giambattista
Vico / by Giuseppe Mazzotta.
p. cm.
Includes bibliographical references and index.
1. Vico, Giambattista, 1668–1744. I. Title.
B3583.M39 1999 195—dc21 98-26421 CIP

ISBN 0-691-00180-4 (CL : alk. paper)

This book has been composed in Galliard

Princeton University Press books are printed
on acid-free paper and meet the guidelines
for permanence and durability of the Committee
on Production Guidelines for Book Longevity
of the Council on Library Resources

http://pup.princeton.edu

Printed in the United States of America

1 3 5 7 9 10 8 6 4 2

To my brother Guido

CONTENTS

PREFACE

IN THE TWENTIETH century the work of Giambattista Vico has been the focus of sustained attention from a variety of disciplines. Though a text such as the *New Science* has never really sunk into oblivion, renewed interest in Vico's thought was triggered by Benedetto Croce's *La Filosofia di G. B. Vico*, originally published in 1911. Croce's monograph provided piecemeal clarification of the entire range of Vico's speculations and laid the foundation for the interpretive debates that inevitably were to come.

Croce characterizes the central questions of Vico's thought with the aim of casting Vico as a legitimate interlocutor in the philosophical conversation of modernity. He isolates a number of Vico's concerns that decisively engage the problematics of modernity: Vico's critique of Cartesian cogito; his insight into the radical historicity of all human reality; his departure from the classical forms of Western philosophical thought (metaphysics and theology) to the domain of a man-made world; his unintended but de facto secularization of Providence; his theory of esthetics, highlighting the belief in man's possibility of creation and self-creation (though for Croce it never reaches the decisive stage of a self-conscious conceptualization).

Croce's epoch-making interpretation of Vico has come to be viewed as a thinly veiled alibi for and prefiguration of Croce's own immanent theory of history and, as such, it has been questioned from top to bottom without being, however, completely discarded. In the wake of Croce's "rediscovery" of what he takes to be the main features of Vico's philosophical concerns as well as of Fausto Nicolini's painstaking philological reconstruction of Vico's historical circumstances, Vico has become in the twentieth century something of a cultural phenomenon. Yet, the many sides of his work—he is variously a visionary, an antiquarian, a philosopher, and a theorist of law and literature—escape the critical efforts to reduce it within a single, overarching formula or coercing him within the taste and modes of a single historical period.

The echoes emanating from the depths of his mind can still reach us, it seems, on condition that we view him as the precursor of a number of thematics (mythology, linguistics, anthropology, etc.) that have been engaging the intellectual discourse of our times. Casting him as a precursor of our intellectual fashions is in reality a way of acknowledging his historical untimeliness, of which Vico was aware and which readers over the years have interpreted in a variety of ways.

The visionary energy of his fabulations, which transcends the decorous, neoclassical conventions of academic discourse, has been the object of fascination since the Romantic age. Authors such as Manzoni, Foscolo, Hamann, Herder, Goethe, Marx, Michelet, Joyce, Beckett, Ungaretti, Pavese, and Carpentier, drawn by the enigmatic quality and the tantalizing obscurities of Vico's imagination, have grasped a prophetic, untimely, and anti-historical aspect in the heart of his historical thought or have quarried his texts and myths as if they contained nuggets of secret wisdom. Because of the seemingly irreducible strangeness of his vision, in their quest for a vital mythology of the future, these writers have elevated him to the role of spiritual mentor, the very embodiment of the intellectual as seer who blazes new trails for the future.

With some exceptions, however, Vico's self-conscious visionariness has been neglected by sober-minded intellectual historians on both sides of the Atlantic. Philosopher-scholars ranging from Cassirer to Grassi and Verene, from Lowith and Apel to Mooney, from Auerbach to Garin and Badaloni, from Tagliacozzo to Costa, from Vasoli to Piovani and Struever, from Berlin to White and Bergin, from Battistini to Fletcher (both of whom have actually probed the visionary-prophetic strains of Vico's thought) have succeeded in putting Vico studies on a solid philosophical-historical footing. Vico is no longer seen simply as the oracle whose utterances unavoidably place him always ahead of us. Rather, he appears now as a first-rate philosopher. And he is studied through the prism of the historical realities of Naples and seventeenth-century Europe. Such a recuperation of Vico as an original thinker who is rooted in the concrete traditions of Renaissance and baroque learning has eclipsed the visionary, anti-historical burden of his thought. It has removed him, at the same time, from the role of antiquarian, of the forlorn intellectual who looks always backwards and whose thought remains unassimilable into the debates of the present.

In spite (and because) of these self-contradictory debates, thanks to Croce, Berlin, and Grassi, Vico has become a major figure in the history of European consciousness. Actually, the consensus is steadily emerging about Vico's lucid awareness of the crisis of seventeenth-century culture in Naples and the rest of Europe. Thus, scholars have been increasingly occupied with the complex context of ideas within which Vico forges his thought. The main pieces of this mosaic have been identified as the traditions of Renaissance thought (Neoplatonist, Machiavellian, and the neo-Aristotelean arguments over the *Poetics*); the scientific, philosophical, and political debates (Cartesian and natural philosophers) raging in seventeenth-century and early-eighteenth-century Naples (a city that was truly one of the most intellectually vital centers of Europe); the styles of baroque literature and art; scholastic theology about nature and law, etc.

The thrust of these scholars' research, even if not explicitly stated, is that Vico's relentlessly austere and demanding thinking comes forward as an alternative to the rampant scientific-technological consciousness of our time.

Impossible in actuality, Vico's anti-scientific ideas are basically considered to be the product of an intellectual nostalgia by a latecomer on the stage of modernity. Guideposts to such nostalgia are the turns of Vico's thought toward poetry, rhetoric, and the world of the imagination.

It is possibly the marginalizing of the humanities in the American academic world that has led to redrafting the boundaries of traditional disciplines and their relation to the positive sciences. Such an exigency has made Vico, this solitary thinker who, paradoxically, held "monastic" thinkers in contempt, a necessary *lieu-de-passage* for overcoming the fragmentation of the various intellectual disciplines. It is increasingly clear that Vico's apparent artificial system, in fact, proposes a universal *scientia scientiarum*, a comprehensive project that weaves together into unified totality disparate questions of literature, rhetoric, history, religion, language, myth, philosophy, politics, law, and so forth.

A generation of younger scholars (including Harrison, Bedoni, Schaeffer, Lollini, Mali, Stone, Pietropaolo, Lilla, Goetsch, and Miller) has been examining in recent years (and in continuity with their predecessors) the fundamental themes that figure prominently in Vico's production. This book, much like these scholars' elucidations, seeks to provide a preliminary reconnaissance into the specific cultural context nurturing Vico's thought. It places his writings within specific articulations of early modern history generally neglected by previous scholars: his complex relationship to Bacon, Campanella, and Bruno; his grasp and critique of the baroque; the politics of Naples and his reading of modernity (its politics and sciences, from Machiavelli to Galileo). It retrieves the theological texture (both the Augustinian and Thomistic elements) of his vision and the liminal role of the Bible. It proposes the importance of the myth of Egypt in the economy of the *New Science* and sheds new light on the idea of the *ricorso*. More precisely, my argument aims at gauging the proximity and divergence in Vico's philosophical and poetic thinking, hopefully without blunting the edge of his extraordinary visionariness.

Above and beyond the claims of specific, new themes proposed by this study, *The New Map of the World* centers on the pursuit of the whole or the unification of the arts and sciences as the question lying at the heart of Vico's fragmentary thought. To do so, it focuses on the major positions Vico explicitly advances: "Cultivate knowledge as a whole" (*On the Heroic Mind*, p. 244); the *New Science* is a "rational civil theology of Divine Providence" (NS/2); it provides a philosophy of authority (NS/350); poetry is the master key of his intellectual discoveries (NS/34).

A steady interrelationship holds together these four of Vico's assertions. This book argues that his unification of the arts and sciences into an encyclopedic whole is the other side of a project to forge a new political science—and its limits—for the needs of the modern age.

Organized as a journey of discovery from the self (or that which is close at hand) to the archaic depths of history and to the future, this book has a tripartite structure. It starts with the question of education: the making of the self, the political role of the university, and Vico's reading of the politics of the modern age. The middle section (Chapters 4–6) hinges on the *New Science*'s educational project (the reconstruction of a fragmentary culture into an encyclopedic unity of the arts and sciences). Chapters 5 and 6 evoke the worlds of myth and poetry, and they are the two points around which, like the foci of an ellipse, the argument of this book revolves. Chapters 7 to 9 focus on Vico's elaboration of a new political/theological science that would confront science's premises about chaos and reconcile all political divisions. Chapter 10 lies by necessity outside of this tripartite structure. It deals with Vico's understanding of the Bible and the limits of totalizing politics.

The key to the unity of all the arts and sciences is poetry. Poetry, which Vico never forces within the narrow limits of one doctrinaire formula, as if it were a question that could be answered once and for all, is the prism through which he looks into the time-bound, multifaceted aspects of reality. It is variously seen, for example, as the art of *making*, as a sublime or visionary experience, as a consequence of the figurality of language and its tropes, or as proximate to rhetoric. This complex view of poetry imaginatively shapes, underlies, and alters all forms of thought. Because of its constitutive ambiguities, poetry forces us to think simultaneously in all directions and joins in its compass all contradictions, chaos and order included. But by the very virtue of its intrinsic openness, which resists one-dimensional ways of thinking, poetry has the power to subvert all efforts at totalizing closures.

The New Map of the World is unified by some recurring concerns (bodies, places, limits, thresholds, margins, the "tragic," death, wonder, etc.). The main one is the place of poetry and its role within other structures of discourse (autobiography, the university, history, science, law, politics, theology, etc.). There are in Vico scholarship several important thematic studies dealing with various aspects of his understanding of poetry. But there is no sustained reading of the *New Science* (1744), of which I am aware, that is carried out from within the essentially literary or poetic viewpoint that Vico claims as the key to his science. This is the lacuna I have tried to fill by focusing on his prismatic idea of poetry.

More precisely, each chapter probes poetry's ever-shifting, ambivalent, but undeluded mode of knowledge. It should be stressed, however, that the poetic mode is not just another, more or less ornate, way to say what philosophy says. If that were the case, one of the two disciplines would be superfluous. Poetry certainly shares in the pursuits of the sciences and philosophy, but it remains unassimilable to the parameters of discursive, rational systems. To state it differently, Vico is ambivalent about the new project he heroically envisions for the modern age. Accordingly, he makes biblical theology the perspective for his critique of totalizing political projects. In short, Vico is a political thinker constantly aware of the tragic limits of politics. But tragedies need heroes. He thought he was one.

In such a necessarily literary-philosophical reading, the traditional *querelle* between ancients and moderns describes a complex story transcending the static confrontation between two antithetical views of history; the rational facade of Vico's thought is the fortress of the imagination; the *arbor scientiae* has magic roots; jurisprudence is the fable of the *arcana potestatis*; dim memories of the past are reversed into the archive of the future; poetry and rhetoric are the necessary way of thinking for politics; the idea of totality is flanked by the consciousness of an outsideness escaping the discursive mode and representation of the whole.

There is an emblem that best illustrates my interpretation of Vico's thought: the double-faced Roman god of thresholds, Janus, whose inflected name is revered in Naples and by Vico himself. Like Janus, who looks forever forward and backward, Vico is the thinker-poet who ushers in the vision of the past as the gateway to the future, and who is at the boundaries of a new time which is the future of the past.

ACKNOWLEDGMENTS

BEGINNINGS ARE obscure and uncertain, and so is the beginning of my interest in the thought of Giambattista Vico. My memory takes me back to Cornell University, when my student and now colleague, Robert P. Harrison, asked me to read Vico with him. Since those years Yale University has been a place especially suited for working on Vico. What can be called the American revival of Vico studies had as its trailblazers three members of the Yale faculty: Ernest Cassirer, Erich Auerbach, and Thomas Bergin. At Yale several students, who are now my dear friends, were my Vico interlocutors, and I gratefully acknowledge them: Massimo Lollini, Antonio Melchor, George Trone, Arielle Saiber, Gabe Pihas (who contributed a memorable line), and Nancy du Bois. I am especially indebted to Sherry Roush, Jennifer Wamser, Marcello Simonetta, and Stefano Baldassarri, who diligently and critically read the whole manuscript. My deep gratitude also goes to friends and colleagues, here and in Europe, who patiently listened and often responded as I discussed my Vico work. I still grieve as I recall my conversations with the late Gregory Lucente, who shared with me his extraordinary insights into Vico's "historical imagination." There are other friends to whom I am indebted: Antonella Giacoia, Robert Harrison, Emilio Pasquini, Mihai Spariosu, David Ruderman, Ty Miller, Paul Geyer, Ernesto Livorni, Giovanni Sinicropi, Stefano Velotti, David Lovekin, Roberto Gonzalez, Jacques Lezra, Nuccio Ordine, David Quint, Louis Dupré, Anthony Kronman, Gianni Vattimo, Keith Baker, Cecilia Miller, and, above all, Andrea Battistini, who generously took time from his many commitments to comment on the Italian version of the manuscript. Don Verene, Angus Fletcher, and Donald Kelley were most helpful with their enlightening comments. And, as always, Luisa Dato was wonderful in helping me prepare this manuscript.

It is a pleasure for me to acknowledge several institutions that have invited me to lecture at length on Vico over the last few years: the University of Bologna, where as *professore a contratto* in the spring of 1993, I had the privilege of holding a number of graduate seminars on Vico; the Center for Vico Studies at Emory University, where at the NEH seminar directed by Donald Verene in the summer of 1993, I gave five seminars on material included in this book; and the Istituto per gli Studi Filosofici of Naples (and its director, Gerardo Marotta) for twice having me hold a series of seminars on Vico, in the summers of 1994 and 1996, respectively at Diamante and Vatolla.

Some pages of Chapters 4 and 8 are reprinted from two articles originally published in, respectively, "Vico's Encyclopedia," *The Yale Journal of Criticism*, vol. 1, no. 2 (Spring 1988), pp. 65–79; and "Machiavelli and Vico," in *Machiavelli and the Discourse of Literature*, eds. A. R. Ascoli and V. Kahn (Ithaca: Cornell University Press, 1993), pp. 259–74. Permission to reprint is acknowledged.

NOTE ON VICO'S TEXTS

Unless otherwise stated, all Italian quotation from Vico's texts are drawn from the following editions:

Opere, ed. Andrea Battistini, two volumes (Milan: Mondadori, 1990). Battistini's edition contains the following works I have cited: *Vita di Giambattista Vico scritta da se medesimo; De Nostri Temporis Studiorum Ratione;* "Affetti di un disperato"; "In morte di Donn'Angela Cimmino"; "De Mente Heroica"; "Le accademie e i rapporti tra filosofia e l'eloquenza"; *Scienza nuova prima* (1725); and *Scienza nuova* (1744).

Orazioni inaugurali I–VI, in *Opere di Giambattista Vico*. Centro di Studi Vichiani. Vol. I, ed. Gian Galeazzo Visconti (Bologna: Il Mulino, 1982).

De Antiquissima Italorum Sapientia Ex Linguae Latinae Originibus Eruenda (1710), in *Opere filosofiche*, introd. by Nicola Badaloni. Ed. by Paolo Cristofolini (Florence: Sansoni, 1971).

Opere giuridiche: Il diritto universale, introd. by Nicola Badaloni. Ed. Paolo Cristofolini (Florence: Sansoni, 1974).

Studi storici, ed. Fausto Nicolini (Naples-Bari: Laterza, 1939). The text contains *La congiura napoletana* and *Vita del maresciallo Carafa*. I have also followed *La congiura de' principi napoletani* (1701). Centro di Studi Vichiani. Vol. II, Part 1, ed. Claudia Pandolfi (Naples: Morano, 1992).

"Discoverta del vero Dante ovvero nuovi principi di critica dantesca," in *Scritti vari*. Ed. Fausto Nicolini (Bari: Laterza, 1940), pp. 79–82.

For the English translations I have cited from:

The Autobiography of Giambattista Vico, trans. Max H. Fisch and Thomas G. Bergin (Ithaca: Cornell University Press, 1944).

The New Science of Giambattista Vico, trans. Max H. Fisch and Thomas G. Bergin (Ithaca: Cornell University Press, 1968).

On the Study Methods of Our Time, trans. and introd. by Elio Gianturco. With a translation of "The Academies and the Relation between Philosophy and Eloquence," by Donald P. Verene (Ithaca: Cornell University Press, 1990).

On the Most Ancient Wisdom of the Italians Unearthed from the Origins of the Latin Language (including the "Disputation with the Giornale de' Letterati d'Italia"). Trans. and introd. by L. M. Palmer (Ithaca: Cornell University Press, 1988).

On Humanistic Education: (Six Inaugural Orations, 1699–1707). Trans. by Giorgio A. Pinton and Arthur W. Shippee. Introd. by Donald P. Verene (Ithaca: Cornell University Press, 1993).

On the Heroic Mind. Trans. by Elizabeth Sewell and Anthony C. Sirignano in *Vico and Contemporary Thought*, eds. G. Tagliacozzo, M. Mooney, and D. P. Verene (Atlantic Highlands, N.J.: Humanities Press, 1979), pp. 228–245.

"The Discovery of the True Dante," in *Critical Essays on Dante*, ed. Giuseppe Mazzotta (Boston: G. K. Hall, 1991), pp. 58–60.

ABBREVIATIONS

The quotations from the *New Science* are indicated in the text as NS followed by the number of the paragraph. The *Scienza Nuova Prima* is indicated as 1NS followed by the number of the paragraph. The other texts are identified by the page number in the Italian or Latin or English editions.

The New Map of the World

INTRODUCTION

THE TITLE of this book, a variant of the *mappamundi*, the map of the world, recalls first of all the globe on the frontispiece of the *New Science*. Vico explains that the spherical globe, called "*globo mondano*" (NS/2), supported by an altar, is girt by a zodiacal belt, and it functions as the footstool for a woman with winged temples, who is identified as Metaphysics gazing at the luminous triangle with an all-seeing eye. The emblem is deciphered as the mind's contemplation of God's Providence in the civil world or the world of nations.

The *New Science* is explicitly concerned with another globe, the *orbis scientiarum* (the orb or sphere of the sciences), for the universe of the sciences is the obverse side of the political sphere. Accordingly, at the outset the text calls the political world the point of reference for the sciences. And although it makes here no mention of mapping, the metaphor of mapping is prominent in the *New Science*. Seventeenth-century cartography and mapping are preeminent Cartesian forms, analytical geometry's techniques for plotting coordinates and defining cross sections of places. Vico calls his version of mapping "chorography" (NS/774), which is literally the geographer's practice of making the map of a place and giving a name to the earth.

As a description, or road map, of the terrain, chorography is one of the two parts of geography (the other is nomenclature), and both are the "eyes" for the representation of history (NS/17). Mapping is tantamount to Vico's surveying the far-off regions of a history that begins in the vagrancy and navigation of peoples, of which the rudder is the symbol (NS/17) and the itinerant Mercury its presiding divinity. Vico's text, in turn, charts the boundaries and curves of his intellectual voyage around the commonplaces of history so that the map is also the graph of Vico's own intellectual adventure into the landscape of memory. His epic voyage proceeds by following seemingly haphazard but extraordinarily precise routes in the path of the migration of ideas and people. He maps the *orbis scientiarum*, marks out the ways, locates the shoals and currents along the way so that we enter the imaginative space traced by his mind like diviners who take "auguries and observe(d) the auspices" (NS/9).

Vico's poetic/philosophical journey takes place in time and space. The *New Science* has as its point of departure the probing of the dark beginnings of mythic consciousness (Book II). His quest comes to an end in Book V with a discussion of modernity (NS/1096) that is raised in the context of the so-called *ricorsi*, which are the new beginnings or recourses of history. Taken in the generality of its overall rhetorical structure, the text maps a voyage of discovery to the roots of man's memories in order to divine the laws of history and the shape of the future. It is the narrative of the author as hero who travels by eccentric paths along the high seas of memory, gathers fossils of time, and interrogates the enigmas of ancient wisdom. He comes ashore in the present to refound the discourse of modernity.

There is no doubt that modernity is the true destination and the real, abiding concern of Vico's thought. That this is the case is made evident by the title of a pedagogical tract, *On the Study Method of Our Time*, that he compiled as professor of rhetoric at the University of Naples. Furthermore, his two historical texts, *The Neapolitan Conspiracy* and *The Life of Antonio Carafa*, taken together, constitute a complex and highly original political history of modernity. At the same time, the *New Science*, by the title's unabashed announcement of novelty in the pursuit of science, textually bears the sign of a deliberate rethinking of modernity's predicament. In fact, the *New Science* is obliquely described as the fulfillment and epochal event of modernity itself (NS/1096).

Nonetheless, there has long been perpetuated, and it lingers still, an image of Vico as a thinker outside of his own time. According to this view, he is an erudite hopelessly embroiled in undecipherable, calcified anachronisms, indeed is himself an anachronism of pieties who is unable to grasp the intellectual challenges of the new modern sciences. Such a platitude about Vico is utterly false. He is outside of time as much as he is in his own time, and he makes a virtue of this ambivalent condition. In its deliberateness, Vico's antiquarianism allows him the vantage point from which to grasp the limits of the dominant, modern paradigms of knowledge. Antiquarianism, more precisely, affords him the perspective of "untimeliness" from which to gauge the deeper, ancient forces shaping the spiritual structure of the modern world. But because he knows that a blanket opposition to the spiritlessness and decay of the modern world is ultimately sterile, he does not just retreat into the cult of antiquities. Rather, he chooses to counter the modern world with his own alternative version of modernity.

Vico knows well that he is not one of the founders of modernity. The founders of modernity are for him Machiavelli, the Tacitists of the seventeenth century, Galileo, Descartes, Bacon, and Spinoza. In Naples their epigones are legion. For Vico the theories of these founders of modernity, rather than solving the crisis the new sciences had ushered in, made it worse. These founders believe that the wisdom of the ages is inadequate for the modern project. They enshrine the present in the persuasion that the world begins with them; they revel in religion's clash with the new empirical sciences, foment civil dissent, and underwrite conspiratorial theories of absolute power. In short, they see the world only through the prism of the natural order and, thereby, they see only broken pieces or a portion of the whole (NS/2).

The *New Science* is written against the theories of the founders, and it purports to be a new discourse for modernity or a *ricorso*—a recourse or appeal, as one might say, using Vico's term in its primary juridical sense. This new discourse is also, though not exclusively, a counter-discourse addressed to the universities of Europe, the academies, and the Republic of Letters (1NS, Dedication). The educational rhetoric of the *New Science*, which is crystallized by its encyclopedic structure and, at the outset, by its dedication to an academic audience, casts Vico as a teacher of (among) teachers (which is what Dante calls Aristotle) or a scholar among teachers. The pedagogical rhetoric unveils Vico's intent: to correct the intellectual errors of the moderns, purge the scholars of their conceit and of the tyranny of self-love, trace a new map of the sciences, especially political science. The new project of learning had to be a universal *scientia scientiarum*, an encyclopedic order of all the arts and sciences.

Vico is aware that his effort to salvage the relics and detritus of a broken world and a broken knowledge is not in itself original. The quest for a synthesis has been the legacy of antiquity and is the challenge of modernity. In the Renaissance and in his own times one gleans versions of this synthesis, which explicitly shapes baroque pansophism and panlogism, from the works of Giulio Camillo and Giambattista Della Porta, from Giordano Bruno's art of memory to Tommaso Campanella's encyclopedism, not to mention the encyclopedism of Vico's own friend in Naples, Giacinto Gimma. But Vico does not follow their examples.

Their encyclopedic ideals were meant chiefly to promote a new cultural order, a Republic of Letters within which the provinces of learning could be unified. The politics of such an aristocratic project is immediately clear, and yet it does not reach into the foundations and causes of history's institutions. What prevents Vico's quest for an intellectual synthesis from being a chimerical search for an elusive totality of knowledge is his Socratic sense that knowledge originates in and is bound to political history. The encyclopedia, which is the sinew of his response to modernity's culture of fragments, is for him a model for the recomposition and reconciliation of political society. In order to achieve this aim, Vico had to turn to and rethink the works of his four "authors": Plato, Bacon, Tacitus and Grotius. Tacitus stands in Vico's mind for the empirical, viscous realities of politics and history. The other three authors have elaborated versions of Vico's own intellectual-political project. The interaction between two of these authors, Plato and Bacon, one ancient and one modern, moves to the center of Vico's thought.

Bacon had decided that Greek wisdom, which to him meant the wisdom of Plato, was inadequate to the needs of the modern world. The distance that yawns between Plato and Bacon is marked by the new sciences and by the political science of Machiavelli and the Tacitists. What Machiavelli indicates for Bacon (or Galileo for Hobbes) is the sense of necessity of a new political philosophy. It also means the realization that the novelty of the Machiavellian political science lies in its unavoidable rejection of classical forms of utopias (*The Prince*, Chapter XV) in the persuasion that modern political reality needs a realistic new science and realistic-utopian political projects (which *The Prince* articulates in Chapter XXVI). Why would classical utopias be inadequate for modernity? The answer is that the modern age (and Machiavelli as its knowing reader) has no room for moderation, which is the essence of Plato's classical project in the *Republic* (NS/130). The modern age is under the aegis of Christian understanding of desire, and Machiavelli makes the Augustinian metaphysics of infinite desire and the inexhaustible appetites of bodies the focus of a modern political science.

Bacon's *De Augmentis Scientiarum* and the *New Atlantis* wish to replace Plato's *Republic* in the light of the new sciences. In point of fact, Bacon's *New Atlantis*, which is patterned on Campanella's *City of the Sun*, is simultaneously a Platonic *and* Machiavellian utopia, just as Campanella's *City of the Sun* is simultaneously a Pythagorean, Ficinian, and Machiavellian utopia. Because modern science, such as Galileo's, has titanic ambitions and even redefines the map of the heavens, Campanella's and Bacon's visionary texts make modern science the paradigm of their new utopias. By addressing the question of science's boundless scope, both want to update and replace Plato's idea of the polis. Yet Bacon, with his utopia of the sciences, with his utopian promise that the sciences will restore the bodies from corruption, does not solve for Vico the rifts and the moral, political, and theological contrasts that are the profile of modernity.

Vico certainly agrees with Bacon's idea about the limits of Plato's *Republic*. He knows that Plato's ideal Republic and indeed philosophy itself "can be of service to but very few," to those who do not wish to fall back into the dregs of Romulus (NS/131). Vico's statement, which expresses his conviction about the limitations of utopian discourses and, concomitantly, the necessity of bringing philosophy down to history, echoes Cicero's view, expressed in the *Tusculan Disputations* (Book V, pars. 10–11): Socrates, Plato's teacher, calls Philosophy down from the heavens, sets her in the cities of men, and compels her to ask questions about life, morality, and things good and evil.

From Vico's viewpoint, Bacon's brand of political philosophy, which yokes utopia and realism, follows and indeed updates Socrates' teaching. His political realism, however, is not immune to criticism, for as Vico points out, Bacon's scientific-educational project essentially pursues a Machiavellian conquest of nature. The world of Bacon, like the world of Machiavelli, Spinoza, Hobbes, and the Tacitists, is for Vico the world of absolute power, of simulations, dissimulations, and irony. This world's thinkers theorize the *libertas philosophandi*, yet their "liberty of philosophizing" has become the alibi for tyranny. The Spinozists, as Vico states in one of his memorable aphorisms, cannot really reason of commonwealths or laws. Their political philosophy is suspect as much as that of the Epicureans and the Stoics, "who [in this respect the Spinozists of their day] make God an infinite mind, subject to fate, in an infinite body" (NS/335 and 130).

In their metaphysics of subjection and determinism (God, as Vico pointedly says, is subjected to fate) the Spinozists argue for a freedom that functions exclusively to legitimize the privilege of libertines, who are both tyrants and slaves of pleasures. Giordano Bruno's *Cena delle ceneri* (*The Ash-Wednesday Supper*) epitomizes this cluster of paradoxes: it discusses Copernicanism and infinite worlds; authority as the source of justice and order (and not the other way around); the dangerous unruliness of the English lower class; the mortal risks the alien philosopher himself runs; and, finally, it exalts the absolute English monarch. In short, even when claims of freedom have a metaphysical foundation, as is the case with Bruno, a self-contradiction ensues: these claims end up envisioning a politics of absolute power.

Confronted with the self-deceptions and irony of the modern discourse, Vico perceives the necessity of a new discourse, of a *New Science*, which has to refound modernity and reintegrate the sciences in a new totality. The new discourse has to yoke together the classical idea of moderation with the modern idea of boundless liberty. In order to trace with precision the articulations of Vico's mind, we need to explore the interstices of his language and the metaphoric patterns of his prose with the close attention usually reserved to the analysis of literary texts. *The New Map of the World* focuses on the "writerliness" or philology of Vico's works and offers close readings of the text. In contrast, historians of ideas and of philosophy often read these works to test the logical and conceptual coherence of his thought, but bracket the literariness of his discourse and merely extrapolate isolated nuggets from his text's complex argumentations.

Vico's own writing style is not a merely formal issue nor is it simply a clue to the maze of his thought. If anything, it articulates with dramatic economy the substance of his intellectual and political project. He forges a poetic and philosophical style punctuated by fragmentary entries, literary and mythological allusions, references to and citations from erudite scholarship, repetition of arguments, pithy conceptual recapitulations, proleptic statements, formal symmetries and antitheses, and apparent digressions that recall the technique of the *entrelacement* and errancy in epic narratives.

At the heart of this way of writing lies the realization that the logical grammar and the linear geometry of rational demonstrations of traditional philosophical expositions are inadequate. They do not adequately express the configurations of a mobile, open reality in which the most contradictory experiences are simultaneously co-implicated in a steady conversation.

Thus, a supple poetic discourse is needed to confront these new realities. To this end, Vico adopts the mobile curves of the baroque style. Such a style is a necessity of his thought. It makes available the repertory of figures for exorcising the deceptions, self-deceptions, and obliquities of modern discourse. This self-conscious style, which implies the power of poetic language to render the problematical and contradictory perspectives of reality, allows us to perceive Vico's own investment in the making of himself as an author. By pursuing oblique paths and serpentine lines of thought, he shows himself as possessing the authority and knowledge to grasp the reality both of the new sciences, with their elliptical paradigms, and of modern political science, with its arcane practices of power. In the process, he reinvents the language and purposes of philosophy, which, because of Vico, can no longer be considered an enterprise of pure theoretical speculation. It is a poetic philosophy, a translation of knowledge into activity or making.

The question of Vico's "writerliness" inevitably entails the issue of poetry, and its place, in the *New Science*. No doubt, there is a reason fundamental to his thought that has induced him to call poetry or myth (the *universale fantastico*—the imaginative universal) the path to knowledge or, as he puts it in a phrase that recalls the vocabulary of hermeneutics, the "master-key of [his] Science" (NS/34). The problematical relation between poetry and science, which lies at the heart of the *New Science*, could not have been captured with more sharpness. In what way is poetry the master key to Vico's *New Science*? One answer is that poetry is the path for those, such as Vico, who quest for wisdom and think of it as reason's defense from itself, from the technological and ratiocinative excesses that stifle the life and freedom of the imagination. But more is meant by the present emphasis on poetry as the foundation of the text or hermeneutical *clavis* giving access to it.

By the statement, the distance from Vico's earlier efforts to establish a juridical "new science" in his treatise on law, *De Uno*, is plain. What does he mean by poetry in the *New Science*? What are its origin and power? Poetry is said to originate in the passionate and violent imagination of archaic man from an "ignorance of causes" (NS/375). But the imagination, which is a free and spontaneous faculty, is neither productive (there is a pathology of the imagination) nor, consequently, can it be hegemonic. In this sense, the imagination is not at the center of Vico's universe of knowledge. At the center stands poetry, *poiesis*, which is making and creating, or the imagination that becomes a work of art. Because it fundamentally expresses humankind's imaginings, perturbs the mind, contains and educates the turbulence of the passions (NS/376), poetry, as the act of making, is the basic ground of all knowledge.

To be sure, Vico had long intuited poetry's centrality in the act of knowledge. In his discussion of the university curriculum, he places it at the exact center of the fifteen chapters of *On the Study Methods of Our Time* just as later he will place the "Discovery of the True Homer" at the exact center of the five books of the *New Science*. This idea of poetry's centrality is rooted in its sublime essence, which, in turn, depends on the constitutively poetic and metaphorical origin of language. From the sublime, non-ratiocinative property of poetry a principle follows: poetry, as the language of the imagination, is not a lie. Indeed, men believe what they imagine (NS/376). Such a radical assumption, which scholars have long acknowledged and the consequences of which Vico rigorously explores, shapes his consciousness of the novelty of his discourse.

He is aware that these views about poetry set him apart from the philosophers of antiquity, such as Plato and Aristotle, as well as the Renaissance theoreticians of poetry, such as Patrizi, Scaliger, and Castelvetro (NS/384). They also set him apart from baroque poetics (e.g., Marino's *Adone*). This poetics reduces poetry to an idyllic contemplation of illusory beauty and to a false esthetic game played, with some ironic self-consciousness, on the stage of the world. Against baroque theories of art as illusive, ironic artifice; classical philosophies of art as mimesis or discursive allegory; and neoclassical rhetoric that simulates the retrieval of Greek antiquity, Vico proposes an ancient and yet new esthetics whereby the imagination and the passions are no longer sundered from reason. This poetic passionalism, for all its Romantic aura, echoes St. Thomas Aquinas's definition of art as a virtue of the practical intellect in the order of making. In this Scholastic view of art as work (endorsed by Dante), the true and the made are yoked together. In brief, Neoplatonic ideas of the imagination merge with neo-Aristotelian notions of art. Both are grafted on Cicero's assertion about the civilizing power of the word and Longinus's theory of elevation or the sublime.

From the standpoint of this synthetic insight into poetry the *New Science* mounts a sustained critique of the most traditional esthetic arguments and their reductive tenets: the neoclassical debates about poetic verisimilitude; the neo-Aristotelian notion of art as merely a technique with specific rules and methods; the cult of simulacra peddled by baroque poetics; the musings about the meaning of *fabula*, which for Vico's friend, Gianvincenzo Gravina, was the receptacle of Egyptian wisdom; the speculations by a Cartesian philosopher of art, such as Caloprese, for whom truth is the prerogative of science, while the beautiful is the domain of art; the nature of myth, irony, and the tragic—these questions, which the *New Science* re-thinks, *The New Map of the World* extensively probes.

But Vico's insight into the origin and nature of poetry is not a purely ac-ademic pursuit nor is it a way of merely accounting for the variety of puta-tively autonomous or self-enclosed esthetic phenomena. What is peculiar about Vico's understanding is that poetry is the key of access to the very foundation of humanity's time-bound existence, to the workings and cul-ture of the mind. It reveals the mind not as a delimitable, discontinuous entity that stumbles into an impasse. Its mobile faculties, rather, are all im-plicated in the act of knowledge, just as the configuration of its experiences is ever shifting. The modifications of the mind are refracted through (as) the very mobility of metaphoric language. In turn, poetry is the knot of threads that reach out into all parts of Vico's intellectual and moral world. This insight into poetry makes possible his quest for the whole of knowl-edge (and for knowledge as a whole), which is his new discourse for the modern age.

Poetry's foundational status leads Vico to invest it with the power to unify all knowledge into an encyclopedic totality. The reason is plain enough. Poetry—the encyclopedic poetry of Homer and Dante—is not a pastoral form hermetically self-enclosed. It encompasses all the vital lan-guages of the tribe and all forms of knowledge, records its true imaginings, links together the parts that seem disparate, voices archaic passions, and speaks the language of memory and history. Poetry-as-memory (and as his-tory) embodies and is the path for the ongoing education of the soul.

Vico explicitly announces his project for a poetic encyclopedia at the very moment when he defines "poetic wisdom" as the trunk from which branch out all other "subaltern sciences," such as logic, morals, economics, and politics. The other sciences, from physics to astronomy, also stem from an-other limb of this "tree of knowledge," and they are said to be "all likewise poetic" (NS/367). In short, all forms of knowledge are linked together in the circle or spiral of poetic activities. From this encyclopedic standpoint, he begins to show the limit of all self-enclosed and self-referential dis-courses, such as ironic discourse and political practice of simulation. Irony and falseness dominate the politics of modernity and the stylistics of mod-ern poetasters, who are the true enemies of poetry. By casting irony as a privileged, secret, and, a priori, as a fundamental feature of language, the philosophers of modernity take one part for the whole. In so doing, they bypass the sense of the whole lying at the heart of the *New Science*.

The question of the "whole," especially as it is thematically announced as a philosophical ideal in texts such as *On the Heroic Mind* or as the ency-clopedic genre in the *New Science*, has already been pointed out by con-temporary scholars. *The New Map of the World* drafts Vico's periplus around the kingdom of the arts and sciences, and it shows how poetry, as it links them together, modifies the logical coherence of the whole. The intrusion of the passions into the intelligible order of ideas demands a poetic representation of the whole and not an abstract statement of principle. In short, we are not to see in Vico's reconstitution of all knowledge into an encyclopedic unity some vague presentiment of the Hegelian proposition that "the true is the whole." If Hegel means, as I suspect he does, that philosophy's essence is to speculate about the whole, his ideas are far removed from Vico's.

Poetry is not just another way of saying what philosophy says. In making poetry the master key of his science, Vico argues, in effect, that poetry is a unique mode of making and knowing, that the whole must be perceived in the perspective of metaphor's property to join together disparate worlds and of the tropes' power to represent and take one thing for another. In the perspective of poetic representation, nothing is ever literally itself; nor is the configuration of the arts and sciences an end in itself. The metaphorical dislocations, which mark Vico's writerliness, are more than peculiarities of style or relics of the baroque past. They are tropes whereby literature "contains," in the double sense of the word, the world of science, particularly political science.

Because education is the core of Vico's political thinking, just as, in the sense of philosophy, it is the core of both Plato's and Bacon's political projects, I begin by clarifying what Vico understands by it. The first four chapters of *The New Map of the World* examine the question of education from a variety of viewpoints. *Paideia*, or education of one's self; pedagogy, as is practiced in academies and universities; and encyclopedias, that are ideal prolongations of the university, are the formal structures through which he articulates his constant meditation on literature, on the sciences, and on their methods and finalities. He does not shun discussing technical questions, such as the curriculum of the liberal arts or the relation between particular disciplines and corresponding parts of the soul. What underlies these discussions, however, is the interaction, derived from the Renaissance rhetoric of education, between education and political consciousness.

The point of departure (Chapter 1) for identifying Vico's own process of education is his *Autobiography*, a literary text whose focus is the problematics of subjectivity. The question of the subject, from which modernity and the new philosophy stem, and which modernity celebrates and disseminates, was not thematized in the *New Science*. Now, Vico interrogates the question of the "place" of the subject and of the philosopher within the economy of the polis. It will be by following his complex rhetorical strategies and his literary-narrative techniques that one gets a clear sense of what I call Vico's *exotopy*.

The Autobiography ends with the evocation of the death of Socrates, the philosopher who dies for (and because of) the polis. The myth of Socrates, the educator of Greece, reappears in the explicitly pedagogical texts Vico writes. Chapter 2 shifts to his idea of the university and focuses on his Inaugural Orations, *On the Study Methods of Our Time*, and *On the Heroic Mind*. These texts approximate a definition of what Vico takes to be the horizon of the "political." He never defines this concept. Yet, from these formal speeches one evinces that the "political" does not merely describe a political entity, such as the state with its public powers, its laws, and its practices. The political sphere is circumscribed within the vast compass of the domain of culture (which is the polity's "mental dictionary," or totality of beliefs, institutions, laws, intellectual styles, etc.). Vico's effort lies in defining the possible mode of confrontation between a sovereign idea of culture and the state's claims of sovereignty.

The *New Science*, which identifies politics and culture, will move beyond the identification of the two spheres. The university affords Vico the polemical standpoint both for assessing the narcissism and provinciality of the present and for contesting the despotic power structures of the political world. Nonetheless, like Machiavelli, Bacon, and Hobbes before him, Vico is drawn to the contentious, chaotic, and forever antagonistic realities that are the soil and the essence of political life. His sober assessment of the political realities of modernity is expressed in *The Neapolitan Conspiracy* (1703) and *The Life of Antonio Carafa* (1716), which are discussed in Chapter 3. The historical chronicle of the conspiracy shows Vico's debt to a whole tradition of histories and theories of conspiracies (Cicero, Politian, Machiavelli, and Bacon), and it highlights Vico's consciousness of the threatening nature of secret political action. By contrast, the account of Carafa's political life, which features the formation of a courtier and a general at the imperial court of Vienna, stages Vico's mature reflections about politics in the modern age and, obliquely, about his own political ambitions as the possible educator of rulers. The biography, as Vico states in his own *Autobiography*, was written at night, and the textual detail connotes the dark and secret edge of Vico's meditations.

We are now ready to begin an investigation of the *New Science* (1744). Chapters 4 through 10 seek to interpret the text as an articulated totality—an imaginative interrelationship of metaphors and ideas and not by a random extrapolation of "relevant" passages, as is unfortunately the critical practice followed by several readers of Vico. Chapter 4 of *The New Map of the World* tackles the *New Science*'s baroque form as well as the preliminary political implications of this structure. It shows Vico's pursuit of an encyclopedic and poetic sphere of knowledge, wherein fragmentary experiences such as politics, theology, law, history, and so forth, cannot be viewed in isolation from one another. Each entity overlaps with the other and together they are fused in a historical and poetic totality. Chapter 5, on the other hand, analyzes the links binding together myth and science, and, by focusing on Book II of the *New Science*, it reflects on the imaginative convergence between the myth of the Earth, its boundaries and territories, and agrarian laws. Chapter 6 discusses the "Discovery of the True Homer" (the sense of poetry), which occupies Book III of the *New Science*.

The problem of political simulation Vico deploys in *The Life of Antonio Carafa* is not abandoned. On the contrary, he reflects steadily on it as the particular domain of the Spinozists and as a form of the rhetoric of irony. What has changed, if anything, is that the problematics of simulation is for Vico part of the larger issue of figurative or poetic language, the *clavis universalis* of its new way of thinking. Only after discussing Homer's poetic encyclopedia can Vico turn to questions of law, politics, and history, which are the explicit subject matter of Books IV and V of the *New Science*. What exactly is the relationship between law and poetry? And how can the merging of science and politics, peddled by the new philosophy, be replaced by linking together poetic theology and politics? Chapters 7 and 8 focus, respectively, on Vico's rethinking of Grotius's idea of jurisprudence and Machiavelli's political science and his theory of the appetites and chaos. Machiavelli must be neutralized by the new political science; yet, Vico knows that "Machiavelli" is forever part of his vision.

Chapters 9 and 10 attempt to clarify the fundamental point and the novelty of the *New Science*. The *New Science* is a new way of seeing the world and ourselves in the world. This new way of seeing the world is articulated through Vico's boldest theory: the theory of the *ricorsi*, or recourses, of history in Book V. Such a theory, discussed in Chapter 9, is made possible by a metaphysical, visionary perspective that transcends particular experiences, gazes at the completed totality of a historical cycle, and divines the new beginning of history. The *New Science*, as a matter of fact, descends into the mythical origins of history; as an archaeology of knowledge it provides the "principles" (which are beginnings, criteria, causes, foundations, etc.) of such a history. Vico knows, as did Plato and Machiavelli, that every myth of origins is an essentially political myth. Humans return to the beginnings and foundations to revive them or purge the corruption of the present. Vico also knows that all beginnnings (except for the history of the Jews) are unknowable and are rooted in fables from which claims of originality, conceits of scholars, and conceits of nations derive.

Vico's counter-discourse to modernity compels us to confront modern eristics and proposes the reconciliation of the shreds of our knowledge into an irenic whole. This reconciliation, which is possible as a project of learning, may work within the universe of knowledge. But Vico realistically knows that there is a gap between who we are and what we understand, and that we are what we do *not* understand. He also knows that what we think *is* fundamental to what we are, and this assumption about humankind divided from itself justifies his intellectual discourse. As an intellectual discourse the *New Science* wills to remind us of the passions and brutish potential at the heart of the noblest human constructions of reality. It reminds us of man's doubleness in the clear perception that a greater danger lies in wait, were we to forget it. Were we to forget the real foundation of our being, we would fall prey to abstractions, would have reason justify all contrivances of reason, and would lose nothing less than the future. In Vico's historical vision the itineraries of memory reverse into openings to the future.

Given the temporal, open-ended framework of Vico's science, nothing is ever just itself and everything is under the gaze of shifting viewpoints. Thus, theology itself cannot be circumscribed within the orbit of a mere political theology (which would be another Machiavellian gesture of reducing it to an *instrumentum regni*). Theology, in its tripartite division, is for Vico the foundation of the "political," yet Chapter 10 shifts this book's ground and it argues for his critique of totalizing politics and culture from the standpoint of biblical theology. The biblical insight into fragments emerges as the other side of encyclopedic wholes.

The *New Science* has told us all along that the Bible does not record human history, and it must, therefore, be left out of the purview of history as if it were irreducible to it. The Bible, which is a text of exile, is itself exiled, as it were, to the margins of history. Yet, the *New Science* contains in its folds a reading of biblical history wherein what is marginal and unassimilable to history becomes the object of thought. The *New Science* has also told us that there is a world which is outside the projects and the consciousness of each individual, and this residue, which appears as a form of otherness, is also the place where every human project begins.

Marginality and liminality, which anthropologists distinguish from each other, are crucial categories of Vico's thought. As his version of utopia, the notion of marginality and liminality sets Vico apart from Plato, from Bacon, and from Machiavelli. The two terms describe the existential, exilic apartness of the philosopher in his native Naples; they challenge the tyranny of historicism that, above all in Naples, wills to coerce all experience within the boundaries of the contingent and leaves no real room for metaphysics; they define the ambivalent role of the university within and yet outside of the city; they recall the idea of Platonic-Pythagorean justice at odds with laws; they evoke the role of Providence, God's all-seeing eye, which is outside of history and yet periodically enters history to save it from its recurrent tragedies. The tragic, let me finally say, is incessantly the edge flanking Vico's thought.

As an alternative to the tragic, Vico theorizes his theology of Providence. As is known, he substitutes for the name of Christ that of Providence. In a way, theology marks the limit of philosophy. "Providence" also expresses the limits of a Christian Europe within a universal whole as well as Vico's will to reconcile warring religious factions. Against all sectarian and partial divisions Vico's thought seeks the piety of a poetic and philosophical conversation. As it does so, it retrieves the subjective and literary dimension of experience put forth in his *Autobiography*.

Chapter 1

THE LIFE OF A PHILOSOPHER

WE ARE ALL FAMILIAR with the external circumstances that led Vico to write his *Autobiography*, whose title actually is *Vita scritta da sè medesimo*. An adequate account of its origin is available in the *Autobiography* itself: Count Gian Artico di Porcia had launched a "Proposal to the Scholars of Italy" (*Progetto ai letterati d'Italia per scrivere le loro vite*) in which he urged them to write their own autobiographies (or in the term Carlo Lodoli coined, "periautographies"). The overt impulse behind Porcia's editorial initiative was unequivocally educational. The aim of each autobiography, as he envisioned it, was to make intelligible a scholar's scientific practice and achievement and find a way, as Vico says, "da indirizzarvi con più sicurezza la gioventù nel corso degli studi, sulla vita letteraria di uomini celebri in erudizione e dottrina" (to promote a new method in the studies of the young, which would make their progress more certain and more efficacious) (p. 68). Had it been realized as a series, the project would have provided a map of the intellectual landscape of contemporary Italy by retrieving the more significant scholarly voices—indeed the spiritual energy—of the times.[1]

Vico's *Autobiography* was the only one to be published in the series Porcia had conceived.[2] He had just published his *Universal Law*, which had won him some recognition, but out of real or simulated modesty, he hesitated for a time in accepting the invitation to contribute the story of his life. Once he agreed to do it, however, he carried out his commitment with constancy. Not that by doggedly keeping his end of the bargain did he really think that the enterprise ever would (or could) be merely an unproblematic exercise in self-confession. Nor, even worse, did he think it an attempt at naive, deluded self-representation. Quite the contrary.

He saw it through, first of all, because he grasped that Porcia's invita-

---

[1] For a thorough study of the autobiographical genre in the eighteenth century see Andrea Battistini, *Lo specchio di Dedalo: Autobiografia e biografia* (Bologna: Il Mulino, 1990).

[2] Ludovico Antonio Muratori, whose work about the reform of culture, the education of the young, the retrieval of antiquities, etc., parallels in many ways Vico's, was also invited to write about the "method" he had followed in his studies. He found "public confessions" dangerous and never sent the manuscript to Porcia. See his "Scritti autobiografici" in *Opere di Lodovico Antonio Muratori*, eds. G. Falco and F. Forti (Milan-Naples: Ricciardi) I, pp. 3–42. On Muratori and eighteenth-century culture see Ezio Raimondi, *I lumi dell'erudizione: Saggio sul Settecento italiano* (Milan: Vita e Pensiero, 1989).

tion amounted to a much coveted, and for him long overdue, public recognition of his leading role within the turbulent and often melodramatic theater of Italian letters in Naples in the early part of the eighteenth century. Now he had a choice public forum—the savants of all of Italy (especially Venice) and Europe, which is where he believed his true interlocutors were to be found. To them he could explain himself as well as the presumed obscurities of his thought, that made his work seem intractable and altogether impenetrable to many readers. No doubt, in reaction to what he took to be a "vile impostura" (*Vita*, p. 73)—a base and false account—of the *New Science*, that appeared in 1727 in the *Acta Eruditorum Lipsiensia*, the bulk of the final section of the *Autobiography* becomes a fairly detailed commentary on the architectonics and substance of the *New Science*.

Vico understood that Porcia's invitation gave him a unique, historical opportunity to look at the self and at the question of the subject, its presuppositions and possibilities, in the light of the broader framework of ideas and principles he had been forging. He also understood that writing the story of his life for a wider national audience was necessarily going to be the story of how he came to be an author. Thus, he quickly grasped the opportunity to confront larger challenges, such as the structure of the self, the question of the self's (and his own) authority, and the problem that both encompasses and grounds them all, namely the relationship between philosophy and literary representation. The *Autobiography* addresses all these self-implicating issues in a detailed and deliberate manner.

Vico had already written biographical pieces, such as the oration for the death of Donn'Angela Cimmino, which is a eulogy on the woman's life and character. He had written the *Life of Marshal Carafa*, which is the celebration of a heroic character in modern times as well as a meditation on war. And he had written one powerful lyrical poem, "Gli affetti di un disperato," in which the lyrical "I" (which is not necessarily an empirical "I") descends to the innermost realm of the mind's anguishes. The *Autobiography* makes no reference to it, as if its dark core were a temporary aberrant posture. Composed in the mode of Dantesque and Petrarchan canzoni and shaped by Lucretian and Epicurean doctrines, the song draws a picture of the self with no essential bonds to anything around it: this self is tragically adrift, forever led to acts whose consequences remain opaque and unintended.

Vico never really completely bracketed the questions of biography, character, and subjectivity. He knew with great clarity that what is missing in the *New Science* is a precise, sustained discourse on subjectivity—how the self enters, shapes, and is itself shaped by the fabric of history. It is no wonder, then, that one should view his writing the *Autobiography*, which is carried out while he is revising the *New Science*, as a vehicle enabling him to reflect on the problematics of the self (its origin, the relation between contingent experiences and transcendent knowledge, the issue of whether or not the self can attain the vantage point from which it knows itself and knows the world, etc.) which the New Philosophy had long been disseminating.

The claims of the New Philosophy are crystallized in Descartes's conviction that a certain and indubitable basis of knowledge lies in the self-certainty of the knowing subject.[3] Vico's specific, polemical reactions to this idea of the self will be documented as we go along. For now suffice it to say that for Vico the self is not an a priori given, no more than the cogito has an unalterable fixity: there is a history of the self and there is a history of the mind in that both steadily experience alterations and shifts. Consistently, he will write the *Autobiography* as a novel of a time-bound education of his mind, as an inventory or history of the sundry stages of his intellectual growth toward the virtue of self-knowledge. Vico's intellectual itinerary will providentially lead to the production of the *New Science*, so that the *New Science* makes him, gives him authority, at least as much as he makes the *New Science*. Or, to say it differently, the *Autobiography* gives the genetic history and commentary of the *New Science*: by writing this book, Vico puts his signature as an author in the book of history.

This understanding of self as a succession of historical stages is, at least in part, both reflected and generated by the circumstances under which the text was composed. It was written and revised over a period of eight years: it was started in 1723; a subsequent section was added in 1728, and a final one in 1731. The desultory, temporally disconnected modality of the text's composition—one necessarily writes about oneself as one lives—sheds light on one of Vico's major insights into the structure of the self. The issue can be for now described in historical terms. In opposition to Montaigne's skeptical "Que sais-je?" the Cartesian model of subjective individualism, set forth in the *Discours de la méthode*, defines the self in terms of its timeless, innermost mental realm. Vico, who sees linked together both the Cartesian and the skeptical notions of self, dramatizes the historical consciousness of self as ceaselessly time-bound, shifty, and always in the process

---

[3] In the *Discourse on Method* Descartes writes: "I had recognized in my travels that those who have feelings very contrary to ours are not, for that alone, either barbarians or savages, but that many of them use reason as much or more than we do; and I had considered how the same man, with the same mind, being raised from childhood among the French or Germans, becomes different from what he would be if he had always lived among the Chinese or cannibals. . . . Therefore I was unable to choose anyone whose opinions were preferable to those of others, and I found myself forced to undertake to guide myself." The quotation is taken from *Discourse on Method, Optics, Geometry, and Meteorology*, trans. P. J. Olscamp (Indianapolis: Bobbs-Merrill, 1965), pp. 14–15. Descartes is attempting, plainly enough, to stave off the relativism that someone like Montaigne, who gave currency to the "Que sais-je" of Pyrrhonism, had ratified in his *Essais*.

of being formed and reformed. And if in the Cartesian universe the self reaches a global understanding of itself by turning into a spectator and by disengaging himself from any active involvement in the world, Vico's first move is to show that the self is not given an essential or autonomous individuality, but it is radically constituted by his work. These issues are overtly staged from the very start of the *Autobiography*:

Il signor Giambattista Vico egli è nato in Napoli l'anno 1670 da onesti parenti, i quali lasciarono assai buona fama di sè. Il padre fu di umore allegro, la madre di tempra assai malinconica; e così entrambi concorsero alla naturalezza di questo lor figliuolo. Imperciocchè, fanciullo, egli fu spiritosissimo e impaziente di riposo; ma in età di sette anni, essendo col capo in giù piombato da alto fuori d'una scala nel piano, onde rimase ben cinque ore senza moto e privo di senso, e fiaccatagli la parte destra del cranio senza rompersi la cotenna, quindi dalla frattura cagionatogli uno sformato tumore, per gli cui molti e profondi tagli il fanciullo si dissanguò; talchè il cerusico, osservato rotto il cranio e considerando il lungo sfinimento, ne fè tal presagio: che egli o ne morrebbe o avrebbe sopravvivuto stolido. Però il giudizio in niuna delle due parti, la Dio mercè si avverò; ma dal guarito malore provenne che indi in poi è crescesse di una natura malinconica ed acre, qual dee essere degli uomini ingegnosi e profondi, che per l'ingegno balenino in acutezze, per la riflessione non si dilettino dell'arguzie e del falso." (p. 5)

(Giambattista Vico was born in Naples in the year 1670 of upright parents who left a good name after them. His father was of a cheerful disposition, his mother of a quite melancholy temper; both contributed to the character of their child. He was a boy of high spirits and impatient of rest; but at the age of seven he fell head first from the top of a ladder to the floor below, and remained a good five hours without motion or consciousness. The right side of the cranium was fractured, but the skin was not broken. The fracture gave rise to a large tumor, and the child suffered much loss of blood from the many deep lancings. The surgeon, indeed, observing the broken cranium and considering the long period of unconsciousness, predicted that he would either die of it or grow up an idiot. However by God's grace neither part of his prediction came true, but as a result of this mischance he grew up with a melancholy and irritable temperament such as belongs to men of ingenuity and depth, who, thanks to the one, are quick as lightning in perception, and thanks to the other, take no pleasure in verbal cleverness or falsehood.) (p. 111)

The main thrust of the exordium is to give both the chronography and topography of the self, the history of the self's origin in a world one has neither chosen nor can determine. In the opening sentence ("Il signor Giambattista Vico egli è nato in Napoli l'anno 1670 da onesti parenti. . . .") the apposition "signor," strategically placed at the beginning to suggest that even grammatically it sustains the organization of the sentence, would denote that Giambattista Vico is the subject of experience, as if he had lordship over the events of his life. But the presuppositions of the self as the subject of experience, as a self-grounding basis of occurrences and decisions, are dismantled both by the grammatical structure of the first sentence and by the conceptual movement of the paragraph. Never before or since in autobiographical narratives has the term "signor" appeared to be the hollow, institutional formula that in effect it is. This self has neither lordship nor power over his own world and, for that matter, over his own purposes. After giving his own name, Vico writes of himself in the third person singular. The technique is not unusual. A member of the Arcadia Academy, Chiabrera, had deployed it in his *Vita di Gabriello Chiabrera scritta da lui medesimo*. No doubt, Chiabrera's rhetorical model certainly had its impact on Laufilo Terio, which is the Arcadian mask of Vico himself.[4] This procedure had been employed also by Hobbes in his short Latin autobiography. But for Vico the narrative technique turns into a basis for a rigorous epistemological argument: in his handling of it, the point of the third-person narrative is that *I* am forever another, that I am not now the person I once was, that I am what I have become or shall become, that I am always ahead of myself, for my past lived experience is foreign to my present reflective consciousness, and I am the object of my own thoughts.

The non-coincidence of the self to oneself is the result of one's time-bound life, and the temporal self-distance is crystallized by the fact that Vico now writes from the point of view of the author of the *New Science*. The narrative strategy he deploys deserves a close look. As the author (in a narrative that steadily seeks to determine how he himself comes to acquire authority), he looks back at the spiritual-intellectual foundations of his widening education and relates how his philosophical text comes into being. From this standpoint, the *New Science* is the real subject matter of the text: it is, at the same time, a symbolic event which, in retrospect, gives coherence, direction, and intelligibility to the apparent randomness of Vico's intellectual quest. It is for him the epochal achievement that justifies his casting himself as an author as well as a heroic, innovative individual whose work, however misunderstood, determines the inevitable paths of our knowledge. It is, furthermore, the perspective which allows him to present the strands of his fundamental thoughts and to show how his thoughts evolve into the discovery of a "new science."

Vico's narrative strategy of a doubling of self (the one who writes as author and the one who was a child) is bound to recall the parameters set by

---

[4] For a history of Arcadia and its vicissitudes see Giovanni Mario Crescimbeni, *Storia dell'Accademia degli Arcadi in Roma* (London, 1803). See also Giuseppe Toffanin, *L'Arcadia: Saggio storico* (Bologna: Zanichelli, 1958); Amedeo Quondam, "L'Arcadia e la Repubblica delle Lettere," in *Immagini del Settecento in Italia* (Bari: Laterza, 1980), pp. 198–211.

the archetype of all subsequent autobiographical novels, St. Augustine's *Confessions*. The reference is not arbitrary, for St. Augustine is Vico's patron saint, as he pointedly notes at the conclusion of the 1731 continuation of his *Autobiography*.[5] St. Augustine writes the *Confessions* in the necessary mode of retrospection: the author, who writes in the first-person singular, looks back at his past with detachment as if he now were a different person from the one he once was. The assumption behind this narrative posture is that an authentic autobiography is a confession: it is a way of making sense of one's life, and, as such, it can be written only when one knows the end of his life. The knowledge of the end, which coincides with one's own death, *defines* and imparts a significance to the blurred contours of the chaotic events of daily living.

Vico's *Autobiography* marks a radical departure from the Augustinian autobiographical model in one crucial sense: he alters St. Augustine's structure of narrative retrospection. Unlike eighteenth-century memoirs and autobiographies (Spinelli, Giannone, Muratori, the *Vite degli Arcadi illustri*, etc.) or unlike Dante's autobiographical *Vita nuova*, which is stylized as a book of memory, Vico's *Autobiography* is told proleptically without a hint that the author already knows the end. And much like the *Vita nuova* and Petrarch's *Epistle to Posterity*, which end with an open-ended trajectory of the poet's visions of the future, Vico's *Autobiography* starts from the time of the protagonist's birth, relates his growth and ordeals, and it extends to an open-ended present. No doubt, from the start there is the intimation of a providential design to Vico's life; yet, as this work-in-progress unfolds, the narrator does not quite know the shape his life will take. Thus, the prolepsis, which is a technique whereby the memory of the past turns into a narrative of the future, is a trenchant critique of death and of retrospection. Life may only be understood backwards by an act of memory, but it must be lived forwards in a radical redirection of time to the future (as Dante's *Purgatorio* has it). The critique of death and of the cult of death is, more precisely, the dismantling of any possible belief that death is either the "conclusive" or the irreducible revelatory event in a person's life. That event is one's work.

The fiction of telling about one's past as if it were the future dramatizes Vico's essential point that life is a future-oriented project and that mem-

---

[5] For a refined analysis of the rhetorical-theological structure of St. Augustine's *Confessions* see John Freccero, *Dante: The Poetics of Conversion* (Cambridge, Mass.: Harvard University Press, 1986). The reference to St. Augustine in this context is not gratuitous. Vico himself writes of his narrative: "Terminata la vigilia di santo Agostino (27 agosto), mio particolare protettore, l'anno 1731." *L'autobiografia, il carteggio e le poesie varie*, eds. B. Croce and F. Nicolini, 2d rev. ed., *Opere di G. B. Vico*, Vol. V (Bari: Laterza, 1929), p. 377. See also Donald P. Verene, *The New Art of Autobiography: An Essay on the Life of Giambattista Vico written by Himself* (Oxford: Clarendon Press, 1991), p. 92.

ory is a recollection-forward of the scattered fragments of one's existence. This idea of a historical time, within which one's life is represented as an open-ended adventure, is the standpoint from which Vico is sharply polemical against autobiographies written as documentary or naturalistic accounts of past events. A first clear sign of such a polemic is visible in the opening paragraph of the *Autobiography*, which seeks to place the subject within a network of firm facts or in what could be called the *natural history* of the self. It recalls the legal name of his natural family, Vico, and it goes on to state the place, the time, the parents' hereditary or humoral disposition, and the family circumstances of Giambattista's birth. From the start, then, the self appears placed within a social context to which he belongs and which shapes and defines his "naturalezza" (nature).

This pattern of self-location within the legality and history of one's family with the aim of grasping one's nature seeks to evoke—and quickly discard—the materialistic belief that the future destiny of the self is contained within a deterministic context of natural causes. (Cardano's *De Vita Propria Liber*, which is the story of a physician/natural philosopher, could be seen as belonging to this mode.)[6] From this standpoint, the reference to Vico's own predominant humor, melancholy, is a discrete reference to Ficino's *De Triplici Vita*, in which melancholy, the humor that descends from Saturn, is the material mark of intellectuals and philosophers given to contemplation and destined to excel. Yet, this naturalistic pattern is disrupted by a number of textual details. The story of the seven-year-old child who has fallen down from the staircase, lost consciousness for five hours, and is expected by the attending physician to die or grow up "stolido" (not fully alert) stages Vico's polemic with naturalistic and generally Cartesian representations of self.

The physician, who is the natural philosopher, misreads the signs of the sickness according to a mechanical law of cause and effect or the laws of evidence (what Vico will later call "autopsy"). The principle of causality is not given a priori, as the natural philosopher believes. It is discovered afterwards, as Vico suggests, and once it is discovered, it comes through as a providential plan. The natural philosopher, in effect, short-circuits history's openness by interpreting events according to a mechanical scheme of causality. More than that, his misreading signals that natural sciences deal not with firm self-evidence of empirical facts but with the divination of probabilities and hypotheses.

[6] By contrast, see the rhetorical organization and the shaping ideas behind the *Autobiography* (or *De Propria Vita Liber*) of Gerolamo Cardano, ed. Paola Franchetti (Turin: Einaudi, 1945). Cardano writes the story of his life in 1575 (he will die a year later—September 21, 1576—in Rome) largely to clear his name from sundry moral charges and perpetuate his fame as encyclopedist: "Quale sia stata la ragione che mi ha indotto a scrivere . . . fu il desiderio di perpetuare il mio nome" (p. 161).

Furthermore, the metaphor of falling, which, no doubt, is meant to recall the theology of man's fallen condition, allows us to assess the ground, as it were, on which Vico's notion of the subject rests. In contrast to the Cartesian view of the subject as essentially disembodied mind or consciousness (*res cogitans*) and as the firm, certain foundation of all knowledge, Vico drafts a picture of the subject in its full etymological, anti-Cartesian force as *sub-jectum*, as literally thrown under, without a firm foundation, losing control of oneself, and provisionally without consciousness. If the naturalists are wrong in reducing life to a question of humors, the Cartesians are wrong in thinking that life is reducible to pure thought. From the viewpoint of the wounded child, ironically, the naturalists, for all the limits of their vision, are, after all, right in maintaining that one is hooked up to a body, that the body determines whether or not one is alive or dead.

This critique of the two major theoretical models about the constitution of the subject does not end here. Vico turns quickly to an interrogation of what we are to understand as "facts" in his narrative. Right at the outset he gives his birth date as occurring in 1670 rather than, as documents show it did, in 1668.[7] Is this an error or a misrepresentation? Much is at stake in this move. Yet, ultimately it matters little whether or not the error is an involuntary slip of the pen or the writer's conscious falsification of the record. In one sense, however, it matters greatly, for there are no chance occurrences in Vico's understanding of the providential design of his life.

The misrepresentation serves several narrative purposes. If it is deliberate, the error primarily shows Vico's ironic will to power over time, the heroic and futile effort to break out of time's tyranny. This thinker of time and of the *ricorsi* comes to discover that what is decisive in one's life—one's own birth date—lies beyond any possible determination by oneself. Whether deliberate or not, moreover, the error shows that there is never a sufficient, indubitable knowledge to guarantee the truth of one's self-representation. The essentially innocuous, and even humorously vain, misrepresentation of one's year of birth stages, finally, the hazy domain of the self's origin. In Vico's archeology of the self and of history, beginnings are fabulous approximations; genealogies are a faltering memory or a likely story wherein facts take on the uncertain hue of life's fictions, of a knowledge which cannot be based on direct experience of the object it wills to represent. The misrepresentation, in short, reveals the literary foundation of autobiographical and historical fictions. In the process, literature offers a dreamy knowledge for the philosopher's meditations.

The *Autobiography* tells essentially the life of the philosopher, and it turns into a reflection on a philosophy of life wherein old questions about

---

[7] Donald P. Verene, *The New Art of Autobiography* (see note 5), p. 165ff., has a different reading of this "slip" of Vico's pen.

the philosophical life are raised afresh, in the guise of the sense of the theoretical, Socratic life, the good life, or the Augustinian *beata vita*. From this standpoint, Vico wants to find out how to live: he seeks to grasp the significance of character in the forging of one's life, how apparent defeats are providentially reversed into new opportunities, and whether or not the life of the *sophoi* and the *phronimoi* is best for us. This quest for the authentic sense of one's life puts Vico's autobiographical writing in areas that far exceed Chiabrera's self-representation, Cardano's naturalistic view of self, and the Arcadian, fictional masks of the self. But the error about the birth date is also a pretext that allows Vico to gauge the exact relation between literary fictions and philosophy. He does so by directly confronting and taking to task the philosophical, Cartesian figuration of self and its version of the road the self has to take in order to make oneself.

The question of autobiographical self-representation figures at the forefront of the *Discours de la méthode*. Vico alludes directly to this text, by deploying the name of Descartes, in order to contest his analytical dismemberment of the traditional method of studies. Nonetheless, Descartes's own autobiographical experiences have been adumbrated earlier in the *Autobiography*. Toward the beginning of his account, Vico recalls his school years and he records what he takes to be the feebleness of his mind in coping with the demands of Chrysippean logic. The failure was a bitter disappointment, which induced him to give up for about a year and a half on the studies he had pursued in the school of the Jesuits. A little earlier he had taught himself grammar and rhetoric, following the *De Institutione Grammatica* of the Portuguese Jesuit Manuel Alvarez. But all of a sudden he is forced to discover the limits of his mind: his relative youth cannot yet endure the intellectual rigors of propositional logic. When he resumes his philosophical studies under the tutelage of another Jesuit, Father Giuseppe Ricci, who is "a Scotist by sect but at bottom a Zenonist" ("scotista di setta ma zenonista nel fondo" [p.8]), Vico finally manages to grasp the sense of modal logic's abstractions, such as substances and points. The success convinces him to leave school once again and to stay home for a year to study the *Disputationes Metaphysicae* by the Spanish Jesuit Francisco Suarez, again by himself.[8]

These references to his attending the schools of the Jesuits echo and parallel Descartes's own educational experience with the same religious order. At the same time, the detail of being continually in and out of school marks his distance from Descartes's decision to break definitively with school and to learn from direct experience. Vico, whose own name, ever since Dante's

---

[8] The importance of Suarez for Vico has been stressed by Elio Gianturco, "Suarez and Vico" in *Harvard Theological Review* 17 (1934), pp. 207–10. More recently, the issue has been studied afresh by Cesare Vasoli, "Vico, Tommaso d'Aquino e il tomismo," in *Bollettino del Centro di Studi Vichiani* 4 (1974), pp. 5–35.

Paradiso, evokes the way or method of the philosophers,[9] has lost or simply has not yet found his way or personal method of studies. By a logical shift the *Autobiography* reflects on Descartes's "method" and establishes a direct link between the Cartesian understanding of self and Vico's educational principles:

> Da sì fatta disperazione (tanto egli è pericoloso dare a' giovani a studiar scienze che sono sopra la loro età!) fatto disertore degli studi, ne divagò un anno e mezzo. Non si fingerassi qui ciò che astuta-mente finse Renato delle Carte d'intorno al metodo dei suoi studi, per porre solamente su la sua filosofia e mattematica ed atterrare tutti gli altri studi che compiono la divina ed umana erudizione; ma, con ingenuità dovuta da istorico, si narrerà fil filo e con ischiettezza la serie di tutti gli studi del Vico, perchè si conoscano le propie e naturali cagioni della sua tale e non altra riuscita di litterato. (p. 7)

> (His despair made him desert his studies—so dangerous it is to put youths to the study of sciences that are beyond their age!—and he strayed from them for a year and a half. We shall not here feign what Rene Descartes craftily feigned as to the method of his studies simply in order to exalt his own philosophy and mathematics and degrade all the other studies included in divine and human erudition. Rather, with the candor proper to a historian, we shall narrate plainly and step by step the entire series of Vico's studies, in order that the proper and natural causes of his particular development as a man of letters may be known.) (p. 113)

The passage is a direct reference to Descartes's foundationalism, to the decision, recounted in the autobiographical section of his *Discours de la méthode*, to abandon the study of disciplines not built on solid rational foundations. The philosopher will no longer be subjected to the false promises of alchemists, to the deceptive predictions of astrologers and the impostures of magicians. In contrast to Descartes, who altogether quits school, Vico never leaves the precincts of school for too long. He becomes a tutor to the children of the Rocca family in the fastness of Cilento and, later, a university professor, and his thought gets its vital shape by disciplines Descartes finds scientifically unreliable. The intelligibility of the world will depend on his foundationalist project, the notion that a firm foundation to the fabric of our beliefs must be grounded in the rationality of the self. Thus, he sets himself apart from all entities, removes his self to the chamber of his consciousness, and travels around the world:

> as soon as I was old enough to emerge from the control of my teachers, I entirely abandoned the study of letters. Resolving to seek no knowledge other

---

[9] I am thinking of "vico de li Strami," the Parisian street where Siger of Brabant "silogizzò invidiosi veri." *Paradiso Canto* X, 136–39. For a gloss on the scene in Dante in terms of *vico* and *via* as metaphors of the philosophical method, see Giuseppe Mazzotta, *Dante's Vision and the Circle of Knowledge* (Princeton, N.J.: Princeton University Press, 1993), pp. 110–12.

than that which could be found in myself or else in the great book of the world, I spent the rest of my youth travelling, visiting courts and armies, mixing with people of diverse temperaments and ranks. . . . For it seemed to me that much more truth could be found in the reasonings which a man makes concerning matters that concern him, . . . than in those which some scholar makes in his study about speculative matters. . . . And it was always my most earnest desire to learn to distinguish the true from the false in order to see clearly into my own actions and to proceed with confidence in this life. (Part I, pars. 9–10)

The two passages by Vico and Descartes highlight the drastic opposition between their two respective ideas of the self and their respective methods of study, which could summarily be called the historical *ratio studiorum* and the analytical *ratio studiorum*. Vico's plan valorizes the principle of history, which is a totality of memory and tradition, as the ground in which the education of the self is unavoidably rooted. Descartes's method rejects the study of the languages, of the orators, historians, and poets; it privileges self-knowledge as self-reflection and, above all, mathematics as the paradigm of the sciences.[10] The Cartesian hierarchy of intellectual values is said by Vico to be a narcissistic self-serving ploy to claim the superiority of Descartes's own system over all others. The reference to mathematics as Descartes's privileged science emphasizes the point. In Greek, *ta mathemata* designates that which is known in advance, and, from this point of view, this sort of mathesis is grounded in the subjectivism of the cogito. In short, from Vico's standpoint, in the Cartesian universe of discontinuity the claim of superiority of mathematics is a fiction masking the exaltation of one's self. This narcissistic self-projection is nothing more than a crafty lie.

The phrase "Non si fingerassi qui ciò che astutamente finse Renato delle Carte" pointedly discloses the Cartesian affirmation for a search for truth as if it were separable from falseness to be Descartes's conscious literary fiction. Descartes's disclaimer notwithstanding, fiction is inexorably woven in the architecture of his discourse. Furthermore, for Vico only the historical method gives access to a unified science ("all studies included in divine and human erudition"), and he intends to narrate his life as if he were the historiographer of himself. The term, "istorico," has wide resonances. In a primary way, the "ingenuità dovuta da istorico" implies a degree of candor

---

[10] See the following passage from the *Autobiography* in which Vico addresses explicitly these concerns in Descartes: "le *Meditazioni* di Renato Delle Carte, delle quali è seguito il suo libro *Del metodo*, in cui egli disappruova gli studi delle lingue, degli oratori, degli storici e de' poeti, e ponendo su solamente la sua metafisica, fisica e mattematica, riduce la letteratura al sapere deli arabi, i quali in tutte e tre queste parti n'ebbero dottissimi, come gli Averroi in metafisica e tanti famosi astronomi e medici che ne hanno nell'una e nell'altra scienza lasciate anche le voci necessarie a spiegarvisi." (*Autobiografia*, p. 29.)

and self-detachment whereby the self is enabled to judge itself in an un-adorned manner. But to be a historiographer of oneself also implies a view of the self, not floating in a timeless, supra-historical realm of essences, as Descartes would have it, but a self caught in the unfolding and carnality of time, and shaped by errors and failures.

Later in the text Vico obliquely calls his *Autobiography* a philosophical novel, which at first he resists writing, but then he writes it as a philoso-pher ("scrissela da filosofo" [p. 69]). The phrase (as well as the anaphoric "meditò" [he meditated] used to convey philosophy as meditative lan-guage) encapsulates Vico's awareness of the necessity of a hybrid discourse whereby literary representation is necessarily inseparable from both history and philosophy. What joins these disciplines together is the question of education.

The picture of man's powerless condition, dramatized by the child's fall and sickness, constitutes the Augustinian backdrop against which Vico etches the process of the making of the self within the context of the prob-lematics of education. As we know, this process of intellectual education, which the text proceeds to relate, will have no end. If for modern theories of subjectivism there is a self-defining, pure, inner self that the outside world can never darken, for Vico there is no a priori essence for the self: one is what one makes of oneself, and one makes of oneself what one knows, so that being, knowledge, and making are ceaselessly interwoven in an endless recirculation. And if for Plato, and for Plato's Socrates, edu-cation is philosophy itself, the *paideia* that traces the privileged path to the acquisition of justice in one's soul, for Vico, education does to the self what laws do to the state: they both bring about a new way of looking at one-self and at history. Finally, Vichian self-education does not get off the ground by introspection and self-reflection. True self-knowledge for him is never the idealized stripping away of social masks in order to find the au-thentic, pure "I" underneath the simulacra of public conventions. If any-thing, the *Autobiography* understands education as the experience that pre-pares us to be place-holders in the historical structure of what the Greeks would call the *oikos* and the *polis*.

The journey of education and self-instruction follows some predictable guideposts (grammar school, the university), but on the main it proceeds, though not quite like the Autodidact in Sartre's *La Nausée*, as a random pursuit of an encyclopedic totality. Vico represents himself as a perpetual autodidact who, paradoxically, will submit to the discipline of the tradi-tional *ratio studiorum* of the Jesuits. The dramatic detail of himself as au-todidact seeks to sketch the self-portrait of a man who knows he does not quite fit any existing molds or preestablished categories. The text proceeds to tell the inventory of books he reads. After convalescencing from his head wound, the child opens his eyes and lands upon a wondrous world—the world of books and of the discovery of the mind's limits. The young boy returns to grammar school; his mind is quick, but the teacher, a grammarian, refuses to teach and treat him in a class by himself (one wonders if this is not already a presage of logic's insufficient classifications). The pupil acts as his own teacher ("un fanciullo maestro di sè medesimo" [p. 9]) and he will leave school again. One inference is unavoidable: the belief in clear, distinct, and immobile abstractions of the mind is belied by this history of self-consciousness with the mind changing, stumbling against itself, growing, and refashioning itself continuously. It is as if for the boy, and for the mature narrator alike, nothing else matters except for living out his powerful intellectual passion.

The other passions that probably entangled their threads in his mind, the phantoms of the heart likely to remain untouched by time, the bewildered cluster of dreams and reveries (registered in a poem such as "Affetti di un disperato") are all bracketed as the boy studies the arts of the *trivium*, metaphysics, law, and poetry. Eventually Vico's process of education will be marked by a profusion and confusion of books, by the will to traverse the whole field of knowledge in its vast heterogeneity as if to justify the compliment of "autodidact" the Cartesian philosopher Gregorio Caloprese, who doubted everything and who yet valued the principle of the self as ground, assigned to him.[11]

We are approximating the definition of the crucial tension of Vico's *Autobiography*: the physical and historical limits of the self are set within the self's ambition for a global knowledge. In a way, this tension is contained within the very assumptions of the encyclopedic knowledge he pursues, in that to know everything means to know oneself. Nonetheless, Vico's production of an encyclopedic text is made possible by his traversing a series of what can be called liminal and marginal experiences. At its core, as a matter of fact, the *Autobiography* is an extended reflection on the thinker's inability to define (and not out of intellectual inadequacy) the legitimate "place" the philosopher/man of letters can occupy within the economy of the polis. Where does one really belong? What is the place of literature in philosophy and vice versa? Where does the "self" belong in Vico's own "science"?

Let me, first of all, shed some light on the new terminology I am introducing. Anthropologists have long spoken of ritual processes in terms of marginality and liminality.[12] Marginality designates a life forever lived out-

---

[11] See this other remark by Vico on Caloprese: "E, infatti, sul maggiore fervore che si celebrava la fisica cartesiana, il Vico, ricevutosi in Napoli, udillo spesse volte dire al signor Gregorio Caloprese, gran filosofo renatista, a cui il Vico fu molto caro" (*Autobiografia*, p. 22). An inference is unavoidable: as Caloprese calls Vico an autodidact, he is drawing him within the perimeter of Cartesian intellectuals such as himself.

[12] For a recent discussion of various critical positions on this issue and for their moral im-

side the structures of history from where one can challenge and counter the myths of the world. The prophet, the poet, or Socrates himself are figures living at the margins of the social order. Liminality, on the other hand, designates the threshold, the possible transition to higher or different states of consciousness or social degree. A university education or the church, for all the radical differences between them, can be understood in terms of the experience of liminality. To be sure, it is always difficult to determine whether literature is marginal or liminal, whether or not it remains unassimilable to history, and the determination is simply likely to betray our own biases. But there is no doubt that Vico's *Autobiography* collapses the mechanical opposition between marginality and liminality proposed by the anthropologists. Vico is always outside of history and he lives as an irreducible exile; yet, at the same time, the movement of the text and of his life leads him to an ever-deepening awareness of the historical role of his project and life.

The ambivalent state of the self concerns, to begin with, his inner psychology. He appears dejected, and he revives his enthusiasm, thanks to his constant passion for thinking rekindled in him after a session held at the "accademia degli Infuriati" (p. 7). And he quits school only to return to school. We could view his quitting school for a time as sheer intellectual impatience, as the sign of the untamed restlessness of a gifted and yet errant mind with its dark presages of a great future. This scene of life could even be taken as a not-too-subtle fashioning of the self as a young genius who is never altogether where he should be, who is either ambitiously ahead of himself or undeservedly held behind by unnamed (as if they were obscure) teachers, but who does not lose sight for too long of his natural vocation and final intellectual destination.

We would probably be right in extrapolating such a reading from this whole passage of the *Autobiography*. I suspect, however, that we would be closer to the truth if we were to read this initial oscillation in his being in and out of school as nothing less than the prefiguration of a life-long pattern of experiences by a thinker who lives forever at the edges of history, who is forever destined to be in and out of public structures and institutions, whose recognition, ironically, he highly covets (as he must), but from which he feels excluded. These existential experiences, which Vico recalls with scrupulous deliberation, will turn out to be the sinew of a complex idea of space and a sense of liminality of the self that his *Autobiography* represents with utmost clarity.

From the start, Vico's imagination is constantly drawn to well-defined

---

plications see Mihai I. Spariosu, *The Wreath of Wild Olive: Play, Liminality, and the Study of Literature* (Albany, N.Y.: State University of New York Press, 1997.) The sense of the "outside" has been studied in a Vichian, lyrical-philosophical vein by Robert Pogue Harrison, *Forests: The Shadow of Civilization* (Chicago: University of Chicago Press, 1992).

private and public places. These are both open and closed spaces, which, like concentric circles, delimit and define the self and which variously include and exclude other selves. The places are, firstly, the household, in which Vico is surrounded and sheltered by his family and friends; the forum or the world of the court; the exclusive academies—such as that of the Infuriati—that gather together the local intelligentsia; private libraries such as that of Valletta; bookstores, such as the one owned by his father, in which books are treated as commodities and as values, and which are loci of exchanges and of decisive encounters; the university, which is simultaneously a liminal and a marginal place; Naples, which to Vico looks like a planet unto itself; Vatolla, which he imagines as if it were out of this world; and Europe both as a distant dream and a nearby horizon of vital discourse.

The thought of these places punctuates the unfolding of the *Autobiography* and largely determines Vico's fate and sense of self. I am who I am, Vico says, because of my irreducible geography and chronology. Yet, Vico's historical thought, which is here to be understood as his consciousness of the mutability and possible otherness of all things, always evokes other places and other times, which are both real and imaginary—faraway correspondents in Rome, Venice, and Leipzig; the separate worlds of Augustine, of the Italian Trecento, and of the Renaissance. In effect, the constellation of disparate issues traversing the *Autobiography* and giving it its conceptual coherence—education, the questions of laws, the self, the relationship between literature and philosophy, the critical reception of Vico's work—is determined by the radical ambivalence characterizing his sense of place and, more generally, his life experience. Vico, the proponent of a topical philosophy, of the *ars topica*, rethinks the place of the self and of what could be called the topology of the self, and in the process he allows us to catch sight of the life and death of the philosopher.

After the years spent in grammar school and the stint at the Academy of the Infuriati, Vico attends the University of Naples to study law. Eventually, he meets in a bookstore Monsignor Geronimo Rocca, who urges Vico to go as a tutor to his nephews in a castle of the Cilento. Here he studies theology; he cultivates, under the influence of Lorenzo Valla's *Elegantiae*, Latin; he reads the classics of Italian literature (Dante, Petrarch, and Boccaccio) alongside Vergil, Horace, and Cicero; he applies himself to the reading of the Greeks, from Plato's *Republic* and its vision of justice to Aristotle's *Ethics*, to the Epicureans and the Stoics.

When he had left Naples, the philosophy of Epicurus, in the version of Gassendi, was fashionable. By contrast, Vico, who loves to project himself either as one who is out of place or out of step with his own times, studies it in Lucretius. But it is Plato's metaphysics that provides the standpoint to discard the mechanical physics of the Epicureans, the atomism of Gassendi, and the sensualistic morality or morality of pleasure ("una morale del piacere" [p. 19]) of John Locke.[13] Descartes's *Les passions de l'âme*, which are written *en physicien*, are rejected as a specimen of the technology of the soul (more useful to medicine than to ethics, as Vico wryly remarks). In effect, the Platonic metaphysics of freedom is the foundation for Vico's intellectual quest for unity, and this quest, no doubt, is the ironic counterpoint to his steady sense of existential apartness.

His separateness from various philosophical trends is forcefully dramatized by the account of the nine years spent in what he wants us to perceive as the absolute seclusion of Vatolla. Vico returns to Naples "come forestiero nella sua patria" (p. 23) (a stranger in his own land). He will not hide his disappointment with the intellectual climate of Naples epitomized by the tyranny and monotony of the Cartesian discourse now at the height of its popularity among the established men of letters. His sense of what I would like to call the *exotopy* (displacement) of self is highlighted by his awareness of the intellectual dead end of the present, which is embodied by sectarian prejudice and philosophical fashion. The metaphysicians and polymaths of the fifteenth and sixteenth century—Ficino, Pico, Nifo, Steuchio, Mazzoni, Piccolomini, Acquaviva, and Patrizi—who had contributed so much to poetry, history, and rhetoric, are now in disrepute, as are the medieval interpreters of civil law, the style of Della Casa, and good Tuscan poetry. Given these trends Vico is forced to accept a radical *a-topia*: the fact that "non solo viveva da straniero nella sua patria, ma anche sconosciuto" (p. 26) (he lived in his native city not only a stranger but quite unknown).

The metaphorics of place and displacement offer a sharp sense of the contradictory complexity of Vico's thought both in the *Autobiography* and, as I will show in the successive chapters, in the *New Science*. It is in a second encounter in a bookstore, for instance, that he is asked if he wants to become a Theatine. His vocation, however, is teaching, and he will become the Professor of Rhetoric at the University of Naples. Just as, at an earlier stage of his life, it was in the Academy of the Infuriati that he decided to go back to school, now in the Academy of Medinaceli (inaugurated in 1698 and disbanded in 1702 because of the conspiracy of Macchia) he decides to apply himself wholly to the profession of humane letters.

The job he lands at the university marks the watershed of his life. Up to now, even as a tutor, he had been a disciple. Now he is the teacher—and a largely unacknowledged author—who will seek to investigate man's knowledge in its encyclopedic totality and who will try to discover the vital dimensions philosophy had left out of the field of knowledge. That which lies outside of thought and determines the configuration of all of science is for Vico the dim, phantasmagoric world of passions, fictions, and dreams,

[13] Giovan Battista de Benedectis's *Philosophia peripatetica* (Naples, 1687) is a fierce attack against Leonardo di Capua's Gassendism. See also Matteo Giorgio, *Disputa intorno a' principi di Renato delle Carte* (1713) for a reading of Descartes in terms of Epicurus.

the mute and archaic mythology of the collective imagination that inexhaustibly projects its illusory shadows on the theater of rational reflections, the horizon of time that dissipates the frozen Cartesian cogito in the elusive geometries of universal history. What has been left out is, in one word, poetry. How can Vico make a *science* out of these eminently literary materials that perpetually evade all discursive formulations? How can literature and philosophy be thought of together without compromising the presumed integrity of each? Are they really entirely different from each other? Or, to say it differently: is literature the privileged language of the self, and what is the point of the *Autobiography*?

The study of history, literature, law, and philosophy that he has been pursuing has allowed him to discover the proximities and distances in all the forms of knowledge, whereby the present is best understood by uncovering its intersections with the past. From the time he becomes a university professor, he will be intent on drafting the yet blurred map of the totality of man's experience. There is an overt, if oblique, link in Vico's mind between encyclopedia and university, and what links them is the belief that the present cultural disintegration of the world can be contained by providing a unified model of new knowledge, which the university and the encyclopedia embody. By means of his insight into the encyclopedia, he aims to articulate a science that cuts through Platonic and Cartesian dualisms and that overcomes the crippling restrictions put forth by logicians, naturalists, and literary purists. The immense reorganization of culture he undertakes must draw together all the hybrid disciplines that constitute the world in a historical, provisional totality—poetry, myth, law, religion, history, and so forth. This sovereign aim is the *New Science*, which intends to provide a scheme wherein an ideal eternal history will be traversed by the universal history of all times. What helps him to conceive of this encyclopedic project that would represent and bind together the multiple spheres of man's activities is the encounter with the world of Bacon, who was to be named one of his *authors*.

Because the text stages the making of the self into an author, in the sense of a legitimate, authentic, and authoritative voice, Vico goes into an extended meditation on his four authors, whom, in contrast to the modern rejection of all outside authorities, he studies throughout his life. The four authors are Plato, Tacitus, Bacon, and Grotius, who are mentioned as if each figure constituted a necessary rung in his ever-widening perspective on the complexities of history. Each is a stepping stone in Vico's plan to reconstruct the ancient house of knowledge from its very foundation. It is clear that to claim authority one must have knowledge of the whole.

With his universal science, Plato contemplates man as he should be; Tacitus contemplates man as he is; Bacon's *De Augmentis Scientiarum* provides a model for the representation of encyclopedic knowledge, for he does justice "a tutte le scienze . . . e a tutte nel consiglio che ciascuna conferisca del suo nella somma che costitovisce l'universale repubblica delle lettere" (p. 30) (to all the sciences and always with the design that each should make its special contribution to that *summa* which the republic of letters constitutes). The fourth author will be Grotius, who brings a defining focus to Vico's search for a *mathesis universalis*. Grotius's *On the Law of War and Peace* opens up for Vico a whole field of knowledge by correlating philology and philosophy, history of facts, both fabulous and real, to the study of the three classical languages, Hebrew, Greek, and Latin.

Taken together, all four authors re-propose to Vico the necessity of a harmonious, totalitarian discourse, the outlines of which begin to emerge from the synopses the *Autobiography* gives of Vico's works. As Professor of Rhetoric he is called upon to deliver annually from 1699, the university's Inaugural Oration. The six lectures he prepares are a series of public reflections on the structure and uses of a university education, the aim of which is, according to Vico, "the unification in one principle of all knowledge human and divine". These concerns are further extended, as the next chapter will show, in his *De Nostri Temporis Studiorum Ratione* (*On the Study Methods of Our Time.*) Eventually, he will turn his attention to the study of law in the conviction that the codes of wisdom and of political order are embedded in the fabric and history of Roman jurisprudence.

On the strength of *De Uno*, and lured by the prestige and pay of the chair, Vico decides to run for the law lectureship that had just fallen vacant. He had already understood that the foundation, and indeed the condition, for any possible representation of order lay in language, for language preserves the deep and buried sediments of the ancients' wisdom. Bacon's *On the Wisdom of the Ancients* and Plato's *Cratylus* allowed him to rethink the premises of the grammarians' etymologies and to reflect on the semantic stratifications of Latin. The sense of this insight, however, emerges fully in the course of Vico's quest for the law chair at the university.

He prepares the lecture the night before he is to deliver it, working, as he says, until five in the morning while his friends conversed and his children cried. This domestic picture of Vico captures the essence of his thought, whereby "family" can first of all be understood as the conceptual metaphor for the cluster or web of relations defining each entity and rescuing it from the circle of separate or frozen self-sufficiency. His etymologies, let me say in passing, are imaginative, interconnected ramifications of one word rooted in the natural metaphor of "family." Also disciplines, like members of a family or cluster of words, are related to one another.

At the same time, however, the image of the philosopher at home pulsates with a different, subtler energy. The earlier work, "Affetti di un disperato," is now no more than a distant, even irrelevant, flicker of memory as the philosopher is surrounded by the vital affections of his family. If for philosophers, from Plato to Parmenides to Descartes, to think is to undertake a dialectical journey or to find the right method, for Vico to think is part of the hearth, part of the nurturing and compulsions of domesticity. But if thought is at home with Vico, the scene also evokes the philosopher's lonely, estranged activity even in the midst of the familiar landscape he inhabits. He can never be anywhere but at the margins.

Vico's quest for the law professorship turns out to be futile. In a sense, it was necessary for him, the thinker of the *legality* of authority, who also grasps that the determination of sense is a question of legality, to seek this appointment. But his failure allows him to shift from the conviction of the sovereignty of the law to the priority of language. The story Vico tells of his failure has an extraordinary dramatic economy. While delivering his lecture he mispronounces a Greek word. He had already fully grasped the power of language as the discourse of history and he had understood the value of the finest Greek expressions to convey his legal erudition. Now, in the academic performance of his life, he stumbles against what can be construed as a remnant of the medieval *Graecismus*. Because of the difficulty of the term, Vico mispronounces *progegrammenon:* he tries to make use of an elegant Hellenism, *antitupia*, in order to save the day, but he is forced by the circumstances to withdraw his candidacy from the law chair.[14]

The involuntary slip of the tongue in the delivery of his speech recalls and retrospectively casts light on Vico's misrepresentation of his birth date. It also ratifies Vico's new consciousness both of the status of error in the process of knowledge and of the nature of self. The two are connected. We are approximating here the deeper reasons for Vico's sense of the necessity of writing his *Autobiography*, that is to say of a literary representation of the philosopher's life. Error, says Gravina echoing Spinoza, consists in the privation of knowledge, which is brought about by inadequate and confused ideas. For Vico, one's origins are unknown; error happens, as if the tongue or language had a logic of its own that exceeds the rational control of the subject. The involuntary mistake leads Vico to perceive the extent to which the mode of existence of the self turns into an open-ended adventure, an "errare," as the *Autobiography* recorded earlier, wherein the voluntary and the fortuitous coalesce in what appears as a providential design. But the error is never final, because nothing is ever final or self-enclosed in Vico's thinking. This error, in point of fact, is productive for Vico's theory: as a result, he will grasp the value of fictions and simulacra in the determination of all wisdom and morality.

I have so far drawn attention to a number of mutually implicating issues in the *Autobiography*, which can be thus summarized. Vico writes about

---

[14] Vico's failure at the examination has been explained by Croce and Nicolini in the plausible terms of academic politics. Cf. Vico's *L'autobiografia, il carteggio e le poesie varie*, eds. B. Croce and F. Nicolini (see note 5), p. 118.

himself as if he were simultaneously inside and outside his own world, and his mind reaches or retreats to places unknown to other minds. Life is a life of the mind in the sense that one lives with books. But we are not limited to a representation of the solitary glitter of his mind. If anything, the story of his bodily sicknesses, as much as the inventory of his education, shows Vico within a historical context: he moves through the various institutions in pursuit of an institutional recognition and a totalizing science, by which he himself will become an authority. The *Autobiography* is the place where the claims to and the acknowledgment of his own authority will be transacted.

The text reports the publication of the first *New Science* in 1725 and describes in detail its contents (the recognition of sacred history; the invention of a critical art; the discovery of history and time as the framework within which knowledge is to be assessed; the role of poetry and language in the process of knowledge; the links between metaphysics and politics; the reinterpretation of the principles of jurisprudence and natural law). The work's description is the preamble to the account of its contradictory public reception, which is at the same time a parable of the disfiguration of Vico's self in the public arena. Sparse recognition of the value of the *New Science* came from abroad (Le Clerc) and from Venetian intellectuals, such as Conti, Lodoli, and Porcia, and this praise was neutralized both by anonymous attacks published in a Leipzig journal and by the almost total neglect in which it was held at home. Not without self-irony and in contrast to his academic failures, Vico goes on to record his social success as a local writer for various occasions: he is asked to pen funeral orations, inscriptions for funeral rites and nuptials, orations on the death of Donn' Angela Cimmino; and his own *Vita scritta da sè medesimo*. He revises the *Second New Science*, which was begun, as Vico says, on Christmas Day, 1729, and was finished on the evening of Easter Sunday, 1730.

This sequence of public events places Vico in the agora, in the public space where, as in the bookstore, knowledge is a market commodity, and where, like the Sophists Socrates despises, one writes for money. There is a transparent self-irony in the frivolous profile of a Vico suddenly fashionable for all the wrong reasons: a rhetorical gun for hire and the acknowledged celebrant of the comedies of worldliness. This worldly success hides the painful reality of the unacknowledged philosopher, who has portrayed in his *Vita scritta da sè medesimo* the ceaseless weave of life and death, the ceaselessly ambiguous weave of failure and success, of disappointments and violence to which one is subjected.

On the one hand, we are given the grand, recurring rituals of life: Christmas, Resurrection Sunday, weddings, and funerals, which together cast the *Autobiography* as a literary and philosophical meditation over the ongoing cycles of life and death. On the other hand, Vico is painfully aware of the pettiest aspects of life and of the ridicule he arouses: the most shameless of the pseudo-learned, he says without a shadow of self-pity, call him a fool; the more courteous say he is obscure, odd, eccentric; others pay him the ambiguous, damning compliment of being a teacher of teachers (a statement that casts him as Dante's Aristotle, but is an underhanded suggestion that he is an irrelevant figure for those who already know). The *Autobiography*, which began with the author's own misrepresentation of his birth, as if he were a stranger and unknown to himself, ends symmetrically with the account of a general misrepresentation or misunderstanding of Vico.

Is there a place, then, for the man of letters/philosopher in the city? Is one doomed to do what others want one to do? Vico's answer is clear. Confronted with these disappointments he withdraws from the marketplace to what seems to be the Cartesian space of his mind, to a desk, "come a sua alta inespugnabile rocca . . . per meditar e scriver altre opere, le quali chiamava 'generose vendette de' suoi detrattori'; le quali finalmente 'l condussero a ritruovare la *Scienza nuova*" (p. 83) (as to his high impregnable citadel, to meditate and to write further works which he was wont to call 'so many noble acts of vengeance against his detractors.' These finally led him to the discovery of his *New Science*).

No doubt, the "alta rocca" which Vico ascends symmetrically reverses the falling with which the *Autobiography* began, and, thus, it seals what to his mind appears as his spiritual redemption. Moreover, the metaphor of the desk as "rocca" recalls the retreat to the edge of the world, to the seclusion of the Rocca estate in Vatolla. Through these textual echoes of past figurations, one infers that it is part of Vico's wisdom to know that the past is never past, that it is a disguised figure of the future, that the future itself is an act of memory and a metaphoric dislocation of the past. From these metaphorical heights, above the fray, as it were, he will plot his "generose vendette." The phrase, with which he qualifies his works, is something of an oxymoron and it demands a special gloss.

In his *Passions of the Soul* (articles 153; 156–161), Descartes speaks of generosity as the key to all virtues. Akin to Aristotle's magnanimity, it is the virtue of the natural master, for it signals the consciousness of one's strength and elides any egalitarian perspective. Generosity is strength and nobility of mind acquired from birth or a moral virtue that can be taught (*Nic. Ethics*, 1124a). Revenge, on the other hand, defines one's submission to someone else's prior acts, and, as such, it ratifies one's slavery to the past. As Vico links generosity with revenge, the phrase gives us a glimpse into his ambivalent inner thoughts. While revenge can be construed as a form of equality and retributive justice, as a way of being equal to one's enemy, generosity implies that one is more than just, that one dishes out less than one has received. As shall be shown in the following chapters, the oxymoron—whereby acts of mastery and slavery are fused together—crystallizes Vico's politics. For now let me point out that "generose vendette" uncovers his original sense of time. If generosity, etymologically, suggests a productive, future-oriented action, vengeance is a figure of the tyranny of and nostalgia for the past: in taking revenge one acknowledges the hold of the past and the prestige of one's rival on one's mind. As such, writing, the "generosa vendetta," is for Vico a recollection forward, a *corso* and *ricorso*, one could say, or the future of the past and the past of the future. This insight by Vico is the very essence of literature.

But philosophy is not left out, for the philologist's dialogue with philosophy can never be abrogated. The figure of Socrates, with which the *Autobiography* comes to a close, puts into focus the radical sense of the philosophical strand of the narrative: "Dopo la quale [i.e., in the *New Science*], godendo di vita, libertà ed onore, si teneva per più fortunato di Socrate, del quale, faccendo menzione il buon Fedro, fece quel magnanimo voto: *cuius non fugio mortem, si famam assequar,/ et cedo invidiae, dummodo absolvar cinis*" (p. 83) (And when he had written this work, enjoying life, liberty, and honor, he held himself more fortunate than Socrates, on whom Phaedrus had these fine lines: I would not shun his death to win his fame; I would yield to odium, if absolved when dust.)

The lines from Phaedrus give a Petrarchan twist to Vico's *Autobiography:* the triumph of fame over death is the way the self, in the immortality of one's name, becomes an author and posthumously enters the world of history or, like Petrarch, "posterity." But the figure of Socrates resonates with a complex mythology that stretches from Plato to Cicero, from Petrarch to Erasmus and Bruno. Socrates is, at one and at the same time, the stray dog, always elsewhere and always out of place, the educator who links rhetoric and knowledge. In *On the Study Methods of Our Times*, he is the figure who possesses universal knowledge. In the *Autobiography*, however, it is the philosopher's death that is recalled. Socrates dies for and at the hands of the city: he dies both to preserve his freedom to philosophize and the legality of the city. Thus, through Socrates Vico emblematically ratifies his Socratic estrangement from his own city as well as the irreducibly political intimations of his philosophical discourse. As Vico mirrors himself in the figure of Socrates' death, philosophy comes through as a style of life, his life.

This insight into the self was not—and could not have been—advanced in the *New Science*, which purports to articulate a theory of the cycles of life and death of the world. It could be written only in the *Vita scritta da sè medesimo*, which is a literary text about the sense of a life. But the life of the philosopher is also a philosophical text about the philosophy of life as a life philosophy, in the sense that life is the horizon against which Vico's science has to be seen. In the wake of Valla, Ficino, Telesio, and Campanella, Vico knows that a philosophy can only be a philosophy of life or an ethics, that is, a taking care of one's *ethos* or character. He unequivocally stands in this line of wisdom, to which one might add Tacitus's *Life of Agricola* and Bacon's *History of Life and Death* with its reflections on how best to preserve natural bodies from death. From this standpoint, Vico's *Vita* is the story of a self-education aiming at preserving life against the encroachments of political and natural destructions, at carving a space for oneself as an authority living in liberty and honor. His philosophy of life is condensed in three words: "vita, libertà ed onore" (p. 85).

The phraseology echoes some key terms of John Locke's doctrine of ethical rationalism. In the *Second Treatise of Government*, written, under Bacon's influence, as a meditation on liberty from arbitrary government, there is a section on self-preservation as the "fundamental law of nature." Locke's notion of preservation of life includes "Life, Health, Liberty, and Possession" (par. 6) or "Lives, Liberties and Estates" (par. 123). But Locke's view of life as a utilitarian pursuit of wealth is not Vico's. Rather, Vico's "vita" has to be seen against the backdrop of Socrates' death and as a critique of death, while both "life and liberty" have to be viewed in the light of "honor" as if it were life's aim.

The word "vita" takes us back to the text's title and, in this sense, it conveys the text's deliberate transfiguration of a biography into a theory of life and into the life of the theory. Its proximity to Socrates' voluntary death suggests that Vico's sense of life is fraught with the consciousness of mortal dangers hovering over the philosopher. On the other hand, "libertà," which is the perspective of Vico's criticism of naturalism in its various disguises, is the moral precondition of life. The authority of the self is at one with his freedom. But what about "onore"?

In the sixteenth and seventeenth centuries, there is a ream of treatises on honor. As a worldly value, it is at the center of, say, Giambattista Possevino's concerns in his classical *Dialogo dell'Onore* (1553).[15] For Plato, man longs for honor. Yet, honor is an experience showing us on the stage of the world as we yield to the tyranny and we acknowledge somebody else's power (*Republic*, 620c). For Vico, the term is a double-edged proof of one's own self-consciousness. In a primary way, honor designates the first stirring of oneself to oneself as well as the stark recognition of oneself in relation to others. As in Plato's representation of the timocratic ethos, it is quickened by and, in turn, quickens in us the sense that each of us does not stand alone. *Onore*, as a principle of martial competitiveness (NS/277), undercuts the idea of autonomous self, for it is a most theatrical virtue in that it shows that one is what one is perceived to be by others. Tragic texts, es-

---

[15] One could also mention Flaminio Nobili's *De honore* (1563); Antonio Massa's *Contro l'uso del duello* (1553), which was written against Possevino; or Annibale Romei's *Discorsi* (1585). See also Francesco Ersparmer, *La biblioteca di don Ferrante: Duello e onore nella cultura del Cinquecento* (Rome: Bulzoni, 1985).

pecially in the Spanish theater, focus on *honra* both as a way of thinking how one ought to live one's life and as a diabolical yielding of oneself to appearances. By stressing *onore* as the crown of life, Vico summons us to the risks of the moral life and its unavoidable entanglements with the simulacra of the world.

Chapter 2

THE IDEA OF THE UNIVERSITY

FEW INNOVATIVE INTELLECTUALS of the seventeenth century produced their work from within the structure of an academic institution. Bacon, Hobbes, Descartes, Spinoza, and Leibniz—to mention the names of the epochal figures of that period—were deeply committed to a new way of thinking about knowledge. They even took part in its worldwide dissemination, but they shunned the politics and constraints of the universities. The intellectual autonomy and diffusion of knowledge many of them sought was to be best achieved, so they thought, by following different routes of investigation and communication of knowledge. Some of them would compile, for instance, encyclopedias. All of them would endorse and practice the aristocratic principles embodied by the so-called Republic of Letters or Republic of Scholars. The logical link between these two institutions and tools of learning is in many ways self-evident, but it bears some clarification.

In historical terms the Republic of Letters is a Petrarchan and Renaissance reformulation of the Ciceronian *ratio litterarum* and of the commonwealth of *litterae publicae* and, ultimately, of the Platonic Republic. Its aims are to reconstruct and promote a new, cosmopolitan atlas of knowledge, to allow the existence of multiple and dissenting viewpoints and yet to free intellectual debates from sectarian dissensions, and to pursue the ideals of harmony and unity of knowledge.[1] By the same token, the new encyclopedism of the seventeenth century also addresses these very concerns. Like the Republic of Letters, the principle of encyclopedism entails what can be called an ethics of knowledge in that its finalities and criteria of organization reflect the desire for a harmonious, universal scope of knowledge. A primary and highly influential example of the new encyclopedic project is Bacon's *Advancement of Learning*, written in 1605 but later revised in Latin as *De Dignitate et Augmentis Scientiarum* in 1624. Conceived as an introduction to the *Instauratio Magna* (of which only one section, the *Novum Organum* was completed), *De Dignitate* is chiefly a survey of the contemporary state of knowledge. Because it seeks to give a

---

[1] *De sui ipsius et multorum ignorantia* puts forth the notion of the morality of philosophical education and debates. See Leonardo Olschki, *The Genius of Italy* (New York, 1949), pp. 199–212. More generally see Enrico de Mas, "Associazionismo cristiano e prospettive ireniche agli inizi del Seicento," in *Studi in onore di Luigi Firpo* (Milan: Angeli, 1990), Vol. II, pp. 109–32.

representation of the *unity* and *variety* of knowledge, Bacon's encyclopedism is legitimately to be viewed as an extension of the criteria and assumptions shaping the Republic of Letters.

If these structures of education and knowledge were zealously endorsed, universities, which were long-established European institutions for such goals, were bypassed. Bacon's own *Cogitata et Visa* ponders on and sharply indicts the educational methods followed within the universities.[2] The chief objection leveled at the universities is that their antiquarianism and erudition, the two central features that characterize the academic discourse in its role of guaranteeing the transmission of the wisdom of the past and the discovery of new knowledge, in fact, stifle an openness toward the thought of the new.[3] "Knowledge," Bacon says in his *Advancement of Learning*, "is like waters" (Book III, Chapter 1), and the image, grammatically given in the plural, accurately conveys the idea that knowledge finds its own level and that its main body is made up of many tributaries. Against those who view it as a fixed, stagnant, or solid body, Bacon juxtaposes his sense of the fluidity, plurality, and openness of the various forms of knowledge. These he calls the "liquid regions" of philosophy and the sciences (and the implication of their mobile, uncontainable vitality is unequivocal). If for Giordano Bruno, who in a play such as *Il candelaio* calls for the melting of all rigidities, be they sexual or scientific, in the belief that knowledge is malleable wax, for Bacon the liquidity of knowledge carries still another implication. The frozen or vaporous forms of academic discourse, for all the apparent antinomy of the two physical states, converge on the same point. Whereas one dissipates knowledge's energy, the other contracts it into the guise of a scientific rigor which is really a *rigor mortis*.

There were, predictably enough, notable exceptions to this sort of opposition to university education, just as there were serious doubts about the practicality and real nature of the ideals peddled by the Republic of Letters. Many texts address these issues: from Ludovico Muratori's sketch of the "Repubblica letteraria d'Italia" (dated at Naples in 1703) to Diego de

---

[2] In the *Advancement of Learning* Bacon writes: "So if any man think philosophy and universality to be idle studies, he doth not consider that all professions are from thence served and supplied. . . . Scholars in universities come too soon and too unripe to logic and rhetoric, arts fitter for graduates than children and novices. For these two, rightly taken, are the gravest of sciences, being the arts of arts; the one for judgement, the other for ornament. . . . The wisdom of those arts, which is great and universal, is almost made contemptible, and is degenerate into childish sophistry and ridiculous affectation. . . . Another [defect] is a lack I find in the exercises used in the universities, which do make too great a divorce between invention and memory. For their speeches are either premeditate, in *verbis conceptis*, where nothing is left to invention; or merely extemporal, where little is left to memory." (Book II, pp. 8–12). Bacon's critique finds an echo in Hobbes's *Leviathan*, Part IV, Chapter 46 ("The Kingdom of Darkness").

[3] Vico mentions Bacon's "*cogitare videre*" in a different context (NS/359).

Saavedra-Fajardo's satirical *La republica literaria* to Jonathan Swift's *Battle of the Books*, from the debates between Perrault and Boileau on the quarrel between the *ancients* and the *moderns* to Leibniz's figuration of literary glory as tobacco smoke[4] (which, no doubt, was a gesture of recognition of the recent "discovery" of the American colonies). The myths sustaining the literary republic appeared to be undercut by the unavoidable sectarianisms making up the quarters of the international citadel of the new knowledge.

If the Republic of Letters was seen as the humanists' naive illusion barely masking personal and intellectual divisions, efforts were made to reform and promote the university as the framework within which knowledge as both tradition and innovation could be cultivated. A quick glance at the intellectual life of early eighteenth-century Naples reflects the generally European uneasiness about the value of the cultural discourse articulated within the universities, and it also shows the efforts directed to improving the quality of that discourse.

As elsewhere in Europe, in Naples the academies played a major role in the city's cultural life.[5] The Accademia degli Investiganti, the Accademia degli Oziosi, and, later, the Accademia di Medinacoeli were the freer, more vital meeting grounds for intellectuals such as Tommaso Cornelio, Francesco D'Andrea, and Leonardo di Capua, who were interested in what can roughly be called a Cartestian-based scientific research. The relative success of the academies was symmetrically seen as the unmistakable sign of the decadence of the university. The letter exchange between Federico

---

[4] Although the battle between ancients and moderns is originally a problem that occurs in Italy, only in the late seventeenth century does the phenomenon acquire a European dimension. See *Parallels des anciens et des modernes*, four vols. (Paris, 1688–97), reprinted with introduction by H. R. Jauss (Munich, 1964). For further bibliography see Joseph M. Levine, "G. B. Vico and the Quarrel between the Ancients and the Moderns," *Journal of the History of Ideas*, 52 (1991), pp.55–79. For Leibniz see Leroy E. Loemker, *Struggle for Synthesis: The Seventeenth-Century Background of Leibniz's Synthesis of Order and Freedom* (Cambridge, Mass.: Harvard University Press, 1972), p. 44.

[5] The bibliography on the extraordinarily lively intellectual life in Naples is rich. Among others, see Giuseppe Ricuperati, "A proposito dell'Accademia di Medina Coeli," *Rivista storica italiana*, 84, n. 1 (1972), pp. 57–79; Silvio Suppa, *L'Accademia di Medinacoeli fra tradizione investigante e nuova scienza civile* (Naples: Istituto Italiano per gli Studi Storici, 1971). More generally see Nino Cortese, *Cultura e politica a Napoli dal Cinquecento al Settecento* (Naples: ESI, 1965); Vincenzo Ferrone, *Scienza, natura, religione: mondo newtoniano e cultura italiana nel primo Settecento* (Naples: Iovene, 1982); Salvo Mastellone, *Pensiero politico e vita culturale a Napoli nella seconda metà del Seicento* (Messina-Florence: D'Anna, 1965); Biagio De Giovanni,"La vita intellettuale a Napoli fra la metà del '600 e la restaurazione del regno," in *Storia di Napoli* (Naples: ESI, 1970), Vol. VI, Part I, pp. 401–534; cf. *Saggi e ricerche nel Settecento* (Naples: Istituto Italiano per gli Studi Storici, 1968); Jerry H. Bentley, *Politics and Culture in Renaissance Naples* (Princeton: Princeton University Press, 1987); Harold S. Stone, *Vico's Cultural History: The Production and Transmission of Ideas in Naples* (New York: Brill, 1997).

Cesi and Cassiano del Pozzo about establishing the Accademia dei Lincei shows the crisis enveloping the traditional structures of learning.[6] And although some of these same scholars straddle both academies and university, in 1714 Filippo Caravita officially requests a reform of the *studium* of the city and laments that the most distinguished talents are kept away from university life.[7]

The perception of a generalized crisis of the universities notwithstanding, there were in Naples and in Europe figures who unequivocally acknowledged the educational and scientific importance of the universities and carried on their research within their frameworks. One such figure was Galileo, who taught at the University of Padua and also gave life, along with Cesi, to the Accademia dei Lincei. Another was Amos Comenius, himself a student of the encyclopedist Alsted at the University of Herborn. In the wake of Bacon's speculations about learning as an empirical method, but against Bacon's belief that the universities are outmoded, fossilized structures for the transmission and discovery of knowledge, Comenius yokes together the aims of the encyclopedic project with the idea of a new university. His *Pansophia* theorized a new and purposeful university curriculum that had to be characterized by an encyclopedic, universal scope and had to come into focus by an "anatomy" of reality. Vico elevates the medical term *autopsia* (drawn from anatomical theaters) to a category of history and philosophical knowledge in the *New Science*. The term means for Vico "l'evidenza de' sensi" (the evidence of the senses) (NS/499) or a direct vision of things as the Epicureans practice it. For Comenius autopsy is the route of knowledge beyond what he takes to be the useless stories of the ancients (*gentilium nugae*).[8]

In Naples Vico belongs to the category of scholars that includes Galileo, Gravina, and Comenius. Vico's thought spawns and breathes fresh life into all structures of learning—academies, universities, and encyclopedias—and it seeks to correlate them as components of an overarching educational vision. His *Autobiography*, as the preceding chapter has shown, details the role and importance of these institutions in Vico's and his city's life. On the other hand, the speech he delivered at the Accademia degli Oziosi in 1733 ("Le accademie e i rapporti tra la filosofia e l'eloquenza" ["The Academies and the Relationships between Philosophy and Rhetoric"]) shows his awareness of the academies' functions and limitations. The oration sketches a history of the high points of the academy, from Socrates' olive

---

[6] On the intellectual role of Cesi and the influence of Bacon on his ideas see Ezio Raimondi, "Scienziati e viaggiatori," in *Il Seicento: Storia della letteratura italiana,* eds. Emilio Cecchi and Natalino Sapegno (Milan: Garzanti, 1969), Vol. V, pp. 225–318.

[7] On Caravita see Biagio De Giovanni, "La vita intellettuale a Napoli tra la metà del '600 e la restaurazione del regno" in *Storia de Napole* (Naples, ESI, 1970).

[8] For Comenius see his *Pansophia Prodromus* (Lugduni Batavorum, 1644), p. 19ff.

grove to Cicero's academy, and defines the academy technically as an aggregate of lettered men engaged in the pursuit of erudition and doctrine.[9] Within the narrow but prestigious boundaries of the academy, the educated man of proven accomplishments in a particular domain of knowledge can roam freely over the wide fields of wisdom.

But because at the heart of his philosophical thought lies the question of education of the young and its extension into the public domain of practical needs, Vico centers many of his speculations not on the academies, which are by definition made of select elites gathering in self-enclosed social circles, but on the structure of the university. There are three texts that record Vico's ongoing speculations about the crucial role the universities play or ought to play in modern life and, specifically, in the political world.[10] They are the Inaugural Orations, which he delivered ex officio at the annual opening of the Royal University; *On the Study Methods of Our Time*, which rethinks the structure and rationale of the curriculum and takes to task the assumptions shaping Bacon's encyclopedism; and *On the Heroic Mind*, which explores the possibility of a heroic intellectual life in the prosaic modern age, recapitulates his thought on education, and reflects on the possibility of originality and discovery in the sciences.

In a sense, given the fact that Vico spends his entire adult life as Professor of Rhetoric and Literature at the University of Naples and that he develops his major works within and in opposition to the perimeter of Naples' academic structure, it was inevitable that he should come to view the university with such passionate, steady, but essentially ambivalent, involvement. His idea of the university, as we shall see, is highly contradictory, and, indeed, Vico theorizes the university as the ambiguous but vital locus of multiple, necessarily contradictory voices in the process of education.[11] No

[9] "Questo nome 'Accademia', che abbiámo preso da' greci per significare un comune d'uomini letterati uniti insieme affin di esercitare gl'ingegni in lavori di erudizione e dottrina. . . ." in "Le accademie e i rapporti tra la filosofia e l' eloquenza," in Giambattista Vico, *Opere*, Vol. I, pp. 405–09.

[10] Scholars have analyzed these texts by Vico in order to stress the importance of rhetoric in his thought. See Ernesto Grassi, "Filosofia critica o filosofia topica: Il dualismo di pathos e ragione," *Archivio di Filosofia* (1969), pp. 109–21; Cesare Vasoli, "Topica, retorica e argomentazione nella 'prima filosofia' del Vico," *Revue Internationale de Philosophie*, 33 (1979), pp. 188–201; John D. Schaeffer, "Vico's Rhetorical Model of the Mind: 'Sensus communis' in *De Nostri Temporis Studiorum Ratione*," *Philosophy and Rhetoric*, 14 (1981), pp. 152–67; see also Rosario Assunto, "La prolusione *De nostri temporis studiorum ratione* di G. B. Vico e la difesa della fantasia nella cultura di oggi," *Realtà del Mezzogiorno*, 13 (1973), pp. 315–33. Of note are George de Santillana, "Vico and Descartes," *Osiris*, 9 (1950), pp. 565–80, and J. Chaix-Ruy, "J. B. Vico et Descartes," *Archives de Philosophie*, 31 (1968), pp. 628–39.

[11] For the modern debate about the university see Jaroslav Pelikan, *The Idea of the University: A Reexamination* (New Haven: Yale University Press, 1992), which is a reflection on cardinal Newman's classical text about a modern Catholic university; and Frank Turner, *The Idea of the University* (New Haven: Yale University Press, 1996). From a historical viewpoint

doubt Vico's own professional experiences had much to do with the ambivalences present in the theoretical model of the university he constructs. His academic failures certainly made him aware of the morally dim political mechanisms governing the institutional life of a university such as his own. The account of how he was denied the much coveted law professorship and had to stay put in the chair of rhetoric, as the *Autobiography* tells us, shows that he had few reasons to harbor illusions of the ethics shaping the life of the academic community. He knew first-hand the power games academics play, and he played some himself.

Yet his personal experiences cannot quite explain why Vico should continue to think of the university as a privileged structure of knowledge. Furthermore, there is no evidence in his past to explain why Vico shares Galileo's and Comenius's conviction that erudition and adventurous innovation are not mutually exclusive dimensions of knowledge. It is clear, however, that the university is for Vico a privileged structure. It can be surmised that from a purely personal viewpoint, Vico stayed at the university simply because there was no other reasonable choice for a young and self-consciously gifted scholar, such as he was, who needed employment and who craved intellectual recognition.

The university, however, came to mean much more to him than what the narrow focus of his personal experiences would lead one to suspect. All his pedagogical writings, taken together, bring to a head central questions that have nothing to do with likely personal peeves or career concerns, though these triggered his selection of topics. The complexity of his theoretical speculations can be gauged by recalling the central issues on which he steadily muses. The first issue is the sense, which is the legacy of Roman culture, of the role of an institution as a historical construction, as the crucial locus of the sediments of historical memories. But there are other issues figuring in Vico's mind: the nature and uses of knowledge, the ethics of research, the relationship (necessarily full of mutual distrust) between university discourse and political power, and, more overtly, the links between tradition and intellectual discovery or originality. This last point is to be understood as the sense and possibility of epochal rupture in the interpretation of knowledge and in the representation of history.

Predictably, these questions cannot be found simultaneously in each of his texts nor are they necessarily treated in a thematic or consistent way, as if Vico knew all along and never had to alter his ideas about the university. Because they were written over a long period of time, the Inaugural Orations, which were delivered from 1699 to 1707, *On the Study Methods of*

---

see Jacques Verger, "Remarques sur l'enseignement des arts dans les universites du Midi a la fin du Moyen Age," *Annales du Midi*, 91 (1979), pp. 355–81; John Gascoigne, "A Reappraisal of the Role of the Universities in the Scientific Revolution," in *Reappraisals of the Scientific Revolution* (Cambridge: Cambridge University Press, 1990), pp. 204–60.

Our Time, which was composed in 1708, and *On the Heroic Mind*, which was written in 1732, map a series of shifts in Vico's views on university education. He never really wavers, however, in his commitment to the Platonic ideals that ought to shape university life. From the standpoint of these noble ideals, whereby education is essentially a question of the education of the soul and is itself the very incarnation of philosophy, the university remains for him a structure ever complicitous with political power and yet consciously marginal to it. In brief, the university marks the ambiguous boundary of the city, and it comes forth as a real and yet imaginative place where society's social and moral values are both preserved and radically challenged and subverted.

To be sure, Vico never articulates explicitly these ideas about the university's marginal/liminal and yet central status in the life of the polis. Yet, there is hardly any doubt that he is fully conscious of the multiple roles the university plays in shaping the cultural values of society. One such role, as *On the Study Methods of Our Time* shows, is historical or institutional. This institutional role can be summarized as the power of the university to preserve and transmit for the future the past's unfathomable accumulations of knowledge. It can be said that from such a viewpoint the university structure crystallizes Vico's sense of historical knowledge, the knowledge that grasps what is timely and untimely in modernity's consciousness of tradition. But the university's primary role is sharply delineated in the Inaugural Orations, which start off and unfold in the wake of Neoplatonic ideals about man's divinity.

The Neoplatonic principle of man's boundless poetic energy and inner divinity leads Vico to underwrite Plato's idea of philosophy as being itself nothing less than education, as a spiritual process whose end must be the enlargement of the intellect for the pursuit of "the knowledge of things human and divine" (*The Autobiography*, p. 146). More specifically, Pico's theory about man as the *copula mundi* in *De Dignitate Hominis* constitutes both the core and the point of departure for Vico's reflections in the Inaugural Orations on the utopian and political nature of a university education. As we shall see later, a mature text, such as *On the Heroic Mind*, will ponder the discrepancies between utopian principles and political realities of the university structure. The Inaugural Orations, on the contrary, will posit a possible harmonious continuity between utopia and politics.

The first oration defines the nature of knowledge as Socratic self-knowledge, and self-knowledge is cast as the point of destination of all the branches of learning. The second oration, on the other hand, addresses the utopian ends of a university education. By deploying a terminology that resonates with Plato's *Republic*, the *City of the Sun* by Campanella, and the *New Atlantis* by Bacon, Vico argues that the universe is a cosmopolis, a great city regulated by divine laws. Education is the process by which wise people, those who know the laws of nature, are granted the privilege of citizenship in this universal city. This overt transcendence of the cramped confines of one's political membership achieved through education certainly echoes the principles of broad-minded cosmopolitanism of the Republic of Letters. More than that, this utopia of the mind formed by the process of education is reached by expelling from one's soul what Plato calls *pleonexia*, spiritless greed. Retrospectively, we see what knowledge of the laws of nature entails: the knowledge of bodies, the natural inequalities of bodies, their proneness to excess, and their uncontrollable urges. Vico refers to them as vices to be contained by moderation, by waging a "tragic war" against sloth, luxury, malice, and imprudence.

In spite of their powerful utopian rhetoric, the Inaugural Orations do not remain caught up for too long in abstract metaphysical speculations. The quick account of their thematic content, available in the *Autobiography*, stresses how these orations "delivered in successive years at the annual opening of studies in the Royal University [would] propose universal arguments brought down from metaphysics and given social application. . . . The first three treat principally of the ends suitable to human nature, the next two principally of the political ends, the sixth of the Christian end" (pp. 139–40). The summary statement of the translation of metaphysics into politics and theology accurately reflects the shift of Vico's conceptual focus. Quite explicitly, the fourth and fifth orations proceed to transpose the Platonic abstractions into the immanent domain of politics. At stake is Vico's political understanding of education which he carries out by taking his cue from different but correlated sources.

Classical theories of education, such as those by Cicero and Quintilian, who theorize that man must perform his function as a citizen; humanist theorists, such as Salutati, Bruni, Vergerius, Guarini, and Vives, who variously believe that the *studia humanitatis* find their truth in the Logos of the city and that rhetoric must shape the civic consciousness of the individual; Aristotle's *Politics*, with its central insight that man is a political animal gifted with speech: these are the aspects of Vico's vision of education. The fourth oration, thus, exhorts the young to direct their efforts toward the "glory and good of the community" (p. 142).[12] This joining together of politics and education dispels any possible illusion that the autonomy of the university could be a self-enclosed entity devoted to pure research. Vico agrees that the university exists primarily to serve the interests of the state. At the same time, the university itself emerges as a *politeia*, as the place where the entire range of public concerns is to be debated.

This double idea of the university as having both utopian and political ends is not really Vico's own elaboration. A brief synopsis of the archeol-

[12] The epitome of such a traditional concern about politics and education in classical and Renaissance thought is available in *Quintilian's Institutio Oratoria*, Book I, Section iv, p. 5.

ogy of the idea is needed as a way of shedding light on Vico's thought. The chief impulse for his recognition of the institutional value of the university is to be found in his Roman and juridical conviction that an institution is the locus of historical continuities, the stable and yet temporal archive of public memories. The particular history of the University of Naples, on the other hand, partially accounts for the political focus in the orations he addresses to the students of that university.[13]

It is certainly well known that modern universities were established, concomitantly with the phenomenon of medieval encyclopedism, in the twelfth century at Bologna and Paris, which together constituted the models for all other European universities. It also known that most Italian universities—Padua, Modena, Vicenza, Reggio—come into existence out of a schism from the University of Bologna.[14] So does the University of Naples. Founded as a law school in 1224 by decree of the Emperor Frederick II (and conceived by Pier delle Vigne), it was intended to offset the hegemony of the jurists and scholars of canon law housed at Bologna since the days of Irnerius. A number of prestigious figures, including Thomas Aquinas, taught at the University of Naples, but the purpose of its foundation was unequivocally secular and political: Frederick II needed experts in statecraft, agents for diplomatic missions, jurists for the chancery, and lawyers to settle the empire's sundry controversies. The University of Naples, thus, is the first state school of Europe and it never lost the traces of its institutional origin: political censorship over the professors and their oaths of loyalty to the royal chancellor, who was its superintendent, made it abundantly clear who worked for whom.

If the specific history of the University of Naples constitutes the concrete, material background for Vico's musings on the links between education and politics, it is clear that the philosophical rationale for the idea of the university poised between utopia and politics comes to him from elsewhere. From the figures he loves most of the remote and recent past—Plato, More, Campanella, and Bacon—Vico has learned that all traditional speculations on education are monotonously placed within a utopian setting.

In Plato's *Republic*, which is primarily a text about the various theories,

---

[13] An account of the University of Naples is available in Giangiuseppe Origlia, *Istoria dello studio di Napoli* (Naples: Giovanni Di Simone, 1753). See also Pietro Napoli-Signorelli, *Vicende della coltura nelle due Sicilie* (Naples: Presso Vincenzo FI, 1784), ii, 244ff.; iii, 28, etc.; Hastings Rashdall, *The Universities of Europe in the Middle Ages* (Oxford: Clarendon Press, 1895), II, pp. 21–26. Cf. Michelangelo Schipa, *Il regno di Napoli descritto nel 1713 da P. M. Doria* (Naples: L. Pierro, 1899). Cf. also the more recent *Storia della Università di Napoli* (Naples: Ricciardi, 1924); Alberto Marghieri, *Studium generale ed università dei nuovi tempi* (Naples: Giannini, 1924).

[14] Paul O. Kristeller, "The University of Bologna and the Renaissance," *Studi e memorie per la storia dell'università di Bologna*, n.s. 1 (1956), pp. 313–23.

practices, and decadence of Greek *paideia*, he found the conceptual origin of the idea of the university. I shall examine other aspects of Plato's work in the chapters that follow. Here I shall limit myself to remarking how the *Republic*, which among other things investigates the relationship between education (or philosophy) and politics, provides nothing less than the Western blueprint for the establishment of the Academy or university curriculum. In earlier books of the *Republic*, Plato sets out the program for primary and secondary education or *mousike*. In Book VII, on the other hand, Plato adopts the Pythagorean plan of higher education, which is to be understood as the process whereby the soul's eye turns away from the facts of the material world to immutable objects of pure thought. The process is effected by teaching the *mathemata* (geometry, arithmetic, astronomy, and music), which are the disciplines encouraging reflection on the Forms.

In the wake of Plato and More, Campanella tells of the *City of the Sun* through a member of Columbus's crew who had returned from one of his journeys of discovery into new spaces of the mind and of geography. Bacon travels to a new continent, to Bensalem, in order to locate in that scientific utopia, a *novus orbis scientiarum*, a new rational principle, whereby peace, justice, truth, and honor can be rescued from general destruction. But Bacon does not mechanically repeat Plato's ideals in the *Republic*. Rather, he knows that those ideals are no longer adequate to modern times and that modernity is under the sway of Machiavelli's view of infinite desires and of the titanic ambitions of the sciences. More precisely, he knows that Plato's myth of moderation, essential to the order of the polis, is abrogated by Machiavelli's Augustinian theory of desire. Bacon, thus, rewrites Plato's utopia by placing it within the context of Machiavellian politics.

Unlike Machiavelli, Vico insists on the necessary moderation of bodies. But he thoroughly subscribes to the trenchant critique of political utopianism that Machiavelli unleashes in Chapter 15 of *The Prince*, in the persuasion that man must govern ideals just as much as ideals must govern man. And unlike Plato, More, Campanella, and Bacon, Vico never places his educational views within the rhetorical genre of utopias. If anything, it is as if the university structure, which is so much within the city and so blatantly subjected to the king and to the ecclesiastical authorities, were his only possible utopia, the place where history and utopia confront each other.

We can be sure that Vico never really thought that the *Republic* or the *New Atlantis* or the *City of the Sun* were merely visionary tracts in utopian political theory. But he was certain that they were about politics, though in a special way. They are about the educability of tyrants, about establishing values on the basis of a scientific rationalism, or about contesting and perpetuating the myths of the polis. They are political works, more to the point, in the measure in which they are chiefly about education: Plato, Campanella, and Bacon understand only too well that the health and the future of the city are decided by the city's educational programs. Nor does Vico have any second thoughts about the centrality of education in the life of the polis. The university is for him the all too real landscape where utopias find, as it were, their only possible topicality. In this idea of the university that Vico elaborates, utopias and political realities are kept distinct and yet are tangled together, while the continuity between utopian principles and politics, which punctuates the unfolding of the early Inaugural Orations, becomes increasingly recognizable as a form of illusory optimism.

These general conceptions shape the movement of all of Vico's Inaugural Orations. The third oration, as a matter of fact, reflects on the ethics of university life, but as it does so, it manages to cast the university, if not as a utopia, as a potentially moral universe where the common practices of the ordinary world are reversed. The oration's explicit theme, as it is announced in the *Autobiography*, is that "The society of letters must be rid of every deceit, if you would study to be adorned with true, not feigned, solid, not empty, erudition" (pp. 141–42). The virtue of *honestas* in scientific research—which is the ideal of seventeenth-century education— moved Bacon, Descartes, Spinoza, and Leibniz to posit it as the true aim of moral knowledge.

Vico retrieves this tradition. But this virtue, if practiced in the university, would make it an anti-world that challenges the myths and values of the ordinary world. The worldly values are here evoked unequivocally, though indirectly. Historically, in fact, the *homo honestatis* is the figure opposed to the skepticism or dissimulatory practices of the erudite libertines. Whereas the libertines assert the despotic dominion of their own selves over the entities of the world, *honnetete* is founded in and recognizes the boundaries and limits of self. More than that, *honestas*, which means variously *pietas* or *equitas*, action based on the good and the desire for the good, is the acknowledgment of others; it is the virtue of Castiglione's courtier and it marks the acknowledgment of different viewpoints in the Republic of Letters. Vico makes this virtue the ideal ethical rule of the university.

It is possible to find elements of proximity and distance between the "world" and the university even in the fifth oration. Overtly, its focus is the practical value of a humanistic education from the viewpoint of the traditional relationship between military glory and the study of letters. The judgment on the humanities is one of their usefulness to the state, which is represented in terms of a martial ideology. Vico's encounter with Grotius's *On the Law of War and Peace* will take place years later. But in this fifth oration he already constructs the relationship between military glory and the study of letters as if they were two opposed ideologies of, respectively, war and peace, power and justice.

In the *Florentine Histories*, Machiavelli had asserted the temporal priority of arms over letters (Mars over Minerva) and of captains over philosophers (V, 1). Hobbes in his *Leviathan* (XLVI) agrees with this Machiavellian genealogy of values. The ethos of competitive action and power, crystallized by the divisiveness of war, engenders and determines for both of them all other social values. Vico brackets and dismisses the hierarchy of values set forth by these two political philosophers, and he argues for the necessity of yoking together, as the humanists of the Italian Renaissance had done, the tenets of *vita activa* and *vita contemplativa*. Without the irenic tones of Erasmus's *Laus pacis*, Vico maintains that the world of letters is also a world of action, and it ought to be promoted in order to set limits to the unbounded practice of war and to displace the settlement of controversies from the battlefield to the tribunal.

Doubtless, Vico believes in the ultimate heterogeneity of the two pursuits. The mentality of war, which for Vico is the core reality of the libertine and a strategy of Machiavellian politics, is the denial of the world of letters. War unavoidably makes a partisan and single viewpoint into an absolute; while humane letters oppose the violent closure of all possible discourses and are irreducible to the demands of one single viewpoint. But Vico retrenches from the insight into the antithetical outlooks of the two enterprises, and the retrenchment acknowledges the university's complicity with the value system embodied by military glory. Thus, Vico will argue that the study of letters, which is set apart and constitutes the very boundary of the values of war, can coexist with military values and, indeed, it can favor greater military glory.

Vico's perception of the radical ambivalence of the university as having both political ends and the power to transcend, to question, and to reverse the boundaries of the political domain is extended in the sixth oration where he reflects on the essential ambiguities of man's own nature. Vico now places the question of education within a scheme of universal history, but he effectively rethinks the optimism of the Neoplatonists concerning the *dignitas hominis*, which the first oration had articulated.

For Pico the ambiguity of man is metaphysical and it depends on the fact that his nature has neither a fixed essence nor fixed boundaries. Nothing can define or contain man's being, which, paradoxically, is in a state of steady becoming. The image Pico uses is that of the chameleon to signal man's adaptability to shifting circumstances as well as his power to become an angel or descend to bestiality. For Vico, who elaborates a genealogy of history in terms of the *insensati bestioni* who roam the face of the earth until they are tamed into becoming men, ambiguity is no longer a question of simply two contrasting ontological options available to man.

The either/or dilemma of Pico's grand vision, whereby he celebrates the infinite freedom of the individual to forge one's life in the shapes of one's own choice, is for Vico sorely inadequate. What makes it inadequate is that in its radical optimism this myth of self-creation ignores the tragic constraints of the natural order, which Vico relentlessly evokes in this oration. The picture of the wretchedness of man and his natural imperfections because of original sin is for Vico the other side of man's greatness. The perception of man's ambivalent nature recalls the contradictions of man formulated by St. Augustine's theology and its prolongation in Pascal's *Pensées*, his sense of man as a fragile tangle that cannot be unraveled and as a being who is simultaneously the glory and the refuse of the universe, at one and the same time the depository of truth and the "cloaque d'incertitude," (*Pensées*, p. 184). Education, according to Vico, is grounded in the Pascalian domain of the will to reverse the tragic consciousness of the fallen condition and to view life as the day of training on the earth. Consistently, "all the orb of the arts and sciences" (Oration VI from *On Humanistic Education*, p. 129) constitutes for Vico a university education, which engenders eloquence, knowledge, and virtue—the three remedies to man's fallen nature.

From this metaphysical standpoint the sixth oration proceeds to detail the university curriculum Vico envisions. His point of departure is the definition of wisdom—"Sapientia." The foundation of all wisdom, says Vico, following the traditional medieval arrangement of the seven liberal arts, is grammar, which guarantees correct speech. But wisdom also comprises the knowledge of human things (mathematics, physics, and medicine) and divine things (which are the human mind and God and include metaphysics, theology, and ethics). The divine things perfect and give full knowledge of the natural things. The true wisdom encompasses, more precisely, science, prudence (which is an eminently political virtue), and eloquence. Vico goes on to connect the various disciplines to the faculties of the mind, as Bacon suggests in his *Novum Organum*, and thereby he accounts for their necessity and order. Since memory is strongest in children, schooling must begin with the teaching of languages (Greek and Latin).[15] The imagination of the young is very powerful and this is the stage for teaching mathematics. Metaphysics and theology, which are the more abstract disciplines, are to be studied last when rationality is firmly established.

These pedagogical-curricular questions are treated once again and in an extensive and rigorously technical manner in *De Nostri Temporis Studiorum Ratione*, or *On the Study Methods of Our Time*. The tract develops a speech, which was first delivered at the University of Naples on October 18, 1708, and which, on the face of it, purports to be a comparison of the

---

[15] One should recall that in the *City of the Sun* Campanella presents an educational scheme in which the abstract studies of metaphysics and theology also come last, after the language and the alphabet (which the Solarians learn when they are three years old), after the natural sciences (to be learned after seven years of age), and after mathematics, medicine, and other sciences.

educational method of the present and that of antiquity. Vico does not really offer a sovereign method of universal applicability, as, say, Descartes does with his mathematical-geometric method, which seeks the truth in the sciences. Rather, Vico intends to vindicate the intellectual legitimacy and rigor of a program of studies centered on poetry, which is for him the spirit of memory and the language of the imagination (Book VIII of *On the Study Methods of Our Time*).

Vico, who understands poetry as a particular way of thinking and as a particularly moral way of seeing the world, erases the traditional antagonisms posited between the truth of the poets and the truth of the philosophers and makes the world of law the point of intersection of philosophy and poetry.[16] From this standpoint, the term "ratione" in the treatise's Latin title, which has its semantic matrix in logic and law (ratio), discloses these disciplines' proximity to each other. This word, in fact, can be translated as method, procedure, or even as rationale for the ordering of university studies. At any rate, the conceptual breadth of the tract can be gauged both by the other resonances available in the title and by the polemical targets Vico confronts head-on.

De Studiorum Ratione alludes to the commonplace *ratio studiorum*, the course of studies or disposition of disciplines, such as the one the Jesuits prepared and continually revised in the sixteenth century at the Collegio Romano, where scholars such as Suarez, Bellarmine, Vossius, and Kircher taught. The phrase *De nostri temporis*, on the other hand, foregrounds Vico's sense of modernity as a break from the past, as the advent of a new historical discourse that differs from that of the past. The issue of modernity will be developed, quite consistently, throughout the essay in a variety of ways, as if the real challenge of the university rested precisely in its power to shape the discourses of the present and to judge the present from the viewpoint of the past. Thus, Vico explicitly recalls and gives a significant twist, for instance, to the age-old *querelle des anciens et de modernes*. He opposes modernity's disintegration and departmentalization of the unity of knowledge in the name of an overarching harmony of the whole; he evokes Memory, who is, mythically, the mother of the muses and, metaphorically, the figure of gathering and recollecting the sediments of history, as a scandal to the practice of analytical criticism and geometric method rampant in the scholarship of the present. From the viewpoint of

---

[16] "I believe that the goal which today is most particularly pursued, i.e., ideal or universal truth, is exceedingly serviceable to poetry. By no means do I share the opinion that poets take special delight in falsehoods. I would even dare to affirm that poets are no less eager in the pursuit of truth than philosophers. The poet teaches by delighting what the philosopher teaches austerely. Both teach moral duties; both depict human habits and behavior; both incite to virtue and deter from vice." *On the Study Methods of Our Time*, trans. Elio Gianturco, pp. 42–43.

memory, the modern educational project is not as original as its proponents believe.

For all his overt opposition to the new fashion of the geometric method of the logicians, Vico himself adopts the rhetoric of the "new": "Unless I am mistaken," he announces at the outset, "this theme is new" (p. 5). Its novelty lies in the comparison of the method of studies of antiquity with that of modernity. Obliquely, then, the university comes forth as the privileged space where the necessary confrontation between the new and the old turns into an object of reflection. If in the Inaugural Orations the idea of the university provided an ethical, theological, and political perspective disengaged from, and yet subordinated to, the actualities of history, *On the Study Methods of Our Time* casts in epistemological terms what can be called the marginal and liminal status of the university in relation to the demands and fashions of history.

The text's argument unfolds under the aegis of *De Dignitate et de Augmentis Scientiarum*, where Bacon proposes to reconstruct the entire fabric of the arts and sciences and break away from the paths of tradition. Vico acknowledges that the English chancellor discovered "a new cosmos of sciences" and "a completely new universe" (p. 4). The phrase translates and adapts Bacon's *novus orbis scientiarum*. The emphasis on Bacon's novelties, which are said to consist of his revision of Aristotle's division of the sciences, suggests that in principle Vico is opposed neither to modernity nor to modernity's claims of innovation. In the wake of Plato and Bacon, Vico certainly believed that one lone man could undertake the task of total, heroic renovation of culture. Plato in the *Republic* seeks to overhaul the Homeric encyclopedia and replace it with a theory of education centered on a dialectical method. Bacon's *instauratio* is a self-conscious vision of a radically new reorganization of knowledge for "minds washed clean of opinions" (*Natural and Experimental History for the Foundation of Philosophy* [English, Vol. 5, p. 132]). Vico's own *Scienza nuova*, plainly, dramatizes Vico's self-conscious role as an innovator in the mode of both Plato and Bacon. Thus, Vico is not opposed to modernity as such, but he opposes the narcissistic erasure of the past in the complacent assumption of modernity's wholesale superiority over the past. This assumption led Bacon to recast the terms of the historical *querelle* between the "ancients" and the "moderns." Vico sees in Bacon's apology of modernity's scientific conquests nothing less than a version of a Machiavellian strategy of power.

The vindication of the value of modernity is proven for Vico by the institution of the university. *On the Study Methods of Our Time*, in fact, locates in modernity the origin of and the need for contemporary universities. Vico is in this way theorizing against Bacon's dismissal of universities in *Cogitata et Visa* in the name of the myth of the isolated thinker. It is impossible, Vico claims, for an individual in our times to retrace and master

the entire range of the human sciences. In antiquity, "the Ancients possessed universities for the body, i.e., baths and athletic fields"; in intellectual matters, however, "a single philosopher synthesized in himself a whole
university" (p. 74). The reference is to Socrates, but in modern times the
traditional role of the lone philosopher can only be played by a university,
where "all branches of knowledge are taught by a number of scholars, each
of whom is outstanding in his particular field" (p. 76). The collective mind
of the university must replace, but not cancel, the mind of the individual.
Vico's polemic with Bacon's version of the *querelle* between moderns and
ancients pivots on the sense and value of the past.

   Both in Italy and France the *querelle* recognizes a fundamental paradox
in the processes of knowledge. In the sciences, where progress continues
to take place, modernity's superiority over the past is unequivocal. Vico
agrees with this assessment ("As for astronomy, the modern telescope has
brought within our ken a multitude of new stars, the variability of the sun-
spots, and phases of the planets." [p. 10]). The limit of the moderns lies in
their making reason the rule of knowledge. Yet antiquity's superiority over
the present in poetry is for Vico a fact that cannot be contested. One cannot undo the ancient models in the name of originality, and imitation does
not exclude invention. Homer remains for him the epitome of poets.
Bacon, on the other hand, seeks to get out of the debate by formulating a
powerful conceit on the question of modernity, and he writes in *Of the Advancement of Learning* (Book I):

> Antiquity envieth there should be new additions, and novelty cannot be con-
> tent to add but it must deface: surely the advice of the prophet is the true di-
> rection in this matter, *State super vias antiquas, et videte quaenam sit via recta
> et bona et ambulate in eas.* Antiquity deserveth that reverence, that men should
> make a stand thereupon, and discover what is the best way; but when the dis-
> covery is well taken, then to make progression. And to speak truly, *Antiqui-
> tas saeculi juventus mundi.* These times are the ancient times, when the world
> is ancient, and not those which we account ancient *ordine retrogrado,* by a
> computation backward from ourselves. (Vol. III, pp. 290–91)

The reversal or *metalepsis* of temporal priorities, whereby modernity is the
truly ancient time and antiquity is the youth of the world, prompts Bacon
to cast aside the past as past and to embrace the technological discoveries
of modernity. Accordingly, he weaves the *filum labyrinthi* as the clue to the
maze of nature's inward secrets. The labyrinth's thread leads to the Cartesian world of scientific research portrayed by Bensalem in the *New Atlantis.*
The utopia of science, with its promise that it can preserve bodies from decay
and death, defines for Bacon the essence and hegemony of modernity.

   The intellectual substance of *On the Study Methods of Our Time* lies in
the challenge Vico mounts against Bacon's conceit as well as against the

moral-political implications of the "new universe of knowledge" he heralds for the modern age. That the challenge is deliberate is revealed by the presence of textual allusions to Bacon's language. In Chapter II, while discussing Descartes's analytical geometry and its link to skepticism, Vico writes that "Modern scientists, seeking guidance in their exploration of the dark pathways of nature, have introduced the geometrical method to physics. Holding to this method as to Ariadne's thread, they can reach the end of their appointed journey" (pp. 9–10). The allusion to Bacon's sense that the labyrinth of nature's secrets can finally be deciphered by science is unmistakable. Bacon's scientific ideology, however, is placed in the context of skepticism and Cartesian geometric method. We have here the preamble to Vico's critique of the political core of Bacon's encyclopedic and scientific enterprise.

Knowledge is certainly not an imposture for Bacon. Nonetheless, the utopian-scientific foundation of knowledge that the *New Atlantis* dramatizes is no guarantee for peace among the willows. The new, utopian universe of Bensalem is arguably an alibi for power and a Machiavellian text, and Bacon acts as if he were Machiavelli's prince: "[he] acted in the intellectual field like the potentates of mighty empires, who, having gained supremacy in human affairs, squander immense wealth in attempts against the order of Nature herself. . . ." (p. 4). Why does Vico explicitly link Bacon's scientific discovery and his will to power? Bacon's chimerical and utopian totalization of the sciences is de facto a will to conquer nature, and, in this sense, his scientific project is modernity's grand political scheme. For Vico, modern science and its Promethean desire to play a divine role over nature acknowledges man's infinite desire, but it brackets the reality of fallen man's imperfections and fallibility. More importantly, Bacon's (and Descartes's) valorization of modernity does not rout, in fact, it encourages the "skepticism of the New Academy" (p. 9).

The oblique link between skepticism and power (or science and politics) as the trait of modernity, with each the source of the other, marks the beginning of Vico's critique of Bacon and is the necessary preamble for Vico's defense of the wisdom of the ancients as the core of the university. The past must be studied, Vico insists, not in the mode of allegorical appropriation for and by the present, but in its pastness, with the consciousness of its radical, irretrievable otherness from the present. Poetry, which is the archeology of Memory and, literally, the posthumous voice of the past is, consistently, placed, I would like to suggest, at the very center of Vico's idea of the university education. As is known, *On the Study Methods of Our Time* is composed of fifteen chapters. The central chapter, Chapter VIII, reflects on poetry as the art of Homer, as if Vico already knew what the *New Science* would articulate: that the Homeric encyclopedia can still educate the soul of Hellas.

Because Vico places poetry's "imaginary figments" at the center of the university, we must focus on it in order to grasp what Vico expects of poetry and of the university. Let me begin by saying that, in making poetry the core of the curriculum, Vico's distance from Plato and Bacon could not have been greater. Bacon's suspicion of poetry and rhetoric recalls Plato's critique of poetry. Bacon admires poetry but does not admit that it is an instrument of discovery in that it never teaches us how to control nature (*Advancement of Learning*, Vol. III, p. 343). Bacon, thus, invests rhetoric, not poetry, with a hegemonic role in politics. On the other hand, Plato banishes poetry and Homer from the *Republic* because Homer encourages his epigones to imitate and not to think anew. And poetry is also said to pose a moral and intellectual danger. As much as the rhetoric of the Sophists, poetry indulges in illusionism and has no idea of the truth. By contrast, Vico privileges poetry because of its morality, which is articulated by its encyclopedic compass, its power to express the heterogeneous and multiple voices of experiences transcending any individual viewpoint.

Vico does not seek to persuade us that poetry necessarily gives us moral guidance. We cannot turn to poetry in order to edify ourselves. Were we to do so, we would reduce its strange and alien powers to tamed, familiar versions of our own selves and we would miss the radical, temporal alterity of its simulations as well as its challenge to the complacencies of the present. The constitutive ambiguities of poetry—its mixing instruction with delight, truth with simulacra, the past with the present—unveil, in turn, the constitutive ambiguities of the idea of the university. Just as poetry, which, as the offspring of memory, contests the illusions of the present, so the university, as the voice of the accumulated wisdom of the past, reminds us that the past is nothing less than the path of the future, for if we were to deny the weight of the ancients, we would actually (and logically) doom ourselves to deny that we could have a future.

Although poetry is the core of the curriculum and the *mise en abime* disclosing the epistemological role of the university, poetry is kept paradoxically marginal to the practical aims of education. Is its centrality, then, only apparent? And how is it connected to its de facto marginality? The structure of the text goes a long way in answering these perplexities. The excursus on poetry is flanked by a discussion on ethics (Chapter VII) and on theology (Chapter IX). As if mindful of the lay origin of the University of Naples, Vico puts the study of dogmatic theology outside of the university curriculum and assigns it to the schools of the Jesuits. Furthermore, whereas in medieval university curricula the point of destination of the liberal arts is theology, Vico makes jurisprudence (which is simultaneously the philosophy of law, the theory of justice, and the theory of the state) the climax of his method of studies. In point of fact, jurisprudence is the point where a university education and the political needs of the state intersect.

To understand the political value of jurisprudence, we must recall Vico's reflections on ethics in Chapter VII. Ethics is understood as prudence in political life. The chapter also focuses on Machiavellian simulations and dissimulations, and it vindicates the necessity of dealing realistically with facts and with Machiavellian fictions by adapting to shifting circumstances. The argument suggests that for Vico a moral theory that is not rooted in Machiavelli's sense of simulations and does not come to terms with their implacable exigencies is of no value. Were it a high-minded set of prescriptions, it would be a mere evasion of reality. To exemplify the inference, Vico mentions the Roman legal scholars, who would introduce all their judicial decisions by the verb *videri*, which means "seeming." The scholars' grammar reflects their grasp of reality as a play of simulacra and fictions. To state it differently, rhetoric, which rests on the recognition of the world of pure appearances and the fact that virtue is inculcated through the education of the passions and the seduction of eloquence, is a discipline fundamental to ethics.

The reflection on ethics leads to the synopsis of the history of Roman jurisprudence (Chapter XI), which unveils the complicities between legal fictions and political power. In Greece the teaching of the philosophy of law was devolved to philosophers. But in Rome, philosophy is politics and the philosophers themselves were jurists (p. 49). This means that the knowledge of the law is the *arcanum potentiae*, "a secret source of power" (p. 50), and the practice of the law is "a deliberate scheme for strengthening the rule of the *princeps*" before it turns into an evil by which that rule is wrecked (p. 69). Vico confronts, quite directly, the fact that "the state will again benefit by the conjunction of the philosophy of law, that is, civil doctrine, with juridical doctrine and theory" (p. 70). In modern times, he goes on to say, jurisprudence is severed from both eloquence and philosophy. It follows that law is no longer a science capable of ordering the state. After evoking the principle of political Machiavellianism about *raison d'état*, he exhorts the prince to connect laws with politics and eloquence.

Placing law as the political aim of education leads Vico to consider two questions which are really two sides of the same coin: first, the question of invention in art and technology (Chapters XII and XIII); second, the role universities play in the modern world (Chapter XIV). The two questions are intimately connected. Vico's remarks concerning the need for universities are known. In Greece and Rome there was no need for universities. The intellectual curiosity of the Greeks was circumscribed within the universe of the polis, and within that vast and yet narrow orbit the philosopher acquired mastery of all learning. The Romans had less need for universities because wisdom for them consisted in the art and practice of the law.

But in modern times universities are needed because the traditionally rigid boundaries of knowledge have been shattered. The new boundaries range from a thorough knowledge of the Scriptures to Eastern languages, with the laws of the Greeks, Romans, and Arabs. The drawback of this modern idea of the universities is that arts and sciences, "all of which in the past were embraced by philosophy and animated by it with a unitary spirit, are, in our day, unnaturally separated and disjointed" (p. 76). As a remedy, Vico suggests that professors "should so coordinate all disciplines into a single system as to harmonize them with our religion and with the spirit of the political form under which we live" (p. 77).

The question the Greeks were wont to ask: "Are thou a Greek or a barbarian?" (p. 74) is the symptom of a conceit, of a worldview that aims at separating Greek from barbarian and, thus, has neither curiosity of the outside world nor doubts about its own ethnocentric myths. Vico's reflections focus on the necessity of universities as a way of dealing with the ever-growing and ever-shifting complexities in the modern world, with the awareness of the existence of worlds different from one's own. The encyclopedic compass of the university is the way of offsetting the fragmentariness and particularisms of separate worlds. More than that, literature, which is the infinite commemoration of past history; which articulates many voices, as epics do; and in which originality is the flip side of tradition, is the model Vico pursues. But this idea of the university, in which memory is central and to learn is to remember, logically entails the question of what place invention and novelty have within the scheme of knowledge.

Invention in the arts (Chapter XII) is tied to the principle of imitation ("if Homer had not existed, there would have been no Virgil; and without Virgil, no Tasso" [p. 70]). But imitation, says Vico, echoing Plato's castigation of imitation, can hinder genius. By the same token, the invention of printing (Chapter XIII) at first is viewed as being "of signal assistance to us in our studies" (p. 72). Yet, such a scientific technology (and the criticism of Bacon is now overt) can be an impediment to true learning, while copying by hand assures the reproduction of truly outstanding works and helps the students' meditation.

Clearly, there is no endorsement of the "new" or invention in *On the Study Methods of Our Time*. In a way, it would seem that the criticism leveled at universities by the likes of Bacon, who believed that antiquarianism stifled the quest for novelties, has some justification. A theory of discovery and of the new, however, is available in the last speech Vico delivered at the University of Naples. The oration, which is known as "On the Heroic Mind," was read on October 20, 1732, in the presence of students, faculty, and civil and religious authorities. It has a recapitulative quality in that Vico retrieves and presents with great clarity positions put forth in the earlier *protreptics*. The title, "On the Heroic Mind," accurately conveys Vico's intent. By the same token, the specific audience listening to the speech partly accounts for Vico's intellectual focus and for the rhetoric of the sublime he deploys for his topic. The topic, as he says, "overflows with greatness, with splendor, with sublimity."[17]

The concept of the heroic, ever since Tasso and Bruno, is intimately bound to the "sublime" and to discoveries. The hero is one who tends to sublime achievements, overcomes the necessities of nature, and aims at immortality. Historically, the sublime, ever since Longinus and the seventeenth- and eighteenth-century debates, marks the limit of empiricism, and it designates the consciousness of an overwhelming force that ruptures the uniform, repetitive patterns of perception. For Vico the sublime, which is an experience of the mind and is tied to the passions of the soul, such as fear and pleasure, is also a historiographic category marking a break between the known and the unknown.

Vico's own discourse steadily highlights the possibility of ruptures and the *new*. Moreover, the *Scienza nuova*, in its very title, announces the practice of a new mode of understanding, a new way of thinking and of looking at life, for this is what the word science means to Vico. In addition, within the *New Science* the term "discoverta" (discovery) (as Chapter 6 of this text will show further) is used for questions of poetry and, as such, it is not different from the *invention* rhetoricians such as Cicero have elaborated. As a discovery of what the past keeps hidden, invention finds and brings to light what is always already there.

In "On the Heroic Mind" new discoveries are said to be possible "for," (and the phrasing alludes faintly to Bacon's *metalepsis* about the present) "this world is still young" (p. 243). The compass, the telescope, the barometer of Torricelli, Boyle's air pump, the microscope, gunpowder, the knowledge of the circulation of the blood, and the building of church cupolas—these are some of the new scientific achievements. The heroes of this new age are "the sublime Galileo," "the towering Descartes," Columbus, and Grotius (p. 244). Because discoveries mark ruptures in the unfolding of history, we ought to consider what exactly they mean in the context of Vico's musings.

In the *Gerusalemme Liberata* (Canto XV) Tasso describes the Christian heroes' journey to the Blessed Isles through regions populated by prodigies and sea monsters. In the economy of the narrative the journey foreshadows the discoveries that a man from Liguria, Columbus, will effect someday (Canto XV, 31–32). The navigation to the Blessed Isles, however, takes place in a boat guided by blindfolded Fortune. The implication of Tasso's metaphor is clear: discoveries are chance occurrences and they concern the workings of the imagination. Vico certainly agrees with Tasso's

[17] I am quoting from "On the Heroic Mind," p. 229.

insight. He would also say that discoveries, which, as illuminations of the mind, are linked to the power of the sublime, mark a "knowledge broken." The phrase is Bacon's, and he deploys it in the *Advancement of Learning* when, to justify the use of aphorisms for the art of discovery, he defines them as "representing a knowledge broken inviting men to enquire further" (Vol. III, p. 405).

In short, discoveries have the power to unsettle the past and the understanding of the past. Vico is at pains to show how discoveries are a consequence of the intellect disciplined to viewing many things at once as a whole and never forgetting that each fragment of experience communicates with and is part of a larger system. While the thrust of the oration is to recapitulate the commonplaces he had voiced in his previous university speeches, a large place is given to the value of scholarship as the area where the "heroic mind" can unleash its powers. More precisely, Vico begins by refocusing on the utilitarian aims of education as he reminds the students that they should pursue their studies not simply out of a love of learning or in order to gain riches, high offices, and influence. The chief purpose of their studies is "to manifest the heroic mind you possess" (p. 230). This heroic life is available in our times, as the case of the Vatican librarian and ecclesiastical historian Cesare Baronio (1538–1607) shows, within the boundaries of the universities.

The reference to an orthodox Counter-Reformation cardinal and scholar is also meant, no doubt, to highlight Vico's sense of baroque erudition's monumental achievements and of baroque hagiographies celebrating man's heroic grandeur in the service of faith. It is a recognition of the University of Naples, where Baronio had graduated. It is also meant as a way of minimizing the possible suspicion that "On the Heroic Mind," which seeks to provide heroic models for the young and stir the heroic imagination beyond the commonplace world of the familiar and the known, may in fact be a call to intellectual and moral transgressions. Accordingly, Vico turns his attention, first, to the senior members of the university who "represent that public education which His Imperial Majesty Charles VI of Austria, King of the Spains, has provided in this place for your instruction" (p. 231); and, second, he acknowledges the presence in the audience of "His Excellency Count Aloys Thomas von Harrach, who with supreme courage and wisdom auspiciously presides as Viceroy over this kingdom of Naples" (p. 232).

Through this series of encomia, Vico draws the picture of a harmonious bond between students, faculty, and political authorities at the university. This political harmony is also an educational end as the university is said to provide instruction "into every form of learning, the general or encyclopedic, the esoteric or acroamatic" (pp. 232–33). Here lies the essence of what Vico calls a "university education," and it consists in the mastering of "all the branches of knowledge" (p. 233). From this standpoint, he provides a moral definition of the university, which the Italians, he says, forcefully call a "Sapientia"—Wisdom (p. 233). The Platonic term discloses what must be called the inner ethics of the university.

Vico sets up a hierarchy of values from this Platonic perspective just as he did in the Inaugural Orations. The unceasing pursuit of knowledge will remove from the students' minds "all dishonesty . . . all puffery and play acting" (p. 234), while true learning will engender "that image and likeness of God" in their minds. Because the students have to acquire "wisdom in its entirety" and resist the tyranny of any one hegemonic discourse, the students "will not have to swear an oath of fealty to any professor, as happens so often in the sectarianisms of the schools" (p. 235). They have to be versed in all the disciplines that compose "the universe of knowledge" (p. 239), wherein "all its parts are seen to come together, answer one another, and stand as one" (p. 239).

These reflections on the unity of knowledge as a conversation of the arts, the emblem of which is the encyclopedia or the circle of knowledge (p. 241), are made possible by Vico's absorption of the Platonic idea of universal knowledge and wisdom which he finds incarnated in the university. The university is also the place where universal knowledge is imparted and man rediscovers in himself God's "image and likeness" (p. 234). But Vico's idea of the ethics of the university shows that there is another dimension to the university other than the one embodied by its social usefulness to the state: the alliance between city and university dissolves as the university forms a moral boundary to the arcana of power. Because it is the place where free discourse is sovereign, the university comes forth as an anti-world, at the margins and threshold of the social structures, whereby it resists and turns upside down the tyrannical practices and values of the world.

In this utopian and yet real other-world embodied by the university, Vico pursues the moral and scientific unity of knowledge. But he is aware of how problematical this reconciliation of broken knowledge can be. The idealized vision of a unified order of knowledge is flanked by a crucial counterdiscourse. Vico's reading of Bacon, as we have seen, has brought to light the core issue of modernity: the new sciences and the new technology have redefined the architecture of the earth and of the cosmos. This is to say that the achievements of the modern world subvert the old models. More than that, the innovations of the sciences, the aim of which is truth, undermine the moral stability of the political universe by subjecting nature to the overriding claims of science.

The questions opened up by the physical sciences do not trouble Vico. If anything, he is perplexed by the errors in the modern understanding of civil prudence or political science, which is irreducible to mechanical criteria of scientific truth. That there is a radical discrepancy between natural sciences and political science had been explored in *On the Study Methods of Our Time*. Natural science frees truth from error and seeks the one cause behind the multiplicity of phenomena. By contrast, civil prudence evokes the theater of entangled plots, secret machinations, and insidious ambitions (Chapter VIII). Civil prudence, thus, places us in the spiral of the conjectural and the probable, of free will, which is always most uncertain, and it seeks likely, multiple causes behind a historical phenomenon. As the sphere of the verisimilar, politics is the boundary of scientific knowledge; it even denounces the impossibility of enclosing knowledge and action within a definite theoretical scheme.

"On the Heroic Mind" picks up this problem. It argues that the university has to educate men for unusual and heroic tasks and train intellectuals who can be useful to the state. As he makes his argument, Vico evokes the names of Socrates, Cardinal Mazarino, and Guicciardini. They are exemplary figures whom students should emulate in their pursuit of civic virtues for they have successfully translated philosophy into practice, knowledge into action. They stand for the bond between education and politics asserted by the humanists.

What can these political philosophers teach about the links between university education and political action? Can they really be said to have a common destiny or have had a common mission? And what is Vico exactly saying about the role of the university in the modern world? The differences among the three figures are flagrant. Socrates, who embodied within himself a whole university, challenges the intellectual complacencies of the polis, is accused with undermining its stability, and, to obey the city's laws, he drinks his poison. On the other hand, Mazarino and Guicciardini embody a non-Socratic knowledge as they totally submit to the absolute exigencies of the political or prudently pursue private ends. Socrates is removed from the life of an intellectual-courtier such as Mazarino, and from Guicciardini's political prudence, just as both of them are removed from Castiglione's myth of the courtier.[18] Vico does not describe them in the terms that he uses in *De Ratione* for courtly philosophers ("filosofi cortigiani,") [p. 137]), who are seasoned in the arts of simulation and dissimulation.

But even in their profound differences, taken together, Socrates, Mazarino, and Guicciardini reflect Vico's idea of the university as the ambiguous place where contradictory aims are pursued: the interests of the state are promoted; the authority of the state is challenged; self-interests sought; and the philosopher may die for or by the state. In a way, all three figures stand for Vico's sense of the possible, contradictory political-

[18] Carlo Ossola, *Dal "Cortegiano" all' "Uomo di mondo": Storia di un libro e di un modello sociale* (Turin: Einaudi, 1987).

intellectual models available to the students. They even suggest that the three models, for all their contradictoriness, are to be necessarily and simultaneously present in the proper conception of the intellectual's role within the state.

Vico's own claims of intellectual-political authority are inseparable from his views of the philosopher as a statesman. By the end of *On the Study Methods of Our Time* (Chapter XV) the argument about modern universities moves beyond abstract questions of epistemology or pedagogy. It turns to G. B. Vico himself, to the legitimacy of his authority, his rhetorical strategies (his prudence in not disparaging colleagues and not placing himself in the "spotlight"), his foolhardiness in treating a subject that "involves a knowledge of all sciences" (p. 78), his "duty" as a professor of eloquence, and his "right" in taking up the subject of his discourse. His claims rest on the Ciceronian principle that eloquence is wisdom that speaks. Bacon's Letter to James I, king of England, from Book II of *The Advancement of Learning* about "the places of learning," is also cited to buttress the view of rhetoric's hegemony among all the disciplines.

In this self-reflexive chapter, tonal questions of rhetorical performance are made transparent, and, at the same time, the author's own willed obscurity, away from the spotlight, is dramatized. One must wonder why Bacon's political context is evoked in this elaborate interplay of light and darkness. From a formal point of view, the reference to Bacon in the final chapter recalls the opening of the text and gives a circular structure to it. It suggests that Vico's thought here is a deliberate response to Bacon's educational-political ideas. More substantively, the ordering of the arts and sciences now refracts itself as an ordering of the political realities. Finally, the tacit equation Vico establishes between himself and Bacon (whose names are mentioned in the same paragraph) discloses the horizon of Vico's prudently hidden political desires: to have, like Bacon, the power to advise the king. Vico's sense of his own intellectual-political authority, here cautiously etched, steadily flanks his "objective" and "scientific" analyses of reality. To probe further the interaction between education and politics we must turn to his extraordinary political reading of the modern age in his historical studies.

Chapter 3

THE HISTORIAN OF MODERNITY

THE FIRST TWO CHAPTERS of this book have shown Vico as a scrupulous, deeply committed historian of himself and of his own times. The *Autobiography* chronicles the history of Vico's mind and the history of his ideas from the standpoint of a self who is by necessity the historian of himself. The necessity for a historical narrative of oneself lies in Vico's own premise that any genuine self-knowledge is historical. Chapter 2, on the other hand, shows Vico's reflections on education. Such a concern had long fascinated the humanists of the Italian Renaissance, whom he largely follows. The question of education, however, affords Vico the focus for reexamining the relationship between knowledge and power in terms of the institutional role of the University of Naples and its interaction with the state.

In spite of the steady attention Vico lavishes on the intellectual debates and institutions of his own time, the most common image of Vico is that of a scholar who all his life stayed out of touch with the historical and political realities of the day. The telling sign that he was basically removed, as is widely supposed, from the windstorms of the eighteenth century, which engender the entanglements of modern thought, is to be found in the peculiar bent of the *New Science*. The *New Science* evokes and is vitally engaged with the intellectual challenges debated a century earlier by the likes of Bacon and the other founders of modern thought, such as Machiavelli, Descartes, Galileo, and Hobbes. In truth, the impact on Vico's mind of Bacon's *De Dignitate et Augmentis Scientiarum* (*The Advancement of Learning*) is duly recorded in the *Autobiography* and it certainly cannot be denied that Bacon's plan of a total reconstruction of the sciences as well as his hope for what he calls a "new philosophy" (to which "the rest is subservient and ministrant") (*The Great Instauration* "Plan of the Work," Vol. IV, p. 32) stands behind Vico's *New Science*. But Bacon is for Vico essentially a political philosopher who shapes Vico's own political thought.

It is also believed that because Vico lived in Naples, a city which Gramsci inaccurately called "un angolino morto della storia" (loosely meaning "a dead end of history"), Vico could only have written a work that evades its immediate historical reality. Feeling, as he did, that he was a stranger in his own native city, he replaces the commitment to the politics of the day by the radical project of making the *New Science* a text that pries into the elusive darkness of mythical and distant origins of humanity and thereby drafts the shifty forms of human consciousness. It must be stressed that Vico's turn to the archeology of the mind and its spectral constructions was never understood—nor could it ever have been understood—as a nostalgia for edenic origins. Rather, it was justly hailed as the consequence of Vico's discovery and introduction of a new tool of thought into the eighteenth-century landscape of ideas. The new conceptual tool, which would account for the ways the world has been and is likely to be in the future, is history.

If one were to define what history is for Vico, one could say, to start off, that he does not simply view history as a mere academic discipline that, ever since Cicero, falls within the orbit of rhetoric and is hallowed as *magistra vitae* (the teacher of life). As shown in Chapter 1, above and beyond these classical platitudes, which Vico nonetheless values, history is for him a mode of being and a way of thinking. To state it differently and perhaps more precisely, history is a perspective on life as well as the temporal condition of life, and these features, taken together, make up his historical consciousness. One could even say that *Vico's "new science"* hinges on the view of history as the record of the precarious, time-bound scripts and pageants of a ferocious and harsh world. Yet Vico's historical sense cannot be consigned, as readers of the *New Science* all too often have done, to the sphere of either existential anguish or of brilliant, if abstract, speculations about the three ages of universal history—the ages of the gods, heroes, and men. Nor does Vico conceive of a historical reconstruction of experience as the disinterment or posthumous *autopsy*, which is Vico's own metaphor, of dead, dismembered memories of the past.

There are writings by Vico that delve into the hidden folds of the political history of his own times. Both the *Neapolitan Conspiracy* (1703) and, especially, *The Life of Antonio Carafa* (1715), which scholars inexplicably continue to neglect as if they were inconsequential exercises of local history, quite marginal, or even foreign to the radical universalizing project of the *New Science*, trace out Vico's historical understanding of the present, of the myths and realities shaping the politics of the modern age. One can claim that actually Vico conceived of them as exemplary synopses of the history of the present. More than the dead end of history or the hiding place from the ever-present dangers of a violent history, Naples, *neapolis*,—the new city—is for Vico the concrete arena of the realistic, de-idealized politics both reflecting and sharing in the political myths, fantasies, and practices of modern Europe.[1]

---

[1] Vico's relationship to modernity has been treated recently, in a useful though partial way, by Mark Lilla, *The Making of an Anti-Modern* (Cambridge, Mass.: Harvard University Press, 1993). See also Cecilia Miller, *Giambattista Vico: Imagination and Historical Knowledge* (New York: St. Martin's Press, 1993). For a complex vision of modernity as a crisis of the theo-humanistic synthesis see Louis Duprè, *Passage to Modernity: An Essay in the Hermeneutics of Nature and Culture* (New Haven: Yale University Press, 1993).

The politics of the modern age—and this chapter will define its expressions and its sources—can be provisionally qualified as the power cult crystallized by the permanence of wars ravaging Naples and the rest of Europe. Vico is deeply convinced that the core of history is political history, and he gives a sharp assessment of the political practices of the so-called *arcana imperii*, the secrets of power justifying the reason of state, and of baroque ideology of absolute power. His history of the present reaches into and decisively confronts these defining issues of the political science of the seventeenth century which goes under the name of Tacitism.

The question of Vico's own political stance that I raise here is certainly not new in the critical debates on his thought. Before turning to a careful reading of his two historical texts, it might be well to review briefly the terms of the argument over Vico's political doctrine in order to clarify them and, if possible, to draw out their implications and gauge their stakes. We should, to begin with, recall Benedetto Croce's hasty characterization of Vico's thought as fundamentally "apolitical."[2] Croce's deep knowledge of the social, intellectual, and political realities of Naples in Vico's times had convinced him that Vico was personally too timid, too pious, and too prudent to ever take risky political positions such as those taken by the rebellious Pietro Giannone.

Croce's views, however, have been recently challenged by Pietro Piovani, who believes, by contrast, that at the core of Vico's philosophy of history lies a social and political vision.[3] On the basis of updated historical reconstruction of the social climate of Naples in the second half of the seventeenth century, we have all become aware of the restlessness of the new social classes, of the emergence of the so-called "ceto civile" (middle class) with its own claims to power and its undisguised opposition to the Spanish rulers of Naples, who supported and in their turn were buttressed by the aristocrats. On the strength of these findings Piovani argues that Vico's work displays an extraordinary awareness of the facts of political power, of the importance of social structures, and of the conflicts within the hierarchy of social classes. One can add that Vico's *Neapolitan Conspiracy* is undoubtedly rooted in the clear perception of the disintegrating fabric of political life in Naples.

Piovani's emphasis on the "politicality" of Vico's thought is fully justified. After all, the single, most comprehensive definition of the *New Science* casts it as a book about the "rational civil theology of divine providence" (NS/2). Each word in this definition is problematical. Nonetheless, the adjective "civile" makes the *New Science* a civil science in the sense

[2] Benedetto Croce, *La filosofia di G. B. Vico* (Bari: Laterza, 1965), pp. 253ff.

[3] Pietro Piovani, "Della apoliticità e politicità di Vico," in *La filosofia nuova di Vico,* ed. F. Tessitore (Naples: Morano, 1990), pp. 139–56; see also Giuseppe Giarrizzo, *Vico: La politica e la storia* (Naples: Guida, 1981).

of a political science under the government of Providence. Because Vico's claims about the *New Science* will be discussed in subsequent chapters, I shall seek to determine here the orbit of meaning of the term "political." Piovani's understanding of what is political strikes me as surprisingly limited. His notion of Vico's "politicality" narrows down to a generalized theory of power that takes two directions. The first direction is the fairly obvious view of society as a structure held together by a hierarchy of power. The second direction has Vico appear as the demythologizer of power, the moralist who exposes the hidden strategies of power and removes the veil of mystery shrouding its exercise. From this moralistic standpoint the attempted retrieval of a political and rational Vico is the pretext to do away with the image of Vico as the restorer of pure metaphysics or as an anachronistic epigone of Plato or, what for Piovani is worse, an anti-Enlightenment thinker.

It is easy to object to Piovani's characterization of Plato as a "mere metaphysician" and one should at least be suspicious of the still widespread opinion, restated by Piovani, that Vico must belong to the rationalist tradition of Western thought, if he is to be counted as a serious thinker. It can be argued that there is no more political a thinker—and possibly no more profoundly political a thinker—than Plato. The reduction of Plato's *Republic* to some sort of mindless abstract speculation is a violent simplification of the extraordinary complexities of this preeminent text of political philosophy. By the same token the view of Vico as a rationalist in the line of the Enlightenment is naive. "Ragione" is not for Vico Cartesian rationality. *Ratio* translates law, with its sediments of wisdom, customs, and common sense, and this understanding of *ratio* in no way implies that the rational philosopher should rule over the city nor does it imply that for Vico the world can be saved by reason.

The fact is that Vico's understanding of the "political" has to be found in the arguments put forth by the art of rhetoric of Cicero and the Italian humanists who believed in the hegemony of the rhetorical tradition and its power over the will.[4] More than that, Vico knows the questions that Plato, Tacitus, Bacon, and Grotius, as well as a host of political philosophers of the modern age—Machiavelli and Tacitists such as Giovanni Botero, Scipione Ammirato, Traiano Boccalini, and so forth—have long asked.[5] In

[4] See Andrea Battistini, *La degnità della retorica: Studi su G. B. Vico* (Pisa: Pacini, 1975); Michael Mooney, *Vico in the Tradition of Rhetoric* (Princeton: Princeton University Press, 1975); Ernesto Grassi, *Vico and Humanism: Essays on Vico, Heidegger, and Rhetoric*, ed. D. P. Verene (New York: Lang, 1990), and Andrea Battistini, *La sapienza retorica di Giambattista Vico* (Milan: Guerini, 1995). See also Karl-Otto Apel, *Die Idee der Sprache in der Tradition des Humanismus von Dante bis Vico* (Bonn: Bouvier u. Co. Verlag, 1978).

[5] The tradition starts with Innocent Gentillet, *Discours contre Machiavel*, eds. A. D'Andrea and P. Stewart (Florence, 1994). Cf. Giovanni Botero, *Della ragion di stato, con tre libri delle cause della grandezza delle città, due aggiunte e un discorso sulla popolazione di Roma*, ed. L. Firpo (Turin: UTET, 1948); Scipione Ammirato, *Discorsi sopra C. Tacito* (Florence, 1594);

fact, Vico moves directly within the boundaries of the political science of the Tacitists and he finds them insufficient. But initially, no doubt, their many questions about politics are his questions: who is fit or wise enough to rule and be allowed to rule? Are the rhetoricians, who can dissemble and who yet either believe in nothing or couple wisdom to their eloquence, to be granted the power to lead men out of the ever impending chaos of the forest? Or should technocrats, such as Antonio Carafa, who is highly skilled in military science but may not have a sense of the whole, be allowed to rule? And what are the prudent choices a courtier or a teacher, such as Vico himself, will have to make in a risky, shifting, and morally problematical world? Should a man of virtue be free from politics or is there freedom in politics? Can an abstract utopian morality that does not come to terms with Machiavellian fictions preserve the state or does it lead the state to ruin by fomenting unrealizable, empty utopian illusions? Is war the natural condition of man's immoderate passions and is peace a mere figment of unheroic minds? This book as a whole seeks to answer these questions of political science. But to start finding out Vico's sense of political complexities, we must turn to Vico's texts and their rhetorical strategies in both *The Neapolitan Conspiracy* and *The Life of Antonio Carafa*.

Though they were written some twelve years apart from each other these two historical works belong to and indeed they evoke common intellectual concerns and a common historical background. Historically, *The Neapolitan Conspiracy*, as this title suggests, has a local, Neapolitan political focus. On the other hand, *The Life of Antonio Carafa* narrates the vicissitudes of a Neapolitan general who finds himself acting on the stage of European global politics, but the city of Naples figures prominently in Vico's concerns. No city—and no particular entity—can be accounted for in terms of its presumed self-sufficiency or autarkical self-enclosure. Consistent with this general Vichian principle, both these historical works, which can be said to dramatize two separate chapters of one story, conjure up the broader configuration of the emerging Austrian designs in Europe as the context for their intelligibility.

Traiano Boccalini, *Ragguagli di Parnaso: Tre Volumi*, ed. G. Rua (Bari: Laterza, 1910–48); Antonio Possevino, *Discorso contro l'impietà e perniciosissimi consigli del Machiavello* in *Il soldato christiano con nuove aggiunte* (Venice, 1604), pp. 181–87; Pedro Ribadeneira, S.J., *Tratado de la religión y virtudes que debe tener el principe cristiano para gobernar y conservar sus estados, contro lo que Nicolas Maquiavelos y los politicos deste tiempo ensenan* in *Obras escogidas del Padre Pedro de Rivadeneira* (Madrid, 1868), reprinted Madrid 1952, with intro. by Don Vicente de la Fuente, pp. 449–587. For a broad and most informative discussion see Robert Birely, *The Counter-Reformation Prince: AntiMachiavellianism or Catholic Statecraft in Early Modern Europe* (Chapel Hill: University of North Carolina Press, 1990). See also Peter S. Donaldson, *Machiavelli and the Mystery of State* (Cambridge: Cambridge University Press, 1988). Still valid is *Cristianesimo e ragion di stato*, ed. E. Castelli (Rome-Milan: Centro Internazionale di Studi Umanistici, 1952).

The intellectual common ground sustaining *The Neapolitan Conspiracy* and *The Life of Antonio Carafa* is suggested by Vico's *Autobiography*. We may recall that from 1703 to 1715, the space of time within which he writes these two historical texts, little is recorded by him. These texts are in many ways the crucible of his thoughts and experiences at a time when he is teaching rhetoric at the University of Naples and is reading the works of Tacitus, Bacon, and Grotius. These are the authors who give Vico the needed push to undertake his grand project of a "new science," his intellectual quest for ordering the whole of the arts and sciences into a unity. In fact, both Bacon's sense of the "dignity of knowledge" (and his radical encyclopedism, which is his utopian model of the empire of the sciences) and Grotius's *On the Law of War and Peace* map Vico's route for his own unification of the branches of knowledge under the aegis of the "poetic" and the productive exercise of the imagination. But Vico's meditation on the "poetic" will come later. Between 1703 and 1715 he still functions, however doubtful he is growing about rhetoric's hegemonic status, as a professor of rhetoric.

His sense of the value of rhetoric as a philosophy of history and as an all-encompassing discipline can be gauged from his disagreement with Socrates. In the *Gorgias* Socrates discusses rhetoric as a non-art for it has nothing to do with the love of wisdom. As one reads in the *Gorgias* rhetoric lies knowingly; like magical art it confuses the real and the apparent; it undermines all authority by pretending to all knowledge; the passions it arouses can overpower the rule of reason; it adorns and makes attractive the bad; it edges toward empty sophistry.

In the Inaugural Orations, as shown earlier, Vico had understood, against Plato's Socrates, that there need not be a quarrel between philosophy and rhetoric: his call for yoking together wisdom and eloquence will remain firm in all his writings. Much like Aristotle, who insists on the kinship between rhetoric, logic, and civil knowledge; and much like Cicero, who shows him that the rhetorician has a place in political life, Vico makes rhetoric the tool of political philosophy. What confers on rhetoric such a privilege is the fact that it is the most comprehensive of the arts since it combines the arts of memory, invention, and judgment; it forges links between reason and will and can mold the passions; and as an art of persuasion it broadens the compass of the audience's imagination. Finally, from the Italian humanists, such as Salutati, Bruni, and Valla, Vico had learned that rhetoric *is* politics (and vice versa), and the double equation implies that politics is an art (and not a science) dependent on prudent discourse, eloquent incitement to the virtues, and flexible judgment in the face of shifting political realities.

These concerns with rhetoric, which engage Vico professionally, punctuate both *The Neapolitan Conspiracy* and *The Life of Antonio Carafa*, not just as techniques of argument, but as central political questions. *The Neapolitan Conspiracy*, written in 1703, comes forth as a retrospective reflection on the failure of a plot undertaken in 1701 by a group of Neapolitan aristocrats against the Spanish rule in the city of Naples. Vico wrote the account at the request of the Spanish viceroy, Villena, and his reconstruction of the events becomes both a harsh indictment of the conspirators' confused aims and a veiled critique of (or weak apology for) the government. To Villena it appeared too impartial to be used as political propaganda and the text remained unpublished. What was the conspiracy about? Why did it fail? Could it ever have succeeded?

The chronicle begins by narrating the origin of a broad European political crisis. At his death on November 20, 1700, the King of Spain, Carlos II, leaves no clearly designated successor to the crown. All the major European powers—Austria, France, England, the Dutch Republic, and the various German states—which live in a permanent state of war with one another have their own hidden agenda. They all perceive the death of King Carlos as the death knell of an overextended Spanish empire, which has long been burdened with wars and had become moribund. His death appears, thus, as the ominous sign of new political instabilities and of a new opportunity to redraft the ever-shifting political map of Europe.

At the first inkling of the crises Leopold of Austria, who overtly harbors the design to diminish the hegemony of Spain in Europe, hatches a secret "Machiavellian" plot. The time had finally come—this was Leopold's cherished and long-range ambition—to get rid of the Spaniards from the whole of Italy and have Austria supplant them. As part of his strategy for taking advantage of the apparent power vacuum triggered by the death of Carlos, Leopold secretly encourages a rebellion in the kingdom of Naples against the established authority of the Spanish rule. His plan is to have his second born, Charles, appointed as the new king of Naples. To this end Leopold sends to Rome, which appears here as the European crossroads of political intrigue, two of his officers, Carlo di Sangro and Giovanni Carafa. Their secret mission is to engineer the Neapolitan "coniuratio"—the conspiracy against the viceroy of Naples, Medinaceli, and they do so by drawing into the conspiracy a disgruntled clique of Neapolitan aristocrats.

The historical origin of the Neapolitan conspiracy of September 1701 that Vico chronicles lies, then, in the imperial fantasies of hegemony of European powers. But the value of the text is in its power to plunge us into the world of political secrets, gossip, solemn oaths exchanged and never kept, and conspiracy. No doubt, Vico is mindful of Machiavelli's discussion of conspiracies in his *Discourses* (Book III, Chapter 6) as well as in *The Prince* (Chapter XIX), which elicited Bacon's reflections on seditions, enigmas of power, and the secrets of knowledge. Machiavelli overtly discourages conspiracies as unmanageable forms of civil disorder. Yet, as the *Dis-*

courses views history as a series of conspiracies by which power is obtained and usurped, it offers a summary of possible techniques to achieve success, as if to advise their practice, and suggests that governments themselves are necessarily conspiratorial. Vico's historical account, by contrast, probes mainly the political and social realities of the city of Naples and focuses on the conditions that make conspiracies inevitable.

Reflecting on the rhetorical structure he will impart to his narrative, Vico claims he will imitate pictorial representations. Just as the painters place the principals of the action in the foreground of their canvases, leaving the secondary figures in the background, so will Vico highlight the major events of the conspiracy. He identifies these as, first, the plan to kill the viceroy Medinaceli and, second, to seize the fortress of the city. The esthetic model Vico pursues suggests that his reconstruction is an artful invention. It also suggests that his text gives visibility to what is hidden. More poignantly, the technique he will deploy is what treatises on painting call the perspective, the representation of reality from a standpoint enabling him to establish values between the various parts of the canvas. The implication is clear: there are no objective perceptions in history writing, and one's standpoint is political inasmuch as it dictates the way in which occurrences turn into significant constructs.

As Vico traces the events of the conspiracy, he depicts them in terms of two major antagonistic forces. On the one hand there is the embodiment of legitimate, established, and dynastic authority, the viceroy Medinaceli, born of the union of two old and distinguished families, the French Foix and the Spanish Lacerda. On the other hand, there is the hydra of conspirators, who are ambitious, hold in contempt the authority of the law, and conspire in pursuit of self-aggrandizement, spurred by avarice or because they see in the plot the opportunity to settle old scores. As a way of dramatizing his sense of the distance between the two poles of the action, Vico deploys—side by side with each other—two spatial emblems. It is as if the topography of the city were the symbolic reflection of the city's politics.

The first is the *arx*—the square fortress with its towers, stone bridges, and bastions. The word *arx* has a remarkable semantic history. It is possibly the root of *arcanum* and it designates a place where sacrifices are performed and kept secret from common view. It is also possibly related to *arca*, an inaccessible strongbox. Vico tells us that the fort stands "in media urbe" (p. 332)—in the symbolic center of the city—facing the sea and flanked by a double moat dug around the rampart. I shall probe later in this chapter Vico's insight into the myth of the siren Parthenope, who is the mythical figure from where the city of Naples originates. Let me remark here on the detail of the fortress erected by the sea. The resonances of this semiotics are unequivocal. As if to mark the link between army and government, the fortress is said to be joined to the royal palace by a bridge. By the proximity of the fortress to the sea, then, it is as if the legitimacy of the government rises not only from the army, but it flows directly from the city's founding myth. At the same time, the fortress is placed as if to guard the city from the dangers and wilderness of the sea, which, as Alciati's emblem has it, are the storms and turbulence of bad government.[6] The symbolic equivocation of this architecture of power has other extensions.

The building's square shape and sturdy appearance convey, first of all, the sense of the solid foundation of the political power it houses: it is a secure, sealed structure, such is the description's overt warning—not to be stormed, entered into, and taken by assault. In this sense, the fortress is the visible sign of political legitimacy protected by its own unassailability. At the same time, the straight equal lines of the square stronghold make manifest to the eye the orderly regularity in the viceroy's exercise of power, which is in drastic contrast, however, to the unruly, hidden, bewildering jumble rampant among the conspirators.

But the symbolism of order emanating from the fortress is not without its contradiction. This transparent emblem of authority and power has its own inner tunnels, circuitous routes, and hidden penetralia. Political power is not altogether reducible to the rational domain of its visible exteriority. Authority, one can also say, depends on wealth—both material and symbolic. In the secret recesses of the fortress the royal treasure was once kept. And we are also told that in the enclosed space of the vestibule there stands the Aragonese triumphant arch, which, ironically from the perspective of the present conspiracy, commemorates a uniquely happy time in Naples' history: the reign of Alfonso II (who built it for Alfonso I), a time in which Naples was a brilliant center of art and culture, home to humanists such as Pontano and Sannazaro.

The second spatial emblem Vico juxtaposes to the fortress is the conspirators' grottos, hidden tufa galleries and chambers where they meet on the night of the insurrection. The place is described at first as an underground cavity in the hollow of a mountain, which in antiquity may have served as an ossarium or vault for the dead, with barbaric inscriptions, rough-hewn sculptures, and painted walls. The lengthy and eerie description of the place and its literally grotesque art is meant to evoke the "cae-

---

[6] Andreas Alciati, *Emblematum Liber* (Paris, 1542); see also Guillaume de la Perriere, *Le theatre de bons engins* (Paris, 1539); Daniel Cramer, *Decades Emblematum Sacrorum* (Frankfurt, 1617); Matthias Holtzwart, *Emblematum Tyrocinia* (Strasburg, 1581); Cesare Ripa, *Iconologie* (Paris, 1644). More generally see Peter M. Daly, *Emblem Theory: Recent German Contributions to the Characterization of the Emblem Genre* (Nendeln: KTO Press, 1979); J. Manning, "Continental Emblem Books in Sixteenth Century England: The Evidence of Sloane Ms. 3794," *Emblematica*, Vol. I (1986), pp. 1–11. In general see Mario Praz, *Studies in Seventeenth-Century Imagery* (Rome: Edizioni di Storia e Letteratura, 1975).

cus horror" (p. 333)—the horror and awe of the dark hour and of the imminent and darker action the conspirators are about to undertake. The
spectral loculi, urns, and crypts also signal the rule of secrecy surrounding
the murderous plan.

In its passion for destruction and secrecy (which will be betrayed), the
conspiracy appears as a mad dream of the night whereby the presumed enlightened rationality of the conspirators' revolutionary fervor is eclipsed.
No doubt, Vico's description of this gathering place in the bowels of the
earth exploits the mythic and yet real topography of Naples as the city of
twisted grottos, hidden rivers (Sebetus), and subterranean cities—in short,
the Vergilian underground landscape of Hades, or home of the dead. Because of the hatreds and lawlessness it stems from, the conspiracy has its
symbolic roots in the depths of a hellish imagination, and it is for Vico the
incarnation of a grotesque art, a fantastic, distorted mingling of incongruous shapes and designs. For all the contrast between this place and the
fortress (which has, as has been shown, its classical art), Vico deploys an
image that makes the two emblems symmetrically parallel to each other.
Vico likens the coiled entrances to the lower parts of the hollow to "the-
atri vomitoria" (p. 333), funnel-like entrances or, more literally, vomitories
of the theater. The image, drawn from Roman amphitheaters, describes the
theater's entrances to the tiers of seats, and it suggests that this conspiratorial, secret action has the theatricality and visibility of a spectacle.

The portrait of the historical drama Vico paints is a chiaroscuro painting, the figurative style known in the late seventeenth century as tenebrism
and cultivated in Naples by the followers of Caravaggio, such as Josè de
Figuera Ribeira (called "Lo spagnoletto"), Francesco Solimena, Mattia
Preti, and Luca Giordano. In the intense contrast between light and dark
which the chiaroscuro or tenebrism heightens, what is hidden in the dark
is as important as what stands visible in the light. This baroque technique,
which Vico applies to the representations on the great stage of history,
makes history a fresco of illusory shapes whose dynamics are without direction and reveals the power of what is shrouded in the dark. Discreetly,
the text opens our eyes to the essence of political power: it is, all at the same
time, the effect of visible contrasts, an optical illusion controlled by the
viewer's perspective and an eerily invisible, enigmatic (and thereby more
fearsome) operation.[7]

---

[7] For the spiritual and political implications of the baroque, especially in Spain, see Octavio
Paz, *Sor Juana* (Cambridge, Mass. Harvard University Press, 1988); Roberto Gonzalez
Echevarria, *La ruta de Severo Sarduy* (Hanover, N.H.: Ediciones del Norte, 1987). For a so-
cial-historical view see Josè Antonio Maravall, *Culture of the Baroque: Analysis of a Historical
Structure*, trans. T. Cochran, Theory and History of Literature Series, Vol. 25 (Minneapolis:
University of Minnesota Press, 1986). A view of Vico in terms of his foreshadowing of the
Enlightenment is by Cecilia Miller, *Giambattista Vico: Imagination and Historical Knowl-
edge*, quoted above, note 1. Cf. Gustavo Costa, *Vico e l'Europa: Contro la boria delle nazioni*
(Milan: Guerini, 1996).

The canvas Vico has drawn shows the material, political disjunctions of the city. At the very start of the narrative we are told that the city of Naples is not a productive, organic whole. The political body is radically dismembered: the low classes, Vico says, are inconstant; the middle class lives in idleness, the "dolce far niente," as the Italians say, which is to be understood as a baroque passion for nothing; the aristocrats hate the forensic class and are themselves consumed by inner factionalism. The separateness of each social class comes to the fore during the insurrection. As if the action were merely theatrical make-believe, the ringleaders of the various bands ride with masked faces ("personati obequitantes" [p. 337]) and address one another as "Prince of Caserta" or "Marquis of Vasto." The masquerade turns the action into a macabre puppet show. What is more, the common people watch the mise-en-scène from their windows or doorways. Their aloofness is not gratuitous: they remember and in their apartness they avenge the defeat and murder of Masaniello in 1647 by the nobles (p. 338).

Vico is still far from making his encyclopedic project of the *New Science* the model for his political vision. In the *Neapolitan Conspiracy* the world of history is experienced through the optics of baroque art: an art that draws the real world into the imaginary world and, thereby, exposes the conspiratorial fantasy as an insubstantial reverie which could never become a reality. No doubt, the conspiracy fails not because of any unreasonable demands put forth by the conspirators. All they ask is the guarantee of rights to citizens; uniform norms in the law courts; the right to appeal verdicts; a monarch that does not rule from the outside. Yet the conspiracy fails for the very reason that it started: a multiplicity of social viewpoints and interests unrelated to each other.

Vico certainly agrees with Machiavelli's analysis of conspiracies and seditions. He agrees with Machiavelli that politics is a serraglio of boundless passions and a theatre of crude power games. He also agrees that the absolute tyranny and aloofness of the viceroy is on the same plane of being as the immoderate licentiousness of the conspirators. In the wake of Machiavelli, moreover, Vico discovers the sovereignty of the secrets of power— or conspiratorial discourse—as the essence of political life. But Vico may well be more radical than Machiavelli as he puts forth his insight into the dangers of presuming the self-sufficiency of each social class or any other entity. A critique of a central assumption of Machiavelli's political philosophy is intimated in the light of the claims of ancient philosophy.

The principle of individuality and anarchy—which for Machiavelli will be satisfied by yielding to a limitless desire for totality—is belied by the claim in Plato's *Republic* that a city comes into being because each of us is not self-sufficient (par. 369b). For Vico, let me say this more clearly, the existence of fragmentary, heterogeneous, and self-enclosed groups causes both conspiracies and autocracies. Each is both the antithetical and the obverse side of the other; each produces and seeks to destroy the other. Small wonder, then, that, after compiling this thoroughly skeptical account of the *Neapolitan Conspiracy*, Vico agrees to write the epitaph for two of the conspirators, Carlo di Sangro and Giuseppe Capece.

The concerns with the nature and practice of power, which the *Neapolitan Conspiracy* has articulated, are never going to be left behind by Vico. *The Life of Antonio Carafa* openly depicts both one man, Antonio Carafa, and a world, late seventeenth-century Europe, both relentlessly devoted to power. If the abortive Neapolitan Conspiracy was represented with the sense that the action was a spasm of agony and a preamble to death, *The Life of Antonio Carafa* will obliquely present Vico's teaching about the best government, which is also a critique of the politics of the modern age, roughly identifiable with Machiavellian realistic politics. *The Neapolitan Conspiracy* can be called a Machiavellian text because it grounds political action in immoderate passions which, in turn, both trigger and forever thwart the classical myths of utopias. Utopias stem from the awareness of infinite desire and the fictional utopian promise of its satisfaction. Both Machiavelli and Vico in his *Neapolitan Conspiracy* have no place for utopias. *The Life of Antonio Carafa*, by contrast, will vindicate, against Machiavelli's strictures (*The Prince*, Chapter XV), the necessity of utopias and will argue for the role an intellectual, such as Vico himself, can play in the management of the state.

The material circumstances of the composition of this text, to which Vico alludes in the Dedicatory Letter, may shed some light on the elusive, covert claims which Vico stakes out for himself as a reliable political thinker, as that which the age of the baroque theorizes—in the full semantic sense of the term—as the "secretary" (cf. *The Prince*, Chapter XXIII).[8] We must read carefully into the folds of the official, openly epideictic rhetoric of the Dedicatory Letter in order to grasp what (and why) Vico keeps concealed from public view.

The Dedicatory Letter is addressed to a young man, Adriano Carafa. Adriano, who had been a student of Vico's, had requested the latter to write in Latin—the common language of cultivated Europe—a biography of his uncle, Marshal Antonio Carafa, in order to perpetuate for posterity the memory of the marshal's extraordinary achievements in the service of Leopold I of Austria. Vico agrees to compile the biography for a thousand ducats which he needs for the dowry of his beloved daughter Luisa. The Dedicatory Letter makes no mention of the emolument. More than a sophist who knows how to flatter the vanity of his audience but who be-

---

[8] For the figure of the secretary see the fine essays by Salvatore S. Nigro, "Il segretario," in *L'uomo barocco*, ed. R. Villari (Rome-Bari: Laterza, 1991), pp. 91–108; see also *Elogio della menzogna*, introd. Salvatore S. Nigro (Palermo: Sellerio, 1990), which has texts by C. Calcagnini, C. Malespini, G. Battista, and P. Rossi; see also Torquato Accetto, *Della dissimulazione onesta*, ed. Salvatore S. Nigro (Turin: Einaudi, 1997).

lieves in nothing; who puts a material price on his knowledge and who posits the commensurability between the academy and the marketplace, Vico casts himself as an educator who raises and upholds the moral, absolute standards of what he calls the historical truth. If he does not want to appear a sophist who would lie about the presumed virtues of the marshal, he will appear as Socrates, the educator who belongs entirely to the polis. As has been shown in Chapter 1 of this text, the *Autobiography* features Socrates as the philosopher who refuses to be identified with the values and the spiritual economy of the existing polis. Yet Vico's own stance in *The Life of Antonio Carafa* lacks the *Autobiography*'s irony, which disrupts the belief in a recognizable place and role of the philosopher-educator in the city. The years Vico spent as a private tutor at Vatolla are long gone, but he still holds public and private teaching jobs in Naples and we are here given a glimpse of his political designs.

The Dedicatory Letter places the text within the arc of Vico's educational activities, but its overt thrust is the encomium of Adriano's virtues. Adriano is a rich young man who lives frugally and prudently. He has deep attachments to his family and to his native city of Naples and wants to keep alive the memory of the past. The text emphasizes that Adriano in part inherits these virtues, and in part he has learned them from his father and the women of his family. For all its apparent banality, the detail serves a double purpose. First of all, Vico acknowledges as his source a book on ancient Neapolitan families by Scipione Ammirato, who is an interpreter of Tacitus and a genealogist. Second, the detail underscores Vico's belief that virtues can be taught. At stake is the dignity of teaching. The indirect suggestion is that, if virtues can be taught, the teachers of virtue and excellence, such as Vico himself, must occupy an eminent place in a nobleman's household.

The memory of the years spent as a tutor at Vatolla hovers over these pages. The copious references to Adriano's wealth, generosity, and good breeding certainly suggest that Adriano is no vulgar employer, one who is likely to think of Vico as no worthier than his other servants. On the contrary, Adriano grasps the value of education and he expects Vico to write nothing less than a "true history" ("vera historia" [p. 6]). Accordingly, this history will be written, Vico says, in the mode of the Roman historians: Livy, Sallust, Caesar, and, above all, Tacitus. In what seems to be another gratuitous compliment, which, in fact, will be a highly significant textual element in Vico's discourse, we are told that Adriano knows Tacitus in detail. After a restatement of Vico's busy life as a teacher—whereby Adriano and we are enjoined to see this text as an extension of Vico's teaching—the Dedicatory Letter ends with the wish that Adriano surpass his uncle's glory. The compliment carries also the clear conviction that the marshal's achievements can be surpassed, that the present can go beyond the imperfections of the past.

Vico's claims that he intends to write a "true history" of Antonio Carafa's life, that his chief historiographic model is Tacitus, and that the young Adriano can be taught to surpass the uncle are all intertwined elements of an elaborate political project, whereby Vico dramatizes his political prudence in managing a narrative of private and public events. Tacitus and Tacitism—which, as has been hinted earlier in this chapter, shape the political discourse of seventeenth- and early eighteenth-century Europe—mark the boundaries, are indeed the sinew of Vico's project, which he carefully unfolds in *The Life of Antonio Carafa*. His rhetorical procedure in this text, let me add, is a subtle blend of indirections and the seemingly impartial, objective stance of a man who wants to appear trustworthy or above the fray as he writes a "true history."

Nonetheless, there can be little doubt about the extraordinary importance Vico attaches to the biography he has agreed to compile. His own *Autobiography* records that in preparing to write *The Life of Antonio Carafa* Vico read Hugo Grotius's *On the Law of War and Peace*. It also records that while writing Carafa's biography he was "travagliato da crudelissimi spasimi ippocondriaci nel braccio sinistro" (*Vita*, p. 43) ("wracked by the cruelest hypochondriac cramps in his left arm" [*Autobiography*, p. 154]). But the pain also racks his soul. The hypochondria, which befits Vico's melancholy temper, describes the painful unease of a mind weighed down by anxieties and depressions. Vico duly registers their occurrence, but he leaves unexplored their clinical or psychological causes. That the *Autobiography*, a text, if there ever was one, of self-confrontation, recalls spasms felt during the composition of *The Life of Antonio Carafa* leads us to a legitimate inference. *The Life of Antonio Carafa*, which assesses successes and blights of a compatriot, affords Vico with the occasion to come to terms with the public purposes, covert fantasies, and designs of his own life in a way that the *Autobiography*, written from a Socratic perspective of the misunderstood thinker, cannot.

These purposes are filtered through Tacitus, who in the *Autobiography* is praised for his practical wisdom and utilitarian vision. Why is Tacitus the main model of *The Life of Antonio Carafa*?[9] Who is Tacitus for late Renaissance and baroque historiography? Because Tacitus's *Histories* portray the savage, imperial politics of Tiberius, Nero, Caligula, and Domitian, his name is often linked with Machiavellian politics. Machiavelli, as a matter of fact, is seen by a Tacitist like Traiano Boccalini as an updated Tacitus. There is no overt trace, however, of a specific link between Tacitus's political history and Machiavelli's political theory in *The Life of Antonio Carafa*. Tac-

[9] See the fine study on Tacitus by Vasily Rudich, *Political Dissidence under Nero: The Price of Dissimulation* (New York: Routledge, 1993); see also Ronald Mellor, *Tacitus* (New York: Routledge, 1993). More generally see T. J. Luce and A. J. Woodman, eds., *Tacitus and the Tacitean Tradition* (Princeton: Princeton University Press, 1993).

itus is for Vico the historian of certain facts, and truth is his standard. From this viewpoint, Vico may be well aware of Bodin's preference for Tacitus as a historian and his concomitant self-distancing from Machiavelli. He may even be echoing—and responding to—Lipsius's wonder whether anyone, except Tacitus, can dare write a history that is true in all details. For Lipsius, Tacitus's moral daring lies in his refusal to be an accessory to Roman tyrants and in his will to make public "as our Tacitus calls them, the *arcana imperii*."[10]

In a technical sense, Vico's intent to write a "true history" in the mode of Tacitus must be taken to mean that he will not write a one-sided, official, and hagiographic biography of Antonio Carafa. The less overt implication is that the historian has a sense of the contradictory complexity of events and aims at completeness: to write the truth is tantamount to writing a complete, whole representation of these events. From this standpoint the historian is a rhetorician arguing "in utramque partem" and he can do so because he has been given access to private documents and archives in the Carafa household. In effect, Vico's claim to write a "true history" is in part a sign of moral ambivalence toward Antonio Carafa. The claim also suggests Vico's awareness of a double discourse—the official and the private—that he must prudently handle. The proem, which follows the Dedicatory Letter, reflects on the relationship between the private and the public, biography and history, as modes of the doubleness/duplicity of political discourse.

The proem's point of departure is the distinction between "official historical treatments"—which arouse wonder in the young but don't teach anything—and biographies that encourage emulation in inferior minds. The political critique of "wonder"—which is traditionally the beginning of knowledge and is figured here as a poetic astonishment paralyzing the mind and foreclosing its power to act—is not developed further. The poetry that Vico will acknowledge is a poetry that can be put to use. For the present purposes he goes on to stress the unique value of unofficial biographies on two counts. The first is that biographies are valuable not because they provide panoramic overviews of great events, but because of the minute, subtle details they contain. The true causes of the "preservation or ruin" of large historical formations, such as the state, are found, Vico adds in what seems a parenthetical remark, in seemingly irrelevant, seemingly negligible details. The second reason why biographies are valuable is that they show how their protagonists have harmonized their public and private lives. This harmonization of one's double life, Vico says, is true wisdom.

---

[10] The quotation is taken from Justus Lipsius, *Epistolicarum quaestionum libri V* (Antwerp, 1557), p. 205. Cf. also *Sixe Bookes of Politickes or Civil Doctrine* (London, 1594).

So richly suggestive is each claim of the proem that one must proceed with great care and not overlook, as it were, seemingly irrelevant details. The thrust of the proem recalls, I like to suggest as a way of starting my commentary, Bacon's reflections on historiography in his *Advancement of Learning*. Bacon classifies the various branches of historiography in four parts: natural, civil, ecclesiastical, and literary. Under the rubric of "civil history" (Vol. II, p. 6) Bacon lists memorials, antiquities, and Perfect History. Perfect History is a generalized category comprising chronicles (such as journals, annals, etc.), narrations (such as the *Conspiracy of Catiline*), and, finally, lives, the peculiarity of which, Bacon says, is to yoke together public and private spheres. The history of lives is for Bacon superior to all others because from biographies modern civil wisdom will derive "profit and example" (Vol. IV, p. 304). Bacon's classification is chiefly a pretext to justify the excellence and virtues of the modern age Bacon consciously heralds. Vico takes Bacon's classification as the excuse for a hermeneutics of political discourse.

I take Vico's emphasis on the importance of textual details and minutiae to be nothing less than his hermeneutical precept addressed to the readers. Regrettably, scholars have traditionally opted to define Vico's large, visible pattern of ideas in order to test their conceptual coherence and rigor, but rarely have they engaged in the careful, close reading of the text he explicitly calls for as an interpretive norm through the subtleties of a textual construct. More cogently, the reference to the wisdom of harmonizing the "double life" of a public persona is a statement that, for all its apparent flatness, signals Vico's consciousness that the sense of a text or of a life is not reducible to official or explicit utterances. The implied rupture of the public and private dimensions of a life (and of a text) reveals Vico's sense of a double political discourse, which Bacon himself practices in, say, *The Wisdom of the Ancients*, and which for Vico is the ironic mode of the modern age. In *The Life of Antonio Carafa* Vico both denounces and prudently practices this mode.

But for Bacon, who joins together esoteric and common wisdom, the double discourse is not merely a question of allegorical interpretations. Under the impact of Machiavelli's *Discourses* Bacon had described the science of government as "part of knowledge secret and retired" demanding the statesman's prudence (*The Advancement of Learning*, Book II, Vol. III, pp. 473–4). There is a necessity for noble lies in the order of politics both for the purpose of controlling immoderate desires and for keeping alive the utopian fiction of the *New Atlantis*. Vico directly confronts the questions of secrets of power, for the knowledge of these secrets marks Antonio Carafa's admission into the tight circle of Emperor Leopold's advisors. The context within which Vico mentions the issues of the "secrets of government" is of some note.

Vico's historiographic self-reflexiveness in the proem leads him to assert the existence of a parallel between the course of a life and the course of the state. The assertion, plainly enough, anticipates a key insight in the *New Science* and it can be thus encapsulated here: the life of a state lapses into decadence as much as the life of Antonio Carafa does. And as much as the state needs secrets or secrets are the paradigm of history, so is Carafa skilled in the hidden counsels of government. Vico's aim, as he states it, is to assess the shape, significance, and vicissitudes of a unique existence which has been devoted to the cult of what Vico calls "regni arcana" (p. 10), the secret craft of government.

"Regni arcana" echoes Tacitus's "arcana imperii" (*Annales* 2:36). For Tacitus the phrase evokes concrete historical conditions wherein the tyrant-emperor claims that he is above the law. In a more general way, the phrase describes the surreptitious, covert practices of absolute power, and it includes within its purview secrets of state, conspiracies, the subtle art of making tyranny appear as a free government, the arcane and unspeakable designs of the prince, and so forth. Further, the "arcanum" is derived from *arx* (a sacred, fortified enclosure, as seen earlier) and this possible etymology makes political arcana a sacred and hermetic ritual. It is as if the business of statecraft can be best conducted by transferring onto its domain the cabalas and tricks of occult magic. Finally, "arcana regni" implies that in the context of a secret and ancient political science this art can be practiced by initiates who know how to pierce the veil: the point is exemplified by Machiavelli's story of the covert teachings the Centaur Chiron imparted to Achilles (*The Prince*, Chapter XVIII). This in turn implies that the path of (to) truth or open discourse, such as the one Vico apparently claims for himself as he writes a "vera historia," is unsafe and imprudent. Consistent with the insight, Tacitus counsels dissimulation and prudence to those who live in the dangerous world of the court of, say, a Caligula, where plain speech is a subversive act. The Scholastics define prudence as a virtue of the practical intellect and this virtue is to be understood as an art, as the skill to gauge steadily shifting and precarious fortunes of and around oneself and to decide well among conflicting claims on oneself.

In historical terms, Tacitus and his theory of the *arcana imperii* inaugurate a new political ethos, which the Tacitists of the Italian Renaissance and European baroque politics debate at length. Jean Bodin links the *arcana imperii* of Tacitus with Machiavelli's illusions and stratagems of power as well as with the views of Guicciardini and Plutarch. For Guicciardini, Scipione Ammirato, and Giovanni Botero *arcana imperii* is the *ragion di stato*, *ratio status*, or reason of state. The phrase, popularized by Botero, epitomizes the doctrine of the absolute, unlimited power of the state and it is defined by Botero as "the knowledge of the means by which . . . a dominion may be founded, and extended. . . . And although all that is done to these purposes is said to be done for Reason of State, yet this is said rather of such actions as cannot be considered in the light of ordinary reason" (*The Reason of State* I, 1, p. 3).

These extraordinary actions that are contemplated by Botero trouble, at least on the surface, the Tacitists, and induce them to ponder their implications. Should there be any moral constraints, they wonder, in the pursuit of the interests of the prince or of the state? Should the principles of natural law, which, from Cicero to St. Paul, from Aquinas to Suarez, uphold the existence of an eternal moral order—common to all, written in man's heart, and discoverable by the use of reason—be put aside in the name of the sovereign necessities of the state? When is war—and this is the issue most treated by political theorists such as Bacon, Botero, Saavedra-Fajardo, and Locke—lawful for a Christian state? These questions, which are the core of Tacitism, shape the structure and movement of Vico's *The Life of Antonio Carafa*.

The underlying model of the narrative, I would like to suggest, is Tacitus's *Life of Agricola*. Vico adopts, to begin with, the numerical structure of his model, which is composed of forty-six chapters. *The Life of Antonio Carafa* is introduced by a Dedicatory Letter and a proem and is divided into four books, each of which is comprised respectively of eleven, twelve, ten, and thirteen chapters, which all together make forty-six chapters. The intellectual reasons for imitating the architecture of Tacitus's text are self-evident. Tacitus conceives the biography of his father-in-law as a tribute to a hero's memory, who lived a virtuous life but is at the end in disfavor with a capricious emperor. Written in the form of a eulogy, the text records Agricola's accomplishments in the unscrupulous age of Domitian where "liberty and empire" are seen as incompatible, and its deeper point is to show how "a great man can live under bad rulers" (Chapter 43) and how a prudent man should conduct himself while sycophants, dissimulators, and flatterers are advising the tyrant.

Vico's adoption of the external architectural design of *Agricola* must have pleased the young Adriano, who is himself introduced as a sort of Tacitist. From this viewpoint it can be said that Vico writes a tribute for Antonio Carafa as if Adriano himself had written it. The symmetry is borne out by a textual detail: Tacitus memorializes his father-in-law; Adriano, who is an orphan, memorializes his uncle as if he were his father. The open symmetry, however, quickly collapses, for Vico prudently intends to establish a critical distance between himself and Antonio Carafa and, through the downfall of this flawed hero, he lays open the radical limits of modern European political theories. What was earlier announced as the historian's duty to draw within the compass of his representation the private and public aspects of the protagonist's life turns out to describe the quandaries of

Vico's own narrative that must pursue a simultaneously covert and open discourse.

The story of the marshal's life begins with the account of a double genealogy. Vico offers, first of all, the mythical origins of Naples, which recalls the poetic fable of the Siren Parthenope as told by Homer. A summary of the genealogy of the Carafa family follows, as if the dynasty of one shared in and reflected the renown of the other. After establishing the mythical foundations of the origins, the biography proceeds to sketch Antonio's character and early education. The rhetorical thrust of the *Autobiography* is the bildungsroman, the ceaseless education of the author's mind. Carafa's biography is instead rightly called *res gestae*, a history of things done, and it portrays the strengths and limitations of a man of action, equally skilled in the intricacies of courtly life and the harsh life of the battlefield. Vico's ambivalences toward Antonio Carafa, however, emerge quickly. Born of a noble family in 1642, the young Antonio showed no inclination to liberal education and this neglect, Vico says, comes forth in the carelessness of his speech, which, nonetheless, is resolute and decorous as befits a soldier. After murdering a man, Antonio repairs to Malta, where he fights Turkish pirates, and eventually he finds sanctuary and success at the court of Vienna.

Vico indulges in a scrupulous description of the making of Antonio Carafa into a seventeenth-century courtier, and the narrative of his worldly education is marked by the deployment of the most flagrant *topoi* of Tacitism. As one expects from a baroque mythology of power, the model for his political education is the prince himself, who is largely invisible in the text but from whom all power radiates. Antonio Carafa becomes a chamberlain in the cosmopolitan royal court of Leopold, and from him and the other court dignitaries he learns and practices the art of hiding, or dissimulation. His esthetic education crystallizes and turns for Vico into a question of a politics of art. In Botero's manual of the *ragion di stato* Tiberius's power of dissimulation is singled out as a feigned ignorance of all he knew. For Carafa silence is his cunning, and it appears as an act of supreme prudence for it throws into doubt what one knows or does not know. This passion for secretiveness is itself the secret route in his ascetic pursuit of power. He quietly studies the mind of the prince, the wiles of ministers, and the whims of the princess, as if to carry out the Tacitists' recommendation of what is essential to governing.

Political life has for Carafa a sovereign prestige and he totally submits to its overarching demands. He has no higher principle than the interests of the prince, and his every choice is determined by this principle. Carafa soon finds the court's rituals of power inadequate to his ambition and he serves in the military campaigns Leopold is waging against the Turks in the eastern enclaves of his expanding Austrian empire. Vico focuses on Carafa's military apprenticeship under the tutelage of an Italian general, Montecuccoli, and he lists admiringly his mastery of the military art, the "belli artes"—logistics, fortifications, providing for winter quarters, studying the terrain for the battle, and so forth. But it is also clear that for Vico, Antonio Carafa is only a brilliant technocrat, who faithfully executes the will of the emperor, in whom alone absolute power resides. Carafa's sphere of competence is the ruthless and efficient machinery of war, and the text is studded with accounts of his intrigues and strategies in his sundry wars. If for Antonio Carafa war is a supreme political art, for Vico war crystallizes the essence of the modern or baroque political project. He places the text, in effect, within the vast orbit of seventeenth-century intellectual debates where war is a constant subject of speculation that puts to the test the very principle of reason of state.

The symbolic warehouse of baroque esthetics, as historians of the baroque have pointed out, is infinitely large. As seen earlier, it includes a taste for secret vaults, grottos, ossariums, arches, ruins, theaters, and, as will be seen later, it encompasses globes, twisted oval shapes, archeological relics, obelisks, pyramids, emblems, and so forth. The cult of the mysterious and the singular—the enigmas of hieroglyphs, the pursuit of the monstrous and grotesque—is the prolongation of the esthetic obsession with the production of marvelous shapes violently breaking out of ordinary closed forms. For Vico, baroque iconography, which he lavishly deploys, is a serraglio of oddities, prodigies, and bizarre fantasies, which find their counterpoint in a conceptual world of shifting perspectives, illusory perceptions, infinite and unexplored openness of space traversed by cosmographical and utopian voyages, vertiginous adventures of the mystics, and bold imaginations of the infinite.

The Life of Antonio Carafa retrieves the vanished traces of history perceived as a finite, time-bound world and probes the hidden, political other side of baroque esthetics. Baroque political philosophy with its theories of the *arcana imperii*, of absolute power, conspiratorial discourse, and grand imperial designs, comes through as an esthetics of an ever vanishing perfection covering and stemming from a reality of violence and power plays. War, which is the central political metaphor of *The Life of Antonio Carafa* and of history, is the crossroads of these routes of power, meticulous scientific technology, death cult, heroic fantasies, elaborate diplomatic rituals, and, above all, a complex, richly articulated discourse of moral-legal speculations. The fundamental question posed by the Tacitists and anti-Machiavellians (from Botero to Ammirato to Saavedra-Fajardo), whether or not war should be waged on religious grounds with the purpose of rooting out the idolatry of sects, figures prominently in *The Life of Antonio*

Carafa. A generalized discourse on the morality and legality of war, in effect, punctuates Vico's text.

The moralists' reflections on war encompass definitions of a "just war," issues of limitations on war, and the problematic relationship between war and the *jus gentium*. Moreover, the anti-Machiavellian moralists, picking up views held by the Cajetan and Cardinal Bellarmine, justify holy wars and find a "just cause" in fighting for the prince and the church. Vico's text responds directly to these moral-theological challenges by turning to Grotius's *De iure belli ac pacis* in his account of Carafa's military career.[11]

We follow his career, first, as he fights the Hungarian rebel, Imre Thokoli, who had asked the Turks for help against the emperor. Quickly the war between Austria and the Turks around Belgrade and at the siege of Vienna carries unmistakable overtones of a religious war between Christians and Moslems, and, at the same time, between Catholics and Protestants. For Vico religion appears as an *instrumentuum regni* (II, 7), at least when he judges the Moslem side of the conflict. But there is no doubt that wars of religion are a cloak for covetousness, and Antonio Carafa himself is driven by the principle of equivalence between might and right.

Vico never opposes war, as Erasmus had done from his irenic standpoint and on grounds that war is so hideous as to be forbidden to Christians. He does have Antonio Carafa, however, argue for war and peace in terms of the theory of "Just War."[12] The just foundation of war, as Spanish theologians such as Francisco de Vitoria and Francisco Suarez saw it, can only be the *jus gentium* and natural law. In *De jure belli ac pacis* Grotius defines natural law as "a dictate of right reason, showing the moral necessity or moral baseness of any act according to its agreement or disagreement with rational nature, and indicating that such an act is either commanded or forbidden by the author of nature, God" (pp. 20–21).

The principle of natural law and the very language of Grotius in *De jure* shape large portions of Vico's narrative. Let me illustrate the claim. The vizier Soliman sends a letter to Antonio Carafa via the Aghá Mohamed. The letter charges that the Christians have violated the right and sanctity of embassies and, with it, the law of nature. The issue of the "Right of Embassy" had been treated by Grotius (*De jure*, II, p. 18), and there are echoes

---

[11] See Dario Faucci, "Vico and Grotius: Juriconsults of Mankind," in *Giambattista Vico: An International Symposium* (Baltimore: Johns Hopkins University Press, 1969), pp. 61–76; Guido Fassò, *Vico e Grozio* (Naples: Guida, 1971); Santo Mazzarino, *Vico, l'annalistica e il diritto* (Naples: Guida, 1971).

[12] See James T. Johnson, *Just War Tradition and the Restraint of War* (Princeton: Princeton University Press, 1981) and *The Quest for Peace: Three Moral Traditions in Western Cultural History* (Princeton: Princeton University Press, 1987); Gerardo Zampaglione, *The Idea of Peace in Antiquity* (Notre Dame, Ind.: University of Notre Dame Press, 1973).

of his views in Vico. To have the Aghá Mohamed deliver the letter is Vico's own ploy to flatly contradict Soliman's protest. But Carafa rejects the charge and his argument resonates with the language of both theorists of Just War and Grotius. Carafa appeals, moreover, to the principle of the Just War the Christian army fights against the Moslem—and this is what makes the war just in defense of other Christians. Later in *The Life of Antonio Carafa* (II, 7) the marshal expatiates on the juridical aspect of the war between the Turks and Leopold. He accuses the Turks of waging a war whose morality is defined by "*civilis aequitas*" (p. 128). A footnote by Vico himself explains that the Latin phrase translates what "the Italians elegantly call *ragion di stato*, reason of state" (p. 128). Such a principle, which underlies the martial conduct of the Turks, Carafa adds, is repugnant to Christians who, on the contrary, are guided by the ideas of the Just War.

Why does Vico have Carafa speak as if he had read Grotius? The chapter on Carafa's early education (I, 2) stresses the imperviousness of his mind to the study of the humanities. Why, then, does Vico now cast Carafa as a theorist of moral philosophy and international law? He casts him, in fact, as if he were a student of Vico or Vico himself, although generally the narrative establishes a drastic opposition between the two of them. Let me recall some elements of the radical differences between them. The first is the ambivalent use of Tacitus. Further, Vico, as we may recall, intends to write a "true history," while Carafa, by contrast, is versed in courtly dissembling. Vico is a man of letters, while Carafa, who has contempt for the classics, is the accomplished man of arms.

As a historian, Vico writes by recalling the classical Roman historians as well as the ancient myth of Parthenope and the dynastic succession of the Carafa family. Vico writes, in short, as if he were the bearer of historical memories that transcend the preoccupations of the present. On the other hand, Antonio Carafa lives entirely in the present and can be said to espouse the values of the modern project: war and the technology of power. The moral and intellectual distance between the historian and his subject collapses when Grotius's treatise on war and peace is introduced. We must probe the reasons for Vico's highly controlled and deliberate strategy.

There are, in effect, two stories woven together in *The Life of Antonio Carafa*, and these two stories dramatize two modes of understanding and practicing politics. One story is overt: the apologia and critique of the achievements and ultimate disappointment of the marshal, who is banished from the court of Vienna on suspicion of embezzlement of public funds, and whom Vincenzo Cuoco, in a memorable opinion, dismissed as a mediocrity. The other is a covert, necessarily subtle story in which Vico narrates his political ideas. In this other story he obliquely suggests the importance of an updated but ancient classical project of political prudence as the alternative that can save a war-ravaged world. In this conception of politics the historian, not the man of arms, is fit to rule. In this conception the marshal's achievements can be surpassed by Adriano, and the marshal would speak as if he had been under the tutelage of Vico himself. But what exactly is Vico's classical project? Why should the historian rule? And how does he substantively differ from a technocrat such as Antonio Carafa?

After making the claim that he intends to write a "true history" of Carafa's life, Vico evokes, as said earlier, the origins of the Carafa family, which, in turn, gives way to the myth of the origins of Naples. On the authority of Homer, who is called "primus omnis memoriae scriptor" (*The Life of Antonio Carafa*, I, 1, p. 15) (the first memorialist of antiquity) Vico, paradoxically, summons a poetic myth: the fable of the Siren Parthenope from whom Naples is believed to have originated (SN/304). The reference to Parthenope is meant to underscore the natural seductiveness of the place as well as the pleasures of Naples' civil life. The word "siren" in Greek means entanglements. Paradoxically, the city's delights threaten to be chains. Vico, however, emphasizes the fabled freedom characterizing Naples' history. Naples—*nea polis*—is an eminently political place, a new city whose unique and essential character is embodied by its mixed Roman and Greek roots.

In early Roman times Naples sided with Rome against Hannibal and she enjoyed a free form of government under the Swabians and during the invasions of the Longobards and Saracens. Naples' bond with Rome was indissolubly forged when Roman patrician families (the Virgini, Proculi, Bruti, etc.) repaired to Naples while Rome was being pillaged by the barbarians. On the other hand, the city's achievements in the liberal arts made her the rival of Athens, a new city of philosophy and learning, the place of choice for the offspring of the Roman patricians. In short, the mythical picture of Naples as a *locus amoenus* and as a utopia in history, where the flowers of art and freedom bloom, is in stark contrast to the city's nocturnal conspiracies, Carafa's act of murder and subsequent life of war.

It is plain that Vico interprets Homer's fable as a political fable. His interpretive gesture, it can be added, is reminiscent of Bacon's *De Sapientia Veterum*, where ancient myths are unveiled as if they were hermetic ciphers for the necessarily veiled, secret knowledge of statecraft. What Vico shares with Bacon at this juncture is the belief that a "true history" cannot shun, indeed it needs, the covertness and obliquities of poetic fictions. Carafa's own practice of dissimulation had, after all, its necessity. History—the world of politics—takes fables as its point of departure, and it narrates the fictional story of the city as a free, utopian place in the midst of a seemingly without-end recurrence of tyrannies and invasions for several reasons.

The first reason is stated directly in the text. Vico recounts how, because of Naples' fidelity to Rome and love of humane letters, the Emperor Tiberius held the city in high esteem. He also says that the Emperor Nero found Naples so agreeable because he could "in Neapolitano theatro musicos agens ludos" (*The Life of Antonio Carafa*, I, 1, p. 16) (perform songs on the Neapolitan stage). The moral is self-evident: the arts, songs, and theatrical representations can tame and enchant, as the Siren Parthenope did with the sea voyagers, the savagery of the tyrants. A second reason is that the historian knows that the foundation of the city is fictional and that politics needs utopian fables. Modern political science rejects classical utopias (see Machiavelli's *The Prince*, Chapter XV) as unworkable flights of fancy. For Vico this is the delusion of modernity that reduces history to a cult of the present. But modern history—he implies—cannot be separated from the past if there is to be a future to the present. Accordingly, a true history needs poetic fictions—such as those Homer tells—because myths are, paradoxically, truer than facts and because they are ancient memories or imaginative whorls on the spindle of time.

As is shown in the case of Nero, who straddles the theater and the simulations of the court, poetic fables may seem to have a kinship to the political theater of simulations staged by a Tiberius and his modern prolongation, such as Leopold and Antonio Carafa. Nonetheless, there is a subtle and important difference between these two modes. Poetic myths can be, indeed they must be, prudently manipulated for a given rhetorical end—as Vico does. But the true historian knows—as Tacitus and Vico know in a way that a technocrat cannot—that no myth can be reducible to one literal signification. The true historian also knows that there are always contradictions within the possible senses of a myth and that there is always an excess to what a myth says and seems to signify.

The fable of Naples' origin in Parthenope exemplifies both Vico's strategic manipulation of the total myth of Naples and his historical knowledge of it. The total story of the myth is complex. From Pontano and Sannazaro we learn that Naples is the offspring of the marriage of the Siren Parthenope and the subterranean river Sebeto, to which, as seen earlier, the *Neapolitan Conspiracy* made a discreet reference. We also know from Homer's account that Parthenope in the *Odyssey* (Book XII, 37–200), which Vico cites in *The Life of Antonio Carafa*, is one of the two Sirens who dwell in the grottos of Capri. She is a sea monster who sings beautifully and who, by the seductive power of the song, leads the voyagers to death. Only Ulysses, who has just escaped the tyranny of Circe, can escape the lure of Parthenope by his extraordinary craftiness: he puts wax in the ears of his companions and ties himself to the mast of the ship. Ulysses' virtue lies in his keeping his knowledge to himself. As if he were Ulysses, who makes his companions deaf, Vico silences these details, and yet they contain an ironic premonition of the tragic fatality attendant upon the voyagers in the waters of public life, such as Carafa, or any other aspirant to positions of leadership. The city with her voluptuary charm can lead the heroes astray, as Parthenope did. To escape the city's really monstrous tentacles of pleasure and death one must not hear the siren call, must bind oneself, or have the wisdom and eloquence of a Ulysses. If Vico is thinking of himself as a Ulysses he probably also remembers that Ulysses—who for Dante, anyway, yielded to the temptation of the Siren (or so she falsely claims)—is a *fandi fictor*, the rhetorician who leads himself and his companions to a tragic end as they make for utopia.

By silencing the dangers of Parthenope, the Renaissance version of the myth of Parthenope's marriage to Sebetus, and the ultimate failure of the rhetorician, who at first conquers Parthenope, Vico dramatizes his extraordinary rhetorical craft. He silences, first of all, the subterranean, or baroque, world of politics as a practice of secrets. But he is not upholding a naive ideology of the transparency or truth of political discourses. He dramatizes, rather, the need for a prudent rhetoric that can overcome both the simulations of the tyrants and the immoderate lure of the siren. The rejection of rhetoric, which a strain of Christian theology calls for, is not possible for Vico, who, like the humanists of the Italian Renaissance, knows that rhetoric is the art wherein man's hard choices are debated. Indeed, if the elimination of rhetoric were possible, it would not be desirable. Eliminating rhetoric is tantamount to eliminating history.

Vico effectively argues that there is no a priori safe way of governing or being in the shiftiness of the historical world. The underlying negative lesson history delivers for Vico is that the heroes of history are doomed and that one is a hero exactly because one is doomed. From this tragic foreknowledge of inevitable failure one cannot be led, however, to inaction. Quite to the contrary. For Vico the question of who is fit to rule in an unmanageable, dangerous, and unruly world becomes more pressing than ever before, and he is steadfast in pursuing it.

Immediately after evoking the myth of Parthenope and of Naples as a free, utopian city (I, 1), Vico moves on to sketch the picture of Antonio Carafa's imperviousness to humane letters and his training in military *areté* (I, 2). All of a sudden this second chapter about military education changes direction and Vico begs to digress. He wishes to investigate, he says, why uncultured men are believed to have a special aptitude for governing the state. The digression turns into a series of questions that lie at the center of Vico's concerns. Because they are central, he puts them as an appendix, as if to hide them or as if they were irrelevant. But the proem has just warned us to pay special attention to seemingly negligible details.

Most of the questions he asks come forth as general perplexities: Must a politician be totally aware of his actions? Must one be able to catch in others the slightest signs of simulation? How does one astutely observe the "arcana" (I, 2) of the state (*The Life of Antonio Carafa*, I, 2, p. 19)? Other questions seem to be more like a prescription: Why do statesmen manage to know the particulars of a situation, whereas scholars neglect minute details which, in fact, are essential to the knowledge of the whole? In answering these questions Vico drafts his theory of who is fit to rule.

Men who are distracted by abstract thoughts on the nature of reality, he states, do not know the examples fit to be followed in the course of an action. Vico's polemical target is unequivocal: contemplative philosophers cannot rule. In the *Republic* Socrates asserts that philosophers should rule, that wisdom should rule the city, and yet he knows that there is a hostility between the philosophers and the city. Vico, who, like Bacon, believes that knowledge and power, philosophy and politics are to be thought of together, would, however, agree with Socrates. If contemplative philosophers are so removed, professionally, as it were, from the concerns of the polis, who knows the examples to be followed in the course of an action?

Before answering the question Vico continues his probings by another exclusion. Those who conceive of political doctrine as a set of fixed, abstract precepts put the state to a disadvantage. Political practice cannot be shut in the tight limits, as if they were gates, of a definitive, dogmatic science ("cumque certis scientiae definitionibus contineri, tanquam cancellis non ferant . . ." [I, 2, p. 19]). One can infer that obliquely Vico is attacking the unbending moralists of politics—Botero, Lipsius, Ribadeneira, Saavedra-Fajardo, and so forth—who, by virtue of their doctrinaire rigidity, still transform politics into a technology of power. By the same token, a little later in the digression, Vico advises the monarch, to whose authority he submits, not to transfer the administration of the state to a man "interioris doctrinae" (I, 2, p. 20), with a doctrine of the secret art of government. Quite pointedly, the political allegorists or cultists of the hidden art of government (the *arcana imperii*), who make the Machiavellian practice of simulation the ordinary rule, are rejected. They are rejected because their allegory—a rhetoric of double-talk—is a political subterfuge whereby one says one thing and predictably means another. Such a systematically selfsame duplicity does not work: it foments a hermeneutics of suspicion; it is predictable; it never aims at the totality of interests, but sees meanings from the narrow perspective of the interpreter's self-interested standpoint.

To be of any advantage to the state one must know how to propose examples drawn from history, one must know how the past impinges on the necessities of the present, how to summon utopias and inventively make pliable for the present the lessons of the past. The historian is juxtaposed to the casuistries of abstract precepts, to the recondite philosophies of the *ragion di stato* and to a scientific understanding of politics, which are all evasive and dangerous in the measure in which they are predictably mechanical and rigid. The historian's prudence lies in the art of confronting the ever dangerous contradictions of history, of harmonizing the public and the private, utopian and realistic schemes, and of reaching into the deep secrets of archives. The historian's rhetorical manipulation, Vico implies, is subtler than any other technology of government, which is always partial.

Vico ends his digression on two points. The first is a general consideration of the prosperity of a state, which depends, he says, on wise counsel dictated by necessity and not by choice. The meaning he attaches to this general platitude is evident from what follows it. By contrast, states collapse either because rulers yield to unrestrained cruelty and avarice, or because of civil wars, or because people lapse into a life of luxury and pleasure. States can be preserved, Vico goes on to remark, by the intervention of divine Providence. The notion epitomizes the dangers of tyranny and the equally dangerous, popular sovereignty of pleasure, which the myth of Parthenope exemplified and which Vico a little earlier eluded. Tyranny and the principle of (Epicurean) pleasure are posited to be equivalent and powerful forces of subversion of the state.

Can the historian—who is a man of letters and a rhetorician—be harmful to the state? The inevitable question, though it is not directly raised, is directly answered in Vico's second point where he, in a seemingly abrupt manner (but this is indeed the logic of his narrative), considers the age-old relationship between arms and letters. The kinship between Vico and Carafa, which Vico steadily eludes in the text, moves now centerstage as Vico vindicates the political value of the liberal arts Carafa had neglected. Vico begins his argument by acknowledging the Augustinian—Machiavellian realistic principle that empires are founded by "vi et armis" (p. 20) (by force and arms). Carafa's historical role belongs and is confined to this foundational moment. Once states are founded, however, they become famous, thrive, and expand through the *studia humanitatis*. Clearly, literary and historical knowledge need not be thought of as harmful to the life of political institutions. Their usefulness lies in their ability to promote new scientific inventions (military science, navigation, etc.) that keep the state from disintegrating. Ancient myths and modern sciences, poetic and critical arts, the public and the private, utopian and realistic politics—all these polarities collapse in the figure of the historian.

Vico's history of the modern age—the age of absolute power—has forged a view of history as the discipline capable of capturing the contradictory and hybrid complexities of experience, and yet capable of transcending them. The historian is fit to rule because he has a grasp of the whole, understands the sovereignty of memory, has the eloquence to stir the passions and submit the passions to reason, and has the prudence to confront choices. The claims are unavoidably a historian's claims. More generally, all this is to say that Vico believes that history must rule, that history with its myths and traditions rules in the life of the states. Accordingly, tyrannical politics and despotic perspectives are questioned.

Eventually, as is known, Vico was appointed royal historiographer of the Bourbons of Naples (1735). He had coveted the job and he went on to write pieces of local history and erudition or to take notes for future works, such as the history of the royal house that employed him. The disparity between the bureaucratic job of historiographer and his ideas about history as they emerge in the *Neapolitan Conspiracy* and *The Life of Antonio Carafa* is self-evident.

Vico's reflections on history, as shall be seen later, find their most mature and deepest expression in the *New Science*. We know that Vico is all along haunted by the desire to produce a magnum opus, and that the *New Science* is the goal to which he relentlessly applied himself. But before he set his hand to writing and constantly revising the *New Science*, he wrote a juridical encyclopedia, *De Uno Universi Juris Principio et Fine Uno*. As a way of closing this chapter let me point out some features of this text that pick up and alter his ideas of history in the two texts discussed above.

Firstly, Vico writes an encyclopedia, which he calls *De Uno*. Against the doctrines of Epicurus, against the views in the *Prince* of Machiavelli, *De Cive* of Hobbes, the *Tractatus Theologico-Politicus* of Spinoza, and the *Dictionnaire historique et critique* of Bayle, which are founded in a utilitarian, skeptical view of justice, Vico writes a true "ἐγκυκλοπαιδεία, hoc est disciplinam vere rotundam, verc universam, vere sine offensione, cui iurisprudentiam, uti Ulpianus definierat, respondere eruditi scribunt. . . ." (p. 39) (an encyclopedia that is a truly completed discipline, truly universal, truly unassailable, just as jurisprudence should be, to use Ulpian's definition, in the opinion of the scholars). Vico writes an encyclopedia, which would embody the whole of legal lore (the laws' metaphysical foundation in God, their lexicon and significance, their accumulated wisdom, their history and changes, etc.). In this sense, the encyclopedia, which is an all-embracing synthesis or harmonization of possible contradictions and divisions, is the logical, unavoidable genre for laws. Rights are, by their very nature, indivisible and each law implicates the totality of laws. Bayle's *Dictionnaire*, by contrast, with its quotations and erudite annotations of Pyrrhonistic, skeptical articles and Epicurean, atheistic commentaries, which went on to shape the subversive stance of later eighteenth-century French *Encyclopedie*, does not aim at a reconciliation of opposed viewpoints. His summary exposition of religious or philosophical entries, for all their originality, wants to rip open as false all traditional claims of unity.

The first inkling of what is at stake in an encyclopedic text came to Vico from reading Bacon, who, as we are told in the *Autobiography*, did justice "to all the sciences" (p. 139). Bacon's conceptual limit—and I shall return to this point in successive chapters—is the question of laws. Vico is deeply indebted to Bacon for his drafting a "sum of human and divine knowledge", but he knows that Bacon fails to grasp the law as the essential compass of universal history (*Autobiography*, p. 155). Grotius, on the other hand, "embraces in a system of universal law the whole of philosophy and philology," fabulous and real history, and, the system contains also the languages of antiquity (*Autobiography*, p. 155). In effect, Vico's transition from his historical works to his legal encyclopedia is a transition from prudence to Roman jurisprudence—from epideictic to forensic rhetoric, from a political context of fractured experiences and double/duplicitous discourses to a system of laws where philosophy, politics, history, and language are joined together. It is a transition to a world where the authority of the law, and its own *arcana potestatis*, would hold sway.

The word for law in *De Uno* is "ius," which in Italian is translated as "ragione" (p. 99). *Ragione* or *ratio* is not an abstract Cartesian reason disengaged from the facticity and materiality of history. Rather, it is important to keep in mind that *ratio* is law, and the domain of the law implies the thick and hybrid sedimentation of concrete historical facts—household economy, politics, customs, notions about the authority of nature, and so forth. Above all, laws imply bodies and they act on bodies. I would claim, as a matter of fact, that the radical novelty of *De Uno*, within Vico's production to this point of his life, lies in the consciousness that politics, history, and laws are primarily questions of bodies. Machiavelli and Bacon—not to speak of Campanella—had understood that the body—its immoderate desires, its ungovernable passions, its "mixed" quality—is the central political issue. For them death is the revenge on the infinite desires of bodies. Vico presents an entirely new perspective. *De Uno* begins by asserting the divine origin of all the sciences and it then proceeds to define man's uniqueness and separateness as a body. "Homo ex corpore et mente constat: et corpore et iis quae sunt corporis, uti sensus, quia finitae res sunt, homo a ceteris ommibus hominibus dividitur. . . ." (*De Uno*, p. 41) (Man is composed of body and mind. The body and the things that belong to the body, such as the senses, which are finite, divide man from all other men.). Unlike Bacon, Vico makes death the ultimate law of bodies.

The treatise continues to probe issues of divine wisdom, fallen nature, the "vis veri" (p. 53), the force of truth, the role of reason and its virtue, the ethics of the pagans, the intervention of grace in human affairs, the essence and history of natural law, the foundation and necessity of human society, and so forth, as preambles to laws and to the principle of "honeste vivere." But Vico does not forego his realistic assessment of bodies— their shifting passions, their unending appetites and storms of affection (pp. 51–53). The archeology and economy of the passions, their dim and

Chapter 4

A POETIC ENCYCLOPEDIA

THE TEXTS SO FAR examined show Vico's mind steadily turning around questions of politics and knowledge. More precisely, the *Autobiography*, *On the Heroic Mind*, and the *De uno* exemplify Vico's conception of an encyclopedic organization of knowledge and his endorsement of the notion that to learn is to attain a global understanding of the world and of oneself. The necessity for weaving the sundry threads of knowledge into one fabric is announced by one phrase: "the whole is the flower of wisdom." However, this search for the totalizing universe of learning is not simply a formal enterprise. As Vico states both in *On the Heroic Mind* and at the opening of the 1725 edition of the *New Science*, "all the sciences, all the disciplines and the arts" are directed to the perfection of the human faculties (1NS/11). The sciences are rooted in the very principles that shape the history of the nations. Thus, as Vico adds in the same paragraph, reflecting on the arts and sciences entails reflecting on the history of mankind.

The same encyclopedic and historical impulse that was articulated in earlier texts shapes the structure and aims of the 1744 *New Science*. The global aims of Vico's search are expressed by propositions and images throughout the text. The *New Science* seeks to retrieve a "mental language common to all nations" (NS/161) as well as "tutto lo scibile gentilesco" or "tutto il credibile cristiano" (NS/51) (all gentile learning and the whole Christian faith). Dictionaries, mythological compendia (e.g., Boccaccio's *Genealogy of the Gentile Gods*), the thesaurus, theaters of memory, libraries, and museums—which are baroque spatial emblems of the gathering of heterogeneous domains of knowledge—are deployed as if they were the formal correlations of Vico's own work.

The *New Science* can be construed as a retrospective and critical summa of Vico's previous intellectual enterprises—law, history, politics, education, poetry, and so forth. The epitome goes beyond, however, the recapitulation of past thematic knots. Quite overtly, the all-inclusive text becomes the ground on which Vico's claim to authority rests. Furthermore, it constitutes the model for a possible political-historical totality or universal monarchy. It purports to provide "a rational civil theology of divine providence" (NS/342) and to describe, by offering philological proofs, an "ideal eternal history traversed in time by the history of every nation"

(NS/349). But the encyclopedic focus of this summary is chiefly crystallized by its representation of the totality of history within which the modifications of the mind and the forms of human knowledge are rooted.

The representation of the global order of knowledge occurs by the text's synoptic tabulation of the blurred and yet visible traces of universal history in chronological succession, from the Universal Flood recorded by the Hebrews, through the Chaldeans, Scythians, Phoenicians, and Egyptians, to the Greeks and Romans. Shifts and resemblances across geographical and temporal patterns are duly stressed, while the story of the Garden of Eden is bracketed in favor of the study of gentile histories. The governing principle in this *syntopicon* of universal history is the concept of the three epochs: that of the gods, of the heroes, and that of humankind. This emphasis on time and history is to be taken, first of all, as Vico's way of providing the concrete context for the general structure of experience—language, myths, institutions, and ideas that, all together, are the alphabet and the signatures for his totalizing project. Furthermore, the sense of contingency and historicity, within which every experience is to be interpreted, indicates that knowledge and its totality are historical and that, for all its totalizing ambition, no discourse can ever acquire a final and absolute knowledge.

The above statement about absolute knowledge does not mean that the focus on contingent, variable experiences keeps Vico from viewing his project as a science and as a *new science* at that. Vico's classical dictum, that philology must be considered in the light of philosophy, implies that he writes a new science of contingencies, and he articulates a vision wherein drastic polarities of reality are made to coexist in the oxymoron of an "eternal history." This is the backdrop against which the sense of the claim of a *new science* is grasped.

On the Heroic Mind highlights science's kinship with beauty to emphasize its order and harmonious scope. In the *New Science* Vico deploys the term "science" in the wake of Aristotle's *Metaphysics* (1003a15). Aristotle's science or *episteme* describes the knowledge of an entity through the principle or cause by which it came into being. For Vico science is characterized by "universal and eternal" properties (NS/163) that provide the principle of regularity in the midst of uncertain knowledge. The eternal properties of science are the universality of burials, marriages, and religions. His universal science, thus, hinges on available principles of knowledge; it studies the laws of an "ideal eternal history," and is immersed in empirical reality. Consistently, immediately after mentioning the *Metaphysics*, Vico cites "the best ascertained method of philosophizing, that of Francis Bacon"—Bacon's inductive, empirical method (NS/163).

The Aristotelian-Baconian scientific matrix casts Vico's science as an empirical science that portrays the uniform course run by the histories of all gentile nations and describes the modifications occurring in the history of the human mind. But, as shall be argued here, Vico views empirical science from the perspective of the sapiential tradition.

Vico's quest for a universally intelligible paradigm of knowledge largely reflects and shares in the modality of the baroque encyclopedic tradition. The Herborn encyclopedists, that include Heinrich Alsted, Amos Comenius, and John Bisterfield, elaborate systems of organization of the sciences and projects of education that were to deeply influence Leibniz's sense of metaphysical order. Inspired by the theology of the Reformation, their encyclopedias were compiled with the intent of leading to a millennial vision of universal harmony.[1] On the other hand, within the Catholic orbit (and mentioning figures who did their work in Italy) encyclopedists such as Francesco Patrizi, Giulio Camillo, Giorgio Valla, Athanasius Kircher, Juan Caramuel, and Giacinto Gimma variously sought to gather in a synthetic unity cabalistic-hermetic theories, esoteric doctrines, arts of memory, and antiquarianism.[2]

Vico's *New Science* shares in the presuppositions, methods, and finalities of a baroque encyclopedia.[3] Its eccentric and elliptical style and its fascination with monsters of the imagination and asymmetrical shapes, which the next chapter will again explore, eschew classical forms of representation. They throw into question Cartesian, rational models of order and draw within the open boundaries of the representation knowledge's hybrid and sprawling latitudes. More than a scientific method of ordering facts, such as those attempted by Giacomo Zabarella's *De methodis* and Leibniz's *A New Method of Teaching and Learning Jurisprudence* (1667), with its logic of probabilities as a way of resolving the uncertainties of knowledge, Vico makes method the route to the archaic, most uncertain beginnings of history (NS/338–60). In this sense, method is paradoxically the very destination of his science.

---

[1] Leroy E. Loemker, "Leibnitz and the Herborn Encyclopedists," *Journal of the History of Ideas*, 22 (1961), pp. 323–38. See also Cesare Vasoli, *L'enciclopedismo nel Seicento* (Naples: Istituto per gli Studi Filosofici, 1978); Walter Tega, *L'unità del sapere e l'ideale enciclopedico nel pensiero moderno* (Bologna: Il Mulino,1983).

[2] A detailed discussion of this tradition is available in Cesare Vasoli, *L'enciclopedismo del Seicento*, cited above, footnote 1. See also Ramon Cenal, "Juan Caramuel: su epistolario con Athanasio Kircher S.J.," *Revista de Filosofia*, 12 (1953), pp. 101–47; Dino Pastine, *Juan Caramuel: probabilismo ed enciclopedia* (Florence, 1975); for the earlier forms of the tradition see Lina Bolzoni, *La stanza della memoria: modelli letterari e iconografici nell'età della stampa* (Turin: Einaudi, 1995).

[3] See the discussion of this issue in Giuseppe Mazzotta, "Vico's Encyclopedia," *Yale Journal of Criticism*, 1 (1988), no. 2, pp. 65–79. The notion, directly or indirectly, has been studied by Margherita Frankel, "The 'Dipintura' and the Structure of Vico's *New Science* as a Mirror of the World," in Giorgio Tagliacozzo, ed., *Vico: Past and Present* (Atlantic Highlands, N.J.: Humanities Press, 1981), pp. 43–51. See also Angus Fletcher, "On the Syncretic Allegory of the *New Science*," *New Vico Studies*, 4 (1986), pp. 25–43.

His chief guides for this baroque journey of discovery are Plato and Bacon. There could hardly be two philosophical perspectives more at variance with each other, and the contrasts between their modes of conceiving encyclopedias are artfully woven into Vico's text. For Plato the key question remains the *paideia* (education) of the soul, but he discards practical skills from his educational ideal. Plato's overarching spiritual aim is kept intact in the *New Science*, but his abstractions (be they political, legal, or educational) must be brought down, so at least Vico feels, to the solid and substantial particularities of real existence. The Platonic foundation of Vico's encyclopedia is articulated at the very beginning of Book II of the *New Science* in the section on "Poetic Wisdom." This stretch of the text ranges from a definition of "Wisdom in General" (NS/364–66) to an "Exposition and Division of Poetic Wisdom" (NS/367–68) and comes to a close with a chapter on "The Universal Flood and the Giants" (NS/369–73). Together, these three chapters encapsulate Vico's understanding of wisdom and science (both the discrepancy and complicity between them), and we must look at them with some attention for they contain the seeds for the formal and conceptual resolution of the *New Science*.

Vico's discussion starts from wisdom, "the faculty which commands all the disciplines by which we acquire all the sciences and arts that make up humanity" (NS/364). The verb "comanda"—commands—unequivocally sets up wisdom or first philosophy as the ruler over the descending hierarchy of disciplines by which we learn the arts and sciences. Wisdom's claimed sovereignty is followed by a definition of its moral aim, and to this end Vico deploys two different sources, a philosophical and a poetic source. In the wake of Plato's *Alcibiades Major* (124b–130e), wisdom is called "the perfecter of man." In what plainly is a gloss on the Platonic quotation, Vico adds that man is made of intellect and will so that, one infers, wisdom must satisfy man's double nature by teaching divine and human things. On the other hand, because wisdom among the gentiles began with the Muses, Vico recalls the *Odyssey*'s definition of it as "scienza del bene e del male" (knowledge of good and evil) (NS/365).[4]

The context of the two quotations sheds light on Vico's purposes. Plato's text narrates the encounter between Socrates and Alcibiades. Socrates, who holds that we are impelled to knowledge by the demon of love, confronts Alcibiades, the ambitious young politician and the protégé of Pericles. Their exchange centers on a crucial Socratic question: the critical relationship between politics and philosophy, action and knowledge. Alcibiades, who does not yet know the distinction between justice and injustice, cannot presume to lead the Athenians. From Socrates' viewpoint,

---

[4] In the *Leviathan* (EW, Vol. III, p. 146), Hobbes defines moral philosophy as "nothing else but the science of what is good and evill." See also his distinction between science and knowledge (EW, Vol. I, p. xiii).

on the other hand, nobody, except the philosopher, is capable of giving the power Alcibiades desires. Socrates' claims on behalf of philosophy over and against the power of political action find a correlation in the Homeric text.

The Homeric passage refers to the blind minstrel Demodokos, "who knows the good of life and evil" (*Odyssey*, Book VIII, l. 63). There is an evident and ironic appropriateness in recalling Ulysses' homeward journey just as Vico sets out on his own journey of discovery into the unmapped regions of the imagination. More to the point, Vico quotes from the description of Ulysses, who, unknown to his hosts, arrives at the island of the Phaiakians. In the presence of the disguised guest Demodokos sings about Ulysses' adventures and yields a little later to the hero's own narrative. For all their differences, the philosophical and the poetic citations are sustained by a common concern: Plato's text announces both the necessary link and distance between politics and philosophy, between the brilliant young man and the wise old philosopher. On its part, the *Odyssey* casts wisdom as an epic quest, and it forces on us the thought of the difference between Demodokos and Ulysses, the difference between the minstrel's blind art and the hero's hidden self-knowledge.

This preamble to Plato's and Homer's views on wisdom (and its difference from science) lets Vico document the historical shading of contours between wisdom and science (NS/365). The vulgar wisdom of the nations was a "science" of divination, and it was available to the theological poets, the seven sages of Greece, and generally to metaphysics, also known as "science of divine things." This definition, Vico says, holds for Jews and Christians, and it appears in modern Italian as "scienza in divinità". The linguistic excursus leads Vico to define the *New Science* as a "civil theology" (NS/366), which translates Varro's *theologia civilis*, or political theology. This branch of theology, polemically dismissed in St. Augustine's *City of God* (Book VI, 5–12), suggests that Vico's political theology is actually a political science. To put it differently, the Aristotelian science of first principles is placed within a moral context so as to make Vico's notion of science part of the sapiential tradition. From this standpoint the science of Alcibiades and the art of the blind Demodokos must be appropriated or controlled by Socrates and Ulysses.

In the *Neapolitan Conspiracy* and *The Life of Antonio Carafa* Vico explores the secret machinations of power and the logic of the coup d'état. Obliquely, he even stages the prudent advice, or *callida consilia*, necessary to governing. By contrast, in the *New Science* there is a coordinated articulation of the sciences in their relation to wisdom. In effect, Platonic wisdom must be corrected by philology, by Bacon's inductive method of philosophizing, which he carries over from experiments in the phenomena of natural science. Vico's description of Bacon as "philosopher and statesman" (NS/499) reflects his consciousness that in Bacon's philosophical discourse there is simply no room for knowledge as mere contemplation. If for Plato's Socrates action is antithetical to knowledge, for it is unavoidably blind about its effects, for Bacon knowledge is action or, in his own terms, "civil knowledge."

Vico underwrites Bacon's proposition. The fundamental principle of the *New Science* is that men can only know what they make: they know the world of civil society, for instance, for it has been made by men (NS/331). If both Plato and Bacon seek pure and reliable forms of knowledge outside the domain of poetry, for Vico the link between knowledge and making is "poetic" knowledge (wherein *poiesis* describes what men make). The *New Science* will elaborate a poetic encyclopedia that combines Platonic and Homeric wisdom with Bacon's reorganization of knowledge on empirical foundations. Vico's representation of poetic wisdom, thus, branches out like Bacon's *arbor scientiae* (tree of knowledge):

[w]e must trace the beginnings of poetic wisdom to a crude metaphysics. From this, as from a trunk, there branch out from one limb logic, morals, economics, and politics, all poetic; and from another, physics, the mother of cosmography and astronomy, the latter of which gives their certainty to its two daughters, chronology and geography—all likewise poetic. . . . Thus our Science comes to be at once a history of the ideas, the customs and deeds of mankind. From these three we shall derive the principles of the history of human nature, which we shall show to be the principles of universal history. (NS/367–68)[5]

The emblem is Bacon's, but it echoes Lull's *Arbor Scientiae* (1515) and it occurs also in Comenius and Descartes among others. It aptly suggests that knowledge grows as if it were an organic, natural process, that its systematization is by necessity forever incomplete, and, finally, that all its branches are vitally interdependent.[6] The idea that knowledge is historical (the genetic metaphors of "mother" and "daughters" as well as that of the tree suggest as much) is grafted by Vico, in a radical departure from

[5] See Enzo Paci, "Vico, Structuralism, and the Phenomenological Encyclopedia of the Sciences," in *Giambattista Vico: An International Symposium*, ed. G. Tagliacozzo and H. White (Baltimore: Johns Hopkins University Press, 1969), pp. 498ff.

[6] The motif is present in Comenius, *Pansophiae Prodromus* (see Comenio, *Opere*, ed. Marta Fattori (Turin: Utet, 1974), pp. 514–47). See also Descartes, "Le Principe de la philosophie: Lettre de l'auteur a celuy qui ha traduit le livre," in *Opere di Cartesio*, ed. E. Garin (Bari: Laterza, 1967), Vol. II, pp. 11–24. See also Bacon's *The Advancement of Learning*, Book II, in *Translations of the Philosophical Works*, I: 206. More generally see Robert McRae, *The Problem of the Unity of the Sciences: Bacon to Kant* (Toronto: University of Toronto Press, 1961), p. 26. See also Paolo Rossi, *Clavis Universalis* (Milan: Ricciardi, 1960). For further bibliography and a discussion of the implications of the image of the tree, see Tagliacozzo, "General Education as Unity of Knowledge: A Theory Based on a Vichian Principle," in *Vico and Contemporary Thought*, eds. G. Tagliacozzo, M. Mooney, D. P. Verene (Atlantic Highlands, N.J.: Humanities Press, 1979), pp. 111–21.

Bacon's myth of knowledge as rooted in nature, onto the notion that history and poetry (human nature) are the soil from which the sciences stem. The question of nature, however, is not forgotten. Actually, Vico reflects on nature and history by tracing history's roots, not to a perfect natural order, as Grotius would, but to their "unimaginable" natural origins, to the chaos of the origins, which lie beyond the certainty of any philology and which is the time of the giants (NS/369–73).[7]

Vico's fable about giants is a fable about natural origins and it begins with the account of the giants' birth. The name is etymologized (in the wake of Dante's *De Vulgari Eloquentia* and *Inferno, Canto* XXXI, 77–81) as the "sons of the Earth" (NS/370), and they are identified as the "founders of gentile humanity" (NS/369). By turning to the representation of natural origins, Vico's metaphysics, which is a "sublime science" (NS/367), touches down and literally retrieves the ground. His discourse about foundations deploys two related disciplines. First, he uses the category of etymology, which is the figure of grammatical origins. Second, he reverts to philology, which is here the science of the material residues from the past (skulls and bones of giants are said to have been found) and, ultimately, of the past's unknowable sources. Together, etymology and philology dramatize the problem of history's beginnings. History begins from the earth and her aborigines, the giants.

In Vico's imaginary account of origins, the original state of nature and the beginnings of history are savage and bestial: the giants wandered through the forests of the earth, had no fear of the gods, transgressed all bounds of nature, and grew excessively big. Their excess and errancy mark them as tropes of a nature without measure, and this hyperbole is Vico's perspective on history. It is possible to see in his imagination of giants an oblique image of his own hyperbolic, baroque philosophical project (just as one sees in the giants of Pulci, Boiardo, and Ariosto an image of their extravagantly large and errant epics). The giantism and hyperbolism of Vico's genealogy, however, are more than formal descriptions of his enterprise. They are explicit reflectors of his political theory.

In their aberrant, hyperbolic size the giants challenge the Neoplatonic principle of man as the measure of creation. Furthermore, as "aborigines" or "autochthonous" creatures (NS/370), they seem on the surface to embody the grandiose, powerful illusion of self-origination (NS/531). These terms, in any case, turn out to be linguistic redundancies for claiming lofty, aristocratic origins. More poignantly, the chaos of the giants' natural state alludes to the gigantomachy and the inexhaustible appetites of Machiavel-

---

[7] Philologically, Vico cites here Chassanion, *De Gigantibus*, in which, as he claims, the "nonsense" spoken on this subject is collected (NS/369). On the Renaissance mythology of giants see Walter Stephens, *Giants in Those Days: Folklore, Ancient History, and Nationalism* (Lincoln: University of Nebraska Press, 1989).

lian or Hobbesian political naturalism. Vico does not remain caught exclusively and absolutely within an anti-historical naturalism; rather, he sees man in relation both to nature and to the divine, and, thereby, he posits another history of origins as man's option. The measure or normal stature (which is moral consciousness or the binding of natural law) was kept by the Hebrews "on account of their cleanly upbringing and the fear of God and of their fathers" (NS/371). As normative figures, they are, paradoxically, an exception. From this society (ruled by Mosaic law) under the authority of Revelation and from the Romans' rituals of sacred ablutions, comes the idea of a civil government, which in Greek is called *politeia* (NS/371). The reference to the normal human measure of the Hebrews may well be an echo of the political speculations by Christian Hebraists of the Renaissance, such as John Selden, Carlo Giuseppe Imbonati, Gerhard Vossius, and Jean Bodin.[8] Vico, who thinks that civilization begins with water, links *politeia* to the Latin *"politus*, clean or neat" (NS/371), as Vossius does in his *Etymologicon*, so that the polity he imagines is not just a rational and scientific construct. Rather, it implies moral and intellectual restraint. As his fabulous history and definition of wisdom have it, the civil world is founded by poetic fables. But it also needs a coherent ordering of intellect and will, the faculties that have respectively been darkened and weakened by the Fall. Where can the yoking of wisdom and rationality be found? How can the *New Science* be a model for such a yoking?

The rest of this chapter will seek to answer these questions by showing Vico's polemical involvement with the paradigms of contemporary science as a way of making new the meaning of science. The path of modern science is blazed by Descartes and Bacon. Vico follows Bacon, who, in the name of experience, questions the values of classical culture founded, as it was, on the primacy of contemplation. From the standpoint of the *vita activa* Bacon mounts a radical critique of the classical encyclopedia or "Circle Learning." The phrase translates the Greek ἐγκύκλιος παιδεία (in Latin *encyclios disciplina*), the cycle of education by which the Greeks pretended to teach "an universal *Sapience* and knowledge both of matter and words." This claim turns out to be an impediment to real knowledge. The Greeks' discourse on the chain of sciences is actually self-contradictory, because in their practice the particular, concrete arts and sciences have been disincorporated from the quest for general knowledge. Cicero, Bacon argues, was right to complain that Socrates divorced philosophy from rhetoric but was wrong to maintain that eloquence, more than a "shop of good words and elegancies," holds the treasure of all knowledge.

In the *Advancement of Learning* Bacon discusses the "vanities" and

---

[8] On the phenomenon of Christian Hebraism see Frank E. Manuel, *The Broken Staff: Judaism through Christian Eyes* (Cambridge, Mass.: Harvard University Press, 1992), esp. pp. 108–61.

"peccant humors" affecting the intellect (Vol. III, p. 295). The first falla-
cies of the mind are "the caves of our own complexions and customs"
(p. 146), and the reference is to the *Republic*. In the *Novum Organum*,
which Vico repeatedly mentions and which is the linchpin of Bacon's epistemology, the Greek philosophical fashion (as well as the gratuitous speculations of Telesio and Patrizi) is said to be objectionable not so much on
account of its aims, which are actually acceptable, but because these "pre-
posterous and volatile philosophies" perpetuate infinite error and are idle
displays of power. For Bacon the doctrine of Platonic forms is past the reach
of man's experience; Aristotle's logic is a corruption of natural philosophy
just as Plato's "natural theology" is an adulteration of nature. The law of
reliable knowledge, then, is the experience of nature, even though Bacon
acknowledges that experience itself is a "mere groping in the dark" unless
it is Learned Experience.

Against the myth of the Greek encyclopedia, which proposes and records
untested metaphysical opinions and which presents tradition as an immobile, anachronistic repository of knowledge, Bacon formulates an empirical understanding of "science." Vico begins his *New Science* by following
and yet revising Bacon's empirical method. Because the text delves into the
confused, unclear archeology of a literally broken world, Vico seemingly
indulges in the typically seventeenth-century science known as antiquarianism. The cult of ruins as *disjecta membra* of a lost past is, to be sure, a
practice widely observed even in the Middle Ages. From the excavations in
the Roman city of Verulanium by the abbots Ealdred and Eadman in the
eleventh century to the *Mirabilia urbis*, from the fourteenth-century
Tractatus de mirabilibus Britanniae to the *Antiquitates Britanno-Belgicae*
(1719), archeology and antiquarianism were tools for establishing the
foundation and the legitimacy of one's own world.

Antiquarianism, which in eighteenth-century Italy is embodied by the
monumental work of Lodovico Muratori, figures at the beginning of the
New Science and plays a basic role in its delimitations of the field of knowledge.[9] The engraving at the opening of the text shows, among other
things, an altar, the statue of Homer, a caduceus, an urn, a rudder, a table
with the letters of the alphabet, and the *fasces* in the middle of a clearing.
These anachronistic bits of antiquity, which come to light from the dense
obscurities where they were buried, are the gateway to any reliable knowledge. Vico takes care to distinguish, however, his own process of excavat-
ing the sediments of the past from that of some of his contemporaries. He
goes counter, he says, to John Marsham's *Canon Chronicus Aegyptiacus,
Hebraicus, Graecus et Disquisitiones* (1670), which argues that the Egyp-

---

[9] One should mention Muratori's "Antichità estensi," "Antiquitates italicae," and the
"Annali". See *Opere di L. A. Muratori*, eds. G. Falco and F. Forti, Letteratura Italiana, Storia e Testi, forty-four vols. (Milan-Naples: Ricciardi, Vol. I).

tians, not the Hebrews, shaped the rites, beliefs, and institutions of the European tradition. Marsham's work, Vico adds, was followed by John Spencer and Otto van Heurn's *Antiquitatum Philosophiae Barbaricae Libri Duo*. Vico disagrees with the theories of these writers because of his conviction that the genuine beginning of knowledge is articulated by texts which are simultaneously poetic and theological.

But Vico's polemic against these antiquarian speculations goes even further than this, and it brings us to the heart of his thought. The limits of the conventional antiquarianism of a Marsham or Spencer lie in its reduction of the fossils and residues of antiquity to fixed, immutable objects which the antiquarian, from the standpoint of the present, collects, classifies, and deciphers in order to give legitimacy and a spiritual and material grounding to his own world. As shown, Vico himself engages in this practice as he records the findings of skulls and bones of giants. Such an archeological procedure and such an aim join the presuppositions of Bacon's empiricism with the Cartesian notion of mind, and Vico offers a severe critique of both philosophical strains of what would constitute pure science.

In historical terms Vico's perception is not altogether off the mark. Antiquarian studies emerged in the seventeenth and eighteenth centuries in Britain among the fellows of the Royal Society under the impact of the empirical method of research formulated by Francis Bacon.[10] At any rate, the joining of the Cartesian and empirical assumptions behind antiquarianism is evident in the two initial "elements" of the *New Science:*

> Because of the indefinite nature of the human mind, whenever it is lost in ignorance, man makes himself the measure of all things. This axiom explains those two common traits, on the one hand that rumor grows in its course, on the other that rumor is deflated by presence. . . . In the long course that rumor has run from the beginning of the world, it has been the perennial source of all the exaggerated opinions which have hitherto been held concerning remote antiquities unknown to us, by virtue of the property of the human mind noted by Tacitus in his *Life of Agricola*, where he says that everything unknown is taken for something great. It is another property of the human mind that whenever men can form no idea of distant and unknown things, they judge them by what is familiar and at hand. This axiom points to the inexhaustible source of all the errors about the principles of humanity that have been adopted by entire nations and by all the scholars. For when the former began to take notice of them and the latter to investigate them, it was on the

[10] For the importance of Bacon on the intellectual life of late seventeenth-century Naples, with special attention to Cornelio and Di Capua, see Max H. Fisch, "The Academy of the Investigators," in *Science, Medicine, and History: Essays on the Evolution of Scientific Thought and Medical Practice Written in Honour of Charles Singer*, ed. E. Ashworth Underwood (London: Oxford University Press, 1953), I, pp. 521–61. For Bacon's cultural project see Charles Whitney, *Francis Bacon and Modernity* (New Haven: Yale University Press, 1986).

basis of their own enlightened, cultivated and magnificent times that they judged the origins of humanity, which must nevertheless by the nature of things have been small, crude and quite obscure. Under this head come two types of conceit, one of nations and the other of scholars. (NS/120–24)

It is these two "conceits" that Vico wishes to dismantle, in part because they allow all nations to lay false claims to primacy. The sole exception to this generalized political delusion is Joseph's *Antiquitates Judaicae* (NS/ 126). These conceits, which are insidious because they make the self or the nation the illusory measure of reality, are a narcissistic effacement of the objective, scientific otherness of the past. Retrospectively, Vico's myth of the giants is a fable of the harsh and alien origins of history. More to the point, the phrase "because of the indefinite nature of the human mind," which punctuates in a variety of ways the *New Science*, crystallizes Vico's critique of Cartesianism.

The epistemological universe of Descartes, rooted as it is in the cogito, assumes that thought is an enduring, stable state, whereas for Vico the mind continuously experiences modifications or what in the Middle Ages were known as *alterationes*. The notion of the indefinite and shifting quality of the mind introduces for Vico the principle of contingency into the assumed stability of the cogito. The Cartesian formula "cogito, ergo sum" ends up in the configuration of the mind as an isolated, nondialectical structure, essentially discontinuous with the constraints of material reality. What is more, the provisional certainty which the act of thinking conveys is made to appear as an enduring, nontemporal totality.

This view of the transparency of reflective consciousness is aberrant because it says nothing about the disturbances of the body on the mind, the inherent alterations of the mind, or, generally, about the dense, shadowy dominion of passions over thoughts.[11] In the wake of Galileo, Descartes mathematicizes the order of nature and assigns to philosophy the task of pursuing the abstract, and thus reliable, shape of experience. Vico instead retrieves the thick shadows of the night, the tumults of the body, the fits of passion, man's dark and incandescent imaginings in the face of nature's perturbations, the "mental dictionary" of history—in short, the world of concrete human things.

Vico's critique of Cartesianism is the flip side of his critique of empiricism. In the *Novum Organum* Bacon sounds a warning about the possible narrow-mindedness of empiricism:

But the empirical school of philosophy gives birth to dogmas more deformed and monstrous than the sophistical or Rational school. For it has its founda-

[11] On the passions see the fine article by Andrea Battistini, "Retorica delle passioni fra Vives e Vico," *Rivista di Letterature Moderne e Comparate*, 47, No. 3 (1994), pp. 197–221. More generally see the highly suggestive Remo Bodei, *Geometria delle passioni: Paura, speranza, felicità: Filosofia e uso politico* (Milan: Feltrinelli, 1992).

tions not in the light of common notions (which though it be a faint and superficial light, is yet in a manner universal, and has reference to many things)
but in the narrowness and darkness of a few experiments. To those therefore
who are daily busied with these experiments, and have infected their imagination with them, such a philosophy seems probable and all but certain; to all
men else incredible and vain. . . . I foresee that if ever men are roused by my
admonitions to betake themselves seriously to experiment and bid farewell to
sophistical doctrines, then indeed through the premature hurry of the understanding to leap or fly to universals and principles of things, great danger
may be apprehended from philosophies of this kind; against which we ought
even now to prepare.[12]

Bacon's caution addresses itself to the need for a rigorous, extensive application of the experimental method and Vico certainly agrees that knowledge must begin with experience (or in his terms, philology). Yet he would
not claim that all knowledge depends on experience, for the mind has the
power to create its own reality. Furthermore, the proposition that there are
knowable, stable objects open to the sovereign control of reason is self-
contradictory since perceptions, which inform the mobile operations of the
mind, are themselves tricky, indefinite, and confused.

If the rationalists and empiricists are so harshly chastised, is there any
positive knowledge to be gained from the *New Science*? Or is the *New Science* a case, however brilliant and inventive, of critical philosophy? And
what is the relationship between critical and positive knowledge in the *New
Science*? There is no doubt that the *New Science* can be profitably (and more
easily) read as a chapter in critical philosophy. It is well known that the
sundry outlooks of classical epistemology and their historical prolongations
are systematically summarized throughout the text. Epicurean thought (as
articulated by Epicurus, Machiavelli, and Hobbes) is, for instance, recognized as a philosophy of blind chance and random atomism that leaves no
room for choice and, consequently, for history; the Stoics, and the Spinozists, who are their descendants, make God an infinite mind subject to
fate; Grotius is criticized for positing original men as simpletons and for
viewing history as a progressive movement toward a state of perfection; the
limits of Cartesian metaphysics as well as of empiricism are uncovered;
tenets held by the Neoplatonists and neo-Aristotelians of the Renaissance
(Patrizi, Castelvetro, Scaligero) are repeatedly attacked (NS/179; 338;
348).

This philosophical critical summa is a crucial ingredient of the *New Science*. But to define Vico's positive knowledge—how he moves, that is, from
a perception of fragments and inadequate intellectual speculations to a
practical theory of law, history, literature, and, generally, anthropology—

---

[12] *Aphorisms* from the *Novum Organum*, LXIV, in *Philosophical Works*, Vol. IV, p. 65.

one must bracket the perspective of the pure philosopher and also take on the role of philologist. This means that one must examine the rhetoric of his philosophy (tropes, style, language). A good place to start this sort of analysis is the title of the work. What is the "Science" Vico undertakes to expound and argue for? What is its novelty?

The title, *Scienza nuova*, certainly resonates with Bacon's *Novum Organum*, which is mentioned at crucial junctures of Vico's text, such as when he defines the aim of his philosophy.[13] To this resonance one may add Galileo's *Discorsi e dimostrazioni matematiche intorno a due nuove scienze*.[14] For Vico, however, Galileo's physics, which is a geometric, a priori construction of the world, is neither metaphysics nor the offshoot of concrete experience. Geometry, considered ever since Plato as the model of ethics because it is a science based on inferences (the positing of a point in space entails other points; quantity is transformed into "e-quality" and value, etc.), bears a partial resemblance to the finality of the *New Science*. "Now," Vico writes, "as geometry, when it constructs the world of quantity out of its elements, or contemplates the world in creating it for itself, just so does our Science [create for itself the world of nations], but with a reality greater by just so much as the institutions having to do with human affairs are more real than points, lines, surfaces, and figures are" (NS/349).[15]

This double historical resonance in Vico's title cannot lead us to assume a mere revisionary impulse in his procedure. On the contrary, Vico's title gains from its convergent historical resonances: it announces, more precisely, a science of theory and practice, of speculation and reality. In effect, there is a pattern of adjacencies that rigorously sustains the unfolding of the text. The principle of adjacency—the figure for which is metonymy—governs, for instance, the deployment of etymologies. The section "Corollaries Concerning the Origins of Languages and Letters," which traces the roots and the structure of grammar as the discipline organizing any possible representation of knowledge, culminates in the history of an eminently privileged word, the *Name*. Among the Greeks, Vico says, "name" and "character" have the same meaning, "so that the Church Fathers used indiscriminately the two expressions *de divinis characteribus* and *de divinis nominibus*." In rhetoric, he adds, *name* and *definition* also have the same meanings. Among the Romans, on the other hand, "names meant originally and properly houses branching into many families." The first

[13] Vico's *New Science* recalls other titles. One could mention Patrizi's *Nova de Universis Philosophia* or Gimma's *Nova Encyclopedia*.

[14] See Eugenio Garin, "Vico e l'eredità del pensiero del Rinascimento," in *Vico oggi*, ed. A. Battistini (Rome: Armando Ed.,1979), pp. 69–93.

[15] On geometry in Vico, and its far-reaching epistemological implications, see the recent, insightful study by James Robert Goetsch, Jr., *Vico's Axioms: The Geometry of the Human World* (New Haven: Yale University Press, 1995).

Greeks—as their use of patronyms shows—also used the *names* in the Roman sense. In Roman law, however, "*nomen* signifies right. Similarly the Greek *nomos* signifies law, and from *nomos* comes *numisma*, money, as Aristotle notes; and, according to etymologists, *nomos* becomes in Latin *numus*. In French *loi* means law and *aloi* means money"(NS/433).

The name remains the portal of access to reality, as it is for Plato and Isidore of Seville, but it does not have either a stable identity or a univocal derivation from a fixed origin. Vico's procedure is patterned not on Cratylism but on Varro's yoking of etymology and *semainomenon*: words, that is, are seen as the empirical, dim residues of signified things.[16] More than that, Vico establishes families of alien fragments, interrelationships of distant echoes which can never be constituted into a unified totality. Names are kept in their plural, irreducible dispersion, and the perimeter of their displacement is marked by their own law of phonetic-semantic adjacency. Their meanings surface in the imagination's encounter with the phenomenal world.

Over the last few years scholars have examined Vico's sense of the imagination, how the imagination works in the process of knowledge.[17] I shall not focus here on Vico's theoretical statements on the imagination and the "universali fantastici" that scholars have studied. I would like, instead, to explore the metaphors the *New Science* deploys to map the origin and mechanism of knowledge. These metaphors, as will be shown, are not simply schemas or procedures to represent concepts. They clarify, rather, the rhetorical-esthetic foundation of Vico's understanding of wisdom and the poetic encyclopedia he envisions.

How is this wisdom acquired? In the "Elements," in a context in which he sketches how from a state of ignorance arise poetic theology, idolatry, and divination, Vico focuses on two properties of the mind, wonder and curiosity. Wonder, he says, is the daughter of ignorance, while curiosity, "daughter of ignorance and mother of knowledge," is the property that "when wonder wakens our minds," asks "what it means" (NS/184 and 189). How are they related with each other? And what kind of blind knowledge do they introduce?

The primary resonance of "maraviglia" (wonder) is to be found in what Aristotle at the beginning of his *Metaphysics* describes as *admiratio* (*thau-*

---

[16] See on this question the important essay by Nancy Struever, "Fables of Power," *Representations* 4 (1983), pp. 107–27; see also Andrea Battistini, "Vico, Joyce e il romanzo dell'etimologia," *Lingua e Stile*, 21 (1986), no. 1, pp. 137–48.

[17] The question has been treated by Ernesto Grassi, "Vico versus Freud: Creativity and the Unconscious," in *Vico: Past and Present* (Atlantic Highlands, N.J.: Humanities Press, 1981), pp. 144–61. See also the important study by Donald P. Verene, *Vico's Science of the Imagination* (Ithaca: Cornell University Press, 1981). Of considerable importance is also Luigi Pareyson, "La dottrina vichiana dell'ingegno," in his *L'estetica e i suoi problemi* (Milan: Marzorati, 1961), pp. 351–77.

masmos), or the astonishment felt by pre-reflective man as he encounters the ungraspable phenomena of reality: as such, it is the point from which the impulse to philosophical speculation originates. Since Vico places his aphorism on wonder within the gravitational field of poetic theology, idolatry, and witchcraft, he effectively echoes the endless debates on the marvelous that figure prominently throughout the whole body of Renaissance literary criticism and baroque poetics. For Mazzoni, for Robortello, and for Tasso in the *Discorsi dell'arte poetica* (to mention only a few names), the arguments on the "Christian marvelous"—the supernatural world of the divinity and of demons, witches, and enchantments—pivot on the rhetorical-theological question of whether the marvelous in poetry is permissible merely as an ornament or as a reflection of a reality in which the Christian believes.[18] For a baroque theorist such as Tesauro or a poet like Marino, the marvelous is understood as an esthetic effect produced by the poet's eloquence: it is a technique of shocking the audience with the deployment of unexpected and extraordinary devices.[19] Vico rediscovers the accumulated historical memory in the term "maraviglia." As the foundation of knowledge, wonder is the state that ruptures the uniformity of an undifferentiated world because it marks the perception of an alterity transcending one's state. One's own world, it can be said, comes forth as no longer an indistinct totality, for wonder wakes the mind to astonishing and overwhelming fragments of that world. In point of fact, the *New Science* features wonder as the category under which the poetic and the religious belong.

The other property of the mind central to the acquiring of knowledge is curiosity. After talking about idolatry, he defines curiosity as the sister of

[18] The interest in the marvelous, which stems from the discussions of Aristotle's *Poetics* and his emphasis on the verisimilar and the necessary, is also present in Castelvetro, *Poetica d'Aristotile vulgarizzata et sposta* (Basel, 1576), who insists on verisimilitude. For a defense of the credible marvelous see Jacopo Mazzoni, *Della difesa della commedia di Dante* (Bologna, 1572); Francesco Robortello, *In Librum Aristotelis de Arte Poetica Explicationes* (Florence, 1548), is more nuanced; Francesco Patrizi, *La deca ammirabile* (Ferrara, 1587), is fiercely anti-Aristotelian. See also *Le prose diverse di Torquato Tasso*, ed. C. Guasti, two vols. (Florence: Le Monnier, 1875). More generally see Bernard Weinberg, *A History of Literary Criticism in the Italian Renaissance*, two vols. (Chicago: University of Chicago Press, 1961). See also Baxter Hathaway, *Marvels and Commonplaces: Renaissance Literary Criticism* (New York: Random House, 1968).

[19] The lines of Giambattista Marino "E del poeta il fin la maraviglia / (parlo de l'eccelente, non del goffo): / chi non sa far stupir, vada a la striglia" are well known. They appear in *La murtoleide*, fischiata XXXII, and may be found in *Marino e i marinisti*, ed. G. G. Ferrero (Milan-Naples: Ricciardi, 1964), p. 627. See also the following statement by Emanuele Tesauro: "Et di qui nasce la maraviglia: mentre che l'animo dell'uditore, dalle novità soprafatto, considera l'acutezza dell'ingegno rappresentante, e la inaspettata imagine dell'obietto rappresentato." "Metafora settima di oppositione" in *Cannocchiale Aristotelico, o Sia Idea dell'Arguta et Ingegnosa Elocutione* (Bologna, 1675), 296–305. Cf. Matteo Peregrini, *Delle acutezze*, ed. E. Ardissino (Turin: Edizioni RES, 1997).

wonder: "[curiosity] has the habit, whenever it sees some extraordinary phenomenon of nature, a comet for example, a sundog, or a midday star, of asking straightway what it means" (NS/189). Whereas the marvelous is essentially, in this context, an esthetic category, a faculty of the child or the sublime poet, curiosity is openly linked to interpretation. Historically, I would like to suggest, curiosity belongs to the vocabulary of critical philosophy.

The etymology of "curiosity," from the Latin *cura*, implies diligence, solicitude, or even pedantry. But traditionally the word has been the locus of contrasting values. For the Church Fathers—Tertullian or St. Augustine— curiosity is always *mala curiositas*, an object of widespread condemnation insofar as it is an appetite for knowledge that, as one wishes to submit one's knowledge to the ceaseless test of experience, leads to a transgression of all established boundaries.[20] This perspective on curiosity as a moral vice can be found even in Dante and Petrarch, but for Galileo and, above all, Bruno and Bacon, curiosity is the decisive drive opening up the path of rational knowledge.[21] Vico certainly would agree with this enlightened scientific understanding of curiosity. For him curiosity, in a way, supplements the marvelous. On the one hand, wonder reveals, in the discontinuity of its occurrence, the existence of a given element of the world sundered from the rest. On the other hand, curiosity closes off the shock generated by wonder by seeking the *sense* of the experience. But curiosity, as the patristic apologists intuited through their moral stance toward it, also signals the mind's inability to hold onto the entities it questions. A phrase in Vico's fragment, "curiosity . . . has the habit" (porta questo costume), suggests the negative power of curiosity. By seeking to impart a definite literal signification to whatever is experienced in wonder, curiosity is a repetitive hermeneutics that immobilizes the enigmatic power of that prodigious and fresh metaphorical experience. In its inherent mobility ("has the habit"), however, curiosity, which has the temporal structure of desire, is not strictly speaking a literalization, for it repeatedly devalues any new object it seeks to possess and, in so doing, it acquires the status of irony: it forever an-

[20] See, for instance, Tertullian, *De Praescriptione Haereticorum*, Chap. 14, *Patrologia Latina* 2; St. Augustine, *Confessions*, Book 5, Chapter 3, par. 3; Book 5, Chapter 3, par. 6, etc. See also Serge Lancel, "'*Curiositas*' et préoccupations spirituelles chez Apulée," *Revue de l'Histoire des Religions*, 160 (1961), pp. 25–46; more generally see Jacques Fontaine, *Isidore de Seville et la culture classique dans l'Espagne Wisigothique* (Paris: Etudes Augustiniennes, 1959).

[21] Bruno's defense of curiosity—as a theoretical issue—is everywhere in his *La cena delle ceneri*. For Galileo, see his *Dialogo dei massimi sistemi*; for Bacon the notion is central to his *Novum Organum*. A further discussion—and bibliography—on the patristic-modern shift is in Hans Blumenberg, *The Legitimacy of the Modern Age*, trans. R. M. Wallace (Cambridge, Mass.: MIT Press, 1983), p. 360ff.

nounces the object's shallowness, the inability of any experience to keep the mind fascinated with it.

It seems, then, that critical knowledge and poetic knowledge, curiosity and wonder, the literal and the metaphorical, which Vico calls "sister" properties generated by the same perturbations of the mind, are locked in an adversary relation. In spite of their essential differences, however, these two forms of knowledge are not mutually exclusive options but constantly feed on each other. Wonder is the temporal condition that breaks down the indistinct uniformity of the world; curiosity, which is the exercise of the critical intelligence, establishes rational distinctions and, at the same time, restores the original uniformity by hollowing out the perception of the marvelous. Although curiosity repeatedly figures out and consumes the revelations of wonder, it cannot obliterate the ghostly materiality of the pieces it analyzes. The gap between curiosity and wonder is punctuated by a lingering, disfigured materiality which feeds the imagination and on which the *New Science* focuses. Accordingly, his reflections on Homer and on the Homeric encyclopedia move around this gap, the ruins, as it were, lying between the poetic and the critical.

Chapter 6 will give a close reading of Vico's Homer. Let me say here that Vico defines Homer as a rhapsode, one of those stitchers-together of songs who collected them from their own peoples and who wandered through the "marketplaces of Greece" (NS/872). The reference to the *mercati* of Greece reverses Bacon's "Idols of the Market-Place," those idols, that is, "formed by the intercourse and association of men with each other. . . . It is by discourse that men associate; and words . . ." always beget other words and stand in the way of knowledge.[22] For Vico, on the other hand, the marketplace is the heart of the poetic song. From festivals, fairs, and marketplaces the *Iliad* and the *Odyssey* (as much as the laws) emerge as the encyclopedia of gentile antiquity, as limitless archives of the dialects, customs, laws, and history of Greece. More precisely, these epics are seen as compilations of fables by the Homeric rhapsodes, who are cyclical, digressive poets, or "marketplace" poets. "Authors of this sort," Vico says, "are ordinarily call *Kyklioi* and *enkyklioi,* and their collective work was called *kyklos epikos, kyklia epe, poiema enkyklikon*" (NS/856).

The *Iliad* and the *Odyssey*—and Vico uses this argument to question the existence of Homer as a single individual—are an encyclopedia composed of two poems which are divided against each other and yet forever stare at one another. They are entirely different from one another, as youth and sublime passion differ from old age and reflection. The differences in outlook between the two poems account for the heterogeneity of their repre-

---

[22] *Novum Organum,* Aphorism XLIII, in *Philosophical Works,* Vol. IV, pp. 54–55.

sentations. But there is a kinship between the two texts, which is to be found in their joint retrieval and preservation of "all the fabulous history of Greece from the origins of their gods down to the return of Ulysses to Ithaca" (NS/856). Passion and reflection, metaphor and irony, which are their respective tropes, are discontinuous from one another, each a digression from the other, each a self-enclosed circle of knowledge adjacent to the other in a movement of periodic returns.

The discontinuity between passion and reflection (or poetic knowledge and critical knowledge, or will and intellect) is the gap within which the major insights of Vico's thought are located. In this gap lie scattered and buried ciphers, inscriptions, devices, etymologies, fragmented texts—the wounded, mutilated, material body of all possible knowledge. This gap is man himself, *homo*, whose etymology from *humo* and *humando*, as Vico says, exploiting Isidore of Seville's own etymology, defines the burial ground as man's essence (NS/537). But there is always an excess and a residue to the finite, partial entity called "man," for death, which divides the self from others, transforms individual projects into an object for other projects by other men. This insight, as this book will argue in the chapters that follow, is the foundation of Vico's politics.

This same insight shapes the imaginative structure and the style of the *New Science*, which is an encyclopedic totality of disjointed parts—not as a rational scientific method, but as a critical and poetic rethinking of history's memories and shadows. As a poetic encyclopedia, it is a model for what humans can make. More precisely, the *New Science* is written in the mixed mode of brief philosophical essays, poetic fragments, maxims, fables, and sentences. Its aim is to give the representation of the modifications of the human mind. Because the way of writing is for Vico a way of knowing, Vico's many styles recall among other texts, Erasmus's *Adagia*, Pascal's *Pensées*, the *maximes* of La Rochefoucauld, as well as the *Aphorisms* of Bacon. These styles constitute Vico as an author whose imagination ties together facts and fictions, philology and philosophy, and whose narrative needs readers to remake the movement of his thought. These many styles that resonate in his text constitute his poetic philosophy, a mixture of lapidary fulgurations, oracular obscurities, and rational criticism that together reach toward a time when a new Homer, the true educator of Hellas and the blind seer of the past, will wage a mighty war against time and thereby reacquaint man with death's pageants.

Chapter 5

FROM THE MYTH OF EGYPT
TO THE *GAIA SCIENZA*

THE PREVIOUS CHAPTER has shown the encyclopedic conspectus of the *New Science*, and it has argued that Vico's new project of learning puts poetry at the center of the various sciences. Yet, although Vico makes poetry the grand key to the *New Science*, the idea of the encyclopedia, as much as the *paideia* of the philosopher or the organization of the university curriculum, is cast within and depends on the framework of reason or on a philosophical scheme of thought. Appearances to the contrary notwithstanding, is Vico then a rationalist, really no better off than his Neapolitan friends whom he berates for treading the fashionable, Cartesian paths of rational models of reality?

The question is far from being arbitrary, and, understandably, Vico scholarship has long attempted to define the sources and the substance of his scientific or rationalist conceptions in order to gauge the degree of his involvement with modernity. Because modernity is generally given a positive valorization by his critics, Vico's success as a thinker is assessed in terms of his ability to uphold rational modes of thought. From this standpoint, there can be no doubt that his early Inaugural Orations, which are articulated in the wake of the Neoplatonic doctrine of the "dignity of man," posit the principle that man's self is his rational life and that reason is the trace of divinity within him. In the *New Science*, reason, as the measure of man's thoughts and as law, remains central to the conception of the third age. After all, the burden of the *New Science* is plainly said to lie in its being a "rational civil theology of divine providence" (NS/342). But, as this chapter will argue, just as there is a world above and beyond reason and knowledge, there is also a shadowy, enigmatic world before reason. The historical experience, which for Vico is not under the sovereignty of reason, is myth. In relation to this enigmatic and pre-rational world of myth the path of philosophy is for him a suburban excursion rather than a distant journey. Thus, there are, by necessity, other circuitous routes to follow in the quest for wisdom, and these routes will take Vico further into the dark heart of archaic language from which philosophy, like a splendid fledgling, took its belated flight.

What for Vico, then, lies before rational thought—that from which all philosophical thought radiates and to which it is traced back—is myth, μῦθος, translatable as a "true narration" or even, as he says, "muteness," just as *logos* is a "true speech" (1NS/249; NS/401).[1] At the end of his protracted reflection on "Poetic Wisdom," Vico also calls myth an "embryo" or a "matrix" (NS/779), and the metaphor, derived from the contemporary seventeenth- to eighteenth-century vocabulary of embryology, draws myth within a pattern of organic growth and development. Like the egg in the uterus of the mother, myth takes us to the threshold of the mind's early stage of life and, indeed, it is the language of that life.[2] The organic metaphor is appropriate for a thinker of seeds and dark beginnings, as Vico is. Yet, there is a transparent irony in Vico's deploying the rhetoric of modern natural science for summing up his historical discourse on a pre-scientific representation of experience.

At this point of the text one can only speculate on Vico's intent in rhetorically bringing together seemingly contradictory registers on *physis* and history. It is possible that through the use of the embryological language he wants to imply that science and myth are the twin products of the same mind perceived at different stages of its development. The metaphor also implies that science's conceptual model follows the shape of myth and that myth is itself a now forgotten science. More importantly, the contrapuntal function of the scientific vehicle of the metaphor for its mythic tenor is a clear sign of the deeper concerns Vico entertains and dramatizes throughout Book II of the *New Science:* the relationship between myth and science, which he will in fact explore, and the imaginative genealogy which links them together. That his thought deliberately turns on the relationship between myth and science is further explored by his prying into the semantic tension lodged within the very term "mythology" (NS/403).

Much like the organic metaphor used for the notion of myth as the origin of knowledge, "mythology" is something of an oxymoron, a paradoxical word that fuses together two antithetical but not mutually exclusive terms, *muthos* and *logos*. Aptly enough for Vico's conception, the word's structure preserves the priority of myth over Logos, as if myth literally provokes and triggers the Logos. What is more, Vico defines mythology the way traditional discussions of the liberal arts define grammar, "the first sci-

---

[1] The bibliography on myth is vast. Of considerable interest are Gianfranco Cantelli, *Mente, corpo, linguaggio: Saggio sull'interpretazione vichiana del mito* (Florence: Sansoni, 1987), and Joseph Mali, *The Rehabilitation of Myth: Vico's 'New Science'* (Cambridge: Cambridge University Press, 1992).

[2] See Walter Bernardi, *Le metafisiche dell'embrione: Scienze della vita e filosofia da Malpighi a Spallanzani* (Florence: Olschki, 1986). See also Howard B. Adelmann, ed. *Marcello Malpighi and the Evolution of Embryology* (Ithaca: Cornell University Press, 1966), esp. Vol. I, p. 209ff. for Malpighi's connection in Naples with Tommaso Cornelio and Leonardo di Capua. Adelmann edits Malpighi's work on the egg (*De formatione pulli in ovo* and *De ovo incubato*). See Vol. II, pp. 931–1013, which argues for the theory's impact on Descartes, Gassendi, Digby, and others.

ence to be learned" (NS/51). At the same time, the paradoxical etymology of the word expresses what the claim of its being "la prima scienza"—the first science—means. Like grammar, the first art of language, as encyclopedists and the primers by Priscian and Donatus or even Dante have it, mythology is a science capable of giving voice to silence. To put it somewhat differently, using Vico's own term, mythology is capable of "interpreting" archaic muteness from the standpoint of the fully articulated self-conscious Logos.

This interpretation of myths is carried out chiefly by conjuring up what could be called the archeology of Egypt, its vast phantasmagoria of myths and mysteries. In the *New Science* the word associated with Egypt is "mysteries" (NS/68; 207). Etymologically, *mystery* defines the web of secret/sacred beliefs of the Egyptians, of which Iamblichus is the avowed mystagogue. Egypt's mysteries center on the myth of Thot, the thrice-great Hermes or Mercury, who is the scribe of the gods and the inventor of laws and letters (NS/66; 232). A number of synchretic intellectual movements are rooted in Hermes myth. As is known, Iamblichus's *The Mysteries of the Egyptians* was translated by Ficino, who saw in Egyptian wisdom, by which he broadly means the wisdom of Zoroaster, Hermes, Orpheus, and Pythagoras, both the true matrix of Christian beliefs and the universal truth of Plato. Ficino's idea of a *prisca theologia*, which is a term blending together religion and philosophy—Mosaic revelation, Neoplatonism, Zoroastrianism, Hermeticism, and the Kabbalah—is rooted in the conviction that these doctrines are all paths acknowledging and leading to the one God.[3] As such, ancient theology bears a remarkable affinity to Vico's poetic theology. The sacred texts of poetic theology are poetic myths and hieroglyphs, which conceal a mystery or secret doctrine. A clear articulation of the power of myths is available in a gloss by Vico on the esoteric content of the Orphic hymns: "Orpheus protected the mysteries of his dogmas with the coverings of fables, and concealed them with a poetic veil so that whoever should read his hymns would suppose there was nothing beneath them beyond idle tales and perfectly unadulterated trifles."[4]

[3] On ancient theology see Daniel P. Walker, *The Ancient Theology: Studies in Christian Platonism from the Fifteenth to the Eighteenth Century* (Ithaca, N. Y.: Cornell University Press, 1972); Charles Trinkaus, *In Our Image and Likeness: Humanity and Divinity in Italian Humanist Thought*, two vols. (Chicago: University of Chicago Press, 1970), Vol. II, 722–60; Charles B. Schmitt, "Perennial Philosophy from Agostino Steucho to Leibnitz," *Journal of the History of Ideas*, 27 (1966), 505–23.

[4] Pico della Mirandola, *De Hominis Dignitate*, trans. E. Forbes in *The Renaissance Philosophy of Man*, eds. E. Cassirer, P. O. Kristeller, and J. H. Randall, Jr., (Chicago: University of Chicago Press, 1948), pp. 223–54. The quotation is on p. 253. On the motif of "poetic theology" see Frances Yates, *Giordano Bruno and the Hermetic Tradition* (Chicago: University of Chicago Press, 1964); Don Cameron Allen, *Mysteriously Meant: The Rediscovery of Pagan Symbolism and Allegorical Interpretation in the Renaissance* (Baltimore: Johns Hopkins Uni-

It should be stated at the outset that for Vico the hermetic wisdom of Egypt makes available to us neither the whole of wisdom nor the absolute origin of all arts. As he pointedly says, only "rottami" (NS/173), scraps, or fragments and relics of Egyptian antiquity have come down to us. These fragments are, above all, the hieroglyphs, which, far from being the exclusive domain of the Egyptians, as Ficino and Bruno hold, are common to the Egyptians and Chinese alike. More precisely, they are sacred characters believed by philosophers to conceal "mysteries of lofty esoteric wisdom" (NS/435). Nonetheless, Egypt, if it is not the locus of prehistoric consciousness and pure origin, embodies for Vico the parable of "pretentious memories" or the "conceit of nations" (NS/53). Predictably enough, Vico is too aware of the complexities of experience to give a univocal view or to totally dismiss Egyptian myth. As we shall see, he retrieves the vital remnants of the Egyptian tradition of hieroglyphs as well as the idea of time and chronology. More important still, the world of modern science is shown to be rooted in Hermetic doctrines. The argument about Vico's status as a thinker, therefore, cannot be reduced to a debate as to whether or not Vico's thought is "scientific" or "anti-scientific," "rational" or "anti-rational." He lucidly understood that thought had to move beyond these static, abstract, traditional dualities, and, therefore, he lures us to abandon our critical preconceptions and venture into a domain of the mind where we can find fresh knowledge about the mind's and history's workings.

Vico collects in the *New Science* the fragments of Egypt's ancient, broken knowledge and uses them, first of all, to launch a critique both of Renaissance Egyptologists and of Renaissance science. Let me recall here, as a way of anticipating the argument this chapter will develop in some detail, that between the fifteenth and seventeenth centuries there was a Renaissance revival of the ancient and secret wisdom of Egypt. I have already alluded to the synchretic "Egyptian"-Hermetic projects of both Ficino and Vico. The phenomenon of Renaissance Egyptianism, however, comes to full bloom in the writings of Cornelius Agrippa, Giordano Bruno, Athanasius Kircher, and Francis Bacon.[5] It is not my purpose to sketch, even in

---

versity Press, 1970); Edgar Wind, *Pagan Mysteries in the Renaissance* (New Haven: Yale University Press, 1958), Chap. 1; David B. Ruderman, *Kabbalah, Magic, and Science* (Cambridge, Mass.: Harvard University Press, 1988).

[5] The bibliography on this question, beside the fundamental work by Frances Yates, *Giordano Bruno and the Hermetic Tradition*, ought to list equally impressive contributions such as Paolo Rossi, *Francesco Bacone: Dalla magia alla scienza* (Bari: Laterza, 1957), especially for Chapter 3 which deals with the "ars memoriae," hieroglyphs, and alchemical-magic-hermetic strains in Bacon; Robert Klein, *La forme et l'intelligible* (Paris: Gallimard, 1970); Adelia Noferi, *Il gioco delle tracce* (Florence: La Nuova Italia, 1979). More generally, and for the light it throws on Pierio Valeriano's encyclopedic *Hieroglyphica*, see Mario Andrea Rigoni, "Un dialogo del Tasso: dalla parola al geroglifico," *Lettere Italiane*, 25, no. 1, (1972), pp. 30–44.

the most general terms, the many important aspects of the rediscovery of Egypt for these thinkers. I will limit myself to pointing out one fundamental element of this debate which is relevant to Vico and to the present discussion.

Bruno's *On magic*, which views hieroglyphs as "sacred letters" invented by Thot and as privileged vehicles through which the Egyptians would pick up, as Pythagoras does with the music of the spheres, the conversations of the gods, finds its extension in texts such as *The Expulsion of the Triumphant Beast* and *On the Shadows of Ideas.*[6] Magic and necromancy are distinctive traits of Bruno's Egypt, and from them all knowledge emanates. In the third dialogue of the *Expulsion*, as he reflects on the wisdom, magic, and divine cult of the Egyptians, Bruno asserts that Egypt is the source from which Mosaic revelation derives: "the Cabala of the Jews," one of the interlocutors of this Italian dialogue, Saulino, is made to say "has proceeded from the Egyptians, among whom Moses was instructed" (p. 241). In *On the Shadows*, on the other hand, Bruno alludes to Plato's *Phaedrus* and its account of Thot's invention of writing. Hermes is for Bruno the inventor of writing as an art of memory, *ars memoriae*, and in this sense, Egypt's dark science has layers of wisdom that are far deeper than the clarity and light shed by the *logos* of Greece.

At stake in Bruno's excitement about magic and Egyptianism is nothing less than the crisis of the Greek rational model of knowledge, which is embodied by Logifer's recalcitrance to accept Hermetic doctrine in *On the Shadows*. A disciple of Bruno, the polymath Athanasius Kircher, follows Bruno in this insight, which truly marks a shift in the taste and intellectual direction of the times. In his monumental *Oedipus Aegyptiacus*, which is a work on Egyptology and on the ancient theology of the Chaldeans, Plato, Hebrew Kabbalah, and Hermeticism, Kircher, like Bruno, casts Egyptian wisdom as the womb of all mysteries.[7] The frontispiece to his *Spinx Mys-*

---

[6] The quotation from Bruno's *De Magia* is taken from his *Opere latine*, ed. Francesco Fiorentino, Vittorio Imbriani et al. (Naples and Florence, 1879–91), Vol. III, p. 412. *Lo spaccio della bestia trionfante* is available in English as *The Expulsion of the Triumphant Beast*, trans. and ed. Arthur D. Imerti (New Brunswick, N.J.: Rutgers University Press, 1964); for the *De Umbris Idearum* see *Opere latine*, Vol. II, Tome I. On Bruno's thought see the recent study by Nuccio Ordine, *The Philosophy of the Ass*, trans. H. Baranski and A. Saiber (New Haven: Yale University Press, 1996).

[7] The text, *Obeliscus Pamphilius*, is the only one mentioned by Vico, although he also refers to Kircher in his *On the Most Ancient Wisdom of the Italians*, Chapter VII, Section 5. Let me say in passing that the *Oedipus Aegyptiacus* was written immediately after Kircher compiled his esoteric interpretation of hieroglyphs on the obelisk that stands in Piazza Navona in Rome and that was published as *Obeliscus Pamphilius* (1650). On Kircher's intellectual project see Joscelyn Godwin, *Athanasius Kircher: A Renaissance Man and the Quest for Lost Knowledge* (London: Thames and Hudson, 1979); see also Cesare D'Onofrio, *Gli obelischi di Roma* (Rome: Bulzoni, 1967); Eric Iversen, *The Myth of Egypt and Its Hieroglyphs in European Tradition* (Princeton: Princeton University Press, 1993); Jacqueline Reder, "L'etonnant pere

tagoga, a book on mummies written in 1672, uses the pyramids of Memphis to evoke a baroque landscape of tombs, obelisks, and hidden subterranean worlds, which for him is best conveyed not by Greek philosophy but by the telluric sciences (such as vulcanism), by allegorical ciphers, and by the enigmas of archeological fragments from Egypt. The oracle for this vast and secret knowledge unifying all realms of experience is Hermes Trismegistus, who announces how the universal ordering of apparently contradictory doctrines can be brought about. From this standpoint, Christian dogmas, which encompass all dimensions of belief, are adumbrated by Egyptian lore.

The shift from the Greek rational model of the Renaissance to the world of modern science and Egyptian *mysteries* is explicitly at the forefront of Bacon's interests. In the *New Atlantis* the ancient religion of Egypt provides the material for the text's symbolism. But, unlike Bruno or Kircher, Bacon is suspicious of Egyptian learning, which he views as false magic. And, unlike Bruno, he argues for priority of Mosaic revelation over Egyptian magic, or, as he puts it, Moses was capable of defeating the "serpents of the [Egyptian] enchanters" (*The Advancement of Learning,* Vol. IV, p. 290). Nonetheless, in the *Novum Organum* (Aphorism LXXI) Bacon still deploys the myth of Egypt to dismiss the hegemony of Greek philosophical speculation (Vol. IV, pp. 72–73). He views the fundamental traits of Greek knowledge as "professorial and much given to disputations, a kind of wisdom most adverse to the inquisition of truth" (p. 72). And he concludes his meditation with the words spoken by an Egyptian priest to a distinguished Greek visitor: "They [the Greeks] were always boys, without antiquity of knowledge or knowledge of antiquity" (p. 73). The statement acknowledges the "modernity" of Greek philosophy and its conceits, which experimental science finally supersedes. Obliquely, however, it also presents Greek thought as growing out of the depths and secrets of Egyptian wisdom.[8]

Vico certainly agrees with Bacon's assessment of Egypt, for he has read in Iamblichus's *The Mysteries of the Egyptians* that the philosophies of Plato and Pythagoras, no less than all other philosophies, had their source in the oracles of the Chaldeans, in the mystery religions, and in the ancient pillars of Hermes. The belatedness of Greek philosophy is stressed in the

---

Kircher," *Planete,* 11 (October 1969), pp. 95–104; and P. Conor Reilly, S.J., *Athanasius Kircher, S.J., Master of a Hundred Arts* (Rome-Wiesbaden: Edizioni del Mondo, 1974). See also Paolo Rossi, "Vico e il mito dell'Egitto," and Antonio Corsano, "Vico e la tradizione ermetica," in *Omaggio a Vico* (Naples: Morano, 1968), pp. 9–24 and 27–36 respectively.

[8] On Bacon and the Timaeic tradition in the sixteenth century see John C. Briggs, *Francis Bacon and the Rhetoric of Nature* (Cambridge, Mass.: Harvard University Press, 1989); see also Charles Whitney, *Francis Bacon and Modernity* (New Haven: Yale University Press, 1986); and Brian Vickers, *Essential Articles for the Study of Francis Bacon* (Hamden, Conn.: Archon Books, 1968).

proem to the *Most Ancient Wisdom of the Italians*. In the "Second Response" to the review of this metaphysical work, moreover, Vico emphasizes that in Italy the school of Pythagoras was more ancient than the philosophy of Greece, and that this philosophy "came from Egypt." In agreeing in this respect with Bacon, Vico can be said to underwrite Bacon's critique of Hellenism. Both Bacon and Vico will discard as inadequate the narrow compass of Renaissance Hellenism in so far as it comes through as an esthetic-rational delimitation of reality. But Vico differs from Bacon's assessment of the myth of Egypt as the realm of false magic to be superseded by modern science. There is for Vico no possible break between the old Egyptian learning and modern science, as Bacon would wish. Bacon's error lies in his conviction that modern science casts the light of truth unto our feet. In fact, for Vico modern science can stake no firmer claim for truth than ancient myth did, and both are necessary simulacra concocted by the human mind.

In an overt polemical gesture against one crucial aspect of the Renaissance cult of Egypt, which is the question of its antiquity, Vico flatly rejects the claim for Egypt's primacy. Such a claim is tantamount to its antiquity, and it is consistently vindicated, as shown above, by Renaissance Egyptologists, such as Bruno, Kircher, and Marsham. Possibly following St. Augustine's virulent denunciation of Egypt's belief in its own antiquity put forth in the *City of God* (Book XVIII, Chapter 39), Vico argues that the first people are the Hebrews. The reasons he gives are historical and not theological; in fact, rather than St. Augustine, Vico explicitly acknowledges the authority of Flavius Josephus and Lactantius (NS/54). For reasons of geography and institutions, Vico says, "the Egyptians, to whom Marsham in his *Canon* accords the distinction of being the most ancient of all the nations merit the fifth place in our Chronological Table" (NS/58). With remarkable punctiliousness Vico goes on to insist that even the Scythians and the Phoenicians, who are granted respectively the third and fourth columns in his Chronological Table, surpass the Egyptians in antiquity (NS/56; 57).

Vico's trenchant denial of Egypt's claim of a foundational status in the historical unfolding of culture implies the denial of the secular foundation of the world: the denial certainly agrees with Bacon's view of "the serpent of Moses" devouring, as hinted earlier, "the serpents of the enchanters" (*Advancement of Learning*, Dedicatory Letter). The statement clearly means that biblical revelation is superior to and predates Egyptian magic divination. Yet Vico's Egypt diverges from Bacon's myth of Egypt in two ways. First of all, Vico's turn to the remnants of Egypt, its pyramidal shadows, cryptic architecture, ruins and subterranean meanders, hieroglyphic riddles, and so forth, must be seen as a turn to baroque esthetics with its fascination for what lies "outside" the Greek parameters and firm boundaries of rational order. The sense of what lies "outside" the overt, rational experiences steadily fascinates Vico's mind. From this standpoint, he is certainly close to Kircher. Like Kircher, he pursues the mythical and magic domain populated by unfamiliar figures, strange shapes and phenomena, the snake of time, and fearsome monsters—in short, the imaginative economy of baroque forms traced with twisted, serpentine lines. Second, and more important, Vico differs from Bacon's understanding of the very myth of antiquity and on how *myth* as well as *antiquity* are to be interpreted.

In *The Wisdom of the Ancients* Bacon takes the ancient poetical fables to be oracles of philosophical sense. They are allegories containing the "mysteries and secrets of antiquity," and he proceeds to unveil their hidden conceptual significance in terms of natural philosophy, morality, and politics, or "civil policy."[9] But if Bacon believes that modern science unveils and supersedes the symbolic contents of ancient myth, Vico reverses the direction of Bacon's line of argument. He will show in Book II of the *New Science* that, *pace* Plato and Bacon's own *The Wisdom of the Ancients*, the rational speculations and achievements of modern science are persistently rooted in the representations of ancient myth and that the dry light of reason is thoroughly permeated, even if it represses this fact, by mythological beliefs.

Ancient fables, Vico wryly notes, "may contain all the recondite wisdom desired by Plato and in our time by Bacon of Verulam in his *Wisdom of the Ancients*" (NS/80). The textual acknowledgment is the preamble to Vico's dramatization of the relationship between myth and science that departs from Plato's and Bacon's brand of mythologizing. The rhetoric of Vico's argument discloses how Vico perceives the nature of his hermeneutical quest. He obliquely casts his procedure, as Boccaccio had done in his *Genealogy of the Gentile Gods*, as a sea voyage.[10] The metaphor is suggested by the promise he makes to avoid tradition's pitfalls, which he calls "treacherous reefs": "questi duri scogli di mitologia si schiveranno co' principi di questa Scienza" (NS/81) (these treacherous reefs of mythology will be avoided by the principles of this Science).

The metaphor announces that Vico's exploration of myth is indeed a journey by sea. As with the journeys of epic heroes such as Ulysses or Aeneas, Vico's journey to the land of myth and mysteries could turn out to be a shipwreck. The *New Science* is, thus, the narrative of the mind's ex-

---

[9] *The Wisedome of the Ancients*, trans. Arthur G. Knight (London: John Bill, 1619), Preface. See, for instance, the reading of the Cyclopes as "Ministers of Terror," (p. 9).

[10] *Genealogia Deorum Gentilium Libri*, ed. V. Romano, two vols. (Bari: Laterza, 1951). The proem of each of the fifteen books has a reference to the motif of epic voyaging: see especially the proem to Book I with its emphasis on "the beginning of our journey." The rhetorical motif has been intelligently highlighted by Thomas Hyde, "Boccaccio: The Genealogy of Myth," *Publications of the Modern Language Association of America*, 100, no. 5 (Oct. 1985), pp. 737–45.

ploration as a heroic and yet dangerous adventure of discovery. There are no prefabricated paradigms, as Bacon's practice suggests, wherein ancient myth is the dark parable of enlightened modern science. For Vico, on the contrary, myths, much as philosophy in our time, were in the beginning "true and severe" ("vere e severe") narrations telling ways of life and death. Thus, he will search for the enigmas of ancient and modern dreams in the dim chronicles of antiquity and the archives of myths and legends of Egypt as a way of finding the mythopoetic phantasmagoria of the present. The thread of continuity between the mind's fictions and scientific "facts" will emerge from his reconstruction of the imaginary world of Egypt.

Outside the *New Science* and the "Response," Vico will make an overt reference to Egyptian traditions only in his *Autobiography*. He reports that he had been reading Bacon's *On the Wisdom of the Ancients* and, unhappy with it, he started looking for the principles of mythical wisdom in the etymologies of Latin words (p. 148). This search leads to his writing his metaphysical work which bears a Baconian echo in the title, *On the Most Ancient Wisdom of the Italians Unearthed from the Origins of the Latin Language* (p. 153). Vico's discovery of the ancient sediments of wisdom available in (and from) language's sediments of memory crystallizes in a metaphysical wisdom which is older, he says, than Greece itself. Such a wisdom comes from Pythagoras, who had been instructed by the Egyptians (p. 148). The Greek and Pythagorean conceptual model, as Bacon had said, is clearly derivative from Egypt. More important, from the double meaning of the word for *coelum*, which means both "chisel" and the "great body of the air," Vico opines that "the instrument with which nature makes everything was the wedge, and that this was what they [the Egyptians] meant their pyramids to signify" (p. 148).

The link between Pythagoras and Egyptian lore, which focuses on the question of etymologies, or the origins of words—such as those debated in Plato's *Cratylus*—leads Vico to search for the principle to which the origin of all things can be reduced. In the *Wisdom of the Ancients* Bacon explains the fable of "Coelum" as a "fable [of] philosophy" (p. 66), as the enigmatic account of "the creation or origin of all things" in terms of Democritus's and Lucretius's theories of the eternity of matter. "*Coelum*," Bacon writes, "denotes the Concave Space, or Vaulted Roof that encloses all Matter; and (b) Saturn the Matter itself which cuts off all Power of Generation from his Father: as one and the same quantity of Matter remains invariable in Nature without addition or Diminution" (p. 62). Bacon's derivation of a materialist philosophy from the poetic myth of the beginnings of the world turns in Vico's *Autobiography* into the notion that Pythagorean thought is at its root Egyptian naturalist cosmology.

More than an atomist in the wake of Democritus, however, Vico comes provisionally through as a Milesian hylozoist for whom *physics*, nature, and all matter have life and are inseparable from the soul. "Just as our soul, being air, holds us together, so do a breath and air encompass the whole world," according to a fragment by Anaximenes, which Vico probably never knew, but which he almost echoes in the *New Science* (NS/695). What matters here is that this vital principle of Ionian science was for Vico crystallized by the Egyptian belief in a living nature. And what matters even more is that Vico extends his linguistic insight into the ramifications of the significance of the pyramid—which signifies at the same time chisel, sky, air, and nature—to venture opinions on the theory of the soul, on the operating principle of all things, on the physics of the magnet, the system of medicine and diseased bodies, corpuscular philosophy, and, obliquely, on Harvey's denial that blood vessels contain air.[11] The vast realm of the physical sciences, from Egyptian antiquity to the present, is thus predicated on the multiple resonances of languages, and these senses of a specific word are the sign of language's memory and wisdom.

If the *Autobiography* gives only a limited but strong inkling of the hold the myth of Egypt has on Vico's mind, *De Universi Juris Uno* refers to Mercury in a somewhat formulaic and conventional manner. Within the context of a general discussion of agrarian laws, Mercury is seen as the god who has given the laws to the Egyptians, as the poetic figure presiding over the transactions of the merchants, and as the giver of laws of peace to those who have been defeated (I, cxlix, pp. 5–6). By contrast, the *New Science* is punctuated with extensive references to the imaginative paraphernalia of Egyptology.

The frontispiece, or *dipintura*, with which the text opens, is composed of a number of "Egyptian" hieroglyphs. One cannot help but agree with a recent view that the model for Vico's emblem is Emanuele Tesauro's theory of the *impresa*.[12] The *dipintura*, it may be added, almost deliberately evokes a number of other visual associations. The globe on the altar, for instance, seems patterned on Tommaso Campanella's description of the globe on the altar in what is a Pythagorean description of the architecture of *The City of the Sun*.[13] Vico's *dipintura* also recalls Kircher's frontispiece

[11] "talchè l'anima, o l'aria, insinuata nel sangue sia nell'uomo principio della vita, l'etere insinuato ne' nervi sia principio del senso; . . . così gli spiriti animali sieno più mobili e presti che i vitali; . . . Chè se egli fosse così, il principio operante di tutte le cose in natura dovrebbero essere corpicelli di figura piramidali; . . ." (*Autobiografia*, p. 39).

[12] Andrea Battistini, "Teoria delle imprese e linguaggio iconico vichiano," in *Bollettino del Centro di Studi Vichiani*, 14–15 (1984–85), pp. 149–77. In the same issue of the *Bollettino* see also Mario Papini, "*Ignota latebat:* L'impresa negletta della *Scienza Nuova*," pp. 179–214. See also Donald P. Vereue, "Vico's 'Ignota Latebat,'" *New Vico Studies*, 5 (1987), pp. 77–98.

[13] "Sopra l'altare non vi è altro ch'un mappamondo, assai grande, dove tutto il cielo è dipinto. . . ." Tommaso Campanella, *La città del Sole: Dialogo poetico*, ed. Daniel J. Donno (Berkeley: University of California Press, 1981), p. 30.

to his *Musurgia Universalis* (1650), marked, as it is, by a triangle with an eye inside, a globe surmounted by the feminine figure of Musica and girded with a zodiacal belt.[14] At any rate, the hieroglyphs, such as the lituus of divination, the caduceus of Mercury, the winged cap, and the cinerary urn with a conic or pyramidal shape, evoke the world of Egypt. More to the point, as befits a baroque museum, or *Kunstkammer,* the *New Science* holds in its purview pyramids, obelisks, labyrinths, hieroglyphs, such as Mercury's caduceus, and syringes, which for Vico are both Egyptian stone tombs and reed songs (NS/467). These traditional ciphers of an occult knowledge are for him all hieroglyphs of power whose mechanism and finality the *New Science* unveils. But as a way of explaining what these enigmatic figurations mean for him, let me briefly recapitulate the array of Vico's contradictory reflections on Egypt and his understanding of the myth of Egypt.

The *New Science,* as hinted earlier in this chapter, begins with the outright rejection of the myth, popularized by Giordano Bruno and endorsed by seventeenth-century archaeologists (such as Marsham, Spencer, and Van Heurn), that Egypt is the land of magic knowledge (NS/44–53). In the hazy, uncertain borderland of beginnings priority is assigned to theology. The fact that Egypt cannot claim to be the beginning of things (what Bacon calls Heaven, or *Coelum*) has in itself a theological reason which Vico will carefully explore. On the face of it, the denial of priority to Egypt is the consequence of Vico's desire to hold in check the conceits of this nation. But there is another reason, which, I believe, goes to the core of Vico's sense of Egypt: the identification of Egypt with time and the cult of memory.

Bruno had theorized that Egypt is nothing less than the begetter of an *ars memoriae.* For Vico, however, Egypt *is* the museum, or memory-theater, of history. Its ancient wisdom is preserved, as Vico says almost in passing, in the celebrated Alexandrian Museum, whereby Alexandria is called "the mother of the sciences" (NS/46). The phrase is plainly meant to hark back to the classical definition of Memory as the mother of the muses. Furthermore, Vico flanks his mention of the Alexandrian Museum with references to the Lyceum and the Academy. But, unlike the grove of academe or the temple of philosophy, the museum, which is etymologically the symbolic dwelling place of the ghosts of memory and of the muses, gathers relics of antiquity, safeguards them, and embalms, as it were, the dead and yet immortal body of the past. As such, like Egypt itself, its museum leads us to the secret threshold of an unknown world. In its recesses, as in the silent folds of the earth, death, which necromancy or the practice

---

[14] A copy of the frontispiece is available in Joscelyn Godwin, *Athanasius Kircher* p. 69. See also Kircher's frontispiece to *Arithmologia* in Godwin (cited in note 7 above), p. 82.

Kircher's illustration of the *Musurgia universalis*, 1650.

of embalming posits as the beginning of things, is preserved as if it were the seed of life. This concern with memory is extended to other features Vico attributes to Egypt.

What the great antiquity of Egypt has preserved (and is crucial to Vico's encyclopedic collection of "tutto lo scibile gentilesco" (the whole gentile knowledge) (NS/51) are "due grandi rottami non meno meravigliosi delle loro piramidi" (two great fragments no less marvelous than their pyramids) (NS/52). In the wake of Diodorus Siculus and, above all, Herodotus (*Histories*, Book II), who reduce the myth of Egypt to history and scientific naturalism, Vico retrieves and adapts to his own end the two rational achievements, which he calls "rottami," literally broken pieces of the Egyptian architecture of wisdom. One of them is the tripartite temporal division of history—the age of the gods, of heroes, and of humankind. The other concerns the three languages corresponding to the three ages: the first, hieroglyphic, with sacred characters; the second symbolic, with heroic characters; the third epistolary, with characters agreed on by the people (NS/52; 173; 432ff.). What joins these two remnants of Egyptian wisdom is, on the one hand, the insight into time and, on the other hand, the idea of science.

Egyptian remnants of the past are cast as "boriose memorie" (pretentious memories or conceits) (NS/53). Memory, which is the preservation of time in its pastness, in turn adumbrates and accounts for the metaphor of the "rottami." The metaphor designates the physical, stony materiality of Egyptian monuments, which are both vanishing and yet surviving, the transitoriness of a world that is under the sway of time, inexorably haunted by death, and death emerges from the very existence of these scraps as the truth of time. From this point of view, the timeless immobility of the pyramids—which can be called literally cryptic geometries holding in their wombs mummies and which are yet wedged into the sky— are the grotesque counterpoint to the scraps of time. For in their awesome, impenetrable secrets the pyramids suggest the will to challenge and escape the shadows time casts by its perpetual erosion. This representation of Egypt as the ambivalent crystallization of time as memory and death is further suggested in the *New Science* by Vico's view of Mercury/Hermes as the *psychopompos*, the guide of souls to the fields of death—the Avernus— and back from Orcus (NS/604). This function of Hermes evokes the subterranean world of the *inferi*, what the Greeks call the *upogeios*, the meanderings of the underground rivers, such as Styx, and the gloomy cavern of Erebus, child of Chaos.

This projection of Egypt in terms of time and its cult of memory, which appears also as an idolatry of death and its grim preservation, recalls and extends a crucial strain of the myth of Egypt, which has never been far out of the orbit of Western consciousness. I have alluded to St. Augustine's attack against Egypt's claims of antiquity in the *City of God*. The imaginative and moral objections to Egypt, however, are available in the biblical account of Exodus as well as in Dante's *Divine Comedy*, which makes Exodus its central figuration. In both texts, Egypt is the literal embodiment of time and death, of time as death, and it stands for the phantasm of nostalgia, for the idolatry of the past beckoning the minds of exiles in the desert. From this standpoint, the Jews' bondage in Egypt, just as Dante's view of his *Inferno*, is their provisional surrendering to the powerful pull of the past and of death. To leave the house of bondage, just as to leave hell, is tantamount to rejecting the cult of death, the mummified preservation of what is dead and its implicit belief that death is the beginning of all things.[15] Vico, whose thought memorializes the world of the dead, grasps what the Jews and Dante saw as the essence of Egyptian idolatry. In fact, the Egyptian syringes, which are memorial inscriptions at the entrance of the temples, are for him delicate, harmonious voices leading, as the Sirens' songs do, into the land of the dead. To this view of dead "Egyptian" memories, Vico juxtaposes the living tradition of the past—the world of science.

There is a scientific side, however, to Vico's perception of Egypt in the *New Science*, and it had been adumbrated by the *Autobiography*. The first sign of a scientific reading is available in his lengthy discussion of hieroglyphs in the context of the "Corollaries covering the Origins of Languages and Letters" (NS/428–40). Vico argues that hieroglyphs, which are icons of the primordial unity of words and things, are not to be found only in Egypt. Rather, Vico registers their occurrence among Ethiopians, Chaldeans, Scythians, Mexicans, Chinese, and even Romans (NS/435). Their diffusion shows that hieroglyphs are not a divine invention or the residue of Edenic language. The cause for this scholarly misconception about the origin of Egyptian hieroglyphs and their impact on other cultures is to be found in what Vico calls, by significantly misquoting the very title of Thomas Baker's *Reflections on Learning* as "*Incertezza delle scienze*" (*Uncertainty of the Sciences*) (NS/442).

We know that the "certainty" is the key issue of Vico's science. By Baker's phrase we are plunged into a conjectural world of indeterminable principles, in the sense that the uncertainty of the sciences accounts for the mistaken assumption about hieroglyphs' original status.[16] For Vico, on the other hand, hieroglyphs' mimetic realism depends on the principle

---

[15] I have explored this question at length in *Dante, Poet of the Desert: History and Allegory in the Divine Comedy* (Princeton: Princeton University Press, 1979).

[16] One unavoidably thinks of Leonardo di Capua's, *Parere divisato in otto ragionamenti ne' quali narrandosi l'origine e il progresso della medicina, . . . l'incertezza della medesima si fa manifesta* (Naples, 1681). Di Capua's text was published under the auspices of the Accademia degli Investiganti. Vico reflects on the decay of medicine into skepticism and on Leonardo di Capua in his *Autobiography*, pp. 24–25.

of the natural signification of language. The fable of Idanthyrsus's message to Darius via "five real words" exemplifies Vico's idea of mimetic realism as a phase in the history of language. Not even the thrice-great Hermes, "who brought the Egyptians letters and laws" (NS/66) is exclusively Egyptian. Like Zoroaster in the East, Orpheus in Greece, and Pythagoras in Italy, he is a "poetical character" and the bearer of a historical, not esoteric, wisdom. This rational interpretation of Mercury continues in the extended discussion of this god (NS/604). In this passage, Mercury's caduceus, winged cap, and wings on his heels are interpreted as hieroglyphs or emblems of liberty, bonitary ownership, or heroic orders.

These symbolic and scientific layers of the myth of Thot are recapitulated in the successive paragraph that also functions as a radical critique of traditional Egyptology:

> Quindi ha a dirsi che questo Mercurio de' Greci fu il Theut o Mercurio che dà le leggi agli egizi, significato nel geroglifico dello Cnefo: descritto serpente, per dinotare la terra colta; col capo di sparviero o d'aquila, come gli sparvieri di Romolo poi divennero l'aquile de' romani, con che intendevano gli auspici eroici; stretto da un cinto, segno del nodo erculeo; con in mano uno scettro, che voleva dire il regno de' sacerdoti egizi; con un cappello pure alato, ch'additova il loro alto dominio de' fondi; e alfin con un uovo in bocca, che dava ad intendere l'orbe egiziaco, se non é forse il pomo d'oro, che sopra abbiamo dimostrato significare il dominio alto ch' i sacerdoti avevano delle terre d'Egitto. Dentro il qual geroglifico Maneto ficcò la generazione dell'universo mondano; e giunse tanto ad impazzare la boria de' dotti, ch'Atanagio Kirckero nell' *Obelisco panfilio* dice significare la santissima Trinità. Qui incominciarono i primi commerzi nel mondo, ond'ebbe il nome esso Mercurio, e poi funne tenuto dio delle mercatanzie; . . . e le ali, che qui abbiam veduto significare ragioni eroiche, furono poi credute usarsi da Mercurio per volare da cielo in terra, e quinci rivolare da terra in cielo. Ma per ritornare a' commerzi, . . . la prima mercede fu, come dovett' essere, la piu' semplice e naturale, qual'e' de' frutti che si raccolgliono dalla terra. . . . (NS/605–606)

(Here it must be added that this Greek Mercury was the Thot or Mercury who gives laws to the Egyptians, represented by the hieroglyph of Knef. He is described as a serpent, to denote the cultivated land. He has the head of a hawk or eagle, as the hawks of Romulus later became the Roman eagles, representing the heroic auspices. He is girt by a belt as a sign of the Herculean knot, and in his hand he bears a scepter, which signifies the reign of the Egyptian priests. He wears a winged cap, as an indication of their eminent domain over the land. And finally he holds an egg in his mouth, which stood for the sphere of Egypt, if indeed it is not the apple which signified the eminent domain the priests held over the lands of Egypt. Into this hieroglyph Manetho read the generation of the entire world, and the conceit of the learned reached such an absurd extreme that Athanasius Kircher in his *Obeliscus pamphilius* affirms that this hieroglyph signifies the Holy Trinity. Here began the first com-*merce* in the world, from which this *Merc*ury got his name. He was later regarded as the god of *merc*hantry. . . . The wings, which signified heroic institutions, were later thought to have been used by Mercury to fly from heaven to earth and then to fly back from earth to heaven. But to return to commerce . . . the first *mercedes* . . . were, as they could not fail to be, of the most simple and natural sort, that is to say in the produce of the land.)

The passage encapsulates the myth of Mercury/Hermes in its complex historical unfolding, and it ranges from archaic myths to the view of the god, under whose aegis, as if he were Saturn's complementary figuration, agriculture or the cultivation of the earth begins (NS/3). If Saturn/Chronos, god of time who embraces all cycles of times and all seasons (or chronology and agriculture), falls from the sky to the earth and, thus, signals the shift from eternity into time, Mercury is a protean, ever-shifting divinity who steadily moves between heaven and earth. The very essence of Mercury makes him the paradigm for Vico's mobile and time-rooted imagination of history. His essence consists in: his eloquence (the invention of laws and letters); his constantly elusive mobility, such as his power to shuttle back and forth between heaven and earth, a detail which links him with all exchanges in the marketplace; his establishing boundaries to the fields; and, paradoxically, his power to trespass the borders of the underworld.

In substantial terms, the passage quoted above begins by implying the presence of a direct link in the compressed references to the fable of the cosmic egg, the mystical interpretation by the Egyptian priest Manetho, and the theological allegories by Kircher. The fable of the cosmic egg (a sort of cosmological embryology) stands for the unity of the universe, for the generation of the world (NS/733), and its self-enclosed totality, which is figured in its endless cycles of birth and death. If in the fable one glimpses at the contours of Bruno's esoteric thought of the movement of life and death, the interpretations by Manetho and Iamblichus's *Egyptian Mysteries* invest Egyptian history with an atemporal, abstract significance and with an immutable truth. From Iamblichus's Neoplatonic standpoint, Egypt is stripped of its historical temporal singularity and is immobilized as an abstract myth or arabesque of the mind.

By the same token, Manetho's allegorical interpretation of Egypt assigns Egypt to the order of the same and abrogates exactly what Vico's Egypt stands for: the principle of historical difference, death, and time. Finally, Athanasius Kircher's *Obeliscus Pamphilius*, as I hinted before, reads Egypt's *prisca theologia* as a prefiguration of trinitarian theology and, in this sense, it is a replica of Manetho's syncretism. In Kircher's hermeneutics, which

Vico dismisses as crazy, he sees baroque universal mathesis as a mad impulse to find arcane correspondences rather than historical differences in
cultures: "a tanto giunse a impazzare la boria dei dotti" (NS/605) (the
conceit of the learned reached such an absurd extreme). Why is Kircher's
hermeneutics absurd? The answer lies in the semiotics of the obelisk, which
is a column with a pyramid at the top, and, as such, it is the sign of the primal wedge or shape of matter, or even a symbol of the ray of the sun and
its cycles.[17] Nonetheless, the pyramid at the top acknowledges death's
crowning presence, and, thus, it gives the obelisk an edge of ambivalence.
Kircher interprets the obelisk as a foreshadowing of the Trinity, and such
a reading amounts to an absurd, impossible petrification of time. By contrast, Vico sees in it the monument to death.

The obelisk discloses, just as the idea of memory and time do (or the
symbolic forms which range from the museum, the pyramids, and the sy-
ringe), the latent core of Egyptian wisdom as the wisdom of the unity of
life and death. Vico dismisses any celebration of death's sovereignty; he discards the Neoplatonic theurgy of Iamblichus, the totalizing allegoresis of
Manetho, and the synchretic theology of Kircher. Their limit lies in the extrapolation of a vain, long-vanished image of connected wholeness from
Egypt's ancient wisdom. But Vico retrieves and explores anew the imaginative possibilities contained in this myth of Mercury as a figure joining together earth and sky and the god of transactions in the marketplace. He
posits a bond between the myth of Egypt's self-regenerative movement and
Mercury's attributes. The fable of the cosmic egg, wherein no clear difference can be seen between life and death, is at one with Mercury's attributes, his travels between earth and heaven. To put it another way, what
Agrippa and Bruno perceived as occult, metaphysical knowledge, Vico extends into unpredictable directions. I am suggesting that at the heart of
Book II of the *New Science* Vico articulates a new mythical science of the
earth, which can be called a yoking of myth and science. In such a yoking
the ancient Egyptian myths of earth and sky, and of life and death, and the
modern sciences of geology, astronomy, and cosmography are construed
with each as the prolongation of the other.

At the center of Giordano Bruno's enthusiastic endorsement of the myth
of Egypt stands the view of the magic cosmos of Hermes Trismegistus as
a sun-kingdom, whereby the sun is the eternal center around which the infinite processes of birth, growth, and rebirth occur. In this open and constantly shifting universe, the rigid geocentric worldview that structures all
our thoughts is ridiculed as a vain conceit. By contrast, Hermes, who, silent
and dark, treads all the secret paths of the earth and escorts the souls into
the underworld, is the figure who shatters all rational boundaries. Thus,

---

[17] V. M. Mercati, *De gli obelischi di Roma* (Rome, 1589).

Bruno's baroque vision entails a new grammar, whereby the calcified formulas of language are shown to be hollow, as well as a sense of a new reality which is best represented by the serpentine line, the curvature of space, and the infinite openness of time. From this viewpoint, it is with Bruno, with his expansion of the frontiers of the imagination, with his enthusiastic embracing of the openness of Copernican heliocentricity and his foreshadowing of Kepler's views of the elliptical motion of astral bodies, that the limits of a closed understanding of space and, generally, of the classical world picture are forever sealed.

Book II of the *New Science* offers a direct and critical response to the world of baroque science. In contrast to this science and to the science of the astronomers, who draft a new map of the heavens, Vico proposes to show the process by which the myth of Egypt becomes the science of the Earth, how the myth of Egypt turns into a modern "geo-myth," so that at its core the *Scienza nuova*, the *New Science*, is truly a *Gaia scienza*. To grasp the sense of the elaborate metaphoric pattern Vico develops, one should keep in mind that natural scientists and *geo*graphers of the eighteenth century—Robert Hooke and Niels Steensen—compiled a scientific history of the Earth. Vico, who understands history as a genealogy of myths, writes the Earth's poetic science.

The textual evidence for Vico's project of elaboration of the "Gaia scienza" is unequivocal. Book II of the *New Science* begins by expounding what is meant by "Poetic Wisdom," and the section evokes, in the wake of Boccaccio's *Genealogy of the Gentile Gods*, the Universal Flood and the giants (who are the "sons of the earth," for the Earth is "mother of giants") (NS/370). We are then told that the giants wandered over the dense forest of the Earth. Book II ends symmetrically with Section XI, "Poetic Geography," wherein geography—literally the science that designs the map of the earth—tells of the Greek and Roman colonizing voyages, itineraries, and passageways over the Earth (NS/741–69). This extended reflection on the overlapping boundaries of culture, which Vico conducts through "chorography" and the "nomenclature of history" (NS/774), leads to a seemingly arbitrary account of Aeneas's coming to Italy after the Trojan War. Actually, the fables of Arcadia or of the Pythagorean communities in southern Italy turn out to be narratives of what I call political territoriality (NS/770ff.).

In between these endpoints of Book II Vico traces the Roman agrarian laws as the consequence of: Roman civil wars; the fables of the origins of the underworld (NS/716–21); the myths of Orpheus, Hercules, and Theseus who fetch Proserpina or Ceres from the land of the dead and which Vico understands as the story of the ripening of grain (NS/546); the Greco-Roman recurrences of the myth of Isis through the Saturnian fables of Cybele, Berecynthia, Pomona, and Vesta (NS/549).[18] These fables, like the Earth they figure, are the crossroads and ground of Vico's thought of the Earth in its uncanny, mysterious familiarity. The metamorphoses and migrations of the selfsame "pagan" myths of the Earth, which the *New Science* registers, are chiefly, no doubt, the sign of both the persistence and precariousness of the Earth's sacredness.

Nonetheless, the ancient mythical figurations of the Earth do not reduce the Earth to a simplified, univocal sense. Vico certainly inherits the mythic tradition of Terra, which Boccaccio's *Genealogy of the Gentile Gods* channels from classical antiquity as Gaia, the nourisher and mother giving birth to all things, and as a motionless center opposed to chaos. Such a view recurs in Campanella's *De Sensu Rerum*, in which the Earth is *mater*. There seems to be no room, however, in the *New Science* for Dante's Earthly Paradise or Sannazaro's *Arcadia*, which can be called, by using a Baconian phrase, the "Georgics of the mind." The absence of such a tradition discloses Vico's conviction that the pastoral cosmos is an ahistorical, deluded utopia. By contrast, Vico foregrounds the fable of Hydra, the nine-headed serpent slain by Hercules, which, when any of its heads were cut off, always grew others in their place (NS/540). Equally foregrounded is the fable of the Hesperides and that of the Chimera (NS/541), the fire-breathing hybrid monster made of serpent, lion, and goat. The untamable monstrosity of the Earth (who devours corpses) is the terrifying other side of Gaia, the mother who gives birth to all things, and of Vesta, the Greek Hestia, goddess of the *oikos* and hearth and fire.

This irreducible, eternal ambivalence of the Earth is viewed in the *New Science* through the Egyptian and Hermetic emblem of the snake, which appears in the caduceus, and is a figure of the spiral of time as well as a telluric symbol. Let us quickly follow this metaphoric pattern of the myth in Book II. The snake that Cadmus slays, we are told (NS/679), stands for the clearing of the Earth out of the great ancient forest; its teeth, which Cadmus sows, are the cultivated fields; and Cadmus himself will become a serpent. There is a foreshadowing of these mythic elements, in the section on "Poetic Economy." The idea of the sphericity of the Earth—the *orbis terrae* or the globe—is derived from and is directly linked with the emblem of the serpent: *orbis*, Vico says, comes from "the ancient *urbum*, curved. Perhaps *orbis* is from the same origin, so that at first *orbis terrae* must have meant any fence made in this way, so low that Rhemus jumped over it to be killed by Romulus and thus, as Latin historians narrate, to consecrate with his blood the first wall of Rome. Such a fence must evidently have

[18] The myths of the Earth—with illustrations of the Temple, Vesta, and Isis, and with references to Sannazaro's *Arcadia*—are treated by T. Blackwell, *An Enquiry into the Life and Writings of Homer*, 2nd ed. (London, 1736).

been a hedge (*siepe*), and among the Greeks *séps* signifies serpent in its heroic meaning of cultivated land" (NS/550).

What emerges, first of all, from Vico's discursive obliquities and from his etymological and mythic patterns is the insight that all secret, Hermetic knowledge is really a science of the language (in the double sense of the genitive). This science is contained in the hypograms of words or within the elliptical, python-like movement of language. More substantially, through this mythical grid, Vico is responding to the epistemological challenges of the scientific discourse of his times. Eighteenth-century geologists, such as Buffon, Burnet, Whiston, Hooke, and Hale who write histories of the Earth (an imaginative version of this genre is the *Timaeus* and, more recently, Kircher's *Mundus Subterraneus*), attempt to harmonize it with the biblical account of the Flood, the existence of the pre-Adamites, and recent archaeological findings.[19] At the same time, other thinkers, such as Copernicus, Galileo, Bruno, and Kepler, had displaced the Earth from its centrality in the cosmos. In fact, as the circle gives way to the oval shapes and to Kepler's ellipsis, the notion of center fades and the curvature of infinite worlds emerges as the new imagination of space. But Vico's thought never leaves the Earth. He draws a geocentric diagram of the physical universe, which may strike one as simply out of step with the scientific revolution and the "new" sciences. Yet, the new scientific frontiers of the imagination themselves never really leave the Earth behind.

The debates aiming at placing Vico either in the camp of the antiquarians, who are hopelessly opposed to the new scientific advances, or of the intellectuals who embrace the challenges of science, are too schematic to be really useful in determining Vico's position toward the world of modern science. In order to avoid lapsing into naive notions that Vico is "anti-scientific" we should recall how in *On the Study Methods of our Time* Galileo's achievements, such as the telescope or his unveiling of the limits of the Ptolemaic systems, and the invention of the press are duly vindicated. As we have seen in Chapter 2, Vico's *On the Heroic Mind* celebrates as heroic the scientific advances of the likes of Descartes, Galileo, and Columbus. In Book II of the *New Science* there is a sustained reflection on physics, which is called the "other branch of the main trunk of poetic metaphysics" (NS/687), and which entails cosmography and astronomy. This reflection,

---

[19] There is an explicit reference to Burnet in 1NS/98. See T. Burnet, *Telluris theoria sacra: orbis nostri originem et mutationes generales, quasi iam subiit aut olim subiturus est, complectens* (London, 1680), and Mirella Pasini, *Una storia del mondo tra ragione, mito e rivelazione* (Milan: Angeli, 1981). Furthermore see William Whiston, *A Vindication of the New Theory of the Earth* (London, 1698). See the important work by Paolo Rossi, *I segni del tempo: Storia della terra e storia delle nazioni da Hooke a Vico* (Milan: Feltrinelli, 1979). See the reading of science in Vichian terms by Stephen E. Toulmin, *The Discovery of Time* (New York: Harper & Row, 1965).

as we shall now see, amounts to a rethinking of the essence of modern science in the light of ancient myths.

The section on "Poetic Physics" begins by evoking the classical and poetic mythology of nature. The original Chaos, which physicists view as the confusion or formlessness of the universal seeds of nature, is followed by the imagination of Orcus, the monster who devours all things. These figures are later elaborated by physicists into Pan, who is viewed as "the formed universe, and in the fable of Proteus, who is first matter and who assumes always new forms" (NS/688). As Vico's text indicates, these myths are metaphors or pre-philosophic representations of the origin of nature. If Chaos and Orcus may be said to recall Bruno's discussion of these two figures in his *Lampas Triginta Statuarum*, the figure of Pan is best explained by reference to Bacon's *Wisdom of the Ancients* (Chapter VI). Pan, the son of Mercury, is the parable of the secrets and mysteries of nature about whose origin, says Bacon, there are two opposing views: the first is that he sprung from Mercury, the divine word; the other is that he emerges "from the confused seeds of things" (p. 235.) The third hypothesis about the origin of Pan "was borrowed by the Greeks from the Hebrew mysteries . . . by means of the Egyptians" (p. 236) and it relates to the present world of corruption and death. Bacon goes on to describe Pan's body or the body of nature.[20]

Vico's representation of "Poetic Physics" rewrites Bacon's speculations about science. Within this context it should be pointed out that even Vico's myth of Proteus, whom, as he says, Menelaus fought in Egypt (and which he culls from Book IV of the *Odyssey* [ll. 455ff.]), recalls Bacon's own treatment of the myth in the *Wisdom of the Ancients*. For Bacon the fight between Menelaus and Proteus symbolizes the new science's efforts to coerce doctrines of elusive atomistic forces within the bounds of order (p. 66ff.). By contrast, Vico retrieves what to him is both an Egyptian obsession and a Baconian concern: the mythical representation of physics turns for him into a physics of bodies and the nature of man (NS/692–702). Vico's musings begin with the redefinition of a metaphysical proposition about "being and subsisting" (NS/693): in a pointed polemic with the Cartesian claim of the body as mere extension, Vico brings out the semantic ambiguity contained in the word *sum*, meaning both "I am" and "I eat" (NS/693). The anti-Cartesian identity of being and subsisting ushers in Vico's reflection on the corruption and decay of bodies, on the soul, the passions and humors of the body, the operations of the mind, the nature of the imagination, and the seats of the passions. Overtly, the discussion hinges on natural philosophy, which makes the soul

[20] *The Wisedome of the Ancients*, pp. 18–38. For a modern interpretation of Bacon from the standpoint of the *Timaeus* see John C. Briggs, *Francis Bacon and the Rhetoric of Nature* cited in note 8.

a material form such as air, and on Descartes's Stoic theory of optics (NS/706). Yet, there is in it an oblique critique of Bacon's natural science and its Egyptian forebears. For Bacon the fable of Proteus promises to bind the elusive forces of nature; for Vico the promises of natural science stumble against the realities of the body. Modern physics and medicine cannot preserve, as the Egyptian practice has it, natural bodies from corruption and death.

The section on "Poetic Cosmography" (NS/710–25) stems from the discussion of physics and ranges from a classical description of the *megacosmos* as a three-tiered hierarchical structure of sky, earth, and underworld, and it ends, with appropriate symmetry, with a reference to the *mundus*, the world. In between there is a reference to the myth of Chaos, the father of Erebus, god of the underworld (NS/717). This is the dark underside of the harmonious order of the universe (NS/725), which conveys the belief that in it all things turn in unison. The cosmology Vico evokes largely follows Plato's *Timaeus* and its distillation of Pythagorean doctrine of world harmony embodied by Astraea (NS/713). From this viewpoint one might stress that the word *kosmos*, which was first used by Pythagoras, designates, as *mundus* does, the harmonious mixing and beautiful arrangement of all things.[21] Vico's reference to women's cosmetics (NS/725) suggests the Platonic-Pythagorean construction of the world as an esthetic design. But "Poetic Cosmography" also evokes the *mathemata* in conjunction with the magic arts of the Zoroastrians (NS/711). As one knows from the Hermetic *Asclepius* or from the *Mathesis* of Firmicus Maternus, *mathemata* describes the magic world of the astrologers and their belief, which Ficino, Bruno, Campanella, and Kepler's own *Mysterium Cosmographicum* share, that the contemplation of the stars is the condition for abolishing man's limitations.

Above and beyond this synopsis of Vico's tight argument and the summary of sources he deploys, the clear objective of "Poetic Cosmography" is to dramatize the way ancient cosmological models shape the constitution of modern discourses. Thus, Vico retrieves what in the *Autobiography* appeared as a Pythagorean-Egyptian disquisition on *coelum* in order to explain that the classical principles of poetic cosmology reappear in the Koran (NS/712). On the other hand, the Platonic model of the underworld shapes the eschatological moral system of rewards and punishment, the notion of hell, purgatory, and paradise, such as one finds in the *Divine Comedy* and Christian doctrine (NS/720). In what one can call the theme of

---

[21] For the link between *kosmos* and *mundus* see Pliny, *Historia naturalis*, Book II, par. iv. For the attribution of the invention of the word *kosmos* to Pythagoras see Plutarch, "Opinions of Philosophers," in *The Morals*, trans. Philemon Holland (London, 1603), p. 818.

cosmology and history, which centers mainly on Vergil's *Aeneid* and its own Pythagorean theories, Vico discusses the politics of cosmography through the founders of nations. Empire, we are told, is linked to the *territorium* and to the boundaries of the *orbis terrarum* (NS/722). Finally, as indicated above, cosmography, whatever its pretension to a scientific status, is a speculative model rooted in Pythagorean esthetics.

The section known as "Poetic Astronomy" begins by acknowledging the inventions of the Chaldeans, Phoenicians, and Egyptians (NS/727). The invention of the *quadrant*, which is a graduated arc with a movable index and an instrument used in both astronomy and navigation to measure altitudes, is singled out as a momentous, epochal event in the history of science (NS/727).[22] Here again as if thinking of contemporary astronomy Vico sketches the various historical views of the cosmos: astronomy/astrology as the ancient science of divination and auspices (NS/727); the Ptolemaic system of planets from the moon (which is recalled through the myth of Endymion) to Saturn, the god of time (NS/730); and the view of the planets "which now revolve in their appointed orbits" (NS/730).

But the chief burden of "Poetic Astronomy" is that the heavens are the earth's projection: people write in the sky the history of their heroes and their "heroic hieroglyphs" (NS/729). As Galileo intuits in the dedicatory letter of his *Sidereus Nuncius* man is, indeed, the historian of the stars. What Vico says is that astronomy, despite its claims to being *the* science of modernity and of the modern redescription of the cosmos, is, like cosmography, a poetic creation, and that the astronomers are historians of the stars. This, after all, was exactly the reaction of both Cardinal Bellarmine or Tommaso Campanella to Galileo's astronomical claims. Both of them write from deeply divergent perspectives on the scientist's revolutionary discoveries: Bellarmine writes from an anti-scientific, theological perspective; Campanella writes his *Apology for Galileo* from the perspective of enthusiasm for the new sciences.

For all their divergent presuppositions, both Bellarmine and Campanella told Galileo, when he presented the scientific proofs which he gathered with the help of his telescope, not to take them as literal truths but as likely stories or metaphors. Let me say in passing that Galileo's response to Bellarmine can be gauged from his discussion of science's truth and biblical metaphor in his *Letter to the Grand Duchess Cristina*.[23] On the other hand,

---

[22] On the quadrant as an instrument of navigational mapping see Robert Recorde, *Pathway to Knowledge* (London, 1551), Folios a 3v.–a 4r.

[23] For the importance of Galileo within the scientific debates in Naples and his relationship with philosophers such as Telesio, Bruno, Campanella, Della Porta, and Foscarini, see Fabrizio Lomonaco and Maurizio Torrini, eds. *Galileo e Napoli: Acta Neapolitana*, 7 (Naples: Guida, 1987).

Campanella's charge that Galileo's insights were not Pythagorean enough and that he had not evinced an ethics of harmony from his discoveries was not to find a response. Vico's view of astronomy resonates with these classical objections to modern science: for him science can never be sundered from myth, and scientific paradigms—be they the mathematical language of Galileo or the pantheistic myths of oneness of Bruno—are ancient myths created by new historical ways of thinking about nature and about oneself.

Vico puts myth at the center of his work and he views modern science through the prism of myth. As he does this he impels us to push back the limits of science and invest it with the inexhaustible imaginative possibilities of myth itself. To acknowledge the persistence of myth in scientific doctrines is to invest myth with a new legitimacy. It is to lay claim on new myths in the light of science, such as the sacred/secret vibrations emanating from the unfathomable depths of the Earth; to come in touch with the terror she inspires, as Vico himself comes in touch when, discussing earthquakes (NS/714), he focuses on the opening up of the earth and her exposing, obscenely as it were, what the Earth holds hidden "to the eyes of men and of gods." To evoke myth or poetic fable, finally, is to gauge the possibility of error attendant on the view of science as an entrenched, fossilized truth. In doing this, Vico has divined, before anybody else in European thought, the dangers of the scientific reduction of the world of man to a disenchanted, mechanical technological structure. He "contains" science, and he unveils the arrogance both in science's claim to truth and in the concomitant claim that science is empowered to establish values.

The *New Science* announces that the world is to be seen in a new light. It announces—and the chapters that follow will insistently return to the visionary, Dantesque burden of this text—a new way of thinking wherein no thought is worth thinking unless it is capable of thinking against itself and no map of the Earth is worth drafting unless it has utopia clearly marked and visible on its surface. To fix his and our eyes on the Earth is not necessarily Vico's way of espousing a geocentric worldview. Rather, realistically, the Earth is where one unavoidably must begin and where unavoidably one returns. Here one must come to grips with the shifting limits and boundaries of the fields, the sacred/secret land of the dead; the gift of seed, grain, and hearth; the recurring eons of time within which the history of the Earth is a breath of wind; and the hidden, subterranean world of tombs and ruins that earthquakes may uncover. This wisdom of the Earth, beyond all techniques polymaths forge, is Vico's *gaia scienza*. Ancient myths have endlessly envisaged such a wisdom, which seventeenth-century chorography, geodetics, geography, and the eternal order of geometry have sought to approach. This wisdom may have come to Vico from poets, such as Lucretius, but it comes to him, above all, as this chapter has shown, from the myth of Egypt.

I would further suggest that Vico's imagination of Egypt is shaped by and resembles his own native city of Naples.[24] We all are familiar with the myth of *Campania felix*, but we may be less familiar with some other mythic traditions of Naples which Renaissance poets, such as Pontano and Sannazaro, rediscover in their accounts of the mythic genealogy of Naples. As hinted earlier in Chapter 3, Naples, a Greek and a Roman city, originates, as Sannazaro, in the wake of Pontano and Boccaccio, says in a piscatorial eclogue, from the marriage of an underground river, Sebeto, and the Siren Parthenope. One can add that the phantasm of Naples is laced with the memory of necromancers and poetic visionaries. It is the birthplace of Lucretius, and, by an eerie symmetry, it is the death place of Vergil. It is a city of tombs, caves, and sulfuric grottos, which evoke the gate of Dis as Vergil imagined it; it is the city of volcanoes and earthquakes; of the buried ruins of Pompeii, which will be dug up a few years later in the eighteenth century; of Roman arches featuring the myth of Hercules, Neptune, the Sirens, ominous and bewitching sea monsters, wild protean forms—in short, the complexities and strangeness of the earth as one comes to know it even in one's own familiar world.

This phantasm of Naples resonates with the myth of Egypt, and both are the substance of the baroque world, of which the sculpture and architecture of Bernini, paintings of Caravaggio and his followers in Naples, the obelisks of Rome, and the allegories of the rivers are the epitome. Baroque esthetics signals the triumph of serpentine lines, multiple and shifting perspectives of earth and sky, hieroglyphs, time's ruins, and fantastic analogies between distant fables, which Vico absorbs and through which he sounds the obscure, shapeless depths of tradition's broken knowledge. This mythic fund of Naples is the imaginary terrain in which Vico's visionary thought is rooted.

Though he always felt as an exile in his hometown, Vico never really left his native city, and, when he went off to Vatolla for nine years to recover his breath, he took the city with him. In point of fact, whether at Vatolla or in Naples, the thoughts of this basically sedentary man never remained caught within the horizon of the *sinus Cumanus*, as the semicircular gulf of Naples, visible from Naples, is called. For all his life being rigorously circumscribed within the limits of his native land, his inspiration comes from

---

[24] On the mythography of Naples from the Renaissance to the eighteenth century see the contributions by George L. Hersey, *Alfonso II and the Artistic Renewal of Naples, 1485–1495* (New Haven: Yale University Press, 1969). See also his *The Aragonese Arch at Naples* (New Haven: Yale University Press, 1973) as well as his *Pythagorean Palaces: Magic and Architecture in the Italian Renaissance* (Ithaca: Cornell University Press, 1976), *Architecture, Poetry and Number in the Royal Palace at Caserta* (Cambridge, Mass.: MIT Press, 1983), and *A Taste for Angels: Neapolitan Painting in North America, 1650–1750* (New Haven: Yale University Art Gallery, 1987). More generally see R. Wittkower, *Studies in the Italian Baroque* (London: Thames and Hudson, 1975).

Mercury, god of laws and letters, and god of travel, who silently treads the paths of the earth, descends to the underworld, ascends to and brings news from heaven, and cuts across all boundaries. It is unsurprising, thus, that Book II of the *New Science* comes to a close with an extended section, "Poetic Geography," on journeys across the arc of the Earth (Section XI).

The discoveries of the Greek geographers (NS/741) turn into an elaborate account of the migration of all myths from East to West. Mars and Orpheus, for instance, are said to have come to Greece from Thrace (NS/744); Bacchus came from the East (NS/747); the dogma of the immortality of the soul came from the Gatans (NS/746). In short, we are given a geography of ideas or an itinerary of myths. The nomadic movement of the myths underlies and unsettles all other stabilizing laws of history and is itself the law of history. Such reflection on the flow of the archaic myths, as the locus of wisdom above and beyond the will of particular human subjects, continues with the retrieval of the epic adventure of Ulysses, who is protected by Mercury (NS/757) and, more poignantly, with the coming of Aeneas to Italy (NS/770). Aeneas's epic journey from fallen Troy to the foundation of a new cultural order and empire brings into the focus geopolitics or the politics of territoriality as the flip side of the myths of the Earth.

The fable of Aeneas reaching the Saturnian land tells the story of migrant, antagonistic tribes, Arcadians and Trojans, who reach Latium separately, but together trigger Rome's "immoderate expansion" over the land. The point in this poetic thought of the Earth that Vico articulates emerges as the insight into the precariousness of political and cultural boundaries and their openness to ever new reconfigurations. The account of the Roman foundation myth also suggests that migrations are actually violent incursions and, as such, they are the precondition of conquest. Finally, the journey of Aeneas is the figure of the philosopher's own intellectual voyage. Aeneas is the founder of a new empire. Vico is the founder of a new discourse for a new political order. In the wake of Aeneas, as it were, Vico sets out to reach farther back into the ashes of Troy and to the discovery of Homer, as the strategically placed Book III of the *New Science* proceeds to do. What this textual movement figures is that Vico's foray into the archaeology of myth yields to a quest for the origin of poetry. It can be said that Vico's imaginative descent into myth and poetry leads him to the disclosure of both the earthiness and extra-territoriality of philosophy.[25]

In a way, he reenacts the Socratic desire to bring philosophy home.

[25] Among recent efforts to redefine the Enlightenment's clarity of reason, noteworthy is Harold E. Pagliaro, ed., *Irrationalism in the Eighteenth Century*, Studies in Eighteenth-Century Culture, Vol. II (Cleveland: Press of Case Western Reserve University, 1972). See also Paul Ilie, *The Age of Minerva*, Vol. I, *Counter-Rational Reason in the Eighteenth Century* (Philadelphia: University of Pennsylvania Press, 1995).

Whereas in the past, wisdom's precincts were the Stoa, the Academy, or the Museum of Alexandria, Vico cultivates an eccentric image of philosophy in conversation with poetry, and of poetry as the mother of philosophy. The circumference of such a project coincides with the very circumference of the Earth. As a hybrid, strange, and protean form, poetic philosophy both belongs and yet does not belong to any particular place. It is not the ground of knowledge, and yet, it is at one with the epic quest for knowledge all over the routes of the Earth's histories. To speak of Vico's quest for knowledge is to say that there is a Vico who knows and a Vico who seeks, and the two are the sides of the same coin, simultaneously visible as a quest for the wisdom and enigma of poetry.

Vico knew, as Plato did before him and as the moderns, such as Ficino, Bruno, Bacon, Agrippa, and Kircher dimly perceived, that we must be Egyptologists. This means for Vico that to know, one must not just quest for what one already knows. One must be willing to move beyond such likely conceits, go like Odysseus, Moses, Dante, and Vico himself deep into Egypt, if only to leave it behind as if it were the unanswerable enigma of life and death, or just a distant and yet compelling memory of one's past. As one leaves Egypt behind, one must dig into immemorial time, into epochs distant and different from oneself in order to find that difference in oneself, or that which always remains foreign to oneself. Even so, we must interrogate the hieroglyphs of our passions, and extract all the wisdom we can from the tablets and riddles of time. All this can be accomplished by following the dim and oblique traces left in the night by Hermes' passage, by Ulysses' homecoming journey, and Aeneas's quest for a home in a foreign land. These three myths are the contours of the Earth's wisdom. As metaphors of the text, however, they map the course of Vico's ongoing voyage, which now leads him to the discovery of the true Homer: the probing into myth logically leads to the exploration of poetry's depths and history's fables.

Chapter 6

THE HOMERIC QUESTION

BOOK III OF VICO'S *New Science* is devoted to what has come to be known as the "Homeric question" and to what Vico calls "Della discoverta del vero Omero" (Of the Discovery of the True Homer).[1] This section of the *New Science*, which in all likelihood is the single most well-known argument put forth by Vico in his text, is divided into two parts. The first part is titled, "Ricerca del vero Omero" (The Search for the True Homer); the second part is the "Discoverta del vero Omero." Together—and the logical transition from the quest to the discovery of the true Homer is self-evident—these two parts play a strategic role in the structure and movement of the *New Science*.

That Vico had intended to make this Homeric question the hinge of his total reflections is suggested by the fact that it is literally the numerical centerpiece of the five books comprising the *New Science*. More substantively, the "Discovery of the True Homer" is placed immediately after the book on "poetic wisdom" (Book II), and it is followed by the historical analyses that make up the conceptual bulk of Book IV, "Del corso che fanno le nazioni" ("The Course that Nations Run"). A series of questions arises: to what extent, if any, is the "Discovery of the True Homer" a necessary *lieu de passage* from the conclusions reached on questions of "Poetic Wisdom" in Book II to the speculations on history and institutions in Book IV? If the Homeric question of Book III marks the logical point of crossing from the realm of poetry to that of history, why is it so? Finally, what is Vico's "discovery" concerning the true Homer? To answer these questions we must turn to the conceptual design of the text.

In and of itself, the section on Homer is unlike any other part of the *New Science*. From the standpoint of the rhetorical construction of the argument, Book III comes forth as a sustained and fairly unified analysis of the topic announced by the title—the identity, role, and significance of Homer.

[1] The Homeric question has been widely treated. See Benedetto Croce, *La filosofia di G. B. Vico* (Bari: Laterza, 1965), pp. 170–82; Antonino Pagliaro, *Altri saggi di critica semantica* (Messina-Florence: D'Anna, 1961), pp. 445–74; and Massimo Lollini, *Le Muse, le maschere e il sublime: G. B. Vico e la poesia nell'età della 'ragione spiegata'* (Naples: Guida, 1994), pp. 79–99. Because Vico places the Homeric question within the broad context of Renaissance poetics, a historical sense of this background is available in Bernard Weinberg, *A History of Literary Criticism in the Italian Renaissance*, two vols. (Chicago: University of Chicago Press, 1961).

In contrast to the fragmentary style of exposition Vico systematically deploys as the necessary style of his philosophical investigation—a style that is meant to fracture the grammar of conventional philosophical discourse—in Book III of the *New Science* Vico pursues the path of what must be called logical thinking. A rhetorical description of the logical and thematic structure of Book III is in order here.

Preceded by a brief introduction summarizing the findings on the vulgar wisdom of ancient Greece articulated in the preceding book, Book III unfolds by giving a double complementary series of proofs. In the first part Vico offers "Philosophical Proofs," which are neatly distinct from the "Philological Proofs," for the "Discovery of the True Homer." He then proceeds to weigh the evidence, submit corollaries, indulge in controversies with the critics of Homer from Plato to the neo-Aristotelians (such as Castelvetro), and consider the contradictions in the Homeric tradition. Finally, in the second section, Vico rethinks the relationship between poetry and philosophy, and between poetry and history, at a highly generalized level of reflection. Book III reaches its conclusion with some considerations on the history of tragic, comical, and lyrical forms.

Within the context of the logical methodology Vico deploys, one could point out the aptness of terms such as "discoverta" and "vero." The term "discoverta" must be seen as a variant of the *inventio*, a category that from Cicero's *Topics* (Section II, par. 6; Section XXI, par. 79) reappears in Ramus, Agricola, Descartes, and Bacon. Bacon, who in his *Novum Organum* makes of *discovery* the principle of any authentic knowing, distinguishes two classes of knowledge: a knowledge based on argument and a knowledge based on a discovery to be pursued through the inductive method. For Vico "discoverta" means the imaginative retrieval of the buried sediment of the past, a bringing to light the hidden truth about Homer by removing, as it were, allegory's integument or the layers of critical distortions weighing on his poetry.

How is one to explain this apparent logical procedure Vico adopts in Book III of the *New Science*? The question is legitimate, especially in view of the fact that a linear argument violates both the more characteristic serpentine movement of Vico's prose as well as his general principles about the spiral, oblique processes necessary to reach knowledge. The prose of the *New Science* is ceaselessly marked by digressions that slow down the rhythm of the narrative, by quick forward thrusts of the discourse through dazzling intuitions, by repetitions and sinuous falling back on formulas previously stated but which are now re-viewed from a new angle. This convoluted narrative technique is occasionally cumbersome but necessary. It conveys Vico's sense of the complications existing within the order of causality. The positive links between cause and effect never function by a linear mechanism in this poetic-philosophical universe.

Book III of the *New Science*, however, does not unfold in an absolutely linear progression. Yet the rhetorical-logical structure of the exposition suggests that Vico intends to adopt a special narrative stance. If elsewhere in the *New Science* his enigmatic and dark utterances cast Vico's voice as a seer who thinks about poetry from within his understanding of poetry's constitutive properties, in Book III Vico casts himself as the philosopher who reflects critically from the outside on the essence of poetry and on the truth of Homer but is not deluded by philosophical claims of philosophy's primacy over poetry.

In terms of its conceptual substance, "La discoverta del vero Omero" unfolds by bringing about a deliberate reversal of the most traditional and authoritative meditations on Homer's poetry. The polemical target for Vico, no doubt, is Plato, whose views of Homer are directly confronted. To discover the true Homer (and what Homer discovers for us) means for Vico to establish the principle that "the wisdom of Homer was not at all different in kind" (NS/780) from the early poet-theologians of archaic Greece. This principle, as Vico goes on to say, counters Plato's opinion articulated in the *Republic:* "yet, as Plato left firmly fixed the opinion that Homer was endowed with sublime esoteric wisdom (and all the other philosophers have followed in his train, with [pseudo-] Plutarch foremost, writing an entire book on the matter), we shall here particularly examine if Homer was ever a philosopher. On this question another complete book was written by Dionysius Longinus, which is mentioned by Diogenes Laertius in his *Life of Pyrrho* [i.e., by Suidas in the article on Longinus]" (NS/780).

In truth, Plato never thought that Homer had been a philosopher. Plato's polemic against Homer, on the contrary, is founded on the conviction that the Homeric encyclopedia, the *Iliad* and the *Odyssey*, has nothing to do with philosophy and that Homer is to be repudiated as the educator of the soul of Hellas. Because the supreme music is philosophy, Plato bans, through Homer, the mimetic and tragic poetry of the theater in favor of a non-hedonistic, rational, and austerely ethical idea of poetry. For Plato, Homer must be expelled from the pedagogical programs of Greece because his poems have become material for purely mnemonic exercises, for inert imitations that never generate essential discoveries.[2]

As Vico attributes to Plato the opinion that the Homeric poems contain an occult wisdom, that they are allegorical ciphers to be decoded in their

---

[2] See on this issue the fundamental contributions by Eric A. Havelock, *The Literate Revolution in Greece and Its Cultural Consequences* (Princeton: Princeton University Press, 1982); *The Muse Learns to Write: Reflections on Orality and Literacy from Antiquity to the Present* (New Haven: Yale University Press, 1986). Of interest is also Stanley Rosen, *The Quarrel between Philosophy and Poetry: Studies in Ancient Thought* (New York: Routledge, 1988).

secret meanings, he seems to contradict the letter of Plato's condemnation of Homer. Taken literally—let me restate the point—Plato expels Homer from the Republic precisely because he believes that Homer is not sufficiently philosophical. But Vico's posture is only superficially a contradiction. In fact, his reading reaches the heart of Plato's judgment of Homer. To judge Homer and his poetry from the perspective of philosophy, as Plato does, is for Vico tantamount to considering poetry as a function of philosophy, to judging its value according to its proximity to the canon of philosophical discourse. By contrast, Vico confronts Homer as a poet, and he resists submitting his poetry to the demands of his philosophy.

Given this Platonic premise about the philosophical value of Homer's poetry, the first chapter of the "Discovery of the True Homer" seeks to refute this very premise. To refute the proposition as to whether there is a hidden allegorical wisdom in Homer's poetry, Vico focuses on two fundamental questions: Is Homer the sole author of the Greek epics? If Homer is not the only author—as Vico, with some qualifications, believes—how, then, did the poems come into being? The answers Vico provides to these questions entail a number of issues he keeps under close scrutiny: What is the origin of poetry? What is the true relationship between poetry and philosophy? And what does it mean to claim, as Vico does here claim against Aristotle's *Poetics*, that poetry is itself history?

These broad issues that Vico raises around and through the figure of Homer are in no way peripheral to the conceptual thrust of the *New Science*. On the contrary, the general introduction to the *New Science* announces what Vico takes to be the chief, decisive discovery of his work. The "master key of this science"—as he lucidly formulates it—consists in the acknowledgment of poetry as the hidden source of all forms of knowledge. The insight that the early gentile peoples were poets who spoke in poetic characters leads Vico to posit the origin of religious and secular institutions within the powerful and often wild workings of the imagination. His reflections on the Homeric question belong exactly and must be seen against this horizon of concerns.

This book, with its focus on Homer, does not catch the reader unprepared. We have been told all along, directly and indirectly, that Homer plays a pivotal role in the architectonics of the *New Science* and in the fabric of Vico's vision. The centrality of Homer to his science was unequivocally foreshadowed by the allegorical emblem featured on its frontispiece. The emblem, which is a figurative technique fairly common even in philosophical texts (see Hobbes's *Leviathan*, Bacon's *Instauratio Magna* and *Sylva Sylvarum*, Alciati's *Emblemata*, etc.), presents a visual resumé of the themes which are the fulcrum of the *New Science*. In the center of the emblem, and in a forest clearing, there stands the statue of Homer who, blind and looking inward, is struck from behind by a ray of light. The light is refracted from the breast of a feminine figure, Metaphysics, who, in turn, receives the light from the eye of heaven. Scattered on the ground without any apparent order, around an altar supporting a globe, and at the feet of Homer who stands on a column a bit above ground level, lie various objects, such as the wings of Mercury, a rudder, the caduceus, the tables of the law, a sword, an urn, and a plow. These objects can be called hieroglyphics of the ruins of antiquity, posthumous and barely decipherable things/signs of past history.

The full significance of this opening emblem is given in the "Idea of the Work," which lays out the overall plan of the *New Science*. Because Vico consistently exploits the semantic sediments of the lexicon, allow me to remark that the word "idea" is not the ahistorical, Platonic *eidos* designating the realm of pure essences. Instead—and the implication of this statement will be evident later—he drafts the history of ideas, ideas that belong to the work and are produced by it. At any rate, in the "Idea of the Work" Homer is glossed as the "first author of the Gentiles" (NS/6), and his poems are referred to as "two great treasures of the natural law of the still barbarous Greek people" (NS/7).

The narrative of "The Discovery of the True Homer" picks up the loose threads and further develops the formulations anticipated both in the emblem and in the "Idea of the Work." Vico's discourse now proceeds at several levels, each tightly connected with all of the others. The point of departure for the wide range of problems the figure of Homer crystallizes is poetry's mode of knowledge and self-knowledge. The issue emerges with the notion that "Homer was endowed with sublime esoteric wisdom" as well as the proposition that "Homer was ever a philosopher" (NS/780). Homer is unrivaled "in creating poetic character" (NS/783), but, as J. C. Scaliger had intuited, there is no evidence that his mind was "chastened and civilized by any sort of philosophy" (NS/785). The refutation of poetry's philosophical value induces Vico to deny that Homer was the sole author of the *Iliad* and the *Odyssey*. Homer's fatherland remains unknown; equally unknown remains his date of birth. That almost all the cities of Greece still claim to be his birthplace shows, Vico goes on arguing, that the Homeric epics contain "words, and phrases and bits of dialect that belonged to their own vernaculars" (NS/790). The funeral of Patroclus (NS/793); the art of engraving on metals and of casting in bas-relief (NS/794); the delights of the gardens of Alcinous, the sumptuous banquets and the magnificence of his palace (NS/795); the embroidered garments (NS/796); the fragrant perfumes of the cave of Calypso (797); the sensuous refinements of the baths in the dwelling of Circe (NS/798); the references to men who care for their hair like women (NS/800); the heroes' meals (NS/801)—these are the textual details that prove that "Homer" as a solitary, unique, self-conscious author, lived in the times of the decadence of the heroic age, about 460 years after the Trojan War (NS/802–3).

The doubts about the hidden esoteric wisdom of the Homeric epics and about the birthplace and date of birth of Homer lead Vico to reflect on the essence of lyrical poetry and its relationship to the comical and tragic theater of Greece. In the wake of Horace's *Ars poetica* (*Art of Poetry*), of Aristotle's *Poetics*, and of the commentaries by Patrizi, Scaliger, and Castelvetro, Vico presents Homer not as the poet of infinitely imitable, calcified mnemonic formulas, but as an "inimitable heroic poet" (NS/807). If he really existed, Homer "may perhaps have been quite simply a man of the people" (NS/806). But as a poet, Homer is the most sublime of all the sublime poets, who "preceded philosophy and the poetic and critical arts" (NS/807). Socratic philosophy and the New Comedy, which is made of artifice, came into being after Homer. On the other hand, tragedy which "puts on the scene heroic hatred, scorn, wrath, and revenge, which spring from sublime natures" (NS/808) was produced in the heroic age of Greece. Homer came at the end of this age. In short, Homer is not contemporary with the events the epics narrate; had he lived in a barbarous time, he would not know how to feign. Homer's is the belated voice of memory, and, as such, he is the ironist necessarily posthumous to all events of the narrative. Furthermore, his name, which in the Ionian dialect means "blind" (NS/870), designates the origin of poetry from the turbulent, dark, and anonymous depths of the Greek people.

If Homer is not contemporary with the events the two epics recount, Vico must logically reflect on the relation between poetry and history, or poetry and memory. The "Philosophical Proofs for the Discovery of the True Homer" (NS/810–38) faces squarely this connection by taking to task Castelvetro's commentary on Aristotle's *Poetics* (NS/812). Vico now touches on the central question of his speculations. The proposition that "men are naturally led to preserve the memories of the institutions and laws that bind them within their societies" (NS/811) starts off the analysis. Memory, which designates the temporal rupture between events and their representation, is the knot which binds together the intricate arguments of the "Discovery of the True Homer" and gives intelligibility and coherence to the other lateral aspects of the discussion.

Vico's denial of a hidden wisdom or esoteric philosophy in the Homeric poems is rooted in the premise that poetry is never a mere allegorical cipher produced by a reflexive, ironic act of the will. Homer is "celestially sublime in his poetic sentences, which must be conceived of true passions, or, in virtue of a burning imagination, must make themselves truly felt by us. . . . Reflections on the passions themselves are the work of false and frigid poets" (NS/825). In the wake of the pseudo-Longinus, the "sublime" is to be understood as a theory of language's performative power to create worlds out of nothing, just as in Genesis God's word brings the world into existence out of nothing. At the same time, to acknowledge a hidden, sublime wisdom within poetry's folds is tantamount to recognizing a break between poetry and history, between life and consciousness.

One can inscribe within this issue, at least in part, Vico's radical critique of the theory of the unique author of the Homeric epics, of the theory, that is, of Homer as a Cartesian subject who observes, dominates, and represents reality from the transcendent standpoint of a consciousness dwelling outside the empirical particularities of the world. The Cartesian reduction of the world to a spectacle is the self-evident counterpart of the belief in a philosophical hidden wisdom of the text. Such an assumption of the poem's sublime wisdom is for Vico a late intrusion of the critical and reflexive arts into the incandescent body of poetry's passions. Both Cartesian and critical strains of thought privilege the reflection of consciousness over and against imagination's spontaneous operations.

If the bond between poetry and philosophy shows itself to be a fictional construction of critical thinking, Vico can and must proceed to argue that the poets are the "first historians of the nations" (NS/820). The insight is attributed to Castelvetro and it is taken to mean that poetic allegories must contain only historical significations. The relationship between poetry and history, however, cannot be explained merely in terms of the elaborations of the sixteenth-century commentaries on Aristotle's *Poetics*. In his *Poetica d'Aristotile vulgarizzata et sposta* Castelvetro rightly intuited that history is the foundation of poetry: "history must have come first and then poetry, for history is a simple statement of the true but poetry is an imitation beside" (NS/812). In his neo-Aristotelian theorization of poetry as imitation of reality, Castelvetro, much like other Renaissance theorists (Robortello, Patrizi, Scaliger down to Boileau), never understood the true origin of poetry.

In his usual and fragmentary but always rigorous style of analysis, Vico launches a threefold critique of the principle of art as mimesis of the real. In the first place, he discards all intrinsic distinctions between poetry and history. His recapitulation of the argument has a crystalline clarity and is grounded in the sharp opposition between poetic characters and the nature of critical reflection. Poetic characters, "in which the essence of fables consists, were born of the need of a nature incapable of abstracting forms and properties from subjects" (NS/816), are the manner of thinking of an entire people. Reflection, by the same token, is "the mother of falsehood" (NS/817).

Because the first barbarians lack reflection, the heroic poems—from Homer to Dante to Petrarch's *Trionfi* to Boiardo and Ariosto ("who came in an age illuminated by philosophy" [NS/817])—sing true histories which are preserved in the memories of the people. Memory—and Vico necessarily devotes a long paragraph to its description (NS/819)—is not only the passive copy of experience, but it is imagination, ingenuity, or even invention. As he formulates it, "Memory thus has three different aspects: memory when it remembers things, imagination when it alters or imitates them, and invention when it gives them a new turn or puts them into proper arrangement and relationship. For these reasons the theological poets called memory the mother of the muses" (NS/819).

In the second place, Aristotle's *Poetics* and the Renaissance commentaries on it posit too drastic a separation between the particularities of history and the universality of poetry in order to proclaim poetry's sovereignty. In opposition to this, Vico juxtaposes the principle of a poetic faculty which immerses the mind within the particularities of sense experience. Finally, he refutes Aristotle's conception of poetry as *techne* which is endorsed by the Renaissance commentaries. Their defense of poetry as *techne* is meant as a way of rescuing poetry from Plato's condemnation of art because art degrades the kingdom of essences. But for Vico the idea of art as *techne* falsifies and narrows within imitable parameters poetry's sublime, spontaneous origin. Vico hastens to mark the radical difference between "industry" and "poetry" in a language which unequivocally alludes to the theoretical and critical debates on the *Poetics*:

> In virtue of the axiom that he who has not the natural gift may by industry succeed in every [other] capacity, that in poetry success by industry is completely denied to him who lacks the natural gift, the poetic and critical "arts" serve to make minds cultivated but not great. For delicacy is a small virtue and greatness naturally disdains all small things. Indeed, as a great rushing torrent cannot fail to carry turbid waters and roll stones and trunks along in the violence of its course, so his very greatness accounts for the low expressions we so often find in Homer. (NS/822)

The critical views of art and the various poetics, with their insistence on industry and diligence, promote small-minded ideas of delicacy but lack an understanding of art's turbulence and powers, which are suggested by the metaphor of the rushing torrent. Furthermore, their metaphysical construction of the essence of art misses the sense of the historicity of poetry which Vico has just painstakingly defined: "The fables in their origin were true and severe narrations, whence *mythos*, fable, was defined as *vera narratio*. But because they were originally for the most part gross, they gradually lost their original meanings, were then altered, subsequently became improbable, after that obscure, then scandalous, and finally incredible. These are the seven sources of the difficulties of the fables, which can all easily be found throughout Book II" (NS/814).

The traditional schematic subdivision between *historia*, *fabula*, and *argumentum* (available, for instance, in the *Etymologies* of Isidore of Seville) is abrogated by Vico. No rigid demarcation between truth, fiction, and probabilities is possible because poetry is not just a question of rhetorical rules to be observed; rather it is a way of thinking. What is more, the above meditation on the archaeology and "wear" of metaphor—its ceaseless movement from the true to the improper to the improbable and the incredible—stages Vico's sense of the temporality and historicity of language. The articulations of time (which Renaissance mythography conceives of as "devouring time" or *tempus edax*) have the power to conceal and alter the original bonds between the fables and the experiences they incarnate. From this perspective poetry is indeed memory—the mother of the Muses—both because it preserves the archaic vestiges of the past and because time's deposits are sedimented in it.

The temporal discrepancy at the heart of all poetic constructions allows Vico to present his "Philological Proofs for the Discovery of the True Homer" (NS/839–72). What are we to understand, to begin with, by "philological proofs"? It is well known how intolerant Vico had been of the pedantries of philologists before he was to announce the luminous principle whereby philosophy is to be steadily joined with philology. In the wake of Valla, Erasmus, and Le Clerc's *Ars Critica*, Vico comes to understand that philology is itself history in so far as philology is a discipline disclosing the nature of time and of texts as time-bound productions. More precisely, philology reveals the pastness of the past, as it were, at the very moment in which it reduces the text to an inert document and seeks to rescue it from the past and to restore its original configuration. What Vico understands by "philology" can be gleaned, finally, by the "proofs" he marshals as a strategy to give a secure foundation to his philosophical speculations.

The "proofs" he puts forth constitute a general empirical context within which his method of generalizing abstraction can appear plausible. The philological proof, that the Homeric poems recount history, is inferred by the contextual evidence that the "Barbarous people, cut off from all other nations of the world, as were the Germans and the American Indians, have been found to preserve in verses the beginnings of their history" (NS/841); that "It was the poets who began to write Roman history" (NS/842); and that "Manetho, high priest of the Egyptians, interpreted the ancient history of Egypt, written in hieroglyphics, as a sublime natural theology" (NS/844); and that, finally, "the Greek philosophers did the same with the early history of Greece recounted in fables" (NS/845). In short, disparate historical experiences are eclectically pulled together to give weight, intelligibility, and coherence to the claims Vico advances for Homer.

The philological context that he drafts is a steady feature of his thought and it bears some clarification. What is a philological context? As a theoretical framework, a context presupposes the belief in an articulated total-ity, in a common field wherein individual entities acquire meaning in terms of a surrounding whole. Such is the view of the Neoplatonists or monists, such as Bruno and Spinoza, who assume the whole of reality is made of in-terdependent, organically linked parts. For Vico, however, the context is not a given, an abstract preestablished totality within which particulars are fitted and become intelligible. On the contrary, the context is a historical network wherein independent experiences—not bound to each other—are rooted and imaginatively articulated. Such an understanding of context does not deliver incontrovertible, scientific, and objective facts, as philolo-gists (of the positivistic school) might like. Historical origins, which philol-ogy seeks to ascertain, remain inaccessible to axiomatic determinations and are stubbornly shrouded in uncertainty. According to Vico, philology can at best be a hermeneutics of the "certain," a science of inferences of fabu-lous origins. At any rate, the various proofs Vico collates are the preamble to the further crucial "philological" analysis of the structure of the Home-ric poems.

On the authority of Cicero (*De oratore*, Book III, Section XXXIV, par. 137), who in turn echoes Pausanias, Vico says that Homer's two epics were sung by the rhapsodes who wandered about the Greek fairs and festivals (NS/851). Etymologically, *rhapsodes* are "stitchers-together of songs, and these songs they must certainly have collected from none other than their own peoples" (NS/852). By the same token, *homeros* "is said to come from *homou*, together, and *eirein*, to link; thus signifying a guarantor, as being one who binds creditor and debtor together" (NS/852). This etymology, Vico concludes, casts Homer as a binder or compiler of fables.

The editorial unification of the Homeric poems, which originally were disjointed, fabulous popular proliferations, was willed by the Pisistratids, tyrants of Athens, who ordered that the poems be sung by the rhapsodes at the Panathenaic festivals (NS/853–55). This insight into the structural features of the compilation, which constitutes the Homeric encyclopedia (*kyklos epikos, kyklia epe, poiema enkyklikon*) (NS/856), gives access to an oblique reflection of Vico's: the link between poetry and politics, which is here represented by the tyrants' decision to unify into a false unity the orig-inally disjunct, heterogeneous, and contradictory Homeric poems.

The tyrants' will to homogenize the autonomous, disparate units of the poem, to coerce them into one pattern, and to erase their constitutive dif-ferences is discreetly highlighted by Vico's suggestion that forty or more separate poems had been stitched together in one composition. The sto-ries sung by Demodokos or by Phemius in the *Odyssey* are, from this view-point, a *mise-en-abime* of the "confused mass of material" (NS/853), of the "infinite difference" (NS/853) still visible in the styles of the two poems. The reason for this editorial falsification of the persistent, irreducible heterogeneity of the poems into a totalizing, encompassing unity is political, and it emerges most clearly from the detail that the poems were to be sung at the Panathenaic festival (NS/854). The festival, established in honor of Athena, the goddess of wisdom, is the privileged occasion when the Greeks, through gymnastic competitions, music, and poetry celebrated their newly found political unity. Vico does not directly explore the implications of the tyrants' coercion on the economy of the polity. He remains well within the boundaries of apparently innocuous philological observations. Yet, as will be seen, the core of his reflections turns on the imaginative relationship between history and poetry, and I shall return to this issue of the "Discovery of the True Homer" later.

These philological-political reflections anticipate some arguments in the "Discovery of the True Homer." In Section II of the "Discovery" (NS/873–904), which has the tone of a general summary, Vico will declare that Homer "was an idea or a heroic character of Greek men insofar as they told their histories in song" (NS/873) and that "the Greek peoples were themselves Homer" (NS/875). The variety of dialects, the many idioms of the Greek people (emended by Aristarchus), the diversity of styles that Dionysius Longinus could not dissimulate; the fact that the Greek peoples vied with each other for the honor of being Homer's fatherland—all of these aspects induce Vico to conclude that the Homeric poems are the history of the Greek people. As the voice of common memories, Homer can justifiably be called the founder of the Greek polity or civility (NS/899) and the father of all other poets (NS/901). But Homer is, above all, the "first historian of the entire Gentile world who has come down to us" (NS/903). His poems are "two great treasure stores of the customs of early Greece"(NS/904).

An appendix, which is called a "Rational History of the Dramatic and Lyric Poets" (NS/905–14) and which is meant to correct the confused history of rhetorical forms elaborated by philosophers, closes the discussion of Book III of the *New Science*. Questions of chronology are revised, and Vico posits—against those who impose a naive genealogical pattern on the development of forms—the existence of two kinds of tragic poets and two kinds of lyric poets (NS/907). By possibly casting a glance in the direction of the musical experiments going on in Naples in the 1720s (Giovanni Battista Pergolesi, Domenico Scarlatti, et al.), Vico places the origin of the genres within the historical mythologies of Greece and Rome (NS/910).

So far I have given an interpretive paraphrase of the major strains of Vico's "Discovery of the True Homer." This argument can be summarized in the following four points. First, Vico repudiates the subjective theory of the author. Authority does not reside in an individual. Political authority determines the shape of the two epics. But Homer is not the Cartesian subject who occupies a disengaged perspective on the events of history; rather,

Homer is the imaginative point of contact of various dictions and *contra-dictions*. Second, the poems are an encyclopedia of Greek dialects. The educational value of Homer's work is thus vindicated against Plato's strictures. Third, poetry is history, rather than a mimesis of reality as both Plato and Aristotle, with different emphases, believe. As history, poetry does not generate atemporal truths as allegorists and makers of philosophical mythologies think. Fourth, poetry, and not philosophy, is the foundation of knowledge and of the city.

These four points, which I have heuristically isolated, are all ceaselessly present in Vico's figuration of Homer. They are the hinge of the radical rearrangement of knowledge pursued in his *New Science* and epitomized by the figure of Homer. From this standpoint, the "Discovery of the True Homer" intends chiefly to demolish the errors and falsifications dominating the interpretations of Homer and of poetry in general from Plato to Aristotle and to the vulgarizations of both, which the Italian Renaissance had produced. The truth, which Vico paradoxically finds in the fables and poetic fictions, consists also in unmasking the self-idealizations and blind beliefs that hamper the sense of poetic wisdom.

Vico's radical revision of the Homeric question must be understood, first of all, as a reaction against the growing European cult of Homer and of the large phenomenon called Renaissance Hellenism. What is, exactly, this phenomenon? Doubts about Homer's existence had existed since early Greek antiquity. In the first century, Dio Chrysostom questions the veracity of Homer's account and advances the argument in his *Trojan Discourses* that the Greeks lost the Trojan War. In the Middle Ages Homer is not really known. Petrarch acknowledges him but cannot read his poems. After the Aldine edition, published in 1507 and 1517, Homer decisively entered the European imagination. One thinks of Chapman's *The Whole Works of Homer* (1598–1614); of the translations of the *Iliad* by Dryden and Pope, until Bentley himself rejects the unitarian thesis of the *Iliad* and the *Odyssey*. In Italy, where the favorite epic poet is Vergil, Homer does not exercise much influence in the fifteenth and sixteenth centuries, but by the end of the seventeenth century the myth of Homer has grown massively.[3] In 1683 the antiquarian (and Arcadian) Raffael Fabbretti (of whom Crescimbeni

---

[3] One might mention the strictures against Homer available in Tassoni's *Paragone degli ingegni antichi e moderni* and in Book IX of *Pensieri diversi* (1627). See also Ludovico Antonio Muratori, *Della perfetta poesia italiana* (Book I, Chapter XI). In France, Charles Perrault, *Paralleles des anciens et des modernes*, accuses Homer of roughness, though Boileau admires Homer (*Art poetique*, Chant III). For a historical delineation of the myth of Homer see Paolo Rossi, *Le sterminate antichità: Studi vichiani* (Pisa: Nistri-Lischi, 1969), which is especially useful for the differences between the myth of Homer and the myth of Egypt. Of great value is Michael Murrin, "The Disappearance of Homer and the End of Homeric Allegory: Vico and Wolf," in *The Allegorical Epic: Essays in its Rise and Decline* (Chicago: The University of Chicago Press, 1980), pp. 173–96. See also C. T. Whitman, *Homer and the Heroic Tradition* (Cambridge, Mass.: Harvard University Press, 1965).

wrote the biography) provided the *Tabula Iliaca* with scenes from the story of Troy. In France the Abbé d'Aubignac (1604–1676) in his *Conjectures académiques ou dissertation sur l'Iliade* (which was published posthumously in 1715 and was not known to Vico) submitted the theory that Homer as a person never existed; that the biographical evidence concerning him—such as his exact birthplace or date of birth—is contradictory; and that the *Iliad* has no unified design or pattern. It is, to the contrary, marred both by incongruous characterizations of the gods and heroes and by contradictions among the various episodes.[4]

Much like d'Aubignac, Vico argues (NS/788) that Homer's fatherland is unknown. The Homer of the *Odyssey* comes from the Peleponnesus, while the Homer of the *Iliad* comes from the northeastern part of Greece. More specifically, the *Iliad* and the *Odyssey*, which the Pseudo-Longinus in *On the Sublime* believes to be poems composed at different ages, express a divergent consciousness of historical realities. The *Iliad*, which represents the pride and the wrath of Achilles, was written by a young man; the *Odyssey*, which narrates the duplicities and prudence of Ulysses, was composed by an old man (NS/803).

This European cult of Homer, which is, at least in part, a symptom of the nostalgic estheticism of the past and, implicitly, a symptom of the auto-idealization of the present, is articulated in Italy for Vico by a friend and frequent interlocutor of his, Gianvincenzo Gravina. Gravina's ideas on Homer and on Dante (whom Vico calls the Tuscan Homer) constitute the immediate polemical context for Vico's metaphorization of Homer.

Gravina, who is himself a jurist and a theorist of literature at the University of Rome, publishes a treatise in 1708 entitled *Della ragion poetica* (*The Nature of Poetry*), in which *ragione* is also to be understood as the Latin *ratio*, which is both reasonableness and law or norm, or as Gravina himself says:

> E questi ambidue libri sotto un comune titolo di *Ragione poetica* ho voluto comprendere. Imperocché ad ogni opera precede la regola e ad ogni regola la ragione.[5]

> (And both these books I have decided to collect under one common title, *Ragion poetica*. For the rule precedes every work and reason precedes every rule).

Vico employs the phrase "ragion poetica" (the nature of poetry) (NS/821) as he discusses the relationship between poet and philosopher

---

[4] On this whole issue see Noemi Hepp, *Homere en France au XVIIeme siecle* (Paris: Librairie Klincksieck, 1968). See also John L. Myres, *Homer and his Critics* (London: Routledge and Regan Paul, 1958); and Michael Murrin, *The Allegorical Epic: Essays in Its Rise and Decline* (Chicago: Chicago University Press, 1980).

[5] Gianvincenzo Gravina, *Della ragion poetica* in *Scritti critici e teorici*, ed. A. Quondam (Bari: Laterza, 1973), p. 199.

or metaphysician. But what exactly is at stake in Vico's polemic with Gravina's theories?

In reaction to the baroque esthetics of overstated theatricality and self-complacent simulations, Gravina projects an idea of poetry as a rational, credible imitation of reality. For Gravina the vice of poetry lies in the cult of mere appearances and empty images, which expresses itself in the taste for the marvelous and in techniques which produce optical illusionism and verbal trickeries. Behind Gravina's ideal of rational order, which is founded on an "idea eterna della natura" (p. 15) (eternal idea of nature), there is the Cartesian legacy of his teacher, Gregorio Caloprese: simple diction, naturalness, decorum, verisimilitude—these are the traits of the neoclassical poetics of Gravina's Arcadia. Indeed, *Della ragione poetica* elaborates what could be called a poetics of geometry, wherein the conspicuous values of the "science" of poetry are embodied in the criteria of symmetry, metrical proportions, syllabic quantities, design, and balances, which structure the rhetorical simulation of textual order:

> [C]ome ogni nobile edifizio è fabbricato secondo le regole dell'architettura, e le regole dell'architettura per sua ragione hanno la geometria, la quale per mezzo dell'architettura, sua ministra, comincia la propria ragione ad ogni bell'opera. Or quella ragione che ha la geometria all'architettura, ha la scienza della poesia alle regole della poetica." (p. 199)

> ([J]ust as every noble edifice is built according to the rules of architecture, and the rules of architecture have geometry as their rationale, for through architecture, which is its servant, every beautiful work finds its reason. Now the rule that geometry provides to architecture is what the science of poetry does to the rules of poetics.) (Translation is mine.)

The chief limitation of this mathematization of poetry lies in the absence of Vico's radical sense of the obscure stirrings of the imagination which, in turn, engenders the poet's dark utterances. Nonetheless, *Della ragion poetica* features a powerful defense of the poetry of both Dante and Homer. In a way, it could be said that Gravina inaugurates the eighteenth-century cult of Dante, just as he brings to maturation the Renaissance cult of Homer. For Gravina, Homer and Dante are spiritually proximate figures who represent passions common to all people. Homer emulates the powers of nature, and, like Proteus, adapts himself to all natures. More precisely, the argument between Agamemnon and Achilles is for Gravina the credible representation of genuine human passions.

Vico agrees with Gravina that Dante is the Tuscan Homer.[6] Vico does

---

[6] In the link he forges between Homer and Dante, Vico is not hampered by the fact that Dante is a real historical figure, whereas Homer is said not to have existed. What matters, however, is that Vico reads Dante the way he reads Homer: as an encyclopedic poet whose

not doubt Dante's historical existence as he doubts Homer's. Dante is the Tuscan Homer, however, because, he gathers in his poetry all the languages and realities of Italy, just as Homer does with all the dialects of Greece. But Vico also disagrees with Gravina. For Vico, the aim of poetry is to tame man's monstrous ferocity. He points out, thus, that the Homeric scene of pitching Agamemnon and Achilles against each other lacks wisdom; in fact, the two heroes act like "servants" in modern popular comedies (NS/782), just as the gods (Mars calling Minerva a "dog fly" or Minerva punching Diana) lack decorum. In short, Homer represents passions that transcend the measure of good sense and civilized behavior.

Vico and Gravina, moreover, differ widely on the assessment of Homer's style. In the narrative of the Greek embassy to Troy, for instance, Menelaus's terse speech as well as the sensory energy of Ulysses in figuring "l'ordine delle cose" (the order of things) appear to Gravina to be exemplary rhetorical representations. He even praises Homer's inventions which are judged as too plain or too simple only by those who enjoy the shadow-show of phantasms or the inexplicable tangles which conceal or disfigure the purity of the natural order. Vico, who from this viewpoint draws from the ideas articulated by the pseudo-Longinus in *On the Sublime*, finds Homer's comparisons "taken from wild and savage things" unrivaled (NS/826). Unlike Gravina, furthermore, he takes the fierce Homeric battles not as the natural product of a calm, cultivated, and gentle philosopher (NS/828) but as the outcome of a taste for the truculent and savage (NS/785).

In proclaiming the passionate, naive foundation of the Homeric world, Vico focuses on and unveils the conceptual limits of the Cartesian framework of Gravina's *Della ragion poetica*. Gravina's poetics, which is rooted in the rationality of seventeenth-century sciences, seeks to account for the surface coherence of Homer's texts and he ends up by acquiescing to the belief that the present and its modern philosophical reflection are superior to the past.[7] The modern appropriation of the past annihilates the *truth* of Homer's discovery, and this truth is also the consciousness of Homer's differences from the present, his outsidedness which is irreducible to the demands of the present.

Divine Comedy encompasses all the languages of Italy. See his "La discoverta del vero Dante ovvero nuovi principi di critica dantesca," in *Scritti vari*, ed. Fausto Nicolini (Bari: Laterza, 1940), pp. 79–82. An English version of the text is available in Giuseppe Mazzotta, *Critical Essays on Dante* (Boston: G. K. Hall, 1991), pp. 58–60. In general see Domenico Pietropaolo, *Dante Studies in the Age of Vico* (Ottawa: Dovehouse, 1989).

[7] See Aldo Lo Schiavo, *Omero filosofo: L'enciclopedia omerica e le origini del razionalismo greco* (Florence: Le Monnier, 1983). A critique of Gravina's notion of imitation was offered by Antonio Conti, who links Gravina's poetics to the treatises of the Cinquecento. To Gravina, Conti juxtaposes Muratori's *Della perfetta poesia*.

From Vico's viewpoint, Gravina, for all his good intentions, is responsible for an even more radical mystification of Homer's poetry. The neoclassical counterfeiting of mythical Greece marks the triumph of a mechanical imitation or reproduction of the past. Gravina's Arcadia— whereby the moderns dress up as ancient Greeks and take on Hellenized names—is the tragicomical illusion of a possible, mechanical retrieval of the past. This illusion is a mockery of the essence of history: in the self-mirroring of the present in the past, it can be added, both past and present are immobilized. To state it simply, behind the theatricality and complacent simulations of the masking of Arcadia there lurks the mask of death.[8]

Vico's thought, which is deeply rooted in the historical consciousness of the inimitable greatness of tradition, vindicates the primacy of creation and Homer's inimitability. Given this premise, Gravina's neoclassical theories, which are based on the principle of rational imitation of the classics, hamper originality and discovery. In his critique of the mimetic theory of art, Vico's conception is akin to Plato's critique of art as *mimesis*. Yet Vico's criticism of the Cartesian Gravina is fundamentally a critique of an altogether philosophical and reflexive mode of conceiving the relationship between philosophy and poetry. Because Vico wants to think anew this relation, he is forced to redefine the sense of the "poetic wisdom" that he identifies with Homer.

Poetic wisdom, Vico says in the introductory paragraph of his "Discovery of the True Homer" is "the vulgar wisdom of the first peoples of Greece, who were first theological and later heroic poets" (NS/780). This wisdom, which Plato finds in Homer, shapes Plato's opinion that Homer was a philosopher. Already Vico had defined "poetic wisdom" by giving an account of the origin of poetry. Poetic wisdom was not a rational nor an abstract metaphysics but was "felt and imagined" by men of robust sense and vigorous imagination. Their metaphysics was poetry, an undeluded and yet blind knowledge which was born "of their ignorance of causes" (NS/375).

This philosophical fable on the origin of poetry as pure creative energy casts the beginnings of wisdom as hazy and blurred. Yet the turbulence of the imagination constitutes the metaphysics and the mythologies of the gentile world across different times and places. Vico finds a confirmation of his insight in the practice of both the American Indians and of the ancient Germans. The American Indians, he says, "call gods all the things that surpass their small understanding." By the same token, the ancient Ger-

---

[8] Vico's criticism can be viewed as a sign of his own critical self-reflexiveness about his Arcadian affiliation. His letters to Gian Mario Crescimbeni about Arcadia and Gravina's schism are now available in Giambattista Vico, *Epistole*, in *Opere di Giambattista Vico*, Vol. XI (Naples: Centro di Studi Vichiani, 1992), pp. 82–86. On the idea of masking in Vico see Massimo Lollini, *Le Muse, le maschere e il sublime* (cited in note 1).

mans would hear "the sun pass at night from west to east through the sea, and affirmed that they saw the gods" (NS/375).[9]

This view of poetic wisdom leads Vico to assert boldly the originality of his vision. With great clarity he confronts how radically his insights depart from and reverse the ideas classical tradition has handed down about poetry and about the foundation of knowledge:

> All that has been said here so far upsets all the theories of the origin of poetry from Plato and Aristotle down to Patrizi, Scaliger, and Castelvetro. For it has been shown that it was deficiency of human reasoning power that gave rise to poetry so sublime that the philosophies which came afterward, the arts of poetry and criticism, have produced none equal or better, and have even prevented its production. Hence it is Homer's privilege to be, of all the sublime, that is, the heroic poets, the first in the order of merit as well as in that of age. This discovery of the origins of poetry does away with the opinion of the matchless wisdom of the ancients, so ardently sought after from Plato to Bacon's *De Sapientia Veterum*. For the wisdom of the ancients was the vulgar wisdom of the lawgivers who founded the human race, not the esoteric wisdom of great and rare philosophers. Whence it will be found, as it has been in the case of Jove, that all the mystic meanings of lofty philosophy attributed by the learned to the Greek fables and the Egyptian hieroglyphics are as impertinent as the historical meanings they both must have had are natural. (NS/384)

These principles, which are formulated in Book II, stand as the basis for the arguments in the "Discovery of the True Homer" as well as in Vico's reversal of Plato's critique of Homer in the *Republic*.

We have already seen that Vico's criticism of Plato for inaugurating the traditional view of Homer as a philosopher is, on the face of it, a flagrant misreading of Plato. Plato never claims that Homer's poems have any esoteric wisdom to convey. Yet Vico's misreading has its own paradoxical logic. Let us follow his rationale with a first question: What is Plato's understanding of Homer? The target of Plato's polemic is poetry as it is represented by Homer, Hesiod, and the tragic poets of Greece. Plato—who does not hesitate to imitate Homer and who casts the myth of Er in terms of Ulysses' descent to Hades—objects to Homer's poetry because it is read by all the Greeks who are ready to recognize him as the educator of Greece. He objects to it mainly because his poetry harms the health of the soul as well as the stability of the polis. The reason why Homer's poetry damages the soul lies in the fact that poetry is not directed to the better part of the soul—reason—but to the ungovernable passions. But Plato's condemna-

---

[9] For a further discussion of the imagination see Donald P. Verene, *Vico's Science of the Imagination* (Ithaca: Cornell University Press, 1981).

tion of Homer is above all political. Plato finds Homer politically and morally debatable in so far as his poetry encourages hedonism and the anarchic despotism of eros. Finally, as a mimetic activity poetry falsifies the original truth of the ideas, forces us to live in the midst of simulacra, and hampers any original discoveries.

In Book X of the *Republic* all of these objections converge in Plato's indictment of the educational value of Homer's poetry. Why the indictment? To put it differently, why does Plato think that his own project is not consistent with Homer's? The indictment of Homer discloses the fact that Plato believes in poetry's accountability in the tribunal of philosophy. The poet does not see nor does he know the truth; he will talk about anything, even about beds, without, however, really knowing how a bed is made. Only the dialecticians, who know the subtle bonds and interactions between the various branches of knowledge, have access to the truth.

More specifically, Plato places the question of poetry within an ethical and political horizon. In Book III of the *Republic* (which anticipates the debate of Book X) the critique of poetry and drama takes place in the context of the young guardians of the state. We recall Plato's reasoning. The mimetic arts, such as tragedy, (as opposed to the narrative arts) are to be banished from the Republic because they are founded on the theatrical principle of illusion. The actors on the stage impersonate truth, encourage falsifications and make-believe, which are all at odds with the *epithedeumata*, the occupations of the guardians. Paradoxically, the social education of the guardians will be effected through their imitation of existing models. In Book X of the *Republic*, on the other hand, the critique of Homer takes place within the context of the discussion of justice and the immortality of the soul. Socrates' point is that Homeric wisdom is not appropriate for the education of the philosopher-king, who must know

> how to keep to the upper road and practice justice with prudence in every way
> so that we shall be friends to ourselves and to the gods, both while we remain
> here and when we reap the rewards for it like the victors who go gathering
> the prizes; to live happily in this world and in the thousand year journey that
> we have described. (621c–d)

Within the perimeter of Plato's educational project, Homer's poetry is not sufficiently Socratic; it is mimetic. It has the power to modify the soul's affections, but because it is confined to mimesis, it seals the divorce between images and reality and forces us within the empire of the simulacrum. But for Vico, mimesis, which is a bane for Plato and a constraint for Aristotle, belongs to a different horizon of concerns.

Vico maintains that poetry, far from being mimetic, is tied to history. More than that, the cluster of problems—poetry, history, and imitation— becomes the object of Vico's sustained meditation in the course of which he tackles Aristotle's own insights into these same issues. In the context of an intense reflection on the genealogy and phenomenology of the passions (the vigorous memory of children, the vividness of their imagination, etc.), Vico formulates the well-known *degnità* LIII: "Men at first feel without perceiving, then they perceive with a troubled and agitated spirit, finally they reflect with a clear mind" (NS/218). In the middle of these psychological reflections Vico considers the role of imitation in children. He states in his *Elements* that "Children excel in imitation; we observe that they generally amuse themselves by imitating whatever they are able to apprehend" (NS/215–16). This axiom shows that the world in its infancy was composed of poetic nations, for poetry is nothing but imitation.

The passage echoes Aristotle's *Poetics* in which Aristotle expounds the origin of poetry and the development of drama: "Thus from childhood it is instinctive in human beings to imitate, and man differs from all other animals as he is the most imitative of all" (par. 1448b). Plato's critique of mimesis is here debunked. Aristotle adds in the same paragraph that "Homer was not only the master poet of the serious vein, unique in the general excellence of his imitations and especially in the dramatic quality he imparts to them, but was also the first to outline for us the general forms of comedy. . . ." Children's imitation is Aristotle's premise for his mimetic theory of art. If for Vico imitation is a spontaneous perception, or, to paraphrase slightly what he says, a perception "in a certain way 'real'" ("in un certo modo reale") (NS/217), for Aristotle imitation, which is instinctive in children and formal artifice in Homer, reflects the awareness that the artistic object is not true. Imitation, in brief, carries for Aristotle the sense of a separation between technique and passion. In the "Discovery of the True Homer" Vico attributes to Aristotle's *Poetics* (par. 1460a19) the notion that "only Homer knew how to invent poetic falsehoods" (NS/809).

It is precisely in this understanding of mimesis as artifice that Aristotle grounds his distinction between history and poetry. Poetry, Aristotle says, is more philosophical than history, in that history relates probable and necessary events and particulars, whereas poetry expresses the universal and need not confine itself to the paradigms of historical narratives. This Aristotelian distinction between poetry and history was correctly understood, according to Vico, by Lodovico Castelvetro in his *Poetica d'Aristotile vulgarizzata et sposta* (1576): "The truth is understood by Castelvetro, that history must have come first and then poetry, for history is a simple statement of the truth but poetry is an imitation besides" (NS/812). Yet Castelvetro's distinction, for all its subtlety, does not touch the heart of the issue: "This scholar, though otherwise most acute, failed to make use of this clue to discover the true principles of poetry by combining it with the other philosophical proof which follows next. Inasmuch as the poets came certainly before the vulgar historians, the first history must have been po-etic" (NS/812–13).

It is time for me to draw some provisional conclusions from this present exposition of "Discovery of the True Homer," which has increasingly ac-quired the shape of a fundamental critique of the history of criticism and theory, from Plato to Gravina, from Aristotle to Castelvetro. Poetry's su-periority over the other various forms of knowledge, which is constantly highlighted by Vico, is flanked by the radical speculation about the iden-tity of poetry and history. What does Vico mean in saying that history is poetry and poetry is history?

At the heart of this identity there lies the insight in the inseparable bond between the *logos* (fable, language) and the idea (NS/238), the thing and the sign. More to the point, one can appropriately suppose that the iden-tity between poetry and history entails the view that history is a sumptu-ous spectacle of memory, a fabulous pageant much like the one Helen shows Priam from the gates of the besieged city of Troy; or even very much like the phantasmagoria of the future and the divination of the past into which Aeneas plunges in the dream of Book VI of the *Aeneid*. Vico, who steadily plumbs the mythical imaginative design of historical facts (and of fictions as facts) would most likely agree with this preliminary suggestion. Nor would he probably challenge the notion that the identity between his-tory and poetry resonates with the Ciceronian insight of humanist histori-ographers, such as Poggio, Bruni, Machiavelli, and Guicciardini for whom rhetoric is history, and history is discourse, the locus of debates and choices that rhetoric embodies, and a tragicomical theater of many voices.

But to say that history is poetry (and vice versa) is certainly to say that history, like the Homeric poems that stand at the center of Vico's thought, is irreducible to a unified plot or to a purely tragic or purely comical ac-tion, as one would infer from the neo-Aristotelian, Renaissance prescrip-tions of comedy. Homer's poetry brings about this discovery to Vico. Like the disjointed, contradictory, episodic structure of the Homeric poems, history is made up of loosely arranged parts, anonymous and discordant voices, and heterogeneous happenings that, in their spontaneous, blind oc-currences, resist a harmonious unified totalization if not imposed by the political will of a tyrant.

Only after examining the Homeric question and only after discovering the truth about Homer is it possible for Vico to move on to political and juridical subjects which are the matter of Books IV and V of the *New Sci-ence*. The transition in no way implies an esthetization of history or a politi-cization of art—two formulas of the current sociological vocabulary which are inadequate for Vico in so far as they signal a homogenous transposition from one order of experience to another. In the *New Science* the distinct categories of poetry, politics, law, history, and so forth, are woven together and overlap. But as the history of dramatic and lyrical forms, which is the appendix to the "Discovery of the True Homer," shows, each form keeps its distinct individuality. From this perspective, Vico could only tell the story of his "Discovery of the True Homer" as a philosopher, from outside of poetry, as if the limits between poetry and the critical arts (and philosophy) could not be erased.

Vico's critical or philosophical distance from the object of his meditation allows him to clarify the divergence between Homer and himself. To say it differently: it allows him to take stock of the ethical and epistemological consequences of his reading of Homer. Plato, as has been shown, overhauls the Homeric encyclopedia in favor of a moral poetry—possibly in favor of his own myth making—that would open the way to the contemplation of justice. Vico does not intend to get past Homer, for the ethics of Homeric poetry lies precisely in its representation of many worlds, worlds other than one's own, which always mark the limits of one's projects and schemes. To be aware of worlds that transcend one's own permits one to attain the vantage point of a global understanding of history. The claim of Homer's primacy in Vico's poetic philosophy intends to rescue the principle of heterogeneity from all forms of authoritarian (political or critical) manipulation. But does Homer really have a global understanding of history? And how can Vico really claim that understanding for himself?

On the frontispiece of the *New Science* the statue of Homer is shown standing among the debris of history. Homer, whose name means "blind," turns his back to the source of light and he seems to look inward. If the fact that his back is turned to the light is a flagrant reversal of the sage in Plato's cave, the blindness suggests that Homer does not have a transcendent viewpoint from where he can see and organize the whole of history. Homer, if he really existed as an individual, would be a common man. As it is, Homer is caught within his own history and his own "world view" or blind vision.

The poet, who is the maker of history, is blind to the origins and effects of his own work. Unlike Homer, however, Vico elaborates a trans-historical science. He has a view, indeed a worldview, and a "style" (since style is a certain way of looking at the world) that presupposes the transcendence of his own particular culture and allows him to discover—as Book IV of the *New Science* does discover—the "course that nations run," which is to say, the general succession of radically different worldviews. If Vico were a philosophical relativist, he would never be able to claim for himself the perspective afforded by his trans-historical science.

Standing above Homer, the emblem of the *New Science* shows God's eye whose rays of light are refracted with perfect geometry on a woman's breast. She is Metaphysics, or Lady Philosophy, and from her the light radiates there on Homer's back. That eye, that viewpoint Vico calls Providence—the *pro*vident light—is simultaneously outside and inside the unfolding of history. The chapters that follow will return to these issues. That eye is the epistemologically necessary, absolute perspective rescuing history from its apparent randomness. Without it human history would be the map of tragic plots which Vico recognized, underneath the fictions of the law, by the name of Machiavelli. The argument by necessity moves to an examination of the politics of law and political pathology.

Chapter 7

THE THEATER OF THE LAW

AFTER DISCUSSING the Homeric question in Book III of the *New Science* Vico turns his attention to the "Course that Nations Run." Once the question of poetry, the Homeric question, has been, so to speak, settled, Book IV can begin to tackle a vast and intricate range of concerns, namely, the question of law, its original foundation in poetry, and its links with force, power, and political forms. Throughout the *New Science* Vico's thinking is at the boundary, at the crossroads where diverse branches of the human sciences—history, political institutions, language—meet and diverge. It is a thought that systematically situates itself at the elusive point where the luster of rational construction is wrapped in the shadows of faint memories and phantasmagorias. Now, in Book IV of the *New Science* Vico moves overtly to consider boundaries themselves, which for him are the focus of the law.

Book III of the *New Science*, let us quickly recall, casts poetry—specifically Homeric poetry—as the imaginative circle within which all knowledge and wisdom of ancient Greece are contained. The section the "Discovery of the True Homer" is followed by—and its concerns are extended in—an appendix that describes the "History of the Dramatic and Lyric Poets." By delving into the history of the most obscure antiquity Vico rejects the philosophers' contradictory views on the birth of tragedy. He dismisses as false the assertion that Amphion discovered the dithyramb (and that the dithyramb was a chorus in praise of Dionysius). The rival claims that Aeschylus was the first tragic poet, that Pausanias wrote tragedies under the injunction of Bacchus, or that Thespis was their originator are equally discarded. Vico holds that lyric, tragic, and comic poetry comes into being during the vintage season with "satura," ancient tragedy about "monsters of two natures" (NS/910), or the satyr play, which originally is a "dish made of various kinds of foods" (NS/910). The satyr play is a rudimentary, omnibus form of drama. In Greek myth the satyr and the Silenus—who is the foster father of Dionysus and who is associated with the Italian Faunus—is a creature of the wild, part man and part beast. The monstrosity of the satyr and the nature of the satyr, such as Pan (who signifies "tutto"—the whole, and whom philosophical mythography interprets as the universe [NS/910], stand behind Vico's impulse to cast poetic and theatrical representation as the foundation of political realities.

Satire's hybrid rhetoric or mixture of modes (it is the *genus mixtum*—the mixed genre—that in Vico's time reappears as the operatic melodrama) accords well, Vico adds, with the heroes' belief about the plebeians' own mixed and bestial nature.

Vico's theory of the *satura* and of the Homeric poems is the backdrop of his discussion of the "Course that Nations Run" in Book IV of the *New Science*. The very title of this section announces the premise of his science: the insight into the mobility of the imagination is flanked by the principle of the mobility of time and history. Nothing endures for Vico in a definitive shape, and he will chart the internal fluidity of each social structure through which all nations in history run their courses. There is a tantalizing phrase by Borges that best conveys the sense of Vico's transition from archaeology of imaginary forms to the history of nations. "Unfortunately," writes Borges, "the world exists. Unfortunately, I am Borges." What Borges laments is the inexorable limit of the reality principle, its scandal for and resistance to merely imaginary constructions.

Vico does not lament over the resistance hard reality presents to the flights of the imagination, as does Borges with his elegiac reflection. For Vico the real is indistinguishable from the simulacra of the imagination and from rational thought processes. The general intent of Book IV, more precisely, is to trace the three stages of history's institutional forms. These three stages—the age of the gods, the age of the heroes, and the age of reflection or the modern age—are three crystallizations of different ways of thinking, which, in turn, express themselves as different social and symbolic forms. By deploying fragments of history, myth, and legend, he shows that there are three kinds of natures, of natural law, of civil states or commonwealths, languages, jurisprudence, authority, and reason. These triadic units, which ceaselessly repeat themselves, are all embraced by one overarching unity, the unity of Providence, which informs and gives life to this world of nations.

I shall return later to the number metaphor (possibly Joachistic and/or Dantesque in origin) Vico deploys here. For now let me remark that the age of the gods is the age of the theological poets, when men were fierce and cruel, and by a "powerful deceit of the imagination" there was a fear of the gods (NS/916). The age of heroes is characterized by men's flight "from the infamous and bestial promiscuity in order to save themselves from the strife it entailed, and had taken refuge in, their [the heroes'] asylums" (NS/917). The third age, on the other hand, is the human, or our own reflective, age, when rational human beings are "intelligent and hence modest, benign, and reasonable, recognizing for laws conscience, reason, and duty" (NS/918). Although the third age is marked by the decay of the imagination, by the rise of methodical doubt and Cartesian pure intellection, Vico also defines it as the age of the human law which is "dictated by fully developed human reason" (NS/924) whereby we understand ourselves and our world.

The link between law and reason introduces another relation, that between law and politics. Corresponding to the realm of the human law there is the time of human governments, "in which, in virtue of the equality of the intelligent nature which is the proper nature of man, all are accounted equal under the laws, inasmuch as all are born free in their cities" (NS/927). This beneficent age of human jurisprudence looks at the truth of the facts themselves and "benignly bends the rule of the law to all requirements of the equity of the causes" (NS/940). In short, law makes all citizens equal: this equality is available under free popular governments and under monarchical rule (NS/927). If elsewhere in the *New Science* Vico dismantles the assumptions of Cartesian rationality for making the abstract cogito the ground of being, he now retrieves the value of *ratio* as *law*, and law, in fact, provides the secure foundation for overcoming the political disintegration engendered by the self-interest dominant in the modern age.

Vico's belief that law could provide a global framework to give coherence to the social realities was laid out, as hinted earlier, in his juridical works, such as *De Universi Juris Uno Principio et Fine Uno* (*Of the One Principle and One Aim of Universal Law*) and *De Constantia Jurisprudentis* (*The Coherence of the Jurist*).[1] These two books are conceived as integral parts of a unitary, inclusive system, an encyclopedia, wherein each part coheres within an entire universe of laws. Written from the perspective of the Augustinian theology of fallen man, the treatise begins by evoking the virtues whereby human corruption is overcome. Natural law, according to the systems of Grotius, Selden, and Pufendorf, was instituted by divine Providence so that nations might be preserved from ruin. And since they had to live without truth and natural equity, Providence allows them to cleave to certainty and to civil equity. The model for this comprehensive study of laws comes to Vico from Grotius's *De Jure Belli ac Pacis*, whose aims, developed within a structure of the totality of the natural law, are seen as countering the reduction of justice to a utilitarian set of values available in texts such as Machiavelli's *The Prince*, Hobbes's *De Cive*, Spinoza's *Tractatus Theologico—Politicus*, and Bayle's *Dictionnaire*. Against Carneades, who argues that laws are social conventions, Vico endorses a Platonic justice, sovereign and transcendent, or "exterior justice."

Although it does not have the systematic structure of *De Uno*, the *New Science* explicitly recapitulates the theories expounded in the earlier tractate. It presupposes its formulations and extends its conceptual trajectory. One shared premise in the two works is that the study of the law consti-

---

[1] For Vico's legal thought and the traditions behind it see Donald R. Kelley, *The Foundations of Modern Historical Scholarship: Language, Law, and History* (New York: Columbia University Press, 1970).

tutes a "new science" ("nova scientia tentatur"). What exactly is "science" in this context? What casts law as a science is the universality of laws, their power to be the locus for a dialogue among disciplines such as politics, ethics, history, and poetry. In fact, the tools of this science are philology, which comprises grammar and history, and philosophy, two disciplines which join together the certainty of facts and the explanation of principles. Because at the heart of law lie questions such as the *truth* of facts, the majesty and solemnity of the law, the authority of counsel, and the political utility of the law, Vico steadily grapples with definitions about authority and power. Authority is originally conferred by ownership (NS/944); it then passes to the authority of solemn, binding formulas of the law (NS/945); and finally to the authority of juriconsults (those who are reputed to have wisdom) and who thrive under monarchies (NS/946).

Vico continues his review of the law by distinguishing between divine reason and reason of state (NS/948–49). In doing this, he focuses on the political wisdom of the Romans who kept laws secret from the common people and allowed them to be known by the few who understood what is essential to the conservation of mankind (NS/949). There is a history of duels, which are a form of divine judgment (and in which he evokes the combat between Menelaus and Paris, who had seduced Helen). Finally, Vico illustrates Roman doctrines about the protection of boundaries, social orders, and laws; he examines the political doctrine of Jean Bodin; and he concludes with a general metaphysical meditation on Pythagorean ideas of harmony and justice.

Clearly, the analytical profile of what could be called the empirical features of the law is a preamble to a thoroughgoing probing of the political origins and necessities of laws. More precisely, the discussion turns to the "Properties of the Heroic Aristocracies" (NS/980–1003). What emerges as the unifying conceptual concern of this section is the casting of the law as the necessary establishment of boundaries between conflicting parties. These boundaries mark the limit of liberties and are, however, ceaselessly encroached upon by contingent, unpredictable interactions of interests and classes. The first concern of the aristocratic commonwealths, as we are told, is to "set up boundaries to the fields" (NS/982) in order to halt the chaotic "promiscuity of things" in the natural, bestial state of the giants and of Polyphemus. The private institutions of family and marriages, and the public institutions of cities and nations were established to bring order out of the chaos and to protect the integrity of one's own world.

This insight into legal order coming out of and as a response to the anarchy and monstrosity of archaic life echoes Vico's earlier musings on the undifferentiated, indiscriminate chaos which is his myth of obscure origins. In his treatment of "Poetic Physics" Vico traces what can be called the mythopoetic imagination of origins, to which I shall return, from a political angle, in the next chapter. In this cosmic mythopoeia, at first there is chaos as the "confusion of human seeds in the state of the infamous promiscuity of women" (NS/688). This chaos is imaginatively figured both through Orcus, the "misshapen monster which devoured all things" and through Pan, the "wild god who is the divinity of all satyrs inhabiting not the cities but the forests; a character to which they reduced the impious vagabonds wandering through the great forest of the earth and having the appearance of men but the habits of abominable beasts" (NS/688). Physicists and philosophers conceive confusion variously as the universal seeds of things or, mistakenly, as the formed universe.

Within this generalized context law comes through as the civil light making visible and imposing a sensible, clear, formal conceptualization on the confusion to which Vico again will refer as the "nefarious promiscuity of things." In the aristocratic commonwealths laws were devised in order to preserve what Vico simply calls "potenza" (power) (NS/985), and by which he means ownerships, inheritance, family relationships, legitimate succession, testaments, and wealth within the order of the nobles. In Roman time, these institutions, however, are unsettled at the time of the agrarian laws when, as a result of intermarriages, the plebeians, who in Rome were first considered aliens, won ownership of the fields and the right of citizenship.

Because the validity of laws appears to be dependent on contingent political manipulations and changing interests, Vico now shifts his focus to what he calls the "science of interpretation" (NS/999) or hermeneutics of the law. In divine times the Roman optimates kept "la scienza delle lor leggi" (the science of their laws) secret. At stake is the power of the law which comes through as the law of power. The secret, or arcana, of the law, which amounts to not sharing privileges and keeping the laws from being appropriated "quanto meno e con tardi passi" (as little and as slowly as possible) (NS/1003), is crucial to maintaining social stability. The same principle, Vico goes on to say, explains why "l'imperio romano cotanto s'ingrandì e durò" (the Roman empire became so large and lasted so long) (NS/1003). Vico's argument, which, on the face of it, unveils the logic of power, turns into what seems a prudent prescription for all times: as all political theorists agree, he says, the Roman model ought to be followed by all states that wish to become large and to last (NS/1003). And he concludes the section remarking that neither Polybius nor Machiavelli really understood why Rome built "il maggior imperio del mondo" (the world's greatest empire) (NS/1003).

The link between interpretation and laws, which emerges from the Roman will to keep the "words of the Twelve Tables" (NS/999) from shifting from their original and proper meaning, suggests that for Vico laws are invested with the power undergirding the performative language of the poetic sublime. As happens with God's sublime language or the rhetorician's incantations, laws have the power to found reality and shape people's moral dispositions. There is, thus, a regime (or rules for the control) of meanings, although meanings are forever shifting. Consistent with this, Vico acknowledges that historical conflicts of legal interpretation both reflect ever-shifting configurations of power and seek to control the turbulence of power struggles. Can this violence among social classes or state of war among classes and nations ever be eliminated or controlled by laws which themselves belong to the coercive order?

Grotius, along with Selden and Pufendorf, elaborates a system of judicial ethics in his *De Jure Belli ac Pacis*. He bases his ethics on the authority of the natural law of the people, which is part of the eternal order and is implanted in man's heart and reason. Through his religious rationalism Grotius seeks to redress and contain the realities of war: in peace nations violate boundaries and they make wars which exceed all limits of the law. The law of nations he drafts, in the tradition of Aquinas, Baldus, and the Spanish neo-Scholastics such as Vitoria and Suarez, derives from Aquinas's notion that "law is an ordinance of reason for the common good" (*Summa Theologiae*, Ia IIae, q. 90, art. 4). As has been discussed in Chapter 3, Grotius intends to legislate war by upholding the principle of the just war (which is allowed in order to secure redress) and its legality.

For Vico, Grotius is a unique thinker in that he perceived the necessity of constructing a system of universal law wherein empirical, certain facts, and true, universal principles shape the understanding of the law. Yet these are severe limitations to his legal thought. Grotius's theory of natural law is anti-historical in that it posits an innocent state of nature, the dwellers of which are the "semplicioni di Grozio" (the simpletons of Grotius) (NS/338), while Vico's historical vision rejects the idea of fixity and perfection of the natural state. Vico is closer to Hobbes's conviction that the state of nature is war, wherein human beings live in a present threat of aggression. Like Grotius, Vico views law as a relation of forces, and he challenges the practice of war not only in terms of legal formulation but also from the standpoint of an irenic consciousness rooted in the Platonic and Pythagorean principle of a transcendent justice.

In the wake of Grotius, Vico knows that, within the sphere of immanence, law is an exercise of force. It belongs to anomalous social configurations and it sanctions the mobile power relations between masters and servants. The law disciplines and seeks to stabilize these relations while at the same time it exposes forces that are in a perpetual condition of change, that act upon one another and that resist one another. In this disciplinary model of jurisprudence, which Vico lucidly lays out in a section on "Pun-

ishments, Wars, and the Order of Numbers" (NS/1020–1026) there is no
limit to the universal, eternal rights of man which Grotius had optimistically posited for man in a state of nature.

Yet for Vico, as for Grotius, laws (which, let me stress this point, are
particular and contingent forces of distribution of power) have the property of bending force. The deflecting of force occurs within monarchical
forms of government. The proposition leads Vico to devote a substantial
portion of his discussion to Jean Bodin's theory that monarchy is the government institution best suited to human nature in the reflective third age.
Vico agrees with Bodin's conviction. He illustrates Bodin's idea with the
historical evidence of a cosmopolis that was achieved under a monarch: the
world was construed "as a single city" (NS/1023) under Antoninus Pius
and Alexander the Great. Vico is at pains, however, to refute Bodin's notion that governments were first monarchical, then popular, and finally aristocratic. Earlier in the text Vico contests Machiavelli's reading of the
Roman empire. Now he debates Machiavelli's categories of fraud and violence (NS/1011), and he argues that monarchies, which desire all their
subjects to be made equal by their laws, come into being as remedies to
seditions and to civil wars produced by competing interests. His argument
is in the direction of mixed forms of government, but his main point is that
political unity is not a given. On the contrary, plurality precedes unity,
which, as the discussion of the unity of the Homeric poems has shown, always comes after the fragmentary heterogeneity of historical and textual
configuration.

The relationships between unity and heterogeneity, justice and laws, empirical history and philosophical principles occupy the last section of Book
IV. As always in the *New Science*, Vico's arguments are at first clustered in
a coherent, empirical context of relations followed by generalized inferences and broader conclusions from within the framework of those piecemeal relations. The first element that structures Vico's process of abstraction and generalization is the corollary that "the Ancient Roman Law was
a serious poem, and the ancient jurisprudence a severe kind of poetry, . . .
and how, among the Greeks, Philosophy was born of the Laws"
(NS/1027–1045). The claim of the identity between law and poetry is
hardly new in the narrative economy of the *New Science*: it was already laid
out in advance in the myth of Hermes who gave laws and letters to the
Egyptians and who brings back souls from Orcus, the "lawless state" where
clients are being scattered and lost (NS/605). But what are the implications of this identity? And what has happened to the notion of "science"?

As a way of clarifying the relation between law and poetry, the corollary
is introduced by a pithy reference to a distinction between the "certain"
and the "true": "Above all, by the axiom that as men are naturally drawn
to the pursuit of the true, their desire of it, when they cannot attain it,

causes them to cling to the certain, *mancipations* began *vera manu*, with the actual hand, that is with real force, since force is abstract and hand is concrete" (NS/1027). In order to grasp the complex structure of this metaphor of the hand as a symbol of power (as well as the relationship between figure and letter—the concrete and the abstract, the certain and the true—that the passage discusses), it is well to recall Vico's definition of the certain and the true.

The certain in the law is defined as "an obscurity of judgement" backed by authority, as the particularized, individual matter, that which in civil equity Ulpian defines as a "kind of probable judgement" (NS/321). On the other hand, the true in the laws "is a certain light and splendor with which natural reason illuminates them" (NS/324). To say it differently, the certain embraces the set of heterogeneous, empirical facts and the particularities of words, which are objects of philological analysis. The true is the universal idea, the perfect form of equity and justice, which philosophers have elaborated for over two thousand years.

This distinction between the certain and the true develops by a reflection on symbolic language (on symbols of power and powers of the symbolic) and it is seen as a variant between the concrete and the abstract. Mancipation, which is the formal act of enslaving, is, at first, a literal empirical hand—*vera manu* or a "real force." (Vico goes on to explore "usucapion," which is the act of claiming title by the physical possession of the thing possessed.) As the savagery of the times began to recede, force became symbolic or figured. Hence, those elected to power had power bestowed upon them by the laying of hands on their heads. In later times, powers already bestowed were acclaimed by the ceremonial gesture of the raising of hands. By the same token, the original, literal practices of reprisals and revenge were symbolically transformed into denunciations, which were a feigning of force or a way of preserving the solemnity of the physical action (NS/1032).

By reflecting on this exchange of properties between law and symbolic acts Vico goes to the root of the discourse on truth. The text repeatedly records the historical decadence of the literal, the originary metaphor of truth which is subjected to time's erosion. In archaic times the metaphoric representations were taken to be literally true, and the statement inevitably grafts the question of truth onto the terrain of signs and language. The concern with symbolic language makes the meditation on poetry and law necessary. Law is a form of sublime poetry because its utterances are believed and because it creates reality. But Vico does not keep his argument within the precincts of a merely formal description. Rather, the text moves to the specifically political sphere.

The temporal movement from literal acts of violence to the world of ceremonies and symbolic representations leads Vico to reflect on the marketplace where mimetic impersonations—akin to the representation, which is the stuff of poetry—occur. In the marketplace, as in a theater, masked figures/characters appear: Vico calls them "persone," persons, who are enigmatically dressed up to be identified in the role they play (NS/1033). Vico stresses that *personare* does not mean "to resound everywhere"; rather, it derives from *personari*, which means to be dressed up in "skins of a beast or even to feed on meat of hunted animals" (NS/1034). Semantically, *persona* is both a theatrical and a legal term. Hobbes in his *Leviathan* (Part I, Chapter XVI) explains the word *persona* as the hollow mask of the actor on the stage and extends it to mean the representation of oneself and one's attorney in a court of law.

Against Hobbes's reduction of the court to a metaphorical theater, Vico derives the word *persona* from *personari* (and not *personare*). *Personari*, as Vico conjectures, means the appearance in the marketplace of what the Italians call *personaggi* (characters) or a hero's wearing of skins or the family coat of arms, such as Hercules did. This *persona* or mask is an imaginative corporeal form, a simultaneously fantastic and empirical representation by a primitive mind incapable of abstractions. The aim of such a mimetic impersonation is both to conceal and reveal the power of the hero's family, and, thereby, open oneself up to the risky possibility of violence. The theatrical stratagem of the actor, moreover, is itself a trope which originates from the real display of power in the marketplace.

Exactly because of this property of employing corporeal forms to communicate abstract concepts, Vico affirms that ancient jurisprudence was originally poetry. Like poetry, jurisprudence simulates as facts stories which have never happened, just as it simulates the dead as if they were alive, or the living as if they were dead, as when it deals with legacies and heredity (NS/1036). Ancient Roman law, says Vico with admirable economy, "was at the beginning a serious poem" (NS/1037) that was represented in the forum. It is in the Athenian agora or marketplace and in the Roman forum that laws originate. In the representations that take place in the marketplace, however, the uniqueness of symbolic signs dissolves not in imposture or theatrical simulation but in the absence of univocal referents. As the open space of traffic and transactions, the marketplace (as Spinoza's mercantilism understands) traces the circle of all possible material exchanges, and it brings to the fore the existence of separate worlds with their possibly colliding viewpoints and interests.

The divinity presiding over the marketplace is Mercury, the hidden god of discourse, who is the bearer of news, who joins together Earth and Hades, and is the inventor of laws and letters. In the marketplace, which is the public forum and theatrical stage marked by its own autonomous order and by the plurality of oblique discourses (and which is where the Homeric epics originate in a contradictory plurality of fables), barriers between competing interests collapse. One thing is clear: in this space laws are devised to rationalize, counter, and limit the possible chaos of exchange. To say it differently, the solemn formulas of the law seek to establish a dialogical or hermeneutical relation between strangers. From this standpoint law, in its rigor and in its majesty, is the acknowledgment of an otherness transcending one's own world, of opposite interests turning together in a harmonious conversation, and of the tragic potential lurking in every encounter.

Vico does not focus here on the relation between law and tragedy, on what could be called the tragic impossibility of the law, or on the recognition that when different worlds or different worldviews come together from their remote distances, the relation between them appears as the impossibility of a relation. Rather, he goes on to forge a clear link between laws and the imagination. In the *Laws* (Book IV) Plato explicitly joins together law and esthetics in order to exalt law's role. The harmony of the city, at which the legislation aims by molding man's character, can be achieved by the teaching of the choral songs and the ancient round dance of the Greeks. For Vico, by contrast, what joins together law and poetry is the imagination. This is the faculty that accounts for the vast machinery of tropes and fictions whereby men appear masked in the marketplace and *iura imaginaria*, rights invented by the imagination, are contrived. The fictions of the law (*antiqui iuris fabulas*) are fables designed to preserve the gravity of the laws. Yet, the origin of poetic jurisprudence lies in the imagination's ability to personify rights, such as inheritance, and in this sense, the fictions of the law are truths under masks: laws are symbols of power.

The concluding paragraphs of Book IV of the *New Science* will further probe the question of the truth of the law by concentrating, as we shall see, on the relation between fiction and truth, laws and justice, the certain and the true. The narrative turns into a history of philosophy of the law (and of the legality of philosophy) told philosophically. This mode of theoretical inquiry, which is appropriate to the third age when intellect is sovereign, sketches out the transcendent foundations of a mathematical or Pythagorean justice.

As if almost to suggest that laws and mathematical justice are the foundation of his idea of science, Vico begins his discussion by raising to prominence the principle of the eternity or "indivisibility of rights" (NS/1039) upheld by the interpreters of Roman law. The legality of the interpretation (and the legality of philosophy) is rooted in the acknowledgment of the eternal nature of rights. More to the point, the domain of laws is projected as a unified, scientific knot of causes, axioms, and facts, whereby the basic propositions of the law are tested by facts, and facts, in turn, are explained within the theoretical horizon of the law. This reflection on the problematics of the interpretation of laws announces the genuine direction of Vico's thought, which consists in his effort to work out a new conception of science or philosophy appropriate to the reality of man's historical existence, wherein all truths are historically conditioned. If the Cartesian model of science posits the possibility of objective knowledge, Vico proceeds to write the history of a philosophy, which steadily transacts the relation between particulars and universals. Such a history is a practical activity in its orientation and challenges the possibility of an objective knowledge.

The account begins by evoking Socrates, who adumbrates the consciousness that laws precede philosophy, or as the text has it, Socrates is the figure who found "universals by induction; that is, by collecting uniform particulars which go to make up a genus of that in respect of which the particulars are uniform among themselves" (NS/1040). By induction, which is Bacon's empirical observation of particular facts, Socrates arrives at the general principle of "an equal utility common to all." Plato, on the other hand, by observing the debates in the public assemblies, sees the rationality of justice as the overcoming of particular utilitarian passions. Aristotle's *Ethics* (1132b) picks up Plato's teaching in the *Republic* (Book VII) and articulates an immanent Pythagorean idea of the unity of justice. Vico refers to Aristotle's conceptualization of two forms of justice: distributive justice and commutative justice, "the latter employing arithmetical proportion and the former geometrical" (NS/1042). Arithmetical proportion is depicted through the emblem of the goddess of justice, Astraea, who in Greek and Roman myth is the fabled star of the golden age. Geometrical proportion, on the other hand, regulates the system of punishments either as a double (*duplio*) or as the like (*lex talionis*), and this is called "Pythagorean justice."

This compressed synoptic account of the Platonic and Pythagorean foundation of justice gives way to a reflection that recapitulates the essence of Vico's thought:

> From all the above we conclude that these principles of metaphysics, logic, and morals issued from the market place of Athens. From Solon's advice to the Athenians, "Know thyself," came forth the popular commonwealths; from the popular commonwealths the laws; and from the laws emerged philosophy; and Solon, who had been wise in vulgar wisdom, came to be held wise in esoteric wisdom. This may serve as a specimen of the history of philosophy told philosophically, and a last reproof, of the many brought forth in this work, against Polybius, who said that if there were philosophers in the world there would be no need of religions. For [the fact is that] if there had not been religions and hence commonwealths, there would have been no philosophers in

the world, and if human institutions had not been thus conducted by divine providence, there would have been no idea of either science or virtue. (NS/1043; NS/416)

Once again Vico tells us that all sciences are grounded in the open-ended and yet circumscribed horizon of the shadowy domain of Hermes: the marketplace. He also tells us that laws are prior to philosophy, but all of them have their source in Solon's maxim, "know thyself" (*nosce te ipsum*). Vico's science is not like the natural sciences, which are constituted by making entities fit a preestablished mold of objectiveness. True science is wisdom, as Vico redefines it: it starts with one's own self and one's own historical existence, and it ends with it as its point of arrival.

Solon's "know thyself" certainly intends to echo and correct the principle of Cartesian self-consciousness. The Cartesian atemporal, ahistorical subjectivity is here replaced by the awareness that the particularity of one's own self yields and leads to the generality of popular commonwealths, to laws, and to philosophy. Historically, the injunction, "know thyself," which is said to originate with the Pythagoreans, is associated with the Delphic oracle, Solon, and Socratic self-knowledge or ironic knowledge of one's ignorance. The meaning of the dictum, which is a call for the moral virtue of binding of self or self-control, is made clear by Plato and Plato's Socrates, for whom "*gnothi s'eauton*" enjoins one to be modest and practice moderation. Later in the Renaissance Pico della Mirandola, who is in many ways a theorist of freedom, interprets the oracular phrase in the expansive, Neoplatonic framework of the analogy of microcosm and macrocosm. Rather than marking the boundaries of self, "*nosce te ipsum*," Pico says, "urges and encourages us to the investigation of all nature, of which the nature of man is both the connecting link and, so to speak, the 'mixed bowl.' For he who knows himself in himself knows all things in himself, as Zoroaster first wrote, and then Plato in his *Alcibiades*."[2]

These two strains of interpretation—Platonic and Neoplatonic— converge in Vico who claims that self-knowledge engenders the all-encompassing idea of justice. For Vico law is the search for measure which, as such, emerges from the decorous binding of one's impulses. It can be said that for Vico the movement from self-knowledge to laws and to justice implies a fundamental knowledge: namely, that we never really know ourselves unless we know where we stand in relation to the gods. There is always a gap between who we are and what we understand. Philosophers act in ignorance of the true scheme of things when they do not know, as Polybius, Bayle, Spinoza, and Hobbes do not seem to know, that man is

---

[2] Pico, *On the Dignity of Man*, in *The Renaissance Philosophy of Man*, eds. E. Cassirer, P. O. Kristeller, J. H. Randall, Jr. (Chicago: University of Chicago Press, 1969), p. 235.

nothing before the gods. In this sense, Solon's "know thyself" traces the transition from ignorance to knowledge as the limiting of oneself, and yet, by this self-knowledge man appears as a perpetual enigma to oneself.

No doubt, Vico's unflinching concern with the ways in which we understand ourselves and our world, which is the burden of the *New Science*, edges toward the insights of tragic discourse. It is in the Greek tragic theater (*Oedipus, Antigone, Iphigenia in Tauris*, etc.) that, through reversal and *anagnoresis*, the knowledge tragic characters acquire concerns themselves and the justice of the gods. In the process, the insignificance and arbitrariness of the law is exposed. Vico does not confront in this extended discussion of the law in Book IV what Greek or Spanish baroque tragedy always ends up acknowledging: the impossibility of the law. He concludes his argument by a summary rational clarification and definition of legal obligations in these our human times. The practice of transactions, contracts, pacts, and transfers—which are literally metaphors signaling both the establishment of boundaries and the modality of relations in the chaotic, undifferentiated world of the marketplace—is asserted as the necessary rationality in the politics of the third age. By a reversal of the genealogy of laws from commonwealths, it is as if the authority of the law underpins the authority of the state. Nonetheless, Vico knows only too well that tragic transgressions occur when different realms of experience meet and the rule of law is observed.

One image is evoked repeatedly and almost obsessively in the section on "Poetic Economy": the refugee or guest. In this section Vico's primary aim is to tell the story of the origin of all cities, which he finds in families, colonies, and asylums. The origin of the families is in the *famuli:* at the time of "infamous promiscuity of things and of women" Grotius's "simpletons" and Pufendorf's "abandoned men" could save themselves from Hobbes's "violent men" by having recourse to the altars of the strong (NS/553). The colonies, on the other hand, were originally a "crowd of workers who till the soil for their daily sustenance" (NS/560). Vico goes on to highlight the origin of the cities in asylums. Cadmus, we are told, founded Thebes, the most ancient city of Greece, as an asylum (NS/561). Theseus founded Athens "on the altar of the unhappy," which is the epithet for the unbound world of impious vagabonds. So does Romulus with Rome. "Asylums" were "the first hospices in the world, and those who were there received were the first guests or strangers of the first cities" (NS/561).

The *New Science*, as I have been arguing throughout this study, is punctuated by figurations of separateness, of impenetrable barriers between synchronic and yet distant cultures. The counterpoint to these narratives of separation is the marketplace, the assembly, the university, the ritual games, marriages, and, as is the case in the quotation above, the ageless myth of the strangers, guests, and refugees crossing the threshold of one's own world. In all these experiences of association (economic, political, cultural, etc.) different worlds suddenly draw near to one another, and this is the beginning of the law. As the Roman jurists understood, the law is the sharing of every divine and human right (NS/598).

In the encounter between stranger and host the ancients saw the enigmatic mark of fate. Zeus is the guest-god who stands behind all strangers and avenges any wrong to which they are subjected. When Ulysses unexpectedly arrives from unknown lands to Phaecia, a wonder seizes Nausicaa and the king. The same thing happens in the encounter between Aeneas and Dido (NS/611). The stranger, in Greek texts, is the one who enters the city—the space of defined structures—and with him a new world enters the familiar perimeter of the polis. The stranger's arrival reveals the existence of worlds other than one's own, each world unknown to the other, and yet each accessible to the other. In this encounter, which the god favors, stranger and host exchange the gift of friendship, a precious inviolable gift that would bind them forever. While all this is true, Vico also perceives that the encounter between stranger and host puts in place a strange relation, a relation of strangeness.

After recalling the first commerce in the world (which he takes to be the etymology of Mercury) (NS/606), the meaning of the Greek *nomos*, and the conflicts between Roman nobles and plebeians (who were considered foreigners), Vico drafts the archaeology of civil turbulence, the enmity between citizens and guests in Rome. The necessity of new laws, the shift of the Roman state from aristocratic to popular, and the making of new cities stem from the presence of the strangers and refugees within the walls of the city. With philological meticulousness Vico goes on to say that the word for stranger, *hostis*, "means both guest or stranger and enemy" (NS/611). Language, the element common to law and poetry, does not have a transparent, univocal sense. One word, thus, contains two contradictory and radically divergent senses, two meanings alien to and antagonistic with each other.

From the tragic and dim ambiguity of language we get the most exacting imperative of moral order and piety: the right of asylum. But where the law of boundary reigns there begins the border of tragic violations. Thus, transgressions are the obverse side or invisible secret of laws' moral order. Vico continues by evoking the story of a mythic stranger, Paris, who is both guest and enemy of the royal house of Argos. Welcomed by Menelaus, who observes the laws of hospitality, Paris kidnaps Helen. Paris's tragic violation of the law of hospitality is repeated in the story of Theseus, who kidnaps Ariadne; in that of Jason and Medea; and in that of Aeneas and Dido (NS/611). Tragic depths open up and unsettle the balance of justice at the very moment that the laws of Zeus are observed. The impasse of the law allows Vico to sound the deep sources of the tragic. In a way, the tragic experience of literature, which remains inaccessible to critical reason, begins at the boundary of the law.

This tragic potential of the law is not the endpoint of Vico's discourse. The most conspicuous path of his thought, which always is carved against the awareness of mortal hazards and human ferociousness, leads us beyond the threshold of the tragic and signals how the tragic can be transcended. The Renaissance and baroque vision, from which we glimpse the pitiless, delirious illusoriness of the real that Borges grasped, brings us to a tragic impasse. Grotius had sought to devise ways to hold in the excesses of power by legislating war and peace. For Vico, on the other hand, the tragic, which is a secondary form of representation, can be overcome by a retrieval of the complexity of archaic satire, which is to say, by the restoration of the plurality of discourses available in marketplaces and public assemblies. The tragic, thus, is not abolished; rather, it is located in a broader and transcendent context.

The hybrid unity of the *satura* presides over the unity of justice. Because unity is the matrix of justice, Vico roots his reflections on the two notions, and we must grasp what unity implies. Unity in itself is not a number; it is the source and origin of numbers, and, as such, it is the heart of Pythagorean justice. As Vico's own *De Uno* exemplifies, the unity of justice must be rethought and unveiled as the crossing point of endless contradictions. Macrobius's reflection on unity is a source for Vico: "One is called *monas*, that is unity, and is both male and female, odd and even, itself not a number, but the source and origin of numbers. This monad, the beginning and ending of all things, yet itself not knowing a beginning or ending, refers to the supreme god."[3]

Understandably, the underlying concern of Book IV of the *New Science* is to cast unity as the principle of all things. A broad mathematical grid is deployed to show how the totality of experience can become an intelligible and unified order of relations. The text makes references to arithmetical and geometrical proportions that were analyzed earlier in this chapter; it discusses duels or *duella* (wars) as a quantitative form of justice (NS/959); more poignantly, it refers to Astraea, the myth of the golden age, which is understood as the time when, as Vico says, paraphrasing the *Book of Wisdom*, man became aware of "weight . . . measure . . . and number" so that Pythagoras put the essence of the human soul in numbers. Finally, the order of political institutions is illustrated mathematically by the order of numbers, which Vico calls "the simplest abstractions":

> But lastly we wish to show how, on this concrete and complex order of human civil institutions, we may superimpose the order of numbers, which are the

[3] Macrobius, *Commentary on the Dream of Scipio*, trans. William H. Stahl (New York: Columbia University Press, 1952), Book I, Chapter vi, pars. 7–8, pp. 100–101.

simplest abstractions. Governments began with the one, in the family monarchies; passed to the few in the heroic aristocracies; went on to the many and the all in the popular commonwealths, in which all or the majority make up the body politic; and finally in civil monarchies return again to the one. By the nature of numbers we cannot conceive a more adequate division or another order than one, few, many and all, with the few, many and all retaining, each in its kind, the principle of the one; just as numbers consist of indivisibles according to Aristotle [*Metaphysics*, 1085b 22], and, when we have passed the all, we must begin again with the one. And thus humanity is all contained between the family monarchies and the civil monarchies. (NS/1026)

Let me stress, in passing, the rigor and economy of Vico's conceptualizations. This extensive reflection on number and on the units that compose reality shows that Vico directs his thought—as much as Pythagoras, Solon, Socrates, Plato, and Aristotle had done—to remove all randomness from the thought of justice. The atomistic idea that unity lies in the multiplicity of things and that the one is the many is rejected as a theory of the unceasing war of the elements caught in a perpetual flow, what Vico calls the "Chaos of the nefarious promiscuity of seeds." To the atomists' conceptualizations Vico juxtaposes the Pythagorean and Platonic belief in a unified, intelligible whole which can be grasped by mathematics, because, as Pythagoras knew, "all is number."

Although Vico acknowledges, as the Pythagoreans do, that unity is the essence and substance of all things and that all numbers retain the principle of unity, he, nonetheless, mounts a critique of what could be called the modern version of the Pythagorean idea of political justice. In his mind the chief theorist of such a vision is Jean Bodin. Bodin's *Six livres de la république* discusses the state's "justice harmonique" in terms of an order achievable through the application of Pythagoras's distributive and commutative forms of justice.[4] Vico deeply admires Bodin, whom he calls "equally learned as jurist and as statesman" (NS/952). He is impressed by Bodin's historical work on the institutions of the ancient Romans. And he praises Bodin's redefinition of Machiavelli's and Hobbes's view of power: unlike the prince, the king has to be subjected to the laws of the land. Yet Vico criticizes Bodin for believing that monarchy—the rule by the one—precedes aristocratic commonwealths and that monarchy alone integrates all forms of justice. Bodin's error, more precisely, lies, first, in his not fully grasping the Machiavellian realism in the formula that governments come into being "either by force or by fraud" (NS/1011). Thus, the critique of Bodin foreshadows Vico's complex relation to Machiavelli that we shall ex-

---

[4] See on this Simeon K. Heninger, Jr., *Touches of Sweet Harmony. Pythagorean Cosmology and Renaissance Poetics* (San Marino, Calif.: Huntington Library, 1974). More particularly, see M. Isnardi Parente, "Il volontarismo di Jean Bodin: Maimonide o Duns Scoto?" *Il pensiero politico*, 4 (1971), pp. 21–45.

amine thoroughly in the next chapter. Second, Bodin misunderstood, in
Vico's view, the composite nature of a people, the mixed political body.
Just as unity is not a given, preexistent order, so is a people made of contrasting and heterogeneous parts. The reality of such a mixture belies the
possibility of a primordial unity in the political sphere.

Behind Vico's critique of Bodin's political theory and Pythagorean view
of justice as non-historical and utopian (Book IV of the *Republique* resonates with More's political-utopian concerns) lurk some key method-
ological debates of the sixteenth and seventeenth centuries. These debates
shed light on both Vico's understanding of the law and on his intellectual
project in the *New Science*. Simply put, these debates focus on the possibility of finding a unity among the disparate sciences of history, law, literature, religion, and the natural sciences. They hinge on the relationship between probable and certain knowledge or, to say it in Vico's language,
between the certain and the true. At the center of these debates stand
Galileo, Bacon, and Descartes, who are committed to experimental, empirical science and to mathematics as methods of reaching true, scientific
knowledge.

Bacon's *Novum Organum* sets out to dismantle the Aristotelian world
of logical categories. Their innumerable arbitrary distinctions of the nature
of things pales next to Bacon's sense of science, which depends on induction and on the observation of nature's empirical phenomena. Because
mathematical demonstrations release truths voided of all uncertainty,
Bacon conceives experimental science as a science that can yield universal
true principles akin to mathematical demonstrations. Within the context of
Bacon's science the language of evidence, proofs, axioms, principles, and
demonstrations was mixed with the language of hypotheses, probabilities,
and opinions. Bacon repudiates the probable, which he associates with
rhetoric and, as such, with "fogginess of words." In contrast to Bacon,
Gassendi and Hobbes value the probable exactly because it is conjectural.
There is a price they pay for embracing conjectures: they end up in a generalized skepticism.[5]

The identical epistemological concerns shaping the debates on science
resurface in religious controversies, in historiography, and in legal thought.
Theological arguments were put forth to defend the faith from those skep-

---

[5] One should mention Locke's "On Probability" in his *The Search after Truth* (1674),
Essay IV, Chap. XV. Probability deals here with belief, assent, and opinion, which are outside
absolute certainty. As the opinion of others, probability lies at the heart of his conception of
civil order, while the law of nature is the firm foundation of certainty. Certain knowledge allows Locke to circumvent the danger of skepticism, while probable knowledge lets him de-
flate the claims of intolerance. For Vico there is no room for this optimistic separation between the probable and the certain. The imagination leads us beyond the fictional as opposed
to the true.

tics who denied that any form of truth or infallible knowledge was ever possible. Grotius writes his *The Truth of the Christian Religion* (1675) to show the possibility of rational assent to scriptural truth. In the domain of historiography, which the Renaissance linked with rhetoric, the work of Jose y Acosta's *Historia natural y moral de las Indias* (1590) seeks to describe, as Bacon does, a firsthand experience of the religion, customs, government, and the laws of the Indians. Although Acosta presents his account as if he had been an eyewitness of what he narrates (as a historian is supposed to be), he also knew that historical knowledge could never be established on a certain, indubitable foundation.[6]

Finally, in the study of law the same problems reappear. John Selden in his *Historie of Tithes* holds the view that historical facts, just like the facts accepted by the courts, had to be based on certain foundations if the arguments built on them were to have any validity. For him law had to be a science concerned with degrees of certainty, with truth beyond a reasonable doubt. The inductive method in legal investigation meant care for the particulars comprising the evidence. From this standpoint the intellectual concerns of Bacon, Grotius, Pufendorf, Selden, and Acosta share the same assumptions and predicament.

Vico's *New Science*, and in particular Book IV, hurls a challenge at and responds to these debates of seventeenth-century Europe. He certainly agrees with the claims of the new philosophy that all disciplines overlap and are to be seen as parts of a unified whole. The encyclopedic structure of the *New Science*, as this study has been arguing, depends on and exemplifies the quest for unity. But Vico has a different understanding of how the unity across boundaries of knowledge can be established and can be conceived. The principles of metaphysics, logic, and morals, so he writes, issue from the marketplace of Athens (NS/1043). The agora is the original theater of history, and the law court is the stage where debates are reenacted. At the same time, poetry, law, and religion are the ground on which the certain is rooted. How can the law bring unity to the divergent aims of the various disciplines?

Bacon's empiricism, however rigorous its analysis of the individualized, multiple particulars of the natural world, never really confronts either its own philosophical presuppositions or the fictions of the imagination. It

---

[6] Vico acknowledges the anthropological work of Joseph F. Lafitau, *Mouers des sauvages ameriquains* (Paris, 1724). For the importance of American anthropology in Vico see Amos Funkenstein, *Theology and the Scientific Imagination from the Middle Ages to the Seventeenth Century* (Princeton: Princeton University Press, 1986), pp. 202–89. See also Ramusius, *Navigazioni et viaggi* (Venice, 1556). For the bond between historiography and rhetoric, see Hayden White, *Retorica e storia*, Italian trans. by Sergio Moravia (Naples: Guida, 1978). Of considerable relevance to the question of law is Alain Pons, "Nature et histoire chez G. B. Vico," *Les etudes philosophiques*, 216 (1961), pp. 39–53.

never comes to terms with its own implicit theory of the imagination and language as it clusters together the irreducible, particularized fragments of experience and empirical facts into true universals. The scientific, rational view of the law, articulated by Grotius and Selden, obliterates the shifting complexities of the historical process within which laws are caught. Plato's Pythagorean model of justice and unity is divorced from the reality of experience, though Bodin chooses to stress justice's harmony.

On the other hand, law is the framework of Bacon's natural philosophy. As a formal discipline, law reflects his empirical science of induction. As happens in his notion of interpretation of nature, law gathers "facts," fixes procedures, seeks credible evidence, proves allegations, tests claims, argues out of the maxims of precedent and authority, practices skepticism, and discovers principles of the law. But Bacon also understands the law as the preamble to the structure of the state. From this standpoint, as he writes in his *De Augmentis Scientiarum*, "In civil society, either law or force prevails. But there is a kind of force which pretends law, and a kind of law which savours of force rather than equity" (Vol. V, Book VIII, aphorism 1, p. 88). More than that, he writes about the law as a statesman but, in the process, he brackets the utopianism of the *New Atlantis.*[7]

There is in Vico's conception a utopian or Platonic justice that penetrates and shines through the world of the law. But the relation between law and justice remains unstable. Justice is a remote idea, and laws stumble against seemingly insoluble paradoxes. The final paragraph of Book IV highlights and pulls together Vico's sense of the perplexing relationship between the probable and the true (or the certain and the true), laws and justice, facts and reason:

> To sum up, a man is properly only mind, body, and speech, and speech stands as it were midway between mind and body. Hence with regard to what is just, the certain began in mute times with the body. Then when the so-called articulate languages were invented, it advanced to ideas made certain by spoken formulae. And finally, when our human reason was fully developed, it reached its end in the true in the ideas themselves with regard to what is just, as determined by reason from the detailed circumstances of the facts. This truth is a formula devoid of any particular form, called by the learned Varro the formula of nature, *formula naturae*, which, like light, of itself informs in all the minutest details of their surface the opaque bodies of the facts over which it is diffused. (NS/1045)

---

[7] "All those which have written of laws, have written either as philosophers or as lawyers, and none as statesmen. As for philosophers, they imagine imaginary laws for imaginary commonwealths; and their discourses are as the stars, which give little light because they are so high. For the lawyers, they write according to states where they live what is received law, and now what ought to be law; for the wisdom of a lawmaker is one, and of a lawgiver is another." *The Advancement of Learning* (*Works*, Vol. III), p. 475. Machiavelli's anti-Platonic echoes are made to reverberate here.

This paragraph seeks to determine "what is just" in relation to man's being. Man is both mind and body, which are joined together by language—*pace* the Cartesian principle of discontinuity between consciousness and extension, or the occasionalism of Malebranche. The possibility of justice, just as it happens in poetry, is thus dependent upon speech. The claim is reminiscent of Aristotle's *Politics*, its view of man as the animal who has speech (1253a), and this tool affords him the perception of what is "just and unjust" as well as the practice of politics. In mute times, the body, which only apprehends particulars, experiences the certain. With the evolving of articulate languages man develops ideas of the just, till the just is conceived as a rational idea of the true yoked to facts. Truth is neither in the facts nor does it emanate from them. Truth is like a light shining over the surface of the opaque bodies of facts and gives shapes to them. In the logic of Vico's textual formulation, this light (and the echo from Dante's *De Vulgari Eloquentia* is clear) is speech: as speech joins mind and body, the light joins the particularities of facts (opaque bodies) and the truth of ideas. In the triangulation Vico traces, language makes visible the geometric pattern of facts and ideas.

As one would expect from a practitioner of rhetoric, speech is the unifying principle of knowledge and the world. Through speech the performative power of the law's moral order is established. But the unity is breached by the very nature of discourse and language. It is language's own power to bring stubbornly to the light of reason the mobile contours, the uncertain singularities of events, the ambiguities and polysemies of signs. To say it differently, law reveals the gap between politics and ethics. Vico's insight comes to a focus in his identification of poetry and law, which is the core of his poetic metaphysics. Yet, through language man crosses the threshold of tragic transgressions. The fables of the law unveil its identity to poetry and also tells us that literature has a strange relationship to law. Each is the obstinate stranger to the other, each is the limit of the other, and each is the transgression of the other. How this ambivalent and problematical sense of the law affects Vico's political thought will be the argument of the next chapter.

Chapter 8

THE POLITICAL PHILOSOPHERS

FREQUENTLY IN THE *New Science* Vico refers to political philosophers, whom he calls "filosofi politici" (NS/1109) or "politici" (NS/522; 526; 588; 629). These references occur in discursive contexts (such as the "Conchiusione dell'Opera," the "Iconomia Poetica," and the "Politica Poetica") in which Vico reflects on politics and on the value of ancient and modern political philosophies. This chapter explores both where Vico stands in the tradition of political philosophy and the political theory he carefully weaves in the *New Science*.

Vico's "filosofi politici" is best understood in the light of what he calls "la materia della scienza politica" (the matter of political science) (NS/629), which, as he adds, is nothing other than the "science of commanding and obeying in the state." The definition echoes, I would like to suggest, Aristotle's *politike episteme* (*Politics*, 1282b), the political knowledge or political science that asks what is the best regime for ordering the polis. By the same token, "politici" renders *politikoi* (*Politics*, 1266a), the term by which Aristotle designates both philosophers and statesmen and, thereby, he implies the possible unity of politics and philosophy. In a transparent departure from Aristotle's usage, Bacon in the *Advancement of Learning* distinguishes the "politiques" from the "learned" (Dedicatory Epistle). Vico, on his part, identifies the "politici" as political philosophers, whose prince is not a statesman but the divine Plato (NS/1109).

Unavoidably, in a text that purports to confront politics as a question of political theology as the *New Science* does, Vico's "Conclusion of the Work" (which is titled "An Eternal Natural Commonwealth, in Each Kind Best, Ordained by Divine Providence") is especially studded with both direct and oblique references to political philosophers and their works. Its point of departure is Plato and his fourth or ideal republic (NS/1098). This section of the text unfolds by ranging over Aristotle and his *Politics* (NS/1101); it comes full circle back to Plato, who, along with Cicero, is seen in opposition to Epicurus, Hobbes, Machiavelli, Zeno, Spinoza, the natural law theorists (Pufendorf, Selden, and Grotius), Bayle, and Polybius (NS/1109–10). In short, the conclusive paragraphs of the *New Science* narrate a synoptic history of political philosophy. From such a narrative strategy one infers that Vico stages himself as if he now comprehends the essence and history of political thinking. It is as if he has achieved a vision of the whole presumably because he owns and controls the contradictory perspectives of both ancient and modern political philosophers. As will be argued, at the heart of such a procedure there is the implicit and yet striking claim of Vico's own authority and of the political project that is central to his work.

This final stretch of the text does not simply trace out, however, the intricate roots of Vico's thought. In a gesture that mimes Aristotle's principle that politics is the "architectonic science" (*Nicomachean Ethics*, 1094a), because in it the ends of all other sciences converge, Vico unveils political philosophy as literally the *telos* or "conclusion" of his *New Science*. The statement means that the conclusion confronts the deepest truths of political philosophy that have been advanced all along over the movement of Vico's work and are embodied by Machiavellian fictions, his political theater of rhetoric, simulations, and dissimulations. As he examines the foundation of the theories of natural law, the state of nature, and the moral virtues, Vico reflects on the possibility of a constitutive link between politics and philosophy. More generally, he establishes philosophy as political metadiscourse, as a critical commentary on all discourses.

The conclusion starts by recapitulating the major concerns of the *New Science* and by acknowledging Plato's theorization of the best *politeia*, the just city where the best rule (NS/1097). The reference is to Plato's *Republic* and the five different forms of government it delineates (544a). Throughout the Renaissance, the idea of the just city sparked innumerable utopian political constructions: for instance, Vico's own friend and imitator in Naples, Paolo Mattia Doria, used it as the ground plan for the perfect Platonic-Machiavellian polity.[1] But the perfect rationality of the *Republic*, which earlier Vico has called Plato's nostalgic temptation for a time when philosophers ruled and the kings philosophized (NS/522), is dismissed as unworkable. To show why it is unworkable Vico does not overtly argue, as Doria does, that it needs to be yoked to Machiavelli's political realism. Rather, Vico begins by retrieving Aristotle's critique of Plato in the *Politics* and the political theory contained therein.[2]

[1] For an account of Renaissance utopianism see Frank E. and Fritzie P. Manuel, *Utopian Thought in the Western World* (Cambridge, Mass.: Harvard University Press, 1979). See also Franco Venturi, *Utopia e riforme nell'illuminismo* (Turin: Einaudi, 1970), who emphasizes the republican cast of Doria's ideas. Paolo M. Doria's utopian project is in his *Trattato metafisico, fisico, morale, e politico*, which was burned by ecclesiastical censors. On the whole episode see Paola Zambelli, "Il rogo postumo di Paolo Mattia Doria," in *Ricerche sulla cultura dell'Italia moderna*, ed. P. Zambelli (Bari: Laterza, 1972). See also Vittorio Conti, *Paolo Mattia Doria: Dalla repubblica dei Togati alla repubblica dei notabili* (Florence: Olschki, 1978). For a different understanding of Vico's politics see Frederick Vaughan, *The Political Philosophy of Giambattista Vico: An Introduction to "La Scienza Nuova"* (Nijhoff, 1972); and Bruce A. Haddock, *Vico's Political Thought* (Swansea: Mortlake Press, 1986).

[2] The quotations from the *Politics* are taken from Aristotle, *The Politics*, ed. S. Everson,

Vico turns to the Greek sources of European political thought because what matters to him, first of all, is the origin of political life as well as the concomitant questions of the origins, possibility, and definitions of political philosophy. The *Politics*, which Vico never discusses in a sustained manner, but which provides the frame of reference for his political thought, rethinks from the start Plato's myths of the city. Vico absorbs the salient features of Aristotle's speculation.

For both Aristotle and Vico, Socrates' ideal "city in speech" appears to be completely removed from the confines of natural existence. Appropriately, both Vico and Aristotle (in the first two books of his *Politics*) reject the Platonic disjunction between abstract thinking and practical action. By contrast to Plato, who posits the city as an artifice, Aristotle argues for the natural order of society whereby the state is a natural creation and man is by nature a political animal. Accordingly, he focuses on the politics of the household (marriage, the place of women, property, and slavery) as the foundation of the polis. We are reminded that states, which are always imperfect, come into existence from the "bare needs of life" and "for the sake of the good life" (*Politics* 1252a 30). Vico's "Poetic Economy" (NS/520–81) laboriously analyzes the origin of the cities, first from families, and, later, from the *famuli* or slaves in an effort to draft the transition, against Aristotle's naturalistic claims, from the original state of nature to a historical human society.

In order to gauge further Vico's relation to Aristotelian political theory, other aspects of the *Politics* have to be considered. One of them, following the account of the origin of the city, is the Aristotelian speculation on the virtuous citizens and the various regimes—monarchy, aristocracy, democracy (and their corresponding perversions: tyranny, oligarchy, and mob rule). At stake is the determination of whether or not it is "more advantageous to be ruled by the best man or by the best laws" (*Politics*, 1286a 8). The rule of law, which Aristotle calls "reason unaffected by desire" (1287a 30)—a phrase Vico renders as "volontà senza passioni" (NS/1101)—is said to be preferable to the wild beast of passions—the temptations of tyranny—perverting the minds of rulers. Yet, the rule of law cannot achieve the justice and equity political life promises. From the acknowledgment of defective justice and the imperfections of the city stems the need to rebuild

Cambridge Texts in the History of Political Thought (Cambridge: Cambridge University Press, 1988). On Aristotle's political theory see Leo Strauss, *The City and the Man* (Chicago: Rand McNally, 1964). See Mary Nichols, *Citizens and Statesmen: A Study of Aristotle's Politics* (Savage, Md.: Rowman and Littlefield, 1992). See also Michael Davis, *The Politics of Philosophy: A Commentary on Aristotle's Politics* (London: Rowman and Littlefield, 1996). See also for Book IV, Harvey C. Mansfield, *Taming the Prince* (New York: Free Press, 1989), pp. 45–71. On the anti-Aristotelian taste—and the importance of Plato in the eighteenth century—see Biagio De Giovanni, "Cultura e vita civile in Giuseppe Valletta," in *Saggi e ricerche sul Settecento* (Naples: Istituto Italiano per gli Studi Storici, 1968) especially pp. 20–36.

a workable *politeia* on a new basis. Aristotle's political science, thus, casts the city as a whole of parts to be fit together by the philosopher who also knows the usefulness of music and poetry in making parts appear as wholes (*Politics*, Book III).

Like Aristotle's, Vico's thought does not override the limits of the finite historical world. He brackets the myth of Edenic perfect beginnings and the wishful millenarian illusion undergirding both Renaissance Christian utopias (e.g., the *Christianopolis* of Andreae, the utopia of Comenius, etc.) and the high-flying dreams of Renaissance Platonic republics (the myth of the "città felice," Landi, Doni, Patrizi, More, etc.). As in Aristotle, Vico's point of departure is the natural world. Unlike Aristotle, however, Vico posits a drastic disjunction between natural life and political life. In effect, he looks beyond the scope of the *Politics* and takes to task the question of ethics within nature or the condition of existence to which he refers as the "state of nature" (NS/1098). The phrase, which describes prepolitical human life under the law of nature and prior to the institution of civil society, has notoriously conflicting meanings.

Natural law theorists (from Cicero to Aquinas, Grotius, Suarez, Pufendorf, and Locke), who presume that man is by nature a rational and social animal, view the state of nature as a state of liberty and natural equality. In an overt rejection of the illusion of egalitarianism possibly implied by this doctrine, Hobbes replaces the notion of the "law of nature" with that of the "right of nature," and he defines the "state of nature" as a state of "continual fear," "danger of violent death," of "war of all against all." It is a state, in short, where men are ruled by the mechanics of selfish passions and "a perpetual and restless desire of power" (*Leviathan*, XI–XIII). What matters most in Hobbes's world is the preservation of one's life. In opposition to Hobbes, Locke's moral philosophy recapitulates Cicero's doctrine of the law of nature whereby "true law is right reason in agreement with nature" (*Republic*, III, 22). "The plain difference," writes Locke in *Of Civil Government*, "between the state of nature and the state of war, which, however some men have confounded, are as far distant as a state of peace, good will, mutual assistance, and preservation, and a state of enmity, malice, violence, and mutual destruction are from one another" (Paragraph 19).

Vico's construction of the archaic natural condition is more radical and more thoroughgoing than that of his modern predecessors. To explore this radicality we must briefly turn to the arguments set forth in more detail in the sections of "Poetic Economy," "Poetic Politics," and "Poetic History" than they are in the necessarily compressed prose of the conclusion. "Poetic Economy," as stated above, discusses the politics of the household, and the discussion gets going with an apparently gratuitous digression on education. Vico distinguishes between "educere," which applies to the education of the soul, and "educare," which refers to the education of the body

(NS/520). He adds that the "fisici" or natural philosophers employ *educere* to signify the bringing forth of forms from matter, that is, the form of the human soul from the "vasti corpi de' giganti" (the huge bodies of the giants) (NS/520).

Why should Vico introduce his reflection on "Poetic Economy" with an apparent digression on the soul and the natural philosophers? Vico asserts that the soul is the form of the body, and the definition recalls the classical Scholastic argument of the relation between soul and body as a relation of formal and material principles. Such a view flatly contradicts the various assumptions of the natural philosophers, who make the soul an aggregate of atoms, of the Cartesians, who posit the soul's distinct existence separate from the body, and of the Occasionalists who make the unity of body and soul dependent on God's miraculous intervention. For Vico speech binds together body and mind (NS/1045). It remains to be seen why speech, as the unifying element between body and soul, is necessary to his political thought. For now let me remark that, whereas for Aristotle the unity of the city is achieved through education—habits, philosophy, and laws (*Politics* 1263b 35–40)—for Vico household discipline amounts to an education or management of bodies conducted by the "cyclopean authority" of the fathers (NS/524).

The myth of the Cyclopes, who figure also in the conclusion's depiction of the state of nature (NS/1098), had just been ushered in and glossed by Vico through a tight series of references to Plato, to monarchical rule, to Machiavelli, and to the state of nature (NS/522). Let me quickly review the context. Plato had posited the account of Ogygian and Deucalonian floods—the natural primordial catastrophe disrupting the world—as the reason why the Cyclopes lived in caves. On account of this, "tutti i politici" (all political philosophers), believe that the first form of civil government was monarchic. Such a view, in turn, gave rise to the "principles of evil politics"—and the reference is clearly to Machiavelli and Machiavellianism—that civil government comes about by "violence or fraud"(NS/522) (cf. *The Prince*, Chapter XVIII, 3; *Discourses*, II, 13). If the Machiavellian proposition about the beginnings of politics is erroneous because it presumes rational calculus, albeit in a perverted form, Plato's explanation about the Cyclopes living in caves leads Vico to the recognition of archaic men's separate and solitary horizons. In the atomized, plural realm of Cyclopes who live apart from one another—a picture that recalls Glaucon's solipsistic life of autonomous monads in the *Republic* (258e–359b)—there is no consciousness of a connected human world nor of a unifying monarchical rule. Rather, this is the original world or "state of nature" ("naturale equalità dello stato") in which men, arrogant and savage, emerge from the ruthlessness and chaos of "libertà bestiale" (bestial liberty) (NS/522; 576).

But the allusion to the Cyclopes contains a pointed reference to Aristotle's *Politics*. As hinted above, for Aristotle the city, which is a political partnership constituted for the sake of some good, originates from the structure of the household, which, in turn, is rooted in the natural necessities of reproduction and self-preservation. Women, slaves, and property are the ingredients in this *oikonomia*, or art of the household. Within each household, Aristotle maintains by quoting from the *Odyssey* (IX, 114–15), the father's harsh monarchical rule holds sway (252b 24). The Homeric context Aristotle evokes centers on the Cyclopes, their cannibalism and incestuous practices, and the myth about these children of the earth provides a thread that binds the whole of the *Politics*.

Aristotle's man is by nature a political animal. The maxim presupposes that man's rationality best expresses itself through the exercise of moral and political virtues, or, as Aristotle puts it: "A social instinct is implanted in all men by nature. . . . For man, when perfected, is the best of animals, but, when separated from law and justice, he is the worst of all. . . . This is why, if he has no excellence, he is the most unholy and the most savage of animals, and the most full of lust and gluttony" (*Politics* 1253a 30–35). So careful is this assessment of human grandeur (or perfection by education) and horror that, retrospectively, we grasp the reason for the allusion to the Cyclopes' bestiality and carnivorousness. The city is rooted in nature's moral laws, but there is no thoroughly harmonious life in the state of nature: cannibalism, incest, and robbery—unholy acts of radical transgressions of the rational boundaries of the ethical world—are the original and forever impending dangers, whatever their disguises, hovering over the framework of the polis.[3] Such a consciousness makes Aristotle's philosophical discourse a necessary educational practice, a vigilant commentary on the remote and concealed origins of human society.

The insight into the monstrosity threatening domestic and public life figures at the very start of Vico's "Poetic Economy." In the "state called that of nature" Vico puts the heroic fathers, who are wise in the wisdom of auspices (NS/521), as distinctive emblems of such a state. In effect, Vico insinuates a double idea of the state of nature, thereby making it a historical artifice or a "made" construction. Before the advent of the wisdom of the heroic fathers, there was another unformed beginning, a time when politics was simply a question of bodies: cyclopean, giant bodies who, like libertines later, wandered over the face of the earth and lived in a state of infamous promiscuity. This chaos, which is a recurring possibility of existence, is both a moral condition and a "certain," scientific fact.

Vico states this notion of a primordial chaos in his "Poetic Physics" as

---

[3] The question of cannibalism at the beginnings of culture is also treated by Plutarch, *De esu carnium* in *Moralia*, ed. Hubert and H. Drexler (Leipzig: Teubner, 1959).

he evokes the theological poets who imagined Chaos "as confusion of human seeds in the state of the infamous promiscuity of women" (NS/688). They also imagined Orcus as cannibalizing all of reality: "[he is] a misshapen monster which devoured all things, because men in this infamous promiscuity did not have the proper form of men, and were swallowed up by the void because through the uncertainty of the offspring they left nothing of themselves. This chaos was later taken up by the physicists as the prime matter of natural things, which, formless itself, is greedy for forms and devours all forms. The poets, however, gave it also the monstrous form of Pan, the wild god who is the divinity of all satyrs inhabiting not the cities but the forests; . . ." (NS/688).

The cosmological theory of primal chaos that physicists and poets alike articulate (and which Vico links to the atomism of Democritus, Epicurus, and Lucretius) is the cornerstone for the views of Hobbesian or Machiavellian politics originating in the chaos or constitutive violence of the state of nature. How politics actually confronts (and shares in) chaos, how Machiavellianism is threaded with Epicurean archaisms (and thus it effaces the harmonious proportions of Plato's ideal construction) stands at center of baroque philosophical speculations and dramas of intrigue. Such a notion is also central to Vico's political problematics that effectively responds to the challenges posed by modern atomistic science. Thus, I now focus on the conceptual link Vico forges between physics and politics whereby politics comes through as a physics of insatiable and all-devouring bodies.

Such a link is predicated on the relation between the kingdom of the arts (or the ends and boundaries of the specific sciences) and the faculties of the soul or, more generally, between the *globus intellectualis* (Bacon's phrase) and the world of politics. In historical terms, Plato's *Republic* probes the relation between the arts and the virtues of the soul (e.g., the philosopher king as a man of science). Book IV of the *Politics* announces at the outset the essential affinity between politics and the arts and sciences (1288b 10). In the Middle Ages, there are miniatures (such as the fourteenth-century one of Nicolo'da Bologna) showing the links between, on the one hand, virtues and vices, and, on the other, the liberal arts. In the modern age, Campanella's *City of the Sun*, which has its foundation in the universality of encyclopedic knowledge, makes metaphysics or *prima philosophia* the prince of the city as well as the principle of surveillance over the liberal and mechanical arts.[4] More cogently for Vico, Bacon's *Advancement of Learn-*

---

[4] Campanella's architecture of the arts—in which he follows the ancients—enacts the principle of the purposiveness of the arts as well as the link between the theoretical and practical arts. In this context see a passage from Vico's *Vita scritta da sè medesimo* that has a Campanellian flavor: "Perciò si dovette esso di nuovo portare alla metafisica . . . la metafisica d'Aristotile conduce a un principio fisico, il quale è materia dalla quale si educono le forme particolari, e sì, fa Iddio un vasellaio che lavori le cose fuori di sè. Ma la metafisica di Platone

ing examines both the paradigm whereby the arts and sciences make a whole unified by first philosophy and their places in the world of politics.[5]

The *New Science* evades the predecessors' thoroughgoing schematic intellectualism and rigid commensurability between theoretical abstractions about the liberal arts and corresponding historical practices. If anything, Vico conceives his text as a vast empirical enterprise that gauges the opaque, unwieldy discrepancies between knowledge of the whole and man's postlapsarian fallibility (or *akrasia*). Still, it is sustained by the fundamentally educational impulse to explore the possible translation of universal science into a cosmopolis.[6]

The bond between politics as a question of the bodies' appetites and physics is suggested to Vico by the at once ancient and modern science of corpuscularism. The "corpuscular hypothesis," which is the theory of the corpuscular or mechanical constitution of universal matter common to all bodies, originates in the atomism of Democritus, Epicurus, and Lucretius. In the seventeenth century, moreover, classical atomism is revived by the modern science and the new philosophy of Galileo, Gassendi, Hobbes, and eventually, Boyle and Locke.[7] Vico explicitly delineates the metaphysical

---

conduce a un principio fisico, che è la idea eterna che da sè educe e crea la materia medesima . . . in conformità di questa metafisica, fonda una morale sopra una virtù o giustizia ideale o sia architetta, in conseguenza della quale si diede a meditare una ideale repubblica, alla quale diede con le sue leggi un dritto puro ideale. Tanto che da quel tempo che il Vico non si sentì soddisfatto della metafisica di Aristotile . . . incominciò . . . a meditare un diritto ideale eterno che celebrassesi in una città universale nell'idea o disegno della providenza, sopra la quale idea son poi fondate tutte le repubbliche di tutti i tempi, di tutte le nazioni: che era quella repubblica ideale che, in conseguenza della sua metafisica, doveva meditar Platone, ma, per l'ignoranza del primo uom caduto, nol potè fare" (pp. 14–15).

[5] See on this the excellent discussion by Jerry Weinberger, *Science, Faith, and Politics: Francis Bacon and the Utopian Roots of the Modern Age: A Commentary on Bacon's* Advancement of Learning (Ithaca: Cornell University Press, 1985), esp. pp. 244–59. For Vico's own context see Maurizio Torrini, *Tommaso Cornelio e la ricostruzione delle scienze* (Napoli: Guida, 1977).

[6] In "Poetic Economy" several links between the arts and the political world are posited, albeit in a fragmentary way: the liberal arts are connected to the definition of nobility (NS/537); religion is called the "first principle" of the *New Science* (NS/562); finally, only the philosophers are said to understand *honestas*, or beauty of virtue (NS/565).

[7] Vico's *Autobiography* has a long discussion of Lucretius, Epicurean atomism, corpuscular theories of Epicurus and Descartes: see Italian original, *Vita*, pp. 20–22. The polemic against Galileo (especially his first *Dialogo della scienza nuova*), against the skeptics, and the mechanical philosophers is summarized by Vico in his *Risposte al giornale dei letterati* (1711). For a still valuable general outline of the doctrine see Cyril Bayley, *The Greek Atomists and Epicureans* (Oxford: Clarendon Press, 1928). See also Robert Hugh Kargon, *Atomism in England from Hariot to Newton* (Oxford: Clarendon Press, 1966). Robert Boyle's effort to join corpuscularism and theology (which he thought was also Gassendi's aim) is put forth in his *Some Considerations about the Reconcileableness of Reason and Religion* (1690) available in the *Works of the Honorable Robert Boyle*, ed. Thomas Birch, six vols. (London, 1772; reprinted Hildesheim, Germany: Georg Olms, 1965), Vol. IV. See also Margaret J. Osler, "Baptizing

premises of Epicurean cosmology and connects it with modern corpuscularism.

In "Del Metodo" (NS/338–60), after evoking the principles and myths of philological and philosophical beginnings (the stories of Deucalion and Amphion, the "frogs" of Epicurus, and the "cicadas" of Hobbes), Vico formulates a reflection that is central to his imaginative and conceptual world: harsh and bestial beginnings can hardly be imagined; more than that, they can barely be understood (NS/338). He is not detained at this point by the insight into the tenuousness of our knowledge of beginnings, though it will shape, as shall be argued in the next chapter, his hermeneutics of history. Rather, the text shifts to man's archaic thought, which takes place, as Vico says, under the compulsion of powerful passions, and to the theory of the "conatus," the force that imparts a direction to the passions. This conative thrust of the bodies—which is human choice and free will—is explained by the adoption of the vocabulary of the law of motion in ancient and modern mechanics:

> Perchè dar conato a' corpi tanto è quanto dar loro libertà di regolar i lor moti, quando i corpi tutti sono agenti necessari in natura; e que' ch'i meccanici dicono "potenze," "forze," "conati" sono moti insensibili d'essi corpi, co' quali essi o s'appressano, come volle la meccanica antica, a' loro centri di gravità, o s'allontanano, come vuole la meccanica nuova, dà loro centri del moto. (NS/340)

> (But to impute impulse to bodies is as much as to impute to them freedom to regulate their motions, whereas all bodies are by nature necessary agents. And what the theorists of mechanics call powers, forces, impulses, are insensible motions of bodies, by which they approach their centers of gravity, as ancient mechanics had it, or depart from their centers of motion, as modern mechanics has it.)

The passage tightly compresses the notion of the Epicurean or Lucretian *clinamen* or "swerve" with Newton's law of universal gravitation. To

---

Epicurean Atomism: Pierre Gassendi on the Immortality of the Soul," in *Religion, Science, and Worldview: Essays in Honor of Richard S. Westfall*, eds. M. J. Osler and P. L. Farba (Cambridge: Cambridge University Press, 1985), pp. 162–83; idem, *Divine Will and the Mechanical Philosophy: Gassendi and Descartes on Contingency and Necessity in the Created World* (Cambridge: Cambridge University Press, 1994). In general see Michael Hunter, "Science and Heterodoxy: An Early Modern Problem Reconsidered" in *Reappraisals of the Scientific Revolution*, eds. D. C. Lindbergh and R. S. Westman (Cambridge: Cambridge University Press, 1990), pp. 437–60. For a general view of atomism in seventeenth-century Italy, see Tullio Gregory, "Studi sull'atomismo nel Seicento," *Giornale critico della filosofia italiana*, 46 (1967), pp. 528–41; Eugenio Garin, *Dal Rinascimento all'Illuminismo: Studi e ricerche* (Pisa: Nistri-Lischi, 1970), p. 91ff. But see especially Michel Serres, *La naissance de la physique dans le texte de Lucrece: Fleuves et turbulences* (Paris: Minuit, 1977) and Ilya Prigogine and Isabelle Stengers, *Order Out of Chaos: Man's New Dialogue with Nature* (New York: Bantam, 1984).

state it differently, classical atomism is wedded to the modern mechanics of motion of visible bodies. The route this conceptual tradition follows is well known. Lucretius's *De rerum natura* (Books I and II) recounts the *primordia*, the first beginnings and imperishable foundations of things, *atoms*, which have a blind nature (I, 779). All bodies, Lucretius maintains, are made of atoms forever falling in straight parallel lines (II, 184–215). A random "swerve" diverts the atoms from their rectilinear path, and from their collision the compounds of the sensible world emerge. On the other hand, modern theorists wondered whether or not the motion of particles required external agents; they speculated on how the "swerve" occurs; and they postulated the existence of contrivances whereby atoms are entangled together.[8]

Vico had intellectually "swerved" from Lucretius. Now he objects to the representation of the natural order of things given by the "philosophers's" merely natural theology. Epicureans and Stoics, in fact, "by the physical order observed in the motions of such bodies as the spheres and the elements" (NS/342), draw a mechanical world picture in which material substances are contrivances resulting from a "blind concourse of atoms" or a "deaf chain of causality" (NS/342). Such a Democritean-Epicurean cosmology, vehemently opposed by Plato (as Diogenes Laertes reports) posits the world as matter in endless, random motion without any providential purpose or order (NS/179).

This Epicurean universe of chance and determinism, wherein God is conceived as only a body (NS/335), shapes the realm of politics. Vico has no doubt, as a matter of fact, that Hobbes's political philosophy is a direct extension of Epicurean chance theory: "This [providential] principle of institutions," he writes,

> Thomas Hobbes failed to see among his own "fierce and violent men," because he went far afield in search of principles and fell into error with the "chance" of his Epicurus. He thought to enrich Greek philosophy by adding a great part which it certainly had lacked (as George Paschius reports in his *De eruditis huius saeculi inventis*): the study of man in the whole society of the human race. Nor would Hobbes have conceived this project if the Christian religion had not given him the inspiration for it, though what it commands is not merely justice but charity toward all mankind. (NS/179)

Whereas Christianity affirms and reveals the fundamental connection of all mankind, Hobbes's Epicureanism (or doctrine of "chance") envisions the breakdown of a charitable social order. Within the Hobbesian frame-

---

[8] In his *Animadversiones* (1649), Gassendi, whom Locke follows, accounts for the cohesion of atoms by positing spikes through which they "hook up" (I, 331, 81). Malebranche in his *The Search after Truth* (1674) begins by attributing the cohesion of corpuscles to the pressure of the Ether, but he ends up accepting Newton's theory of gravitational attraction, developed in his *Principia* as the force determining the trajectory of massive celestial bodies.

work of justice without charity human beings are apprehended as isolated entities, as disintegrated multiplicities related by perpetual, random antagonisms and reciprocal fear.[9] Vico would agree with Hobbes's Baconian view that legal order is crucial to the very existence of society and that justice is political order's attendant virtue. But Hobbes—as much as Machiavelli and the natural philosophers—who conceptualizes the politics of the passions and the harsh purposes of nature, and who makes fear of death the passion central to the economy of the body politic, understands only the objective phenomenology of fear.

Like Lucretius and Hobbes (and we can't but recall Machiavelli's maxim that it is preferable to the Prince to be feared rather than loved), Vico acknowledges the sovereign prestige of fear in the domain of politics. But fear is not only a strategy of power, a realistic mode of controlling the imminent dangers and real or imaginary threats besetting the security of one's world. For Vico fear is the ground of the obscure consciousness of a self divided from itself, a terrifying vertigo of self-apprehension that induces man's "swerve" from the bestial chaos of the origins. This fear, which is a founding moral-political experience, is rooted, Vico says, in the awareness of a lightning bolt that forces archaic man, desirous for self-preservation, to seek shelter in the recesses of the cave, acknowledge his limitations, and submit to the awesome, mysterious powers of the divinity (NS/377–79; 689). Because of the fear of bolts of lightning man builds altars, platforms Vico places at the center of our field of vision as signs of the wisdom man possesses: man makes his own world (for the world is the one we make), but the lightnings, which are gleams of a light that quickly appear and vanish, display the cracks in the architectonics of such a world.

From the standpoint of man's subjection to a feared God (as if he were the real prince) "Poetic Economy" mounts a direct critique against both the realistic political philosophers and Plato. Against the Machiavellians, Vico insists twice that archaic man did not understand fraud and violence as strategic tools of political power (NS/522). On the other hand, against Plato, against this philosopher's temptation to view human beings as perfect (which dehumanizes them), Vico evokes a world in which fear brings restraint from original bestial liberty (NS/523). In effect, liberty, far from being an unreserved condition, is tied to duties and to the constraints of

---

[9] It should be recalled that Hobbes's law of nature follows the scientific principles drafted by Galileo (whom Hobbes met at Padua) and by Galileo's student, William Harvey. We are told in the *Leviathan* that the body politic is a mechanical engine in which "every joint and member is moved to perform his duty" (Introduction). Galileo's law of uniform motion is restated by Hobbes in his view of man as a machine in motion driven by imagination and infinite appetites: "when a body is once in motion, it moveth, unless something else hinder it, eternally . . . so it also happeneth in that motion, which is made in the internal parts of a man, then, when he sees, dreams etc" (*Leviathan*, Chap. II, "Of Imagination," ed. A. D. Lindsay (London: Everyman, 1962).

authority. More precisely, "fides deorum," which he translates as the "force of the gods," and which is the counterpart of Orpheus's taming the beast by the power of his song, induces men to obey the laws, discipline their bodies, and turn to labor and industry (NS/523–25). By making the fearful experience of lightning the way to religious belief and politics, Vico bends the vocabulary of philosophy in a theological direction.

Let us quickly recall Lucretius's reflection on lightnings and bolts (*De rerum natura*, VI, 379–422). In his materialist cosmology there is no room for a theological interpretation of these phenomena, which he explains by retrieving Epicurus's philosophical account of their causes. And we should recall that in Greek philosophy the beginning of wisdom is wonder, whereas in the Bible fear of the Lord is the beginning of wisdom. For Vico, who is closer to the biblical insight, fear is the beginning of his political theology, of what he calls—against Stoic and Epicurean philosophers—"rational civil theology of divine providence" (NS/342).

The phrase lucidly conveys Vico's insight into the origin of the state in a pre-philosophical experience. It follows that for Vico the rationality of philosophy is not the paradigm for politics. More precisely, the phrase signals that the *New Science* provides a rational political theory rooted in theological assumptions and that political history is deciphered from a theological perspective. Yet the phrase cannot allay the suspicion that Vico may in fact be indulging in a Machiavellian practice, that the claimed univocal reduction of politics to the parameters of theology is a manipulation of theology for political ends.

These concerns appear in the overtly anti-Machiavellian summation at the very end of the "Conchiusione dell'Opera":

> Adunque, di fatto è confutato Epicuro, che dà il caso, e i di lui seguaci Obbes e Macchiavello; di fatto è confutato Zenone, e con lui Spinosa, che danno il fato: al contrario, di fatto è stabilito a favor de' filosofi politici, de' quali è principe il divino Platone, che stabilisce regolare le cose umane la provvedenza. Onde aveva la ragion Cicerone, che non poteva con Attico ragionar delle leggi, se non lasciava d'esser epicureo e non gli concedeva prima la provvedenza regolare l'umane cose: la quale Pufendorfio sconobbe con la sua ipotesi, Seldeno suppose e Grozio ne prescindè; ma i romani giureconsulti la stabilirono per primo principio del diritto natural delle genti. . . . Quindi veda Bayle se possan esser di fatto nazioni nel mondo senza veruna cognizione di Dio! E veda Polibio quanto sia vero il suo detto: che, se fussero al mondo filosofi, non bisognerebbero al mondo religioni! (NS/1109–10)

> (Hence Epicurus, who believes in chance, is refuted by the facts, along with his followers Hobbes and Machiavelli; and so are Zeno and Spinoza, who believe in fate. The evidence clearly confirms the contrary position of the political philosophers, whose prince is the divine Plato, who shows that providence

directs human institutions. Cicero was therefore right in refusing to discuss laws with Atticus unless the latter would give up his Epicureanism and first concede that providence governed human institutions. Pufendorf implicitly denied this by his hypothesis, Selden took it for granted, and Grotius left it out of account; but the Roman jurisconsults established it as the first principle of the natural law of the gentes. . . . Let Bayle consider then whether in fact there can be notions in the world without any knowledge of God! And let Polybius weigh the truth of his statement that if there were philosophers in the world there would be no need of religions in the world.)

The rejection of political-philosophical atheism (crystallized by the doctrines of Epicurus, Machiavelli, Hobbes, Spinoza, Bayle, and Polybius)—against which Vico juxtaposes the political philosophy of Plato and Cicero—could not have been sharper. In the dualistic, oppositional value system Vico constructs (which generally appears as the polarization of Plato and Machiavelli), Paolo M. Doria's wished-for synthesis of Plato and Machiavelli seems to be dismissed out of hand. More to our immediate concern, Vico explicitly banishes the atheistic philosophers from the realm of political philosophy not because their science is wrong. He banishes them because their incredulity threatens the foundation of the state. The paragraphs obliquely furnish the complex rationale for his forceful *prise-de-position*.

His drastic dismissal of atheological politics, on the face of it, aligns him with the broad tradition of the "anti-Machiavel."[10] Entrenched anti-Machiavellianism, which includes the likes of Tommaso Campanella, Innocent Gentillet, and Jean Bodin, displays a downright revulsion at what it construes as the most frightening elements of Machiavelli's vision: his ideas about the nature of power; his assumption that the world is not exactly the handiwork of God; his belief that words have no necessary relationship to the things they name, and that it is therefore hazardous to take the prince at his word. Campanella's *Atheismus Triumphatus*, to mention a text that belongs to the spiritual climate of the anti-Machiavel, probes the links between religious skepticism and the political idolatry of Machiavellian princes. Vico's reference to Bayle (who in his *Dictionnaire* calls Hobbes an atheist) makes Machiavellianism the synonym for the philosophical skepticism of the libertines. And there is a good reason for connecting philosophers such as Hobbes and Spinoza with Machiavelli, whose founding role in the modern political debate they acknowledge.

Hobbes's *De Cive*, which is thoroughly shaped by the proposition,

[10] See on this Friedrich Meinecke, *Machiavellism: The Doctrine of Raison d'Etat and Its Place in Modern History*, trans. D. Scott (New Haven: Yale University Press, 1962). See also my "Machiavelli and Vico" in *Machiavelli and the Discourse of Literature*, eds. A. Ascoli and V. Kahn (Ithaca: Cornell University Press, 1993), pp. 259–74, from which I have taken some paragraphs.

drawn from Justinian's *Digest*, that "what pleases the Prince has the force of law," is a text that could have been written by Machiavelli himself. Spinoza's *Tractatus Theologicus-Politicus*, the chief burden of which is to reflect on the imperatives of reason and on the desirable shape of government in the world of immanence, cautiously seeks to rescue Machiavelli's thought from the commonplace conviction that his is merely a doctrine of absolutism and coercive power.[11]

Vico's critical distance from this Epicurean-Machiavellian political philosophy reflects in large measure his critique of the central premises of the Renaissance.[12] After pointing out the limits of Plato's *Republic* (NS/13), he sketches the dynamics in the foundation of the polis: the founding vices of Machiavelli's political theory—man's ferocity, avarice, and ambitions—are the presupposition for their turning into the social virtues of the military, merchant, and governing class (NS/132). From Vico's perspective of historical becoming, Machiavelli's much vaunted political realism, it would seem, produces a frozen picture of man's natural existence and thereby robs man of the thought of historical alternatives to the naturalistic course of events.

But there are two other large points of disagreement with Machiavellian political philosophy Vico registers in the paragraphs from the "Conchiusione" cited above. The first point centers on the question of language or discourse, which for Vico is the real foundation of the political arena in its plurality of relations. In this context, the question must immediately be raised as to why Vico banishes atheistical philosophers. For by this gesture of exclusion of "monastic" thinkers Vico runs the risk of violating his own totalizing project; he even runs the risk of appearing a propagandist or a

---

[11] Thomas Hobbes, *De Cive; or, The Citizen*, ed. S. P. Lamprecht (New York: Appleton-Century-Crofts, 1949), Chapter I, Section 4, p. 1. Benedict Spinoza, *A Theologico—Political Treatise*, trans. R. H. M. Elwes (New York: Dover, 1951) writes: "What means a prince whose sole motive is lust of mastery should use to establish and maintain his dominion, the most ingenious Machiavelli has set forth at large; but with what design one can hardly be sure. . . . He perhaps wished to show how cautious a free multitude should be of entrusting its welfare absolutely to one man. . . ." (Chapter V, Section 7).

[12] Vico's relation to the Renaissance has been explored by Eugenio Garin, "Vico e l'eredità del pensiero del Rinascimento" in *Vico oggi*, ed. A. Battistini (Roma: Armando, 1979), pp. 69–93. More generally see Ernesto Grassi, *Rhetoric as Philosophy: The Humanistic Tradition* (University Park: Pennsylvania State University Press, 1980). See also James C. Morrison, "Vico and Machiavelli" in *Vico: Past and Present*, ed. G. Tagliacozzo (Atlantic Highlands, N.J.: Humanities Press, 1979), Vol. II, pp. 1–14. I would point out that the proposition that practically introduces the *New Science* redefines the cardinal doctrine of Italian humanism: "L'uomo per l'indiffinita natura della mente umana, ove questa si rovesci nell'ignoranza, egli fa di sè regola dell'universo" (NS/120). The maxim contains an implicit critique of the Cartesian assumption of the stability of the mind and of humanism's faith in the centrality of man. A few lines down (NS/131) Vico points out the limits of Plato's ideal city, which is followed by a rethinking of Machiavelli's vices (NS/132).

mere rhetorician, as it were, arguing for his own dogmatic Counter-Reformation point of view, rather than as a thinker in pursuit of nonpartisan and non-partial truths.

As a way of answering these legitimate perplexities it should be stated that Vico follows Bacon in considering "atheists" those with a little or superficial knowledge of philosophy (*Advancement of Learning*, Vol. III, p. 267). More substantively, he banishes atheistical and skeptical philosophers because their refusal of or skepticism about the divinity refracts itself as a mistrust of discourse. Ironically for philosophers, such as Machiavelli, who has authorized the *Discourses*, his methodical suspicion about language is a *misologia*, the hatred of the Logos. And the Epicurean sage's withdrawal from the public arena to the "garden of Epicurus," where the philosopher can abide in the pursuit of the mind's pleasure, reenacts the solipsistic enclosure of pre-political life.

Vico's text openly alludes to the mistrust of language that undermines the order of the city and is brought into the city by the skeptics. Retrospectively we grasp why he makes speech the heart, as it were, of the unity of soul and body. Furthermore, his text juxtaposes to the atheistical political philosophers Plato and Cicero, their notion, that is, that a moral-political dialogic conversation is dependable. For this reason Vico stresses Cicero's refusal to "ragionar delle leggi" (discuss laws) with Atticus till he abandoned his Epicureanism and acknowledged the sovereignty of Providence (NS/1109).

Philosophy is divine, says Plato, and the phrase, which Vico endorses, means to him that philosophy must open itself to the divinity. At the same time, the text ends with the claim that the *New Science* has discussed the order of civil institutions ("in questi libri si è ragionato . . .") (NS/1111). Finally, Vico's own rhetorical practice—his passionate rejection of an untrustworthy discourse of the skeptical philosophers, by which he makes no pretense of being an impartial spectator, or perspectival chronicler of history-bound, changing ideologies—makes his own text the metaphoric space of an open discourse in which ideas are critically debated, opinions are judged, political styles of life are examined, and choices are made. In brief, Vico's emphasis on "ragionar" (a term that has not too remote legal resonances and alludes to the debates in the courts of law) returns us to history, to an idea of the city to be ruled by the best and to be made through discourse, laws, and education.

Within this context of materialist philosophy as a blasphemous, divisive discourse that undermines the city and promotes distrust in language, Vico draws attention to the links between language and theology (the Logos in theology), and rhetoric and politics. From the standpoint of the Logos, his "rational civil theology of Divine Providence" retrieves the traditional dimensions of humanistic rhetoric, or *theologia rhetorica*, as the discipline that gathers within its purview poetry, politics, history, philosophy, and theology itself. Rhetoric—as Socrates teaches in the *Phaedrus* and Dante's Ulysses shows (*Inferno*, Canto XXVI)—is also the discipline by which cities are constructed and destroyed. Vico's authority and reliability as a master of rhetoric will be determined by his ability to hold together the irreducible contradictions of this political art. For now let me remark that his staging of rhetoric's sovereignty at the end of his text highlights an essential, politically necessary ambiguity lodged at the heart of the *New Science*.[13]

On the one hand, the *New Science* gives a trans-historical, scientific conspectus of all possible cultural institutions. In this sense, it can never become a tyrannical, technical blueprint for one new social order. On the other hand, the *New Science*, as it discovers the perpetual laws of history, recuperates the rhetorical and political dimensions of philosophy. In effect, Vico's scientific discovery is the obverse side of his rhetorical strategy, his desire to establish his own authority and the authority of his text.

Vico's stance of rhetorical persuasion is consistent with his view of knowledge as engaged knowledge, a knowledge that, far from being pure or without a point of view, is tied to action. Whereas the philosophers who secularize politics (and who, like Polybius, would replace theology with the enlightened rationality of philosophy) provide a philosophy of politics, Vico forces us to the thought of the politics of philosophy or of philosophy as politics. He articulates, thus, a vision of practical knowledge whereby he tells philosophers that the true aim of philosophy is to construct a world, this world; that philosophy never quite coincides with politics; that religious piety and education best actualize the moral and political virtues; that oligarchic aristocracies, which he addresses, trains, and endorses, must be prepared for the perpetual challenges from the lower classes.

The concrete contours of the world Vico imaginatively exhumes from the palimpsest of history are found in the second large point of his disagreement with Machiavellian political philosophy. The last few paragraphs of the "Conchiusione" (NS/1108–10) are scanned by the anaphora of "mondo," world, and "questa terra" or "questo mondo," this earth and

---

[13] For the relationship between rhetoric and politics in the Renaissance see Nancy Streuver, *The Language of History in the Renaissance* (Princeton: Princeton University Press, 1970). For the relationship between rhetoric and politics, and rhetoric and political theology see my *Dante, Poet of the Desert: History and Allegory in the Divine Comedy* (Princeton: Princeton University Press, 1979), especially pp. 66–106. See also my *Dante's Vision and the Circle of Knowledge* (Princeton: Princeton University Press, 1993), pp. 56–74. See also the important reflections on theology and rhetoric by John Milbank, *The Religious Dimensions in the Thought of Giambattista Vico (1688–1744)*, Vol. II, *Language, Law, and History* (Lewiston, N.Y.: Mellen Press, 1992).

this world. The whole world is the horizon of Vico's conclusive vision. In an extension of the rhetorical argument against Epicurus, Hobbes, Machiavelli, and Spinoza, he turns to the Pyrrhonist Bayle and, above all, to Polybius's claim that "if there were philosophers in the world there would be no need in the world of religions" (NS/1110). Why this emphasis on "world"?

"World" has geographic or spatial connotations (unlike *saeculum*, which connotes the time of the world). Polybius's world is the Roman world and the *oikoumene* emerging—as in Epicurean physics—from a random coalescence of atoms impelled by a drive to absorb and possess that which lies outside.[14] Roman imperialism, then, is shaped by a scientific imperialism. For Vico, however, "world" is chiefly one's own familiar world of shared language and memories, of which man is the custodian; it is also the sphere of one's public involvements and the context of one's significant acts. From this standpoint, the central flaw of the political Epicureanism of Machiavelli, Bayle, and Polybius lies in its randomness that defies order and its lack of the sense of the whole.

By contrast, Vico's political theology depends on and elaborates a vision of the whole made of parts. In this sense, it suggests a cosmopolis, which is neither the promise of an impossible utopia nor of a healthy city of mere needs. One puts us too close to the gods, the other too close to the pigs, and both falsify the nature of man. In the "Conchiusione," as he reflects on the institutions of the entire human race Vico calls his cosmopolis "la gran città delle nazioni fondata e governata da Dio" (the great city of the nations that was founded and is governed by God) (NS/1107). The historical, partial, and even fallible incarnations of this City of God are Sparta, Athens, and Rome.[15] These cities' decadence notwithstanding, their public moral virtues persist as residual elements of shared social values, and they are, thus, earthly, imperfect traces of the City of God. Of these three cities, fallen Rome, because of the enduring universality of its laws and its empire,

[14] For questions of cosmology and global politics in Polybius see Harold C. Baldry, *The Unity of Mankind in Greek Thought* (Cambridge: Cambridge University Press, 1965); see also Philip Hardie, *Virgil's Aeneid: Cosmos and Imperium* (London: Oxford University Press, 1986) for Polybius's view of the Roman Empire as the cosmos itself (*Histories*, Book I, Chapter 1).

[15] The historical cities are earthly cities that bear traces of St. Augustine's City of God. For the links between Vico and Augustine see Ada Lamacchia, "Vico e Agostino: La presenza del 'De civitate Dei' nella 'Scienza nuova' in *Giambattista Vico: Poesia-Logica-Religione* (Brescia: Morcelliana, 1986). It should be pointed out that Plato attacks Athens for its class war, bad educational system, and rule by democracy (*Republic*, 488a). His ideal city is Sparta for its economic self-sufficiency and political stability. For the idea of the cosmopolis see Edmund Jacobitti, "Between the *Vita Activa* and the *Vita Contemplativa*: Toulmin's *Cosmopolis* and the Return to (Some) Vichian Concepts," *New Vico Studies*, 9 (1991), pp. 77–85. The article is a review of Stephen Toulmin, *Cosmopolis: The Hidden Agenda of Modernity* (New York: Free Press, 1990).

is the model for a universal monarchy or, as Book V of the *New Science* has it, for what Vico perceives as the emerging shape of a unified Christian Europe in the time of the *ricorso* (NS/1094).

Vico's plan is not to write a chiliastic utopian fantasy about papal rule, as does Tommaso Campanella—to mention a flagrant case of Counter-Reformation baroque and theocratic universalism—in his *Monarchy of the Messiah* (1605). Campanella's apocalyptic project for the conversion of heathens, Mohameddans, and Jews or for the reconversion of Protestants to the Catholic faith under a universal (Spanish) monarchy finds an appropriately parodic distortion in Traiano Boccalini's satire of baroque dreams of universal renovation in his *Ragguagli di Parnaso* (1612). Unlike Campanella, Vico's text, that on the face of it merely aims at bringing historical self-understanding and portrays universal history without a telos, makes not a single Christian confession but Providence the unifying idiom of Europe's violent religious divisions. The reason for what has been seen as the scandalous bracketing of Christ in his political theology lies in the consciousness that Christianity's theological universalism is politically a part of a larger whole. Vico is closer to Dante's imaginative conjunction of Augustinian eschatology of the City of God and Vergilian, Roman empire.[16]

These two large disagreements that Vico registers with Machiavellian political thought would suggest that he intends to align his own political theory with the tradition of the anti-Machiavel. But Vico knows only too well that he must come to terms with Machiavelli in the knowledge that morality and power cannot be thought of as drastically antithetical issues. Such a moralistic dualism would end up as a specular opposition and would unavoidably repropose the question of hierarchy of one term over the other. At stake here, then, is not just deciding how much of Machiavelli's thought Vico assimilates into his *New Science*. The question, rather, is how can he establish his distance from Machiavelli, just as he did from Platonic utopism.

Clearly, the conceptual similarities and differences between them (from their common Augustinian matrix about the fallen human condition to the shared Polybian theory of historical cycles, to their concerns with understanding key terms such as fear, order, religion, and the pair Fortune/Providence) show that Vico is engaged in a steady critical dialogue with Machiavelli as well as in a radical redefinition of his lexicon. The issue for Vico is to determine whether religious morality is subjected to power or, on the contrary, power can be subjected to the sovereignty of moral judgments. From this standpoint, Vico's overt dismissal of Machiavelli is a necessary political and rhetorical gesture.

[16] For a discussion of Dante, and further bibliography, see my *Dante, Poet of the Desert: History and Allegory in the Divine Comedy* (Princeton: Princeton University Press, 1979), especially pp. 147–91.

But above and beyond the conventional dismissal of Machiavelli (but Tacitus is, as it were, his alias) as a teacher of "the evil arts of rule,"[17] we must briefly turn to "Poetic Politics" (NS/582–678) in order to grasp Vico's sense of unavoidable Machiavellian politics and the chaotic world of Epicurean science. This long and largely opaque section of the text is immediately preceded by a reflection on language in the last section on "Poetic Economy": political-poetic fictions are made necessary by the poverty of speech in the first times, although also in the present copiousness of language the same word designates different and sometimes contrary things (NS/581). This caveat about the unavoidable ambiguities of language turns out to be central to Vico's strategy and aim: how can the controlled ambiguity of discourse confront and contain the chaos forever threatening the fragile fabric of political life.

The section begins from the first commonwealths that were born in a most severely aristocratic form (NS/582). Greco-Roman myths and Roman history are arrayed to give evidence of the plebeians' rebelliousness against the commonwealth of aristocrats or optimates. If the myths of Tantalus, Sisyphus, and Cadmus (NS/583) exemplify the plebeians' aspirations, the fable of Cybele or Ops, who conceals the infant Jove from Saturn, who is seeking to devour him, is read as the narrative of what political theorists, such as the Tacitists and Machiavellians, call *arcana imperii*—the obscure secrets of government conducted under cover of darkness (NS/587–88). This social strife—Vico adds by quoting from Aristotle's *Politics* (1310)—proves his assertion that in "the heroic commonwealths the nobles swore eternal enmity against the plebs" (NS/588). This perennially turbulent trait of social history is indelibly carved in the Greek etymology of "*polemos*, war, from *polis*, city" (NS/588).

The perception of perpetual war, which Hobbes posits as the essence of political life, leads Vico to interpret Minerva—directly against the metaphysical meditations of the philosophers—not as the wisdom of the "counselor" (such as, for instance, Vico himself) but as the emblem of predatory arms. When the discussion shifts to Roman history and to its formal symbols of power the same pattern of political history as in the mythical past obtains. Rome's history, which begins with the right of asylum, and not with agrarian revolts, is still marked by the plebeians' seditions over their rights of citizenship and access to the nobles' ceremonies and, more generally, by their political will to change the form of government (NS/609). Appropriately enough, Roman history is viewed through the prism of the relationship between politics and laws (kept hidden to the plebeians) (NS/621), of natural rights, the taxation of nobles, the emergence of the

---

[17] The phrase occurs in the proem to *On the Most Ancient Wisdom of the Italians*, trans. L. M. Palmer (Ithaca: Cornell University Press, 1988), p. 44. The proem dedicates the book to Paolo Mattia Doria.

agora as the place of law making, political representation in the assemblies, and the later structure of society into the hierarchy of three classes. In effect, the survey of Roman history shows it to be a knot of puzzling paradoxes: in it virtue is at one with arrogance, moderation is found in the middle of avarice, justice alongside inequality and cruelty (NS/668).

It is possible to consider Vico's elaborate, labyrinthine disquisition on "Poetic Politics" as a case of diligent archaeology into Rome's wondrous enigma, of a philological scholarly reconstruction of Greece's "perpetual historical mythology" (NS/662) in the wake of Thucydides, Livy, and Tacitus. But Vico's "objective" graph of history, of which only an "obscure memory, a confused imagination" (NS/665) remains, does not completely hide the thrust of his political project, the road map of twists and turns he delineates. What does his rhetoric of objectivity really wish to convey? To answer this question we must look at the extensive metaphoric patterns that sustain the articulation of this stretch of the text.

The pattern emerging from the narrative argues that politics is a cannibalistic and monstrous reality. The tragic figurations for the harshness of political life turn Menenius's classical fable of the body politic (NS/499) into a caricature of the literal, grim practices of devouring one's enemies. A number of political fables focus explicitly on cannibalism and, as such, they recall Aristotle's political realism. The first is the fable of Saturn devouring the infant Jove, while the priests of Cybele or Ops conceal him (NS/587–88). In Vico's hermeneutics the story exemplifies the voraciousness of the servants (Saturn) for the masters' fields to be saved by the secret powers of Ops. Another fable tells of Mercury, who brings the souls back from Orcus (NS/601). Its political meaning is clear: Mercury imposes the law on the mutinous servants, while Orcus embodies the lawless state waiting to "devour" all men. The myth of the labyrinth, where the Minotaur devours infants, as much as the story of Orc seeking to devour Andromeda (NS/635), is understood as the fear of raids by corsair ships into Greek waters. The reflection on barbarians and troglodytes, who kill strangers crossing their borders (NS/636–40), echoes the Homeric account of Ulysses encountering the Cyclopes who kill and eat strangers.

The political economy of bestial desecration of bodies, of their reification as if they were contingent entities to be incorporated and annihilated, is grounded in the science of atomistic physics and its premise of formless chaos, of Orcus who is "greedy for forms and devours all forms" (NS/688). More poignantly, the infernal appropriation of bodies (see *Inferno*, Canto XXXIII), in its horror, strips of all illusions the political philosophies of chance and unalterable, blind fate that elevates disorder to the rule of polis. As a mode of effacement of the principle of otherness, the cannibalistic practice is revealed as the empirical incarnation of the corpuscular theories of nature.

Vico stares unflinchingly at the monstrosity of politics, at its structure of power as a voracious game played by gods and man-beasts alike. He confronts the naked realities of power in the awareness that they cannot be simply ignored by taking the moral high ground as the anti-Machiavellians pretend. Like Machiavelli and Hobbes, Vico recognizes the biology of politics, the bodies' cannibalization of other bodies, that Aristotle himself in the wake of Homer, had presented as the reality haunting the lawless state. And if Machiavelli in *The Prince* casts the centaur or double-natured Chiron as Achilles' teacher of the secret, duplicitous craft of government, Vico invests the Minotaur in his labyrinth, as well as a host of other hybrid mythical shapes, with other significances. The Minotaur is the focus of his representation of the unavoidable ambiguities of political discourse as well as his ambiguous fascination with Machiavellian politics.

The text of "Poetic Politics" shifts into a lengthy meditation on the failure of Spain, "mother" of many bellicose nations, to unite all her peoples in Roman time and set up a universal empire, the "imperio dell'universo" on the banks of the Tagus (NS/644–45). The implication of the genealogical metaphor is that the family of Spanish nations has branched out into discordant and disconnected directions and that they went on to live the solitary and savage life of the Cyclops. Spain's historical failure at political universality (that for Vico, who lives in "Spanish" Naples, adumbrates the modern one) leads him to discuss the conduct of political affairs in kingdoms or cities that are isolated and autonomous from one another. A number of poetic fables are interpreted as narratives of the political world man constructs, as figures of a doubleness that is the condition of political discourse.

With utmost rigor Vico begins by giving the multiple dimensions of the word "canto," song (NS/646–48). Because of the poverty of speech, one word has many, ambiguous nuances and discordant meanings: a song is a prediction, a magic enchantment, such as that of the Sirens or Circe, or a contest. More substantively, he relates the fable of the satyr Marsyas killed by Apollo; of the deceptive song of the Sirens destroying sailors; of the Greek Sphinx killing wayfarers; of the satyr Pan, "mostro di due discordanti nature" (monster of two discordant natures) (NS/654); of Pasiphae and the Minotaur, the beast of death in the heart of the labyrinth; of Hercules who kills the centaur Nessus and who is, in turn, killed by a shirt soaked in Nessus's blood as a love charm; and of Orpheus, "the founder of Greece" (NS/659) who is dismembered by the fury of the delirious Bacchae. Along with these mythical figurations of doubleness, other characters are invested with a double identity, such as the poet Linus (NS/647) or Penelope, who, in some versions of her myth, rather than a chaste wife, is engaged in adulterous promiscuity (NS/654). From this Baconian standpoint, Vico interprets these stories as fictions of the perpetual if ever shifting war between aristocrats and plebeians.

With the advent of a democratic age, when plebeians enjoyed the same juridical rights as the aristocrats, both the heroic age and the wisdom of the theological poets (the "sappienti o politici" [NS/661], philosophers/sages or statesmen) come to an end. Vico lists Orpheus, Amphion, Linus, Musaeus, and others. These poets with their "cantare," with their persuasive songs, have the "scienza," the science, to keep the plebeians obedient to the nobles (NS/661). Science and rhetoric now converge, and the convergence marks the new political science for modern times. The world of chaos and atomistic randomness that modern science posits as the very foundation of the world is best confronted not by Machiavellian political philosophies that feed (on) chaos and present themselves as forms of order, but by the ambiguities of poetic language, by rhetorical incantations, and by the magic power of poetry.

Machiavelli at the end of *The Prince* turns to Petrarch's song and uses poetry rhetorically.[18] Vico picks up where Machiavelli left off. The "Corollaries concerning Poetic Tropes, Monsters, and Metaphors" (NS/404–11) argue that the seductive charm of poetic language consists in fictions' power to be taken as truths. By the magic of poetry, dualisms of minds and bodies appear joined together (NS/ 404); subjects coalesce with forms (NS/405); parts are shown to be wholes (NS/407); and, in the case of irony, truth can be simulated (NS/408). Finally, whereas Platonic and Epicurean philosophies forge a polarization of order and chaos, poetic language exceeds the boundaries of all rigid divisions and dramatizes the constant interplay of chaos and order: it evokes together both the order of the song and the monsters, gathers in its compass all dictions and *contra*dictions, and shows the constant shifts of all forms. More than that, Vico's etymologizing, by which words are broken into their minuscule constitutive syllables and are shown as they recompose into new clusters and proximate words, brings atomistic theories within the pattern of language, as if atomism were the peculiar reality of language.

Only a rhetorician like Vico himself (and his *New Science*)—so he obliquely claims—knows how to confront the hard challenges of the modern age, whose epitome is science's insight into the constitutive randomness of the cosmos. Doria's project of yoking together Plato and Machiavelli, high-minded idealism and realistic politics, does not overcome the scandal of Machiavellianism; indeed, the acknowledgment of Machiavellianism appears now to be a version of Bacon's delusive utopianism. Vico's

---

[18] My *The Worlds of Petrarch* (Durham, N.C.: Duke University Press, 1993) reads Petrarch's poetry from a Machiavellian perspective of power.

stance is to bring Plato down to the real (where Tacitus is to be found), while necessarily seeming to eschew Machiavellian political philosophy. Thus, the *New Science* replaces Machiavelli's simulations in the task of unifying Christian Europe.

This means that for Vico what is needed is a new philosophy of authority (NS/350; 386–90). The new founder is the author of discourse. He is the philosopher-rhetorician who, rooted in divine authority, knows how to bring together within the circle of his vision the ancient discourse of moderation (which Plato grasped) and the modern discourse of liberty (which Machiavelli perceived albeit in a perverted mode). He is a teacher who knows how to interpret the hidden discourses of myths and laws, how to accommodate the contradictory senses of words, how to manipulate songs leaving room for alternate significations, how violence can be rhetorically contained, and order, which is always fragile, can be pursued. In short, the new discourse will produce another, more realistic knowledge about what is to be human and about the limits of politics. Socrates' experience continues to be Vico's model.

As the violent dismemberment of Orpheus and the fate of Thebes, founded by the song of Amphion, exemplify, Vico knows that the political has a tragic limit. He obliquely represents his understanding of the sinister dangers attendant on every founder's claims. The tragic truth is that the dissemination of violence in history is unstoppable and so is the decadence of all historical formations. The decadence can be contained by piety and by the mosaic of sciences and arts (poetry, rhetoric, law, theology, philosophy) on which the map of the *New Science*'s authority is drafted. The limit of the political lies in the inescapable irrationality in Orpheus's violent death and the destructive passions dominant in Thebes, the city of Cadmus, who kills the dragon, but who is himself turned into a snake.

Thebes is the epitome of the earthly city. It sprung from the earth and is the child of impious violence that it is tragically doomed to repeat. The benefits of Europe's civil order notwithstanding, its foundation is in the fable of Jove's abduction of Europa (NS/743), that is, in foundational violence, and its original perimeter was Crete, the site of the labyrinth. Lastly, Vico knows that the limit of the political resides in the necessity of death which, as he stresses by the etymological derivatives of *homo* (man) from *humando* (burial place in the ground) (NS/12), is literally the ground of being human. The tragic limit of politics leads not to a sense of futility; rather, it triggers the conviction of politics as a heroic art that needs heroes.

The *New Science* memorializes history's past, but it also features piety toward and a radical critique of death. As the domain of loss and bankruptcy of self, man's death puts in place a new political economy. It marks the limit of an individual's totalizing project, but, at the same time, it is the new beginning of someone else's project. As a distinctive feature of Vico's politics, moreover, death and its ceremonies constitute the essence of human civilization. They enjoin us to both draw and to efface the sharp line between what is human and what is not human. Vico's political thinking straddles the hazy boundaries between these two interconnected possibilities. There lies his at once heroic and tragic sense of the human polity. As the next two chapters contend, this ambivalence about politics leads Vico both to construct a feasible political theology and to show how theology transcends politics.

Chapter 9

THE *RICORSO:* A NEW WAY OF SEEING

BOOK V OF THE *New Science* focuses on the theory of the *ricorso* of history. At its simplest, the centerpiece of this theory posits the recurrence or recourse, within the spiral movement of history, of the pertinent institutions of the past—forms of government, laws, modes of ownership, and so forth. To make clear that such a theory does not simply underwrite or re-propose the more conventional belief in the mechanically repetitive pattern of history, Vico refers to the recurrences between discontinuous but symmetrical stages of history as "correspondences" (NS/1046). There is a correspondence or recurrence of institutions between the first and the returned barbarian times. Vico draws attention to the way he writes, and he states that evidence of such a correspondence is scattered all over the previous books of the *New Science*. In Book V, however, Vico goes on to give a "luogo particolare," (NS/1046), a special place, to his theory of the *ricorso*.

The brief self-reflection in the introductory paragraph of Book V on the structure of the work, its strategy of composition, and its style—to the effect that what is going to be put in a particular place appeared earlier in the text in a fragmentary and dislocated fashion—will turn out to be central to our understanding of the *ricorso*. Vico will not belabor the rhetorical question of style at this point. Rather, the text proceeds to illustrate the substance of the *ricorso*, which for Vico is tantamount to reflecting on the key questions of the *New Science:* the sense and the necessity of a new discourse, the possibility of the new beginnings of history, the nature of the modern world, and so forth.[1] A glance at the general architecture of Book V shows that at the heart of the *ricorso* lies a sustained analysis of the problematics and dilemmas of modernity, which Vico summarizes as the complex relationship of theology, philosophy, and politics in modern times. The idea of the *ricorso* depends on and responds to the perception of the crisis enveloping modernity.

Divided into three parts, Book V of the *New Science* starts off by evoking the emergence of Christianity as the decisive event that has inaugurated the new beginning of history (NS/1047). By deploying a metaphor of clearing ("schiarita"), which could suggest that history be seen in the clar-

---

[1] For the idea of beginning, developed in a Vichian key, see Edward W. Said, *Beginnings* (Baltimore: Johns Hopkins University Press, 1975).

ity of Christianity's revelatory light, Vico describes Christianity as a religion willed by God. The reference to the divine origin of the Christian religion is followed by a compressed consideration of the historical reasons for its triumph. The heroic virtue of the early Christian martyrs, who are literally "witnesses" and who endured suffering unto death to defend their faith, undermined the political power of imperial Rome. By the same token, the doctrine of the Fathers of the Church and the occurrence of miracles show, by contrast, the hollowness of the philosophy of Greece ("la vana sapienza greca") (NS/1047). These three causes, encompassing theology, philosophy, and politics, make possible the emergence of a "nuovo ordine" of "umanità" (a new order of humanity) (NS/1047). The new order is marked by the new ordering of the disciplines (philosophy is subordinated to theology, and so is politics), and in their new configuration they mark the advent in history of truly divine times. One infers that for Vico such a hierarchy of disciplines has decayed if not entirely collapsed in his own times. Finding the alternative to the morass of the present is a challenge worthy of a heroic mind.

The second section of Book V further thematizes these concerns. The section focuses on the returned heroic times with heroic parliaments, feudal laws, armed courts, and rustic fiefs. Vestiges of these institutions, Vico goes on to say, are found in the "sagro consiglio Napoletano" (sacred council of Naples) (NS/1082) and in the contemporary aristocratic governments of Poland, Sweden, and Denmark. With the obvious intent of recapitulating the conceptual parabola of his whole text as it approaches the end, Vico recalls the beginning of the *New Science*, the "Idea dell'Opera" (Idea of the Work) (NS/1085). The conclusions he now draws, he says, were anticipated at the beginning of the work. There is in the seemingly gratuitous, self-referential statement the claim of a coherent intellectual pursuit. But the self-reflexive writerly recall also signals that, from a formal viewpoint, a cycle is concluded and that a new start is needed. Within this context there is a reference to the revolutionary role played by a modern institution, the Italian universities, in promoting the thought of free commonwealths in the European kingdoms.

In the last section of Book V Vico grapples with the "mondo antico e moderno delle nazioni" (the ancient and modern world of nations) (NS/1088). The title of the section suggests that we are in the presence of a version of the traditional *querelle* between ancients and moderns. But Vico, who has confronted the implications of this rhetorical mode in the *Study Methods of Our Times*, does not lose sight of the central issue of Book V: the role of religion in political life. Thus, he argues that in ancient history Rome's lordship of the world—over and against rival claims to hegemony by Carthage, Capua, and Numantia—was providential and it was characterized by its adhering to and retaining as long as possible each of the three forms of civil states (aristocracy, popular liberty, and monarchy) (NS/1088).

As Vico's attention shifts to modernity, he gives a conspectus of European and world politics from Russia to Ethiopia, from Japan to China, from pre-Columbian America to Europe. In effect, the narrative circles back to the very beginning of Book V as it explicitly focuses on Christianity and on the political ends of Christianity in Europe. By virtue of the Christian religion, which holds "an infinitely pure and perfect idea of God" (NS/1092), Europe abounds in all the good things making for the happiness of human life. This quasi-utopian evocation of European political realities, which Vico knows to be basically chaotic, yields to the statement that Christianity has appropriated the most learned philosophies of the gentiles and cultivates as its own the three languages of its tradition (Hebrew, Greek, and Latin)(NS/1094). The section concludes with the assertion that from the standpoint of purely political ends, Christianity provides the theological justification of authority and reason at a time, one might add, when European discourse witnesses the breakdown of their correlation.

The discussion of modernity climaxes with a form of modern self-reflexivity: he refers to the role of the *New Science* and its radical novelty in intellectual history:

> Ora, con tale ricorso di cose umane civili, che particolarmente in questo libro si è ragionato, si rifletta . . . e si avrà tutta spiegata la storia, non già particolare ed in tempo delle leggi e de' fatti de' romani o de' greci, ma . . . la storia ideale delle leggi eterne, sopra le quali corrono i fatti di tutte le nazioni, ne' loro sorgimenti, progressi, stati, decadenze e fini, se ben fusse (lo che é certamente falso) che dall'eternità di tempo in tempo nascessero mondi infiniti. Laonde non potemmo noi far a meno di non dare a quest'opera l'invidioso titolo di *Scienza nuova*, perch'era un troppo ingiustamente defraudarla di suo diritto e ragione, ch' aveva sopre un argomento universale quanto lo é d'intorno alla natura comune delle nazioni, per quella propietà c'ha ogni scienza perfetta nella sua idea, la quale ci é da Seneca, spiegata con quella vasta espressione: *Pusilla res hic mundus est, nisi id, quod quaerit, omnis mundus habeat.* (NS/1096)

> (Now, in the light of the recourse of human civil institutions to which we have given particular attention in Book V, let us reflect . . . and there will be unfolded before us, not the particular history in time of the laws and deeds of the Romans or the Greeks, but . . . the ideal history of the eternal laws which are instanced by the deeds of all nations in their rise, progress, maturity, decadence, and dissolution [and which would be so instanced] even if (as is certainly not the case) there were infinite worlds being born from time to time throughout eternity. Hence we could not refrain from giving this work the invidious title of a *New Science*, for it was too much to defraud it unjustly of the

rightful claim it had over an argument so universal as that concerning the common nature of nations in virtue of that property which belongs to every science that is perfect in its idea, and which Seneca has set forth for us in his vast
expression: this world is a paltry thing unless all the world may find "therein"
what it seeks.)

The brunt of this conclusive paragraph is unequivocal: at the risk of being
tautological, one can paraphrase it to mean that the *New Science* is new and
is a science. Its scientific status and newness are guaranteed by its original
discovery of universally valid laws of history. More precisely, the newness
of the *New Science* consists in the fact that it goes beyond the particularized, partial, and relative accounts of classical historiography, be it Roman
or Greek history. Quite the contrary, Vico claims to provide in the *New
Science*, by a trans-historical comparison of the "facts" of ancient and modern nations, a unitary, comprehensive consciousness of ideal eternal history.
He has an absolute vision of the whole, and this vision is far removed from
St. Augustine's or Bossuet's salvation history or patristic accounts of biblical history, which center on the vicissitudes of the City of God in history.
Unlike them, Vico has provided nothing less than the pantograph of the
universal history of the city of man. From this standpoint, his representation transgresses the logic of modernity's view of history as a sequence of
discrete, autonomous periods sundered from one another.

The outright vindication of the novelty of the *New Science* at the end of
Book V, as the symmetry of the textual structure makes clear, recalls and
counterbalances the statement made at the beginning of Book V, that a
"nuovo ordine" was ushered in by Christianity (NS/1047). The symmetry, signaled by the recurrence of the word "nuovo" at either end, suggests
the presence of a link between Christianity and the *New Science*. Further,
Vico's claim about his text, advanced, as it is, in the immediate context of
his discussion of modernity and within the larger framework of the *ricorso*,
leaves no doubt that Vico's ultimate, abiding concern is the fate of modernity and the future of history. One can even say that for Vico the *New Science* is the latest epochal event of modernity, a self-conscious fulfillment of
and response to modernity's achievements and blind self-delusions.

The conceptual trajectory of the text traces quite plainly the itinerary and
destination of his thought. A quick glance at the rhetorical structure of his
argument clarifies his purposes. Vico's self-reflective consciousness at the
end of Book V is the point of arrival of a philosophical exploration or epic
journey, marked by numberless detours, turnings, dark passages, and digressions, over the whole history of humanity. The journey began in Book
I in the obscurity of fabulous first beginnings, ranged over the modifications in the structure of human consciousness, and lands in the sunlit plain
of Christian history in Book V. The presence of this overall narrative pat-

tern shows that the view of Vico as a mere erudite hopelessly embroiled in the cult of calcified anachronisms, himself an anachronism in the modern world of technology and science that forever elude his grasp, is utterly false. Vico's understanding of the dissonances and polarizations constitutive of modernity is the premise for his original and bold counter-discourse to modernity. Book V of the *New Science* lucidly articulates such a counter-discourse and the necessity for it.

Within the narrative economy of Book V the account of the *ricorso* symmetrically reenacts and mirrors the general design of the whole of the *New Science*. As was seen from the brief synopsis given above, Book V starts with the theological age of the new Christian history, it goes through the heroic medieval times, and it ends with the modern age and the role of the *New Science* in Vico's own times. The deliberate double structural symmetry—whereby the *ricorso* is the *mise-en-abyme* of history's general movement—draws attention to the presence of an artful design above and beyond the haphazard, disjointed arrangement of hybrid fragments making up the body of the *New Science*. Order can be reached, this is the point, by going through the maze of the text, for behind the tissue of digressions and convoluted lines of argumentation there is the narrator's mind that never loses sight of the argument's direction and final destination. At stake, however, is not merely a formal question of narrative coherence or stylized scheme of dramatic unity. Rather, the clear design Vico imparts to his argument brings into the open a symmetrical "correspondence" between fabulous beginnings and Christian new beginnings of history. The *ricorso* is a bold theory of history's possible new beginnings, of history's second chance, as it were, and the new beginnings occur in the shadow of the new vision delivered by the *New Science*.

On the face of it, Vico conceives of his text as a new discourse or counter-discourse for the modern world. In what way is it new? Is it new by force of its being old? What is modernity to him? What brought the disjunction between antiquity and modernity? And what exactly is the relationship, which the text suggests, between Christianity and the *New Science*, Christianity and modernity, and modernity and the *New Science*? Is the *New Science* the rational, modern endpoint of the new history inaugurated by Christian theology? Is the *New Science* a new or reborn political science, a new theologico-political treatise that prudently wills to replace the dominant and aberrant political philosophies of modernity? Or is there some other path of thought Vico opens up in order to reconcile and reconnect the broken pieces of the present? And what is the relationship between beginnings and new beginnings? Book V of the *New Science* reflects on this traditionally contentious tangle of questions, and only through their analysis will Vico's sense of the role, nature, and necessity of his own discourse be determined.

First of all, what is Vico's version of modernity? The question is fundamental to all other questions sketched above. Vico knows only too well that
he is not one of the founders of modernity. He keeps this in mind—and so
should we—throughout his discussion. As shown earlier in Chapter 3, the
shadowy politics of modernity—conspiracies, dim Machiavellian maneu-
vers, wars, baroque schemes of absolute power at home and abroad—engage him as a historian but not as a founder. The founders of modernity
are for him Machiavelli, Galileo, Descartes, and Bacon, who, along with
their epigones, such as Bayle, Hobbes, and Spinoza, constitute the tradition of modernity. Vico turns away from them and redrafts his own map of
modernity. The gesture of separating oneself from one's predecessors is itself, transparently enough, a typically modern act, but Vico is not hampered by it. Quite the contrary.

Against these first founders, who hold that the moderns are better than
the ancients; who in their pursuit of novelties enshrine the present; who
believe that the world begins with them as sovereign subjects, and who also
posit their own self-origination; who sever the present from the past; who
draft a map of the heavens but mistake their own symbolic constructions
of the mind as objective truths of nature; and for whom the wisdom of the
ages is inadequate for the modern project, Vico places modernity's coil
within the ancient spirals of universal history. He agrees with the founders
that classical political thought cannot solve the realities represented by the
modern phenomenon of Machiavellian politics. Yet, ancient classical
thought remains for Vico crucial for grappling with modernity. This is the
theoretical framework within which the radical claim of the *ricorso* is to be
understood.

More to the point, directly against the founders, Vico proposes a new
foundation, a new project of learning—the *New Science*—that would heal
the divisions wrought by the founders' own theories. As we recall, he addresses his *New Science* to the universities of Europe as if to unveil to his
colleagues the conceptual errors and deluded perspectives in the founders'
thought. The founders are in error because, with all their rational methods
and road maps, they do not really grasp the dangers of the modern world.
Modernity enshrines the cult of power and of self, and this cult leads to divisive, disintegrative practices, of which war is the epitome. What is more,
the founders' very theories, because of the habits of thought they perpetuate, are the source of these dangers. And for Vico the founders are certainly naive in not realizing that the modern world and the new age they
announce are older than they think. It follows that for him their intellectual conceits must be pitilessly dismantled.

Vico's disagreements begin with the very idea of what exactly the "new"
means. Since the thinker who, along with Plato, most exerts a hold on his
imagination is Bacon, we must closely compare their respective under-

standings of the term. In the preface to the *Novum Organum*, for instance, Bacon states that the "honor and reverence due to the ancients remain untouched and undiminished" (Vol. IV, p. 41) in him. His modesty toward the ancients, however, serves only to underscore his confidence in the boldness and originality of his scientific project. From this standpoint Bacon is most like Machiavelli. Bacon knows that he is not simply founding "a new sect in philosophy" after the fashion of the Greeks or of moderns such as Telesio and Patrizi. Rather, his part in the "commencement of the great undertaking" lies in his opening up "a new way for the understanding," (*Novum Organum*, Vol. IV, aphorism 116, pp. 103–41). In providing, that is, a way for modern science untried by and unknown to the ancients. The realm of science, which for Bacon is inductive science, is the watershed between ancients and moderns. As Chapter 2 has shown, Vico has had some inklings of the imaginative links between Machiavellian political science and Bacon's notion of science.

Vico certainly inherits the strong, visionary impulse of Bacon's mind. But, unlike Bacon, and more like a self-ironic philosopher or a novelist with a sense of the quirks of language, Vico plunges us into the polysemous maze the adjective "new" traces in his *New Science*. We know by now that the fulcrum of his thought consists in his exploring the "new," unexpected implications of common words and, thereby, in toppling calcified learned conventions which the word supports. As a metaphor of time's ceaseless mobility "new" suggests that time generates disjunctions and it is the real innovator in history. Antiquity, which Vico never idealizes, cannot actually impede the advent of the new. But "new"—as readers of Dante's *Vita nuova* recall and those of the *New Science* find out—means fresh, modern, young as well as strange or marvelous. The sense of marvelous tilts the *New Science* within the orbit of the fantastic, visionary mode of thought. In factual terms, on the other hand, the "new" of the *New Science* depends on the historical disjunction ushered in by Christianity. Modernity and the *New Science* are branches of a tree whose trunk is rooted in the Christian new beginnings of history. Clearly, Vico's *ricorso* necessarily has to start with a rethinking of theology, and he does this by defining and questioning the substance of the Christian new beginnings of history.

Other theorists of modern political science had identified modernity with the beginning of Christianity. The link had been forged most notably by two of the founders of modernity, Machiavelli in his *Discourses* and Bacon in the *Advancement of Learning*. Vico acknowledges their insights, but he charges that they misunderstand Christianity, which is a way of saying that they misunderstand modernity, and their misunderstanding has tragic consequences for the politics of our time. The error of the founders consists in their viewing both the modern world and Christianity from a secular perspective. By contrast, Vico's project does not aim at the subver-

sion of religion or making it subservient, as his two predecessors do, to political power or the empire of science. His rethinking of the relationship between politics and theology in European history—which stands at the center of his discussion of the *ricorso*—will prudently theologize politics and
politicize theology.

In his *Discourses* (Book II, Chapter 2) Machiavelli, who understood the
spiritual novelty of Christianity but wished to neutralize it, views the Christian virtue of humility as the single most important source of contemporary political weakness.[2] Because the Christian religion places the greatest
good in the contempt for the world and because it glorifies contemplative
rather than active men, it goes counter to the Roman virtues, which are essentially political and martial virtues. The cause of the acquisition of the
empire, Machiavelli says, was the martial virtue of the Romans (Book II,
Chapter 1). This is not to say that Machiavelli underestimates the power
of religious belief in either taming the ferocity of rivaling groups or in en-
gendering the stability of the polis. His awareness of the role of religion in
ancient Rome is steady in the *Discourses* (Book I, Chapters 11–15) just as
Savonarola's prophetic claims in modern times (Book I, Chapter 12) do
not go unacknowledged. But in modern times the Roman Church, which
Machiavelli thinks has strayed from the pure faith of its beginnings, has
brought ruin and disunion to Italy. More generally, for Machiavelli the
pagan religion of the Romans plays a constructive civic role altogether different from the enfeebling religion of the Christians.

Vico begins Book V of the *New Science* by affirming, as Machiavelli never
does, Christianity's divine origin (NS/1047). The assertion, which is true
only in the realm of belief, is quickly followed in the same sentence by the
admission that the "virtue" of the Christian martyrs has dismantled the
power of imperial Rome. By one and the same stroke, in short, Vico acknowledges both the power of the new religion over the political might of
Rome and, thereby, he contradicts Machiavelli's proposition about supposed Christian weakness. The use of the Roman word "virtú" for the
Christian martyrs invests them with the martial attributes that properly belong and are essential to the heroic mythology of their pagan opponents.

The new Christian theology did subvert the old, Roman politics, but,
pace Machiavelli, who in this sense thinks like an Augustinian, there is no
intrinsic mutual exclusion between theology and politics. The establishment of the new Christian dispensation was secured, as Vico proceeds to

[2] For an esoteric reading of Machiavelli and his *Discourses* see Harvey C. Mansfield, *Machi-
avelli's New Modes and Orders: A Study of the Discourses on Livy* (Ithaca: Cornell University
Press, 1979). See also Leo Strauss, *Thoughts on Machiavelli* (Glencoe, Ill.: Free Press, 1958).
Along this power-centered hermeneutical line see also Jerry Weinberger, *Science, Faith, and
Politics: Francis Bacon and the Utopian Roots of the Modern Age* (Ithaca: Cornell University
Press, 1985).

say in the successive paragraph 1048, by setting up "religioni armate" (military religious orders) to counter the proliferation of sects and of other religious confessions threatening its very existence. The signs that the new theological times were warlike is the return of the "pura et pia bella" (the pure and pious wars) (NS/1049) as well as the return of the "Sagra Real Maestá" (Sacred Royal Majesty) (NS/1048). In medieval political theology, from which Vico draws the statement, this is the concept of sacred kingship, which, along with other priestly orders and offices, views the political ruler as the receptacle, mediator, or emanation of the sacred.

Vico's critique of Machiavelli focuses, then, on his skeptical silence about the divine origin of Christianity as well as his false ideas about its power to inspire martial actions. For Vico, Christianity does not break completely with the pagan past but radically redefines its values. That this is so is made clear by a second strong point Vico notes concerning Christianity. Vico states that Christianity opposed "la vana sapienza greca" (the vain wisdom of Greece) (NS/1047) with the doctrine of the Church Fathers and with the performance of miracles. The text now stages the confrontation between theology and philosophy.

The phrase about the vanity of Greek wisdom, which is the vanity of philosophy, faintly echoes St. Paul's remarks about the inadequacy of the "wisdom of the world" vis-à-vis the secret and hidden wisdom of God (1 Cor. 1:18–2:5). By the echo Vico is saying with Saint Paul that the gospel is not merely a new philosophy, and that philosophy is vain because it cannot presume to fathom God's mysterious acts. Furthermore, the echo from St. Paul marks clear boundaries between theology and philosophy: the Christian new beginnings are founded on the disseminating power of belief and not on rational philosophy or eloquent wisdom. In political terms this means that the establishment of a theocracy has no room for reason's doubts and aporias. Thus, the domain of faith expresses itself through the prism of the words of the Fathers (or canonical biblical exegesis), the deeds of the witnesses, and the supernatural signs of miracles.

The reference to patristic exegesis can be taken as an oblique allusion to a past time of hermeneutical consensus on the Bible, which starkly contrasts with the boundless, non-authoritarian, and sectarian subjectivism dominant in modern biblical interpretation. As we come to expect from Vico's quest for a philosophy of authority, both the crisis of the principle of authority and Cartesian subjectivism, which internalizes authority and which he consistently bemoans, go hand in hand. By the same token, the reference to miracles, which are God's interventions in history, or, more literally, wonders performed by God, allows us to gauge further Vico's willed distance from the founders of modernity. The founders are for him natural philosophers, who reduce the world to the parameters of its natural, mechanical functions. Accordingly, their project of knowledge amounts to a rational political philosophy that presumes to order politics but leaves the political realm in the chains of a worse form of despotism.

A political philosopher, such as Bacon, discusses miracles in the context of natural theology or Divine Philosophy (*Advancement of Learning*, Vol. III, Book 2, p. 349). The atheists, so Bacon argues, are unaffected by miracles, and, by saying this, Bacon suggests that miracles are simply natural if odd phenomena or outright implausible impostures. They belong to the casual pattern of life and are likely to convert only idolaters or the superstitious "who acknowledged a deity but erred in his worship." Spinoza, however, devotes the entire sixth chapter of his *Theologico-Political Treatise* to miracles, and he concludes that they are either prodigious works of nature, which surpass human intelligibility, or expressions peculiar to the Hebrew language. While he discounts any supernatural explanation for miracles, Spinoza also quotes the opinion of the Jewish historian Joseph for whom the mystery is a question of opinion. Like Bacon and Machiavelli earlier, Spinoza's statement underwrites a medieval philosophical doctrine known as "Averroism," which, for all its complexity, is viewed as a theory of the double truth, the truth of philosophy and the truth of faith, each separate from the other. For Vico, however, the conceptualization of two distinct, separate domains of truth casts philosophy as the paradigm of divisiveness, which radically undermines the principle of the unity of truth. In Vico's eyes, the political consequences of such a theory are disastrous, as his argument on behalf of miracles makes clear.

Vico's attack against the libertines, the Spinozists, and Spinoza's own theorization of the commonwealth as if it were a "società . . . di mercadanti" (a society of hucksters) (NS/335) regulated, that is to say, by rational transactions of antagonistic self-interests, has already been discussed in Chapter 8. His reference to miracles in Book V, which he mentions without a hint of skepticism concerning their validity, extends his critique of the natural philosophers' reductive view of religious belief. As is suggested by the etymology of miracle, from *mirari*, to wonder, as well as by the epithet "meraviglioso" (marvelous) (NS/1050; 1056), used to qualify the occurrence of the recourse of some institutions in the new divine times, miracles are for Vico signs of a providential intervention in the natural order and part of a semiotics of grace.

The word "grazia" (grace), which is deployed in the introductory paragraph of Book V (NS/1046), has a precise theological connotation. Properly speaking, the word belongs to the grammar of Providence and overlaps with it. The link between grace and Providence has a biblical background—most conspicuously in Saint Paul (Eph. 2:8)—where grace qualifies God's providential act. In the theological tradition, on the other hand, grace and miracles are correlated. Thomas Aquinas claims that grace does not abrogate the natural order but fulfills it. Grace refounds nature, just as miracles are extraordinary invasions of the natural order (*Summa theologiae* 1a, q. 105, art. 4). Like grace, they enter into but do not annul the fundamental autonomy of nature. Vico's view of miracles accords with the most orthodox theological tradition.[3]

These arguments are crucial to Vico's reconceptualization of a unitary political project. Like Providence itself, miracles are for him (as they were for Aquinas) the basis for positing freedom. In and of themselves they are phenomena free (and in the process they free us) from the material determinations of nature. In so far as they are acts of wonder, they are irreducible to the order of nature and, indeed, they shatter the narrow, rational boundaries of natural philosophy. Quite clearly, Vico's emphatic legitimization or rehabilitation of theological discourse and its power is a deliberate strategy to counteract the dangers haunting modernity and its speculative constructions. The fundamental weakness of the modern project is its atheism, which has as its flip side a power ideology as well as the acknowledgment of the absolute sovereignty of the dry light of reason.

Vico has developed from the beginning, as shown in the previous chapter, a critique of philosophical Machiavellianism and the Epicurean philosophy of Hobbes (NS/179; 1109) on the grounds that atheism unravels the fabric of society. In the present context of the *ricorso* his delineation of Christianity upholds the very freedom that the naturalists deny. The irony is transparent: a philosopher, such as Spinoza, argues with disciplined awareness on behalf of the freedom of philosophizing. Yet, he submits to the belief in the tyranny of nature. This radical contradiction, which is lodged at the heart of the natural philosophies of both Stoics and Spinozists, is sharply expressed by Vico himself: these philosophers, he says, "make God an infinite mind subject to fate" (NS/335).

The phrase "subject to fate" has a paradoxical ring to it: without a theology of freedom, the vaunted yet well-earned freedom of philosophizing ends up being a mere cover for subjection to an ideology of power or to political and philosophical tyranny. It turns out, as shall be seen later, that this is precisely the philosophers' blind delusion: to believe that they are ever exempt from the yoke of tyranny. What is more, the moderns' notion that the truth of the philosophers is separable from the opinions of believers sets the two discourses of theology and philosophy on the course of a fatal collision. In effect, the doctrine of a double truth, which the philosophy of dissimulation upholds, hides a tacit hierarchy of values. It makes conspiratorial discourse into an ethics. By the same token, the practice of

---

[3] Giovanni Gentile, "Dal concetto della grazia a quello della Provvidenza," *Studi Vichiani* (Florence: Sansoni, 1969), pp. 145–61.

prudent dissimulation or nicodemism, of feigning belief for the sake of civic order, only masks an ironic claim of dissimulation's superiority over and against the presumed naiveté of belief.

The philosophical thought of the founders of modernity discards and/or misunderstands theology as well as fiction (which they take to be mere simulation), and in the process it fails, as Machiavelli and Hobbes did, to elaborate a new, workable political theology for the modern age. To make his point that theology is essential to the polity, Vico is forced to show by the logic of his argument that the moderns have actually misunderstood the nature of the true relationship between philosophy and politics. As a way of fashioning an alternative to the current construction of modernity and of making his counter-discourse acceptable, Vico thematizes in Book V of the *New Science* the fate of philosophy in its encounter with political power. There is throughout this section an extended pattern of references to the historical failure of classical and modern philosophical discourse vis-à-vis political power, which I now proceed to highlight.

I have already discussed Vico's open reference at the start of Book V to Christianity's triumph over "vain Greek wisdom" (NS/1047). Unlike Greek philosophy, which is so caught within the narrow complacencies and narcissism of its speculations as to appear frivolous or "vain," Christianity is marked by an openness to the divine and by a thrust toward universal knowledge, which is embodied by its open confession and clarity; it is also marked by its impulse to unify its three constitutive cultural traditions and to yoke together reason and authority. Whereas philosophy posits rationality as its beginning, Christianity begins with the recognition of the mystery of origins in the gift of God's making. More cogently, beside Greek philosophy, Christianity at its onset has also defeated Roman political power. The oblique link between philosophy and political power is articulated explicitly later in Section 2 of Book V as Vico alludes both to philosophy's own claims of power over the world of politics and to the disastrous consequences attendant on such claims.

The context for what could be dismissed as only a passing reference to the fate of philosophers is a general problem inherent in the conception of the *ricorso* (NS/1087). In order to exemplify the difficulty of reversing from a monarchical form of government or from a free commonwealth to an earlier oligarchic political system, Vico mentions two stories involving the tragic death of philosophers. The first is the murder of Dion of Syracuse, friend of Plato and enemy of the tyrant Dionysius, for attempting to restore an aristocratic government. The second story, analogous to the first, concerns the Pythagoreans, who were burned alive by the multitude for attempting the same oligarchic plan as Dion. The two references are somewhat cryptic. Yet, the symmetry between them (the tyranny of Dionysius and the ferocious tyranny of the multitude; the philosophical-didactic

utopianism of both Dion and the Pythagoreans; the death of the philosophers) provides a focus for grasping Vico's suspicious views of philosophy's
own temptation of power and concomitant delusion about its pretended
superiority over other forms of knowledge. Possibly he remembers
Socrates' sense of danger in the philosopher's entanglements in political
life (*Republic*, Book VI).

Greek wisdom was thus not wise enough at the onset of Christianity. It
believed, like Rome, in its own power, and it ended up making of its philosophical theater a vanity fair. Classical political philosophy—that of Dion
and of the Pythagoreans—is fired by utopianism, which is a will to power,
a will to impose its own enlightened vision on the multitude, and this
utopianism means that it lacks all political realism. Dion and the Pythagoreans alike presume that their aristocratic dream of establishing an ideal community can be realized by imposing it on the multitude. In effect, Dion
and the Pythagoreans try to philosophize to non-philosophers and to
rulers, but, in their wishful thinking, they forget that rulers, like the multitude, are not philosophers. This philosophical self-delusion does not concern only the past. For Vico it would be a grievous (and yet likely) error of
the moderns to believe that they are better than the ancients and that they
are exempt from ever lapsing into such a philosophical naiveté. The Spinozists, after all, claim that they really have no wish to impart their teaching to those who do not already know it.

Yet, close to Vico's own time, Campanella's *City of the Sun* (on which
Bacon's *New Atlantis* is patterned) stages a totalitarian Pythagorean
utopia, which is founded by philosophers who escape the tyranny of their
world. This utopia hinges on a rational, geometric architecture of power:
it promises to deaden the destructiveness of religious sects, and yet it posits
a hierarchy of power between philosophers, who are in the know, and the
rest of the people. Cogently enough, metaphysics or the science of first
principles rules over this political-utopian fantasy. In point of fact, however,
in *The City of the Sun*, as much as in Bacon's empire of science, all secrets
are forbidden except for the secrets of state or the philosophers' arcana of
power.

It is clear that Campanella's and Bacon's encyclopedic-educational
utopias are projects of political dissimulation akin to (but also unlike)
Machiavelli's and Spinoza's naturalistic schemes of power. In Campanella's
prophetic vision conspiracies of power are tragically entangled with
utopias, and this insight shapes Bacon's strategies in the *New Atlantis*. In
Book V of the *New Science* Vico does not refer overtly to either Campanella
or Bacon, but in the last paragraph of his last book (NS/1096), as he reflects on the novelty of the *New Science*, Vico draws the general context of
philosophy's transgressions and boundaries in a language that resonates
with the moderns' delusion. Let me quickly recall the central point of the

passage. Vico claims in paragraph 1096 that he has not written a particular, fragmentary history. Rather, he subordinates the various fragments of history to the order of the eternal laws undergirding the lifecycles of nations from their rise to their decadence.

This intellectual vindication of the *New Science* is flanked by two textual references. The first is a covert allusion to a theoretician of the infinity of worlds, such as Epicurus and Lucretius, and, in modern time, Giordano Bruno. In the context of a comparison between ancients and moderns, it is reasonable to suppose that the modern philosopher is Bruno. The second is an explicit quotation from a later ancient philosopher, Seneca. The careful rhetorical construction of this paragraph, which was cited earlier in the chapter, leaves little doubt as to its importance for Vico's purposes. The antithesis between "mondi infiniti"—infinite worlds—and Seneca's idea of a little world contained in the Latin phrase "Pusilla res hic mundus"; the naming of the *New Science* in between the two references as if Vico's text were the center of gravity between a modern and an ancient (which is the conceptual burden of this section of Book V); the contrast between the *reticentia* in the anonymous allusion to Bruno's "infinite worlds" and the explicit acknowledgment of Seneca's *auctoritas*—these are all conspicuous signs of Vico's stylistic self-awareness at this climactic juncture of his argument.

The phrase "mondi infiniti" is an echo of Bruno's *De Infinito, de Universo et Mundis*. Bruno sets his theory of the infinitization of the world, a world eternally regenerating itself in time, against Aristotle's *Physics* (Book III, Chapter 4, 203a–b), which argues for a finite cosmos whereby what has a beginning must have an end and a boundary. Obliquely, however, Vico raises the suspicion that Bruno's Neoplatonic view is proximate to his own theory of the *ricorso*, only to dismiss Bruno's boundless cosmology as "false." Plainly, the *ricorso* of the rise, progress, maturity, decadence, and dissolution of nations cannot be understood as a mechanical sequence of endless cycles, as an infinity without finitude.

Vico, the thinker of law's boundaries and of the undefinable infinity, agrees with Aristotle: all that becomes must necessarily come to an end. A sharp distinction is posited: for Vico the *ricorso* is a historical and not a natural process. But for Bruno the rise and fall, to which all forms of existence are subjected, are like the ongoing cycle of the rising and setting of the sun, and the circuit he envisions is akin to the Pythagorean *apocatastasis*. As Bruno's motto has it, "nihil sub sole novum" (there is nothing new under the sun). The motto echoes Ecclesiastes (1:9), and it implies that Bruno's dynamic universe, ironically, is a static tableau for an endless play of oxymoronic reversals: in it, life is identified with death, for death is the obverse side of an infinite rebirth; the limit is identical with the limitless; rise with decadence; the ancient with the new.

There may be another reason for Vico's *reticentia* and dismissal of Bruno's ideas as false. Vico does not refer to it at all, but in the context in which the question of Christianity in the modern age is debated, one cannot but infer that at stake there is Bruno's subversion of canonical theological discourse. If Spinoza, who drew from Bruno, is the very epitome of modern philosophical discourse, Bruno is the hero of modernity. He is the secular martyr, who was put to death for dismantling the central tenet of Christian belief, namely, that finiteness and infinity are yoked by the paradox of the Incarnation. Bruno's ideas are false for Vico because, by decrying the notion of boundaries in the name of the infinite movement of all entities, Bruno, in fact, denies history and difference. Ironically, the very possibility of modernity is abrogated by the thought of modernity's hero.

As Vico distances himself from Bruno's effort to question Christian theology (his "false" opinions symmetrically recall the "vain wisdom of the Greeks" and its failure to cope with the Christian revelation at the beginning of Book V), he turns to the pagan Seneca. Seneca's lines "this world is a paltry thing unless all the world may find [therein] what it seeks," which close Book V of the *New Science*, are drawn from the *Quaestiones naturales*. It is quite in keeping with the general thrust of Vico's argument, let me remark in passing, that his theory of the *ricorso*, which focuses on the modernity of his own thought, should end with the contrapuntal acknowledgment not of a modern but of an ancient classical authority, Seneca. But why would Seneca's phrase—"vasta espressione"—contain and best express, as it were, the claims to science in Vico's title, *Scienza nuova*?

The broad scope of Seneca's *Natural Questions* is to clarify the laws of nature as an orderly, grand arrangement and to draw from it a set of Stoic moral teachings for the conduct of life. Over seven books Seneca discusses a number of speculative theories about the origin and shape of fire, lightning and thunder, waters, rivers, snow, winds, and comets. At bottom, however, the *Natural Questions* is a Stoic *ars vitae* ending in Book VII with a reflection on the foundation and limits of philosophy. More precisely, Seneca opens Book I with the assertion that through philosophy man partakes in the universal order of reason and nature, and that through philosophy man's moral nature can best be defined. In Book VII Seneca's retrospective assessment of his theoretical project concludes with a picture of the dim state of philosophy in his own time. Plainly, Seneca's reasoning bears remarkable similarities to as well as predictable differences from Vico's thought.

Over and against Bruno's eclectic violation of boundaries and all restraint, Seneca's text insists that God has not made all things for man and that he himself remains hidden from our sight (Book VII, 30.3–4). That every knowledge is partial and time-bound is clear from the fact that every age makes its own discoveries, while other discoveries are reserved for ages still to come, when the memory of the present will have been effaced. It is within this exact context of the provisional quality of human knowledge and of nature not revealing her mysteries once and for all that Seneca writes the sentence Vico cites. The sentence, in its turn, triggers Seneca's passionate speech on the moral depravity of the present, on the eclipse of wisdom in his own age, and the decline of philosophy: "Philosophiae nulla cura est" (There is no interest in philosophy) (*Quaestiones naturales,* Book VII, 32.4).

Seneca does not lure us to philosophy with the impossible promise of a perfect and absolute knowledge, as Bruno does. He lures us to the recurrent investigation of the unending secrets lying in the womb of nature. The statement captures the core of Vico's thinking. It is the mark of Vico's conceptual rigor both to assert, with Seneca, that philosophical discourse belongs to its own time and to imply, by using Seneca, that one's own contingent time can only be understood by a turn to antiquity and by seeing the whole of history. More importantly, Seneca's eloquent skepticism about the classical claim of philosophy's sovereignty is no doubt an oblique sign of his consciousness of the mortal danger surrounding him daily at Nero's court. From Tacitus Vico has learned that Seneca, in spite of and probably because of his effort to teach the tyrant, is only too aware of the philosopher's vulnerabilities in the court of power.

Vico, as has been shown in earlier chapters, is steadily aware of the limits of philosophy and is mindful of Socrates' tragic fate. By linking Seneca with Bruno, as the two points of reference for his *New Science*'s final self-definition, he conveys his lucid understanding of the mortal political danger confronting philosophy's immoderate and moderate claims. For all the differences between Bruno's heretical, transgressive thought and Seneca's Stoic conception of limits, the two philosophers share a common fate with Socrates that Vico prudently never mentions: Bruno is burned at the stake by the tyranny of the Counter-Reformation that tolerates no dissent over the nature of its core beliefs; Seneca, unable to control Agrippina's obscenities and transgressions and Nero's mad excesses, commits suicide. Their tragic fate signals the likely fate of philosophy itself in the politics of the modern age.

Against this background, there can be no doubt that Vico, whose work hedges that of Seneca and that of Bruno with their respective sense of boundaries and imaginative transgressions, knows perfectly well that the modality of the political discourse, indeed the tone and style of philosophy must be radically changed. To be sure, he does not altogether reject philosophical rationality; rather, he questions its absolute hegemony in modern discourse, and by doing this he rescues reason from its own worst enemy, which is reason itself. Let us be very clear on this point. Vico is the theorist of language and of rhetoric as the powerful speech of the city. He knows that the danger in positing reason's hegemony consists in the fact that it is capable of rationalizing any outrageous conduct. Further, in denying the cognitive power of the passions, reason blinds us both to the realities of who we are and to the potential, certainly recurrent savagery of our being. Given these dangers confronting rational philosophy, what is the new discourse Vico proposes as adequate to the complexities of the Christian new beginnings?

Vico's own new discourse can only be bifrontal. On the one hand, it encompasses a critique of philosophy's delusion of power: it unveils philosophy's claim to be the privileged and sovereign discourse of the modern age as well as its project to submit Christianity to its critical scrutiny. This pretension is the root of the prudent, philosophical practice of dissimulation. On the other hand, Vico's new discourse, as indicated earlier, idealizes the historical achievements of Christianity: "But Christian Europe is everywhere radiant with such humanity that it abounds in all the good things that make for the happiness of human life, ministering to the comforts of the body as well as to the pleasures of mind and spirit" (NS/1094). In this part of the world alone, because of the sciences, because of the universities and the public debates they promote (NS/1086), and because of aristocratic governments (NS/1087), a new political order, a Christian commonwealth, seems to be emerging and to involve America and Asia (NS/1089–93). Within the logic of Book V such an exalted rhetoric can be explained in terms of Vico's political argument. The paragraph articulates his vision of a European Christian commonwealth; it recapitulates his conviction that Christianity is the stabilizing focus in the play of forces in modern European history.

One may wonder, however, if such a political assessment of Christianity's historical role in the modern age is not to be taken—as befits the discourse of the third age—in the ironic mode of dissimulation or, instead, most literally as a genuine, idealistic assessment of the benign times of the third age. Can it be that Vico, with all his systematic stripping away of the veils of power and deception, and with the pitiless stare he casts at the realities of power, is in fact a supremely subtle theorist of dissimulation? The suspicion is legitimate in the face of Vico's ambivalent judgement of the third age. Book IV of the *New Science*, for instance, views the third age as "benign, reasonable, recognizing for law's conscience, reason and duty" (NS/918). The third kind of jurisprudence, let me add, is defined as one "which looks to the truth of the facts themselves and benignly bends the rule of law to all the requirements of the equity of the causes" (NS/940); and, as a final example, the third kind of authority is "based on the trust placed in persons of experience" (NS/942). On the other hand, Vico's contempt for modernity as weak, rational, and critical, and as the time of "returned barbarism" is equally well known. Is Vico contradicting himself or simply displaying his ambivalences about the third age as a way of hiding his true convictions? Given his constantly ambivalent views of the baroque, his attacks against baroque mimetic falsifications and power-cult, and yet his sense that the baroque articulates the essence of the circuitousness of modernity, the question of Vico's irony is far from arbitrary.

In the barbarism of reflection, after all, irony is the apt figuration of barbaric practices. By viewing the present in the light of ancient teachings, one could say that Vico connects modern irony with the cannibalism of the Cyclopes or one-eyed Polyphemus (NS/191; 447). As a form of reflective consciousness, irony is a one-eyed, illusory, and violent perspective on one's own presumed intellectual superiority. Such a stance is akin to the false seeing of the savage giants; and like the cannibalistic giants of the *Odyssey,* irony splits the mind from the contingencies of history, dismembers the spiritual unity of existence, and devours or annihilates the creations of the spirit. Yet, for all the shipwreck of common sense it engenders, the suspicion about Vico's irony is further justified in the light of his intimation, at the start of Book V of the *New Science,* that the passions of religious belief are destructive: they can undermine the state just as Christian martyrs undermined the Roman Empire. Religion's savagery comes again to the fore in Christianity's unleashing of wars against competing and hostile sects.

The text refers, on the authority of a Church Father, St. Jerome, to the Arian heresy (NS/1048), which, in point of fact, is an adumbration of Giordano Bruno's own doctrine: like Bruno, the Arians deny the consubstantiation of the Son and the Father as well as the Christian idea of redemption. Conscious of religious wars as Vico always is (which in part he chronicled in *The Life of Antonio Carafa* and to which he refers in Book V in the context of the continued hatred between Christians and Turks [NS/1055]), he also lists Moslems (who do not believe in the divinity of Christ) and "altro gran numero d'infedeli" (numerous other infidels) (NS/1048) as dangers neutralized by the force of Christian arms. The question, then, is legitimate: how can Vico display such an awareness of the ferociousness of religious belief and, at the same time, evaluate positively the role of Christianity in the modern age. Isn't he just taking shelter from the possible violence and intolerance ushered in by religion?

The hermeneutical suspicion that Vico subtly deploys a veiled, negative irony toward theology (and, consequently, toward his own overt critique of philosophy and modern esthetics) makes Vico's new discourse no different from the discourse of the "moderns," figures such as Machiavelli, Bruno, Hobbes, and Spinoza, whom he has so sharply attacked. Vico defines irony as the typically modern rhetoric of dissembling.[4] Let me suggest, however, that Vico's irony, which is the other side of passion, is of the Socratic kind. Socratic irony does not depend on radical doubt: it is a form of self-reflexiveness that throws into doubt all certainties by presupposing ignorance. As a form of wisdom, it means that we lack a comprehensive discourse and that we have an incomplete knowledge of the whole.[5]

More precisely, for Vico irony entails a paradoxical sense of contradiction whereby his topical thinking is also *atopic*, which is the sign of a mind always out of place and yet claiming a particular standpoint for his overarching, gigantic vision of the whole. His ambivalences, in fact, are cloaked in a variety of forms: knowledge is not tied exclusively to rationality (as the Enlightenment codifies it); though Vico's thought is shaped by a sense of the Earth, it is extra-territorial; though Vico lives in his home, he is generally so apart that his outside perspective allows him to see, Janus-like, the double aspect behind any one-sided form of reality. In spite of these ambivalences, his thought remains irreducible to and incommensurable with the parameters of the moderns he wishes to supersede. At any rate, as just another example will show, Vico does not share Machiavelli's conviction about religion's generalized destructive and intolerant fury.

In a chapter of his *Discourses* (Book II, Chapter 5) Machiavelli argues that the "changes of sects and language destroy the meanings of things." He holds, on the authority of Pope Gregory, that the Christian sects sought to efface all deeds, images, and representations that would recall the heathen antiquities they meant to supersede. The reason why there was no total effacement of the past, Machiavelli adds, was because the new religion was forced to maintain the Latin language by which it set down the new law. His argument goes beyond the contingent example and involves all religious sects. In his view ancient memories are endangered by the iconoclastic devastation perpetrated by the sects, such as Christianity, whose aim is not universality, but the establishment of an empire under the guise of religion. For Vico, however, Christianity is the custodian of ancient memories. Its religious universality is signaled, and the statement plainly goes counter to Machiavelli, by its cultivation of Hebrew, Greek, and Latin traditions. More generally, Christianity keeps culture alive by preserving the traditions of philosophy and philology (NS/1094).

[4] "L'ironia certamente non potè cominciare che da' tempi della riflessione, . . ." (NS/408). See Aristotle's *Nicomachean Ethics*, 1108a 19–22; *Rhetoric*, 1379b 32.

[5] The modern understanding of irony emerges from Oscar Wilde's "On Lying." For a baroque theory of irony see Torquato Accetto, *Della dissimulazione onesta*, ed. Salvatore S. Nigro (Turin: Einaudi, 1997), in which simulation is seen as a form of irony, a prudential, dignified concealment of one's own superior virtues. For a definition of Socratic irony see Gregory Vlastos, *Socrates, Ironist and Moral Philosopher* (Ithaca, N.Y.: Cornell University Press, 1991), pp. 24ff. See also Søren Kierkegaard, *The Concept of Irony: With Constant References to Socrates*, trans. Lee Capel (London: Collins, 1966).

Rather than practicing an ironic discourse—which is "fashioned of false-hood by dint of a reflection which wears the mask of truth" (NS/408)—Vico hurls the greatest possible visionary challenge at the modern political science of power, its cult of noble lies, and its rhetoric of dissimulation. There is hardly any doubt that his opposition to modernity stems from the perception that modernity cultivates falsehood and nihilism: "Men shape the phrase [i.e., 'Sympathetic Nature']"—so runs one of his memorable statements—"with their lips but have nothing in their minds; for what they have in mind is falsehood, which is nothing; and their imagination no longer avails to form a vast false image" (NS/378). In this overrefined and self-reflexive age, irony is the trope of baroque fragmentary symbolic forms sundered from substances, of a rhetoric without passion, of disembodied minds asphyxiated by intellectual abstractions and by falsehoods. The Pythagorean metaphor of universal analogical relationships (this is the point in Vico's recall of "Sympathetic Nature"), of the relationship of parts and whole in a harmonious system of nature, has turned into a mere conceit. Retrospectively, both Bruno's pantheistic idea of infinite worlds and Spinoza's totalizing rationalization of nature are construed as a false conceit.

Vico's challenge consists in a conscious, deliberate, elaboration of a "new science" that circumvents and even shatters the boundaries of truth and falsehood organizing both the discourse and the crisis of modernity. This "new science" is poetry, and, from the standpoint of poetry, the skepticism of the Epicureans and Spinozists (which afflicts all the sciences in his troubled times) is repudiated. We know that poetry is at the heart of his enterprise and is for Vico the foundation of all the sciences. As can be evinced from his reflections on the "sublime" in Homer, poetry is the powerful activity that creates reality. The "poetic," more specifically, is the distinctively human activity of making and knowing by which man partakes in God's creative acts. In line with Dante's reflections on art as work (*Inferno*, Canto XI) and with the Thomistic concept of art, wherein man is the maker of signs for himself and for others, Vico makes art the other side of prudence. The Scholastic argument is clear: whereas prudence is a virtue of the practical intellect in the order of *doing*, art is the virtue of the practical intellect in the order of *making*.[6] Thus, the adjective "poetic"—from the Greek

[6] For a discussion of Dante's Thomistic understanding of art in the *Inferno*, Canto XI, ll. 94–115 (in the context of a contrast between usury and work) see Giuseppe Mazzotta, *Dante Poet of the Desert: History and Allegory in the Divine Comedy* (Princeton: Princeton University Press, 1979), p. 271ff. A theory of art along Thomistic lines has been elaborated by Jacques Maritain, *Art and Scholasticism and the Frontiers of Poetry*, trans. J. W. Evans (New York: Scribner's Sons, 1962), pp. 10–22. For Vico's relation to Scholasticism see Cesare Vasoli, "Vico, Tommaso d'Aquino e il tomismo," *Bollettino del Centro di Studi Vichiani*, 4 (1974), pp. 5–35. But see especially the richly suggestive philosophical and Thomistic analysis by John Milbank, *The Religious Dimension in the Thought of Giambattista Vico 1669–1744*

poiesis, to make—qualifies all the branches of the sciences in the *New Science*: there is a *poetic* metaphysics and a *poetic* logic, a *poetic* politics and a *poetic* history, and the same holds for astronomy, geography, and so forth. The "poetic" draws the sciences, or science as a whole, within the realm of the *made* or of *fact*: in this sense, art, or that which is made, yokes together making and knowing (by keeping the priority of the making over knowing), the *verum* and the *factum*, the true and the made. In this view of man as *homo faber* of the world and oneself, and of the work of art, which applies to all human constructions, the dualisms between truth and contrivance no longer hold. What are the political implications in this valorization of making over knowing? Is making to rule over knowing?

Vico's challenge and counterpoint to the pathology and to the stylistics of modernity are conceived within this Scholastic and Dantesque perimeter of thought. From this standpoint, poetry cannot be construed as an ungrounded, self-enclosed fiction. Rather than being shut within itself, it is the very epitome of productiveness; it posits the truth of God's being and making as art's ground; it is necessarily part of a comprehensive vision of all disciplines and faculties of the mind. More importantly, a new worldview is made available by man's *ingenium* or by archaic poetry: because poetry does not lie, it escapes the dualism of truth and falsehood forever woven in the fabric of any discourse of simulation. To say that poetry does not lie is to say that the sublime wisdom, indeed the essence of poetry consists in the fact that it is subjectively always true and is at one with one's own perception and imagination of reality. Thus, paradoxically to us who are in the throes of the ironic modern age, Vico speaks not of the conventional view of poetry as *fictio figura veritatis*, a fiction which adumbrates and gives access to truth. Rather, with sublime visionariness, he speaks of "true fables" (NS/34); of "credible impossibilities" and of "marvels wrought by sorceresses by means of incantations" (NS/383). Poetry, in short, is connected with belief and magic make-believe whose simulacra are time-bound truths. As a true practice and not a mere rhetorical simulation, such as the esthetics that latter-day poetasters peddle, this idea of poetry provides the metaphysical foundation and global intelligibility of all the sciences.

But how can this foundational and ethical view of poetry hope to circumvent, if not to obliterate altogether, the politics of simulation and dissimulation, the prosaic ratiocinations of the sciences, and the myths of utilitarian calculus, all of which are rampant on the stage of the modern world? Does the acknowledgment of its hegemony in the process of knowledge

---

(Lewiston, N.Y.: Mellen Press, 1991 and 1992). Milbank's work, which deserves to be better known, explores Vico's early metaphysics, as well as his ideas of language, law, and history, and puts Vico within a Catholic theological historical context.

imply its political sovereignty? How can it become the foundation of a new and alternate political science? Is Vico actually saying that the poetic imagination, which is free, generalized, spontaneous, but is not in itself a productive art, ought to shape the political order, which concerns the sphere of necessity and choice requiring the exercise of prudence and judgment? And if this were the case, isn't his the all too common, dreamy visionariness of a provincial, eccentric, marginal, and powerless intellectual somewhat out of step with the times? To answer these perplexities we must begin by acknowledging and stressing that Vico is certainly a realist deeply in touch with the crushing exigencies of his own times. But he is also a visionary thinker somewhat out of step with the times.

He understood his condition, made a virtue of it, and therein lies his grandeur. Let us emphasize how, while he occupies a detached perspective, he steadily grounds his vision in a clear-eyed perception of reality. He repeatedly warns us in a variety of ways that metaphysics has to be brought down to physics, that philosophy must be rooted in philology, or that the Republic of Plato has to be yoked to the dregs of Romulus (NS/131). One should add that Vico's forever ambivalent thought retrieves the turbulent vortex of the archaic imagination but does not endorse its wild, anarchic transgressions.

An unstinting theorist of law's boundaries and institutions, a realistic chronicler of the dangers of self-indulgent, unbound pleasures, he has in the past called for the education of the imagination, which implies its liberation from the shackles of logic so that heroic and new discoveries can be made. In the *New Science* he theorizes an imagination which becomes work, which follows the rigorous laws of work's production, and which, in being both free and productive, bears the marks of the discipline, rigor, and prudence needed to make a work of art. Finally, poetry, as the necessary mode of expression of the first poetic nations, is grounded in the truth of God and is the language of history. It both reveals and puts us in touch with the deeper memories of history, the myths of a culture, and the believable fictions of the law; and it always exceeds authorial determinations. In short, his new political science—which, like any other political science, deals with prudent choices in critical times—demands the rigor and prudence of art's production.

But the real answers to all these questions lie in Vico's own power to make the *New Science* itself the persuasive counter-discourse of modernity. Vico knows that his work, his *opera,* as he refers to the *New Science* in the "Idea dell'opera," stands or falls on his ability to dramatize his ideas, to put them, as it were, to work.[7] The work, which is truly and can only be a work

---

[7] The claim confirms Vico's educational project and recalls the claim in the *Leviathan* (Part II, Chapter 30) in which Hobbes looks forward to a time when his work will be officially adopted in the universities.

of art, has been carefully assembled block by block, and its design emerges at the end with Vico's daring projection of the *ricorso* as the thought of the possible new beginnings of history. Because this is the pinnacle of his thought, I call the *ricorso* the boldest contrivance in the *New Science:* it determines the meaning and epochal value of the whole text, just as the whole text is the condition of the possibility of the *ricorso*. What, then, is the *ricorso?*

In order to catch its multiple resonances, let me point out that the word translates the Latin *recursus,* which comes from *recurro,* and etymologically suggests a re-running or a flowing back. The frontispiece of the *New Science* allows us to visualize the spiral, serpentine shape of the *ricorso:* as hinted in Chapter 5, Mercury's caduceus, with the intertwined snakes around the staff (NS/30; 604), is the geometric representation of a spiral. By its interweaving of circle and line, which produces the spiral, the *ricorso,* thus, is the simultaneous figuration of closure and openness of a circle that repeats itself with a difference, is always out of place and is eccentric to the other circles in the series. But the *ricorso* is for Vico also a mode of writing and reading, and, more importantly, it is itself a new way of thinking and seeing. In one word, it is history's second chance or appeal, which the *New Science* discloses and ushers in.

I mentioned at the beginning of this chapter that Vico obliquely connects the periodic, recursive movement of history to the style of his writing, punctuated, as he says it is, by countless passages exemplifying the "marvelous correspondence" between the first and the returned barbarian times (NS/1046). Now, Vico says, he intends to give a "special place" to the question of the *ricorso*. One can infer that by the adjacency of the question of writing and history's recourse, Vico is here describing his own rewriting, his own rhetorical *re-cursus,* as it were, or new *cursus*. The term defines, as philologists well know, the scribe's craft of joining together letters in a manuscript.

Together with the *ricorso,* the *cursus* suggests Vico's spiral style of writing and spiral style of thinking, the poetic art of connecting events or words remote from one another. Both are marked by a steady recurrence of topics, by a desultory mode of argument aimed at shattering the idea of discursive linearity or merely circular order. The eccentricities, obscurities, and convolutions of Vico's language, for which he has been chastised by his readers even while he was alive, are real: it is a language that leaps over conventional connections, that slides, like a cursor, backward and forward, pursues seemingly random but rigorously elliptical orbits in a series, and creates a special place for a discourse whereby a new, all-encompassing configuration of the past, present, and future can appear before our eyes. Tied as it is to Vico's style of writing, the *ricorso* comes through as a rhetorical contrivance, as a perspective rhetorically made or produced by the very *New Science.*

Vico's stylistic self-consciousness at this point of the text leaves no doubt that the *ricorso* is a metaphor and a new paradigm of knowledge, a new mode of vision or perspective. The claim is sustained by the very language of the text: the relationship between the first and returned barbarian times is described as a "corrispondersi con meravigliosa acconcezza," as a "marvelous correspondence" (NS/1046). The terms "meravigliosa" and "corrispondersi" literally echo and adapt the baroque understanding of the "ingenious metaphor." Baroque literary theorists—from Sforza-Pallavicino to Baltazar Gracian, from Matteo Pellegrino to Emanuele Tesauro—view metaphor as the invention of a "correspondence" between apparently disconnected entities. The invention of such a metaphoric correspondence, which is seen through the eye of the looking glass, produces wonder in the beholder.

As a way of buttressing the link Vico forges between the *ricorso* and the perspective or mode of vision represented by the *New Science*, let me briefly recall a text of Vico himself, "Practic of the New Science," which he drafted as the final word of the text but decided to leave out of the 1744 edition of the *New Science*. We don't really know why Vico left it out. He probably felt its inclusion was superfluous, for his "contemplative science" was in itself a "practic" (*Practic/*1405), which is to say that the act of seeing is not simply a contemplative stance. This omitted appendix affirms the aim of the *New Science* to be the political/legal education of the young, and it tells the scholars, to whom the text is addressed, that understanding the *corso* nations run "requires of us that, from these human times of acute and intelligent minds in which we are born, we should here at the end look back [*guardare a rovescio*] to the picture that was placed at the beginning" (*Practic/*1406).

The brief text, in effect, is literally a synopsis of the *New Science*, which, in turn, has given us a whole view of history. Yet it begs the question: what is the vantage point allowing Vico and the scholars alike to see the totality of the *corso* and the *ricorso*? The appendix gives more than a hint. To see the universal movement and the new beginning of history demands "un guardare a rovescio" at the frontispiece. The phrase suggests a retrospection, which is also a reversal of perspective, a turning around or upside down to cast a backward glance, a looking from the ground up, whereby one sees the history of things scattered in the debris, the blind seer Homer, the altar and the globe of the Earth, winged Metaphysics looking up at heaven, and, finally, the eye of Providence from which geometric beams of vision emanate. In this sense, the *ricorso* is an experience that frees us from the chains of time and contingency.

As a metaphor for history's new beginnings, the *ricorso* presupposes a transcendent vision of the whole, and it enacts Vico's sublime, transcendent perspective on history as well as his perspective on the sublime. So that it may not be the falsely transcendent vision of an ironist (who is caught up in the one-eyed conceit of his own superior wisdom), or of a Bruno-like overman (or an all-devouring Cyclops), Vico proceeds most prudently by dramatizing the problem of perspective as a question of textual perspectivism of the *New Science* itself. What exactly is this perspectivism?

As a poetic encyclopedia or *satura* that gathers together all discourses and viewpoints of history, the *New Science* is a total form encompassing all styles, all philosophies, all beliefs and myths, and all poetic genres. It is a hybrid *genus mixtum* such as what Tasso conceives the epic to be: an all-inclusive, expansive book full of similitudes fetched from every thing. Its ancient model is the Homeric epics or, in view of the programmatic (and only apparent) exclusion of the Bible from its *plenum* of vision, the epic prophecies of Dante and Tasso. In its ambitious, overweening embrace of the world's variety of experiences and shifting stages of consciousness, the *New Science* is written or made from the perspective of a man who has ascetically reached majestic heights of vision. From the high tower of his solitude, where he also eschews all solipsistic temptations, he has surveyed all the boundaries of history and of the earth, and he has gained the "diritto e ragione" (NS/1096)—the rightful claim and authority—to convey his vision of the total unfolding of history, to denounce history's errors, man's infinite capacity for self-deception, and to speak with the hard-gained authority of an at once humble and proud visionary.

This visionary impulse, which allows him to make his text, stands at the center of Vico's realistic science and gives it its vital form. The *New Science* begins with an emblem, which deals, as Vico says, with "perspective" (NS/3), and whose focus is a blind seer as well as the act of seeing and being seen. By it Vico wants to open our eyes, either cure or remind us of our own blindness, as we enter an enigmatic, never-before-seen world encompassing the fabulous glitter and darkness of existence. It wants to open our eyes to the workings of Providence, which means both foreknowledge and, as its etymology from *provideo* suggests and the pictorial one eye of God at the top of the emblem renders it, "to see beforehand." Providence is Vico's source of vision: it sees all as he sees all. To have wisdom or prudence, which is, etymologically, the visionary counterpart of Providence, means to lift one's eyes toward it. It would be too easy to show that the language of vision, far from being incidental, extends into and involves central concerns or metaphors of the text such as history and its eyes, memory, images, fantasy, theorems, ideas, *imprese*, autopsy, lightning and all the recurrent motifs of light metaphorics, the dark night of the mind and its daybreak, theater, maps, geometry, tablets, inscriptions, bodies, and also the mystery of oracles and sibylline pronouncements. Taken all together, this language casts Vico as caught between a sort of divinatory, prophetic stance and the humble archaeology of the commonplaces.

It is inevitable that in speaking of Vico's or the *New Science*'s perspective one should recall Plato's eye of the soul, Leonardo's eye of experience, Galileo's and Tesauro's telescope, and Descartes's eye of the mind. The eye is the metaphor on which their epistemologies rest, the foundation for their far-reaching scientific claims. Science seeks refuge from its constitutive uncertainty and conjectural knowledge in inner or contrived vision, for only vision guarantees its powerful claims to truth. By virtue of visionary claims, a visionary turns into a scientist and vice versa. To stress the grid of the ocular metaphors in the *New Science* would seem to be a way of presenting Vico in the role of the contemplative Cartesian spectator he consistently rejects. But his concern with perspective is to be understood in terms that exceed a merely contemplative mode. In the middle of his pictorial emblem, which reflects (on) vision and is a counterpoint to vision, he puts the blind Homer, who cannot turn himself away from simulacra toward the true source of light. Vision is the other side of man's blindness. More to the point, because the source of light is outside of him, Homer's inner vision deals only with simulacra which his sublime poetry makes true.

The scientific status of the *New Science* depends on Vico's imaginative power to connect facts remote from one another, and this power, in its turn, depends on Vico's own visionary and sublime stance. Rhetoricians view the sublime as a formal category expressing hyperbolic, strange, and extravagant claims. Vico makes it the trope of the *New Science* in the idea of the *ricorso,* for, with this idea, he occupies a lofty vantage point allowing him to see the end of a cycle and the resurgence of a new cycle. This is Vico's peculiar stance and peculiar hyperbolic style: at the threshold, looking simultaneously, Janus-like, backward and forward, tracing the memories of our future and divining the future of (in) the past. From this sublime stance, whose forerunners in Italy are Joachim of Flora and Dante, he sees (and calls for) the new beginning of history as the return of divine times, as the time when poetry becomes the radical alternative to the ironies of modernity, and as the time when miracles and marvels recur once again as they did at the onset of Christian history. From this standpoint, seeing and making converge.

More poignantly, Vico, as ever the visionary realist, transposes this notion of the sublime into a politics of the sublime or into a politics of wonder. Descartes, in his optimistic scientism, wants us to wonder at nothing.[8]

---

[8] In classical thought, of course, wonder, as the perplexity of the mind, is the beginning of thought. Descartes would banish wonder and replace it with "astonishment": "I shall re-

Locke, in his Latitudinarian vision, warns against "enthusiasm."[9] Vico retrieves wonder. In the unfolding of the *ricorso* he envisions present history
and he instructs us, against the fanaticism and enthusiasm of sects, to see
the world as a whole; to preserve the uncertain, mysterious aura of beginnings and the miraculousness of new beginnings; to restore a visionary
mode of thought that confronts and reconciles eristic divisions; to uphold
the majesty of the law; and to revive religious piety. Most simply—and by
an aptly hyperbolic statement—he wills to bring back, out of the land of
unlikeness and forgetfulness, what the modern project has effaced. Such a
religious-political project had never been seen in Italy since Dante and
Campanella.

There is one last point to be raised. Why should the *ricorso* or the new
beginning of history be considered a radical invention in the *New Science*?
As a way of suggesting an answer, we should look at the first word of the
work's title: *Principi di scienza nuova*. "Principles" certainly recalls Newton's *Principia*. The concern with the metaphoric extensions of *principles*
(births, nations, rebirths, etc.) decisively removes Vico from the more conventional concerns of most of his contemporaries. His archaeology consists
in a steady reflection on false origins and foundational myths, on the *principles*, which are causes, foundations, constitutions, and beginnings of humanity. Plainly, even his science of etymology belongs to this concern. In
his meditation over principles, Vico constantly stresses that there is no
demonstrable certainty about the primordial beginnings of human society
if not in the modifications of the human mind. He even swerves away from
the myth of the biblical origins of man in the Garden of Eden, and, as the
next chapter will show, he was drubbed for bracketing this myth.

To the documented biblical account of Genesis he juxtaposes a realistic
version of the bestiality and chaos of history's beginnings. This version retrieves the Augustinian theology of fallen man, which had been adumbrated by Lucretius and by the Ciceronian fiction of the first men wandering in the forest like beasts. But if, according to Cicero, the rhetorician, by
virtue of his gift of eloquence, humanizes them, Vico believes humaniza-
tion starts in wonder and terror, when lightning strikes and the archaic
mind asks what it means (NS/195). The new authority Vico has in mind
must bring together rhetoric and theology.

We cannot even imagine history's beginning, and yet we know history's
second beginning, the *ricorso* that was ushered in by Christianity's grace.
Vico also knows that the conceit of nations shows that nations monotonously spin grand fantasies about their origins. The *New Science* diligently

---

veal to you secrets so simple that you will henceforth wonder at nothing" *Oeuvres et lettres*,
ed. A. Bridoux (Paris: Pleiade, 1952), p. 885 (trans. is mine).

[9] "On Enthusiasm" attacks divine, personal calling that foments civil strife and appeals to
religious tolerance. See *Essays*, Book IV, Chapter XIX.

chronicles and undercuts all such illusory and self-serving claims of priority, be they made by the Egyptians, the Greeks, or the Romans in their mythical elision of their real origins in appropriation, violence, and conquest (NS/770–73). The conceit of nations about their beginnings is politically dangerous because it harbors and fosters dangerous political delusions by inspiring men to recreate, return to, or live up to impossible and false mythical beginnings. In fact, this is an old concern of political-utopian philosophy, of prophetic-epic histories, or even romances (see Boccaccio's *Ninfale fiesolano*). Because these poetic-political fantasies are so common, it is quite certain that Vico did not discover on his own the power of the illusion lodged in all political myths of beginnings.

The utopian myth of Atlantis in Plato and Bacon's rewriting of it, and the foundational account of Campanella's Solarians, to mention the most obvious examples, are signs of the myth's pull. But it is Machiavelli who articulates its mechanism and necessity. In the *Discourses* (Book III, Chapter 1) he points out how the renewal of the Church took place when the two founders of fraternal orders, St. Francis and St. Dominic, brought the Church back to its evangelical and pure origin. Machiavelli's further discussion of political founders in the same chapter acknowledges that to imagine a better future and stave off the corruption of the present, kingdoms must go back to the beginning. This is so, one might add, with any story. And yet, more than any of his predecessors, Vico knows that, whereas beginnings are false and unknowable, new beginnings are feasible. The *ricorso* crystallizes the vision of what can be made and remade. Poetry is the *ricorso*. The *New Science* traces the path to a feasible political-theological new beginning for modern times; it promises and brings about the rebirth of philosophy as a poetic work of art; it justifies itself as the bearer of a new mode of seeing ourselves and our history; but it leaves history's uncertain aura intact.

The political theology Vico has delivered does not altogether exhaust his understanding of theology. As happens in the *Divine Comedy*, theology is the perspective from which Vico announces a new discourse and a new politics for Europe's new age. Theology also marks for him the tragic limits of politics. As the next chapter will in fact show, there is a biblical history that scandalously counters and yet sustains the parameters of political history.

Chapter 10

THE BIBLE

FROM THE VERY BEGINNING of the *New Science* Vico rigorously keeps his investigations within the field of human activities. Only secular history, which is made by man, can legitimately be the object of knowledge. The dimensions of this profane knowledge are vast and they comprise, among others: poetry, the archaeology of rites and beliefs, juridical procedures and institutions, languages, customs, education, the vulgar figurations of natural theology, the human origin of religions and their political role. The foundation, indeed the emblem, of all human activities and human knowledge is poetry, which rises up from the anonymous and dark depths of the people.

The Bible and Christianity are excluded from the circle of philosophical investigations. The reason Vico gives for such a demarcation of the sphere of research is plain: the Bible records a prophetic salvation history that is true because it is willed by God. Vico acknowledges that the biblical discourse of truth and the poetic-mythical fictions (which are themselves true projections of the mind) are founded on Providence, in the sense that Providence embraces within itself all possible discourses, those which are true and those which are false. Nonetheless, Vico's strategy at the start is both to leave the Bible and Christianity within their peculiar universe of revealed truth and to insist on the total antithesis between poetry and the Bible, between salvation history and secular history so that the two cannot be confused with each other. In spite of the differences between these two distinct orders of experiences and traditions and in spite of Vico's plan to bracket the biblical discourse in order to develop the principles of a rational civil theology of Providence, there is in the *New Science*, in a necessarily fragmentary way, a hermeneutics of the Bible.

This fragmentation, which for Vico is the mode of the representation in the Bible, turns out to be the path to grasping the religious dimension of Vico's thought. To be sure, over the problem of the "religious" in the *New Science* hang, as a shadow, the punctilious glosses of Giulio Torno, the ecclesiastical censor, who, with suspect paternalism, reminds Vico of his straying into heterodox doctrines. The censor's caveats and perplexities have been all too easily used by several critics as a way of presenting Vico through the anti-religious bias of the Enlightenment. The move amounts to a systematic evasion of the responsibility of coming to terms with Vico's reading of the Bible and of Hebrew history, which is his way of reaching the core of religious consciousness.

It has been said by Croce that the decision to put aside biblical history as the discourse of truth is actually for Vico a technique to devalue it altogether as inessential to the movement of secular history. Vico's doctrines, says Croce, are shaped by "a revolutionary, anti-catholic and generally anti-religious spirit."[1] It is especially Vico's concept of the original savagery and unbridled bestiality of mankind that shakes in its very foundation the Catholic doctrine of Genesis: Vico would show, Croce avers, that human history unfolds without any intervention of a religious and transcendent power and outside of the ambit of the Bible and of sacred history.[2] From this viewpoint the highly frequent references to divine Providence punctuating the *New Science* as well as the definition of it as a "rational civil theology of divine Providence" (NS/342) are to be taken as ciphers for a rationality immanent in history. It is this rationality—and not a transcendent Providence—that rescues history from the abyss into which it seems destined to plunge.

In placing Vico's religious thought in the domain of immanence Croce follows the principles of critical rationalism articulated by Spinoza. In the *Tractatus Theologico-Politicus* Spinoza gives a rigorous critique of the structure and composition of the Pentateuch and reaches skeptical conclusions about its religious claims and foundations. Vico—and this is Croce's suggestion—follows Spinoza's inquiry in his redescription of the "Homeric question." In order to find confirmation for the thesis that Vico, like Spinoza before him, ends up in an epistemic predicament in issues of religious beliefs, Croce makes use of a polemical dissertation that the Dominican friar Gian Francesco Finetti wrote against Vico in 1768. The dissertation

---

[1] For Benedetto Croce (in the typically modern gesture of believing that he knows better than those who lived in the past) Vico is anti-religious in spite of his own intentions. See his *La filosofia di G. B. Vico* (Bari: Laterza, 1911), p. 91. See Franco Amerio's rejoinder in *Introduzione allo studio di G. B. Vico* (Turin: Sei, 1947), especially p. 274. Croce's views in our times have been rearticulated by Leon Pompa, *Vico: A Study of the New Science* (Cambridge: Cambridge University Press, 1975). See Samuel J. Preus, "Spinoza, Vico, and the Imagination of Religion," in *Journal of the History of Ideas*, 50 (1989), pp. 71–93. Fausto Nicolini, *Commento a G. B. Vico: Opere* (Milan-Naples: Ricciardi, 1953) views Vico's Providence in immanent terms. See Paolo Rossi, *I segni del tempo: Storia della terra e storia delle nazioni da Hooke a Vico* (Milan: Feltrinelli, 1979). See Mario Reale, "Vico e il problema della storia ebraica in una recente interpretazione," *La cultura*, 8 (1970), pp. 81–107. See Nicola Badaloni, *Introduzione a G. B. Vico* (Milan: Feltrinelli, 1960) and J. J. Chaix-Ruy, *J.-B. Vico et l'Illuminisme athee* (Paris: M. Dide, 1968). More generally see Frank Manuel, *The Eighteenth Century Confronts the Gods* (Cambridge, Mass.: Harvard University Press, 1959).

[2] Gian Francesco Finetti, *Difesa dell'autorità della Sacra Scrittura contro G. B. Vico: Dissertazione del 1768*, intr. by B. Croce (Bari: Laterza, 1936). The citations are on p. xiv of the Introduction. See Massimo Lollini, "L'autorità della Scrittura," in *Le muse, Le maschere, e il sublime: G. B. Vico e la poesia nell'Età della Ragione* (Naples: Guida, 1994), p. 225–35. More generally see Antonio Corsano, *Umanesimo e religione in G. B. Vico* (Bari: Laterza, 1935).

seeks to expose Vico's misunderstandings, interpretive errors, and deviations from the sediments of canonical Church doctrine.

The all-too-real discrepancies existing between Vico's views of the Bible and the tradition of patristic exegesis cast him, for Finetti and Croce alike, as one who senses the incompatibility between biblical history and secular history (especially in terms of chronology) and who negates revealed truth.[3] Whereas Croce applauds what he takes to be Vico's new secular (or Crocean) way of thinking, Finetti writes his dissertation from his own perspective of rational theology in order to dismantle Vico's deceptive theories: "dimostrare la falsità" (to show the falseness) of his artifices and the libertine matrix of his conceptions. Both Finetti and Croce, however, distinguish between the personal beliefs and religious observance of the "pio Vico" (the pious Vico) and the objective idea of Providence drafted in the *New Science*. Vico's idea of Providence in his *New Science* in no way differs from the idea that could be put forth—so says Finetti—by a "mero naturalista o fatalista" (by a mere fatalist or naturalist) (p. 18).

I shall come back to Finetti's polemics and its presuppositions later in this chapter. For now let me stress that the most decisive point in his controversy is that Vico's imagination of the chaotic, savage origins of mankind—on which he builds the complex edifice of the *New Science*—is absolutely contrary to the account available in Scripture.[4] Let me also say that for Finetti Vico's philosophical inventions cast doubt on Scripture's divine revelation and impugn the solidity of religious beliefs. These inventions are objectionable because they are determined by the vain phantasmagoria of the imagination rather than by the light of reason. Vico's imaginative mode, says Finetti, denies the historical reality of Homer. By the same token, he denies the historical reality of biblical characters. From this standpoint, Finetti does not hesitate to connect Vico's hermeneutical practice to the perverse biblical interpretations by one of the unbelievers of the eighteenth century, M. De Boulanger.[5] To summarize Finetti's objections:

[3] See Michel Bligny, "Il mito del diluvio universale nella coscienza europea del Seicento," in *Rivista storica italiana*, 85 (1973), pp. 47–63. See Don Cameron Allen, *The Legend of Noah: Renaissance Rationalism in Art, Science, and Letters* (Urbana: University of Illinois Press, 1949).

[4] The separation between the two histories is argued for by Arnaldo Momigliano, "La nuova storia romana di Vico," in *Rivista storica italiana*, 72 (1965), pp. 773–90. The heterodox view of Vico is brought within the orbit of La Peyrère. As in his *Preadamitae* Vico upholds the principle of man's original ferocity. See Richard H. Popkin, *Isaac La Peyrère (1596–1676): His Life, Work and Influence* (Leiden–New York: Brill, 1987), and his "Isaac La Peyrère and Vico," *New Vico Studies*, pp. 79–81. See also Gino Bedani, *Vico Revisited: Orthodoxy, Naturalism, and Science in the "Scienza nuova"* (Oxford/Hamburg: Berg, 1989).

[5] Franco Venturi, *L'antichità rivelata e l'idea del progresso in N. A. Boulanger* (Bari: Laterza, 1947).

his polemic is a response to what he takes to be Vico's historical reduction of the Bible and to Vico's elaboration of a personal biblical hermeneutics which is at odds with the canonical interpretation.

But what exactly is Vico's interpretation of the Bible? What is the general scheme that Vico, however intermittently, delineates? His *De Uno* argues that biblical history preserves traces of long-vanished secular history (such as that of the Persians) (par. 13). It also retrieves the question of the giants by following Samuel Bochart's account. More than that, in a text such as *De Constantia Philologiae* (Chapter 10) Vico, following the narrative of Genesis, identifies four distinct epochs in salvation history ("quattuor primae historiae sacrae epochae") and these can also be found, even if not systematically arranged, in the *New Science*. The first epoch is marked by the creation of the world and it extends to the Flood. What is to be understood by God's creation? God creates the world out of nothing, and the creation is a pure act of freedom—not of necessity—through which God *separates* himself from the world. An otherness and a dislocation are established by the theology of creation: this sense of creation as separation marks in depth, as will be seen, Vico's interpretive reading of the Bible and is the foundation of his notion of liberty.

That creation is explicitly bound in Vico's mind with freedom is clarified by the configuration of ideas the text goes on to develop. The creation of the world, which is an act of divine authority, entails human authority, which is free will. Man's authority expresses itself in Adam who, "enlightened by the true God," imposed names on the various entities of the world (1NS/306). The imposition of names—technically known as *onomasthesia*—is the experience of the primordial and sublime unity between words and things. By the imposition of names, Adam signals his mastery of the world. This myth of the original harmony and unity of words and things that was lost after Adam's fall is for Vico the unknowable ground of human history, the beginning of which is inaugurated by a historical rupture—the event of the Flood. The Flood ravages the order of nature, tears apart all human constructions, erases any vestige of the original prelapsarian unity, and discloses the deepest hostility or separation between nature and man. At the same time, this universal catastrophe signals the beginning of history and it initiates Vico's speculations.

The "Chronological Table" and the "Annotations" on it, with which the *New Science* starts, will to show the "uncertain, defective, or vain" beginnings of the nations and of the sciences (NS/43). More poignantly, the "Chronological Table"—a chart with seven parallel columns in which Vico gives the chief events of Hebrew, Chaldean, Scythian, Phoenician, Egyptian, Greek, and Roman history from the universal Flood to the Second Punic War—presents, albeit in a highly generalized form, the abstract

scheme shaping the construction of the *New Science*.[6] Vico's description
of history's shifts is rooted in the principle of the three ages—the age of
the gods, of heroes, and of man—which Varro deploys and takes from the
Egyptians. The synoptic table also insists—and the notes on the table
reemphasize it—on the drastic *separation* of Jewish history from the history of the gentiles. This separation involves the different understanding
of the natural law by Jews, gentiles, and philosophers (NS/313).

The history of the gentiles (from the Chaldeans to the Egyptians and to
the Romans) is figured as a succession of epochal configurations that comes
to be replaced by new configurations. In Vico's archaeology of history, the
same myths (the golden age, Mercury Trimegistus, the age of laws, the
foundations of monarchies, etc.) keep shifting and reappearing according
to the logic of the tripartite structure of the ages. On the other hand, the
history of the Hebrews unfolds in a linear movement and not in the repetitive cycle of natural history. Vico underscores three capital events: (1)
Abraham called by God; (2) the laws God gives to Moses; (3) the kingdom
of Saul or the epoch of the Kings. No doubt, in this linear succession there
is still a hint of the tripartition of the ages (age of the gods with Abraham
called by God; age of the heroes with the laws given to Moses; and age of
men in the kingdom of Saul). Yet Vico, who is the genealogist of history,
does not stretch the trajectory of Hebrew history to the narrative of the
exile or to the messianic advent (which would be, once again, the recurrence of the age of the gods). He resists, in short, a reconciliation between
gentile history and Hebrew history within the unity of one system. The
difference between these two historical paradigms remains constant. As a
matter of fact, Vico finds in the history of the Jews the figure and the concrete reality of a singularity and of a diversity always conscious of itself.

This principle of a self-conscious diversity of the Jews is already present
within the three epochal phases that for Vico represent biblical history. The
call of Abraham, to begin with, figures unequivocally the destiny and the
sense of what *separation* comes to mean. We recall the threads of the biblical narrative. Abraham has a God for himself, who signs with him an alliance. God promises to give to Abraham a land where he will be a foreigner
and he will live like a foreigner, who spiritually does not belong where he
dwells. His identity depends on his apprehension of his exilic contingency.
Second, the written laws God gives to Moses restipulate the covenant between God and his chosen people, but the laws perpetuate the abyss that

[6] The chronology Vico proposes is not a mere revision of Scaliger's account. See on this
issue Donald J. Wilcox, *The Measure of Time Past: Pre-Newtonian Chronologies and the
Rhetoric of Relative Time* (Chicago: University of Chicago Press, 1987). Cf. Anthony T.
Grafton, "From 'Die Natali' to 'De Emendatione Temporum': The Origin and Setting of
Scaliger's Chronology," *Journal of the Warburg and Courtauld Institutes*, 48 (1985), pp.
100–43.

will separate Jews from gentiles. Third, the kingdom of Saul, on which Vico gives no other information, evokes the demon of madness that hovers over him and induces him to succumb to a hatred that will separate Saul from his children, his people, and his God.

In the series of events scanning the immutable inner mechanism of biblical history one can grasp Vico's phenomenology of religious consciousness as consciousness of the radical distance or rupture existing between man and God, man and nature, belief and the "world." This distance is articulated through the primordial opposition between nature and man figured by the Flood; through the self-binding of Abraham, Moses, and Saul in relation to other peoples, to God, and to oneself. Religion originates in fear, Vico says echoing Lucretius. In the light of biblical history we can understand this fear as the anguish for a world man cannot dominate, from which he is divided, and which he sees hostile to himself. This fear, in which the experience of the sublime is rooted, is a powerlessness that ends in the infinite desire for God. The fear is the mark of religious man's perpetual dislocation in alien and unfamiliar grounds. The Bible records this exilic history, and Vico theorizes it in his discussion of some of its aspects.

The "Annotations on the Chronological Table" focus on both biblical and gentile history. Let us look at the text more closely. The starting point for Vico is the archaeological foundation in knowledge. More precisely, his speculations in the *New Science* go counter to the epistemological claims made by John Marsham, in his *Canon Chronicus Aegyptiacus, Hebraicus, Graecus* (1672), by John Spencer, in his *Dissertatio de Urim et Thummim* (1670), and by Otto van Heurn and Herman Witz:

> Furthermore it [the *New Science*] proposes altogether contrary to the *Canon chronicus aegyptiacus, hebraicus, and graecus* by John Marsham, where he wants to prove that the Egyptians in both culture and religion preceded all the nations of the world and that their rites and civil laws, exported to other peoples, were received by the Jews with some changes. John Spencer followed Marsham's opinion in his dissertation *De Urim et Thummim* where he thinks that the Israelites learned from the Egyptians the whole science of divine things by means of the Cabbala. Otto van Heurn in his *Antiquities of Barbaric Philosophy* praised highly the work of Marsham. In the book, which bears the title "Chaldaicus" he writes that Moses was taught the science of divine things by the Egyptians and he carried them over into his laws to the Jews (NS/44).

Against the worldviews of Marsham, Spencer, and Van Heurn, who—as Bruno had done—posit the *priority* of the Egyptians over the Jews, that is, of profane over religious knowledge, Vico proposes to follow a different path. He delves into the debris of culture in order to seek a firmer grounding for his philosophy of origins. The conceptual foundation he will provide for his archaeology of culture will demolish the illusion of the primacy of the gentiles over the Jews. It will also strengthen the beliefs and practices of the Christians ("a tutto il credibile cristiano" [NS/51]). The whole of Christian faith is rooted in one underlying assumption: "That the first people of the earth were the Hebrews, of which Adam was the first, who was created by the true God at the creation of the world" (NS/51). Nonetheless, salvation history, stemming from God's creation, can never become for Vico an object of study, since men can know only what they themselves make. He will study, rather, the ordinary vulgar traditions, the "museum of credulity," the superstitions, the rituals, and the magic practices of natural theology available in the conceptions of the poet-theologians.

Why, however, does Vico qualify his rhetorical procedure as a going *against* what he takes to be the false genealogies contrived by Marsham, Spencer, and Van Heurn? Certainly, the image of Vico *countering* the naturalistic explanation of the beginnings of culture belongs to and further disseminates the romantic myth (divulged by Cuoco) of the solitary thinker who rejects and distances himself from the fashions of the times. To think against the cultural paradigms of Marsham, Spencer, and Van Heurn means also correcting their errors in the light of a philology that acknowledges the necessity and inevitability of a philosophical principle of intelligibility. *To think against* also describes the antithetical, critical structure of the *New Science* that always shuns easy harmonizations of contrasting viewpoints. More exactly, Vico's polemical procedure expresses a thought which is consciously different from and alternative to existing scientific conjectures; it recognizes that history is not explicable from the provisional perspective of one's own contingent experience, and that antiquities especially matter because they crystallize realities independent of one's own articulation of the world.

The difference and newness Vico rhetorically claims for his own investigation, as suggested in the previous chapter, is a central category of the *New Science* and suggests that the Bible is its narrative model. The consciousness of the work's apartness is indissolubly linked to Vico's rigorous fidelity to tradition. This self-reflexiveness is thematized both in the "Idea of the Work" and in the "Annotation" as the *diversity* of Jewish history from the history of the gentiles. In the "Idea of the Work," Vico glosses the emblem on the frontispiece of the *New Science* and exemplifies his "nuova arte critica" (new critical art [NS/7]), which recalls the *Ars Critica* of Robortello and Le Clerc.[7]

Vico interprets the central position that the altar occupies in the drawing to mean the recognition that the civil world came everywhere into being through the practices of religion and divinations. These practices or-

---

[7] See Mario Sina, *Vico e Le Clerc: Tra filosofia e filologia* (Naples: Guida, 1978).

ganize and are the source of intelligibility of the symbolic structures of the world. They also account for the "fondamentale diversità" (fundamental diversity), from which derive all other essential differences between the natural law of the Jews and of the gentiles ('l'altre essenziali differenze tra 'l diritto naturale degli ebrei e 'l diritto naturale delle genti" (NS/9). In the *Elements* Vico restates the question of diversity as one of separation: "The Hebrew religion was founded by the true God on the prohibition of the divination on which all the gentile nations arose. This axiom is one of the principal reasons for the *division* [italics added] of the entire world of the ancient nations into Hebrews and gentiles" (NS/168).

The theme of the particularity of the Jews is treated more extensively in the "Annotations." The first column of the "Chronological Table" is dedicated to the Jews, Vico says, because they were the first people of the world, who lived unknown to all the gentile nations and have preserved their memories in salvation history since the beginning of the world (NS/54). The pure preservation of the past (or the recorded permanence of the history of the Jews), while they live unknown to all other peoples, makes of their history a perpetual particle in the heart of the whole, a residue of unalterable memory closed upon itself and haunted by the dangers of the outside world.

The priority of the Jews is also confirmed later in the "Annotations" where Vico states that Moses did not learn from the Egyptians "la sublime teologia degli ebrei" (the sublime theology of the Jews [NS/68]). The Jews' diversity is confirmed by the rejection of the idea that Pythagoras was a disciple of Isaiah. Vico writes that at the time of Homer and Pythagoras the Jews lived unknown to their Mediterranean neighbors. When Ptolemy wondered why neither poet nor historian had ever made any reference to the Mosaic laws, Demetrius replied that some Jews, who had tried to tell the gentiles about them, were miraculously punished by God. Therefore Joseph "confessa generosamente questa lor oscurezza" (generously acknowledges that they are not known) and attributes it to their choice to live separate from and inaccessible to strangers: "We do not live on the shores, nor do we take delight in trading and interacting with foreigners through business trafficking" (NS/94).

This radical historical separation between Jews and gentiles, whereby each world is outside of the other, challenges the very possibility of a totality. Their difference refracts itself as a lack of economic and social interaction and suggests that each culture constitutes a totality unto itself. But this dissociation is not only economic: it has ethical-theological roots that involve the exclusive, historical sense that the Jews have of the destiny of the biblical text. The absolute, self-enclosed quality of the "book" is linked to their desire to prevent the profanation of the religion of the true God through commerce with the gentiles. God's own jealousy is the sign of

love's radical exclusiveness, and it is shown in the establishment of boundaries meant to shelter the purity of the Bible. When the jealous distance between Jews and gentiles is violated, the Jews expiate the violation as a guilt
that demands purification. Thus, the anniversary of the Septuagint, as Vico
says, was commemorated every year with a solemn fasting: "on the eighth
of *Tebet* which is our December; because when it was finished there were
three days of darkness over all the world according to the rabbinical books
referred to by Casaubon in his *Exercitations on the Annals of Baronius*, by
Buxtorf in his *Synagoga judaica*, and Hothinger in his *Thesaurus philolog-
icus*. And because the Graecian Jews, called Hellenists, among them Aris-
teas, who is said to have been in charge of it, claimed divine authority for
his translations, the Jews of Jerusalem mortally hated them" (NS/94).

The Bible, then, is a text that demands and causes a scandalous separation between Jews and gentiles. It is also a text that provokes lacerations
among the Jews themselves, among Jews and Christians, and, *a fortiori*,
among Christians. Vico states this much in the *Autobiography* as he relates
his decision not to comment on the text of Grotius because it would have
been indecorous for a Catholic to adorn the work of a Protestant with his
doctrine. But the confessional split that the reading of the Bible entails does
not generate by necessity antagonisms and hostility. General divisions remain stubbornly irreconcilable, Vico believes, because it is in the tension
of opposed forces that one can find the value of particular ideas. These divisions allow us to fathom the Bible's insight into theological history and
into the divinity.

The most cogent proofs for this insight are to be found in the memory
and sediments of language. In a corollary on "Poetic Wisdom" Vico reflects on the etymological link in Latin between law (*ius*) and Jove (Ious).
The implied original divinity of the law leads Vico to a further meditation
on language. In the wake of the philosophical etymologies of the *Cratylus*
(412d–413c), Vico points out a Greek parallel to the Latin derivation and
stresses the metaphoric identity between the divinity and the heavens:
"Perchè universalmente da tutte le nazioni gentili fu osservato il cielo con
l'aspetto di Giove" (For the heavens were observed as the aspect of Jove
by all the gentile nations the world over) (NS/473). In natural theology
the symbolic unity between God and nature (and one can catch an echo of
Spinoza's *Deus Sive Natura*) is not broken.

The text goes on to enumerate various occurrences of the metaphor: for
both the Chaldeans and the Persians the sky was Jove, "for it signified for
them things hidden from men" (NS/475). For the Egyptians, who believed that the heavens influenced sublunar affairs, Jove was the sky, and
likewise for the Greeks and for the Romans. In short, there is, within natural theology, a literary personification of God and a metaphoric identity
between nature and God. This identity, which is a form of magic-poetic

idolatry, reappears, as Tacitus narrates, among the ancient Germans as well as among the Peruvian Indians. The Indians called their God "the sublime," and to this God they dedicated open-air temples. This identity between sky and God, Vico goes on to say, continues to exist in Italian expressions, such as "*voglia il cielo*" (I hope to heaven), meaning God in both expressions. Parallel forms are present in Spanish and in the French "*morbleu*" (NS/482).

The idolatrous literalization of the nexus between God and nature (or their false pantheistic unity) available in all the languages of the gentiles is entirely absent (or is present in the form of a prophetic denunciation) in the theological discourse of the Bible. In the Bible there is a tenacious rejection of any objective, substantial representation of the divinity: "But the Hebrews worshipped the true All Highest who is above the heavens, in the enclosure of the tabernacle; and Moses, wherever the people of God extended their conquests, ordered the burning of the sacred groves including the *luci* (holy places) that Tacitus speaks of" (NS/481). The uniqueness of such an idea of the divinity as transcendent and hidden transposes on to theology and extends the notion of the Jews' own "obscurity" from other people. Vico echoes Tacitus for such a view. But the idea comes, above all, from his own reading of the Bible, and especially Exodus (40:1) and Deuteronomy (7:5; 12:3; 16:21) in which, since God is said to be out of reach, Moses must consecrate the sanctuary, shelter within its precincts the ark of the covenant, and stretch a veil to hide it.

The prohibitions and the laws present in the Bible are the sign of a scandal, of the Jews' radical contradiction of a secular history perpetually haunted by the temptation to constitute itself as a self-sufficient totality. At the same time, they are the supreme revelation of an unknowable and absolutely transcendent God who is remote from the world, so that the unknowability of God is the proper subject matter of theology. However, there are some places in the *New Science* that radically reverse or temper the assumption of biblical history's priority over and diversity from secular history. In effect, Vico writes a critique of the principle of biblical separation.

One place where the difference between secular and biblical histories is questioned occurs in the paragraph where Vico treats "the Universal Flood and the Giants." Jews and gentiles are different and yet they are said to have a common origin:

> The founders of gentile humanity must have been men of the races of Ham, Japheth, and Shem, which gradually, one after the other renounced that true religion of their common father Noah. . . . As a result of this renunciation, they dissolved their marriages and broke up their families by promiscuous intercourse, and began roving wild through the great forest of the earth. The

race of Ham wandered through southern Asia, Egypt, and the rest of Africa; that of Japheth through northern Asia or Scythia, and thence through Europe; and that of Shem through all middle Asia toward the east. By fleeing from the wild beasts with which the great forest must have abounded, and by pursuing women, who in that state must have been wild . . . they became separated from each other in their search for food and water. (NS/371)

The Flood marks the difference between the giantism of the founders of the gentile nations and the Hebrews who were of normal size. The difference between them is a difference in moral values, and the Jews, in their exception, are, paradoxically, the norm. The absolute heterogeneity between the three races is reversed into the perception of their common fate in a diaspora.

Another textual place occurs in the discussion of the origins of languages and letters in the "Poetic Logic." After treating Egyptian hieroglyphs as sacred symbols and discussing the opinion that hieroglyphs were invented by philosophers to conceal their esoteric wisdom, Vico proceeds to discuss whether the Greeks took their letters from the Hebrews or the other way around:

> There is no merit in the contention of many scholars that, because the Hebrews and the Greeks give almost the same names to their vulgar letters, the Greeks must have got theirs from the Hebrews. It is more reasonable that the Hebrews should have imitated the Greek nomenclature than vice versa. For it is universally agreed that from the time that Alexander the Great conquered the empire of the East (which after his death was divided by his captains) Greek speech spread throughout Egypt and the East. And since it is also generally agreed that grammar was introduced quite late among the Hebrews, it follows necessarily that the Hebrew men of letters called their Hebrew letters by the Greek names. (NS/441)

As we learn later, Vico will reject Erasmus's interpretation of the myth of Cadmus in terms of the finding of letters. What matters here is that, by turning around the principle of the absolute priority of the Hebrews and by attributing the origin of letters to Mercury and to the Greeks, Vico erases the claim of an antinomy or separation between true salvation history and poetic fictions. The Bible seeks to shelter itself from the impure idolatries of the secular world. But this self-enclosure turns out to be a powerful illusion and a misreading of historical realities. In point of fact, poetic secular writing is the material basis of the biblical text, which, thus, edges toward the status of a poetic text. The implied doubt about the existence of the "sacred" being drastically separate from the secular leads Vico to reflect on the ways in which the Bible enters the world of culture: how, indeed, theology becomes politics. This concern lies behind his assertion that Christianity is the true religion that has its foundation in biblical history (NS/1094).

I begin exploring these issues by focusing on some conceptual extensions in Vico's consciousness of biblical history. From the analysis of Vico's interpretation of the Bible it is manifest how much Finetti's *Difesa dell' autorità della Sacra Scrittura contro G. B. Vico* was destined to misunderstand and simultaneously hit the target in Vico's procedures. The causes of the misunderstanding can be quickly formulated. The theoretical premise of Finetti's polemic puts it within the circuit of a prescriptive dogmatic theology. That Vico is fully aware of the nature of this theological strain is made clear by his reflections in *On the Study Methods of Our Time* (Chapter IX), discussed above in Chapter 2. In that context Vico explains the reason for the omission of Christian theology from the catalogue of instruments by which knowledge is procured. Whereas pagan theology entertains a multitude of "contradictory and vague opinions as to the nature of the gods . . . Christianity advocates unassailable dogmas bearing on the nature of God and on the mystery of religion. A new discipline has providentially arisen among us for the disclosure of the divine source of truth as well as for the illustration and interpretation of the sacred books and traditions; it is called dogmatic theology" (pp. 44–45). The discipline, which indeed comes into being in the eighteenth century as a defense of the content of faith from the encroachments of skepticism and rationalism and which counts among its practitioners Baronius, Casaubon, and Vossius, is kept outside of Vico's purview.

Following the Aristotelian-Thomistic tradition of biblical exegesis, which valorizes the literal sense of the Bible, Finetti's dogmatic theology believes that Scripture offers incontrovertibly scientific facts. The reader, thus, can discriminate between, on the one hand, impostors and falsifiers and, on the other, the empire of truth. In brief and paradoxically, for Finetti the Bible is not to be interpreted: its message is unproblematically explicit to the believer. To interpret the biblical text would imply both questioning its self-sufficiency as an intelligible structure of meaning and submitting the narrative to the sovereignty of oneself or one's interpretation. As he confronts the divergences between Vico's biblical elaborations and the letter of the biblical text, Finetti points out that Moses never gives a hint of the division of the earth before the confusion of tongues. Vico, on the contrary, posits the division as occurring long before the Babelic confusion. The Scripture, Finetti adds, "dice quanto basta per far sapere che almeno quattro anni in circa dopo il diluvio i figliouli di Noè erano ancora uniti" (says all that is necessary to make us know that, for at least four years after the Flood, the children of Noah were still together) (p. 16). In short,

Finetti condemns Vico's procedure because in his view Vico believes that "tutta è incertezza, dubbiezza, al più probabilità e verisimilitudine" (all is uncertainty, doubt, and, at most, probability and verisimilitude) (p. 16).

Finetti is certainly right in his perception. For Vico, division is constitutive of the biblical discourse and it is not merely a contingent phenomenon. Furthermore, the probable and the "certain" are fundamental criteria in Vico's quest for origins. Finetti is especially sharp in observing the arbitrariness of Vico's etymologies. As Finetti writes, through the category of etymology Vico

> often, on the basis of the affinity of words and the lightest conjectures, infers consequences and establishes facts of no slight importance: also Boulanger makes large use of the affinity of names and vaguest circumstances to establish his characters, emblems, and symbols. For instance, he wants that Elijah of the Jews, the Ali of the Moslems, and Helios of the Greeks are the same thing, and that the first two are mere symbols of the third, that in that language means the sun. He also wants that Enoch of the Jews, Anach of the orientals, and Inach of the Greeks are the same astronomical symbol. . . . He wants Janus of the Romans and John the Baptist to be the same, etc. (p. 23; my translation)

Finally, in Vico's encyclopedic will to embrace "all that is knowable in a few sheets" Finetti discerns a burning imagination as well as the symptom of an interpretive, synchretistic delirium. His specific aim will be that of delineating "the quality and the character of G. B. Vico" and of catching the source of his errors. The moral-biographical profile of Vico that Finetti traces aims at bringing the interpretive deviations punctuating the *New Science* to the subjectivity of Vico's methods of reading. Vico's interpretive freedom, in short, is for Finetti an example of the libertine morality that one finds among the followers of Epicurus and Lucretius, such as Boulanger.

It is easy to perceive between the position of Finetti and the position of Vico the presence of two diametrically opposed modalities of reading the Bible or understanding tradition. For Finetti, the sense of Scripture is objectively given, because it (the sense) is natural and manifest. For Vico the biblical text never has a literal identity fixed forever nor can it be viewed as separate from the ambiguous concerns of history. As one gathers from Finetti's own remarks about the arbitrary etymologies of the *New Science*, Vico never puts objective limits to the significations of words. The semantic density of words transcends the principle whereby their significance depends merely on their immediate context or on their clear function within a phrase or proposition. There are palimpsests and hidden depths both in the history of words and in biblical history that Vico wants to retrieve. This amounts to saying in a general way that it is never the Cartesian clarity, or the inviolable, rational literalness of texts that interests Vico. Rather, the object of his thought is the obscurity, the shadowy, hidden folds of experiences. Obscurity is also the distinctive trait of his oblique style that some critics have viewed as a systematic strategy to conceal his so-called naturalism.

The critical reading Vico practices, based as it is on his "nuova arte critica" (new critical art), is a *historical* reading comprising philology and philosophy as well as a reading of history. From the historical-philological standpoint, which recognizes the mobility of the literal and of its infinite resonances, texts—and among them the Bible—have neither secret ciphers nor crystallized or reified significations. Vico consistently leaves behind both the allegorizations of ancient fables and the figural-typological exegesis of the Bible. What remains central to his reading is the grammatical principle of etymology, as if this science of origins were the sole portal of access to grasp the sense of things, because the *historia verborum* leads to and discloses the *historia rerum*.

Behind Vico's model of reading there is a new idea of tradition.[8] For Finetti, tradition enacts a selfsame, repetitive pattern that eschews history and time. For him, the spiritual and pure sense of the Bible resides in the *verbum scriptum*. On the other hand, Suarez, who is the theologian whose works Vico reads during his stay at Vatolla, believes in the *regula animata* (the living rule) of tradition. What exactly is the *regula animata*? St. Augustine theorizes in his *De doctrina christiana* that the Bible is the necessary perspective for deciphering the book of the world, and that the science of the Egyptians or the book of the world, in turn, allows us to catch the sense of the Bible. The Council of Trent (fourth session, April 8, 1546) asks if there are divine data outside the Scripture's revelation, and it answers affirmatively. The *traditiones* for the Tridentine Council comprise the vast range of conciliar canons, decretals, patristics, and ecclesial *magisterium*. Vico radicalizes the council's findings when he writes that the poetic "vulgar traditions" in their autonomy from the Bible are still willed by God. They are secular displacements of the Bible, and they give access both to an understanding of the Bible and to the workings of Providence in history.

Such a new, larger, and hybrid sense of tradition is shaped by the awareness of the historical debates about biblical philology going on in Naples among Vico's contemporaries and among some of his friends. A discrete trace of these debates is available in the *New Science*. In the corollary on the origin of languages and letters, Vico, who grasps the divergences and conflicts within tradition, alludes to the "critici bibbici" (biblical critics)— "thus the same heroic origins, preserved in brief in the vulgar tongues, have

[8] On the theology of tradition see Yves Congar, *La tradition et les traditions*, two vols. (Paris: A. Foyard, 1960–63).

given rise to the phenomenon so astonishing to biblical critics: that the names of the same kings appear in one form in sacred and in another in profane history" (NS/445). Diversity and sameness are subtly correlated, and biblical criticism profits by the vulgar traditions. The insight is extended in "Corollaries Concerning the Origins of Poetic Style, Digression, Inversion, Rhythm, Song, and Verse," where Vico chiefly upholds the priority of poetry in relation to prose and discusses difficulties of pronunciations, tropes, heroic verse, and poetic meters in the vulgar tongues. After referring to the oracle of the Pythian Apollo, thus named for his slaying of the serpent Python, Vico turns his attention to contemporary Hebraists:

> Hebraists today are divided in their opinions on the question whether Hebrew poetry is metrical or merely rhythmical. However, Josephus, Philo, Origen, and Eusebius stand as favoring meter, and (what is most to our present purpose) St. Jerome holds (in his preface to it) that the Book of Job, which is older than the books of Moses, was composed in heroic verse from the beginning of the third chapter to the end of the forty-second. (NS/465)

It can be that Vico's reference to St. Jerome is a case of a naive display of knowledge of biblical textual criticism. But, more likely, it must be regarded as a symptom of Vico's mature consciousness of humanistic-biblical philology that starts with Valla; it includes Erasmus, Colet, Spinoza, and Le Clerc and reaches both Giacinto Gimma, an assiduous presence in the circle of Valletta and of Vico himself, and Biagio Garofalo, a friend of Giannone's. This philological line (from Valla to Garofalo) is certainly not homogeneous either in its techniques or finalities. It is even less homogeneous in drawing political implications out of the philological practices.

Valla's philology, which will be Erasmus's, is the matrix of subsequent developments. Valla annotates and amends the Vulgate in the light of the Greek text of the New Testament. Erasmus will later edit the Greek text. For both scholars philology can be defined as the determination of the literal sense of Scripture, and they depart from the medieval biblical exegesis embodied by the glosses of Nicholas of Lyra and Hugh of St. Cher. Valla throws into question the attribution of the Vulgate to St. Jerome. Because of this, Poggio Bracciolini will unleash a violent attack against Valla.[9] For Erasmus, as the title of his work *Novum Instrumentum* suggests, Scripture has no longer the status of a pact in the legal, binding sense of the word;

---

[9] The controversy between Valla and Poggio Bracciolini is illuminated by Salvatore I. Camporeale, *Lorenzo Valla, umanesimo e teologia* (Florence: Istituto Nazionale di Studi sul Rinascimento, 1972); "Poggio Bracciolini contro Valla: Le 'Orationes in L. Vallam,'" in *Poggio Bracciolini: 1380–1980* (Florence: Istituto Nazionale di Studi sul Rinascimento, 1982), pp. 137–61. More generally see Eugenio Garin, *L'umanesimo italiano: Filosofia e vita civile nel Rinascimento* (Bari: Laterza, 1952). See also Jerry Bentley, *Humanists and Holy Writ: New Testament Scholarship in the Renaissance* (Princeton: Princeton University Press, 1983).

Scripture is only a textual document to be described as part of an archaeology in its erasures, uncertain contours, and sense.

Le Clerc provides the reprinting of Erasmus's *Novum Instrumentum* in 1706. He himself writes the *Ars Critica* (1699), which recalls the 1537 *De Arte Critica* by Robortello and in which he advances some proposals for a philological reading of Scripture. Just as the brief reflection by Robortello on the critical methods to be followed for restoring defaced classical texts had done, Le Clerc's *Ars Critica* describes the *recta lectio* of the Bible as a critical inquiry of the culture of antiquity. The task of the critic-reader, says Le Clerc, who will be accused of socianism by Muratori, is to establish the authenticity of the text, its attribution, the exact significance of words, the distinction between proper and figurative senses of phrases, chronology, and the rich cultural context of the times—"cognitio consuetudinum et morum" (De Studii Hebraici Methodo," p. 91).

This philological tradition, which skeptically rejects the dogmatic, a priori emphasis of canonical exegesis, states its unequivocal intent to pursue the spiritual renewal of Christianity and the revival of *pietas*. Yet the philology of Valla, Colet, and Erasmus ends up exercising an influence that far exceeds and even turns around their original intentions. In the seventh chapter of *Tractatus Theologico-Politicus* Spinoza shows philologically, through an analysis of the system of punctuation deployed in the text, that the letter of the Pentateuch is corrupted and that its literal meaning is unclear and confused.

Furthermore, through linguistic proofs, Spinoza denies that Moses was the author of the Pentateuch. His historical-philological analysis generates skepticism on the sacredness of the text, and it induces Spinoza to argue that the Bible must be read philosophically. The Bible, he says, is no longer a book only for the Jews. It is a text, he adds, from which it is possible to extract a rationalist ethics, which will become the basis of his great principles of religious tolerance and which, de facto, reduces religion to moral philosophy and to a political instrument. Spinoza, as is known, absorbs and endorses Hobbes's formula, *cuius regio eius religio*. The formula—stated baldly—means that political authority is invested with the power of determining the sense of the Bible.[10]

In Naples, in the first half of the eighteenth century, Spinozism—a term that embraces doctrines that include Bruno's hermeticism, Spinoza's own philosophy, Epicurus, Lucretius, and Descartes—stands at the center of lively intellectual debates. I shall quickly give a few examples.

Giacinto Gimma writes in 1723 *L'idea della storia dell'Italia letterata* in order to claim that Italy's science and philosophy—and specifically Bruno's

[10] On Spinoza and the Bible see Leo Strauss, *Spinoza's Critique of Religion* (New York: Schocken Books, 1965). On Vico and Spinoza see James Morrison, "Vico and Spinoza," in *Journal of the History of Ideas*, 16 (1980), pp. 49–68.

hermeticism—inaugurate modern thought.[11] The ciphers and secret codes of Kabbalah, Gimma maintains, hide all the mysteries of wisdom. In the hermetic-biblical scheme that he delineates, Adam is the repository of all the secrets of nature, and Gimma proceeds to read the Bible as if it were a hermetic text: "La scienza data da Dio ad Adamo si propagò nei suoi posteri sino al Diluvio e poi Noé coi suoi figliuoli furono maestri di tutto l'umano sapere e da'medesimi derivarono le accademie" (the science given by God to Adam spread among his descendants till the Flood, and afterwards Noah with his children were the masters of all human knowledge, and from them derived the academies).

In his *Considerazioni intorno alla poesia degli Ebrei e dei Greci* Biagio Garofalo analyses the Psalms following the philological criteria put forth by Valla, Erasmus, and Spinoza.[12] Just as Valla and Erasmus do, Garofalo considers the text of the Vulgate wrong and thinks that St. Jerome knows well the allegories of Scripture but that he completely ignores the history of the Jews: "poca conoscenza prendendo della critica. Di modo che al tempo di San Girolamo non avevano ne pure esatta grammatica." (Having little knowledge of criticism at the time of St. Jerome since they did not even have an exact grammar). Garofalo's perspective on the Bible is decisively Spinozist:

> in molti luoghi la Bibbia [è] stata da' copiatori ebrei depravata. . . . Quindi è che alcuni lettori fra gli Ebrei molto rinomati, come Salomone e Moisè, in alcuni luoghi guasti e corrotti sempre si lagnano de i loro copiatori, per aver ordinato la scrittura santa diversa in alcune cose da quello che i profeti la scrissero. (p. 23)

> (In many places the Bible has been distorted by the Hebrew copyists. Thus it is that some very renowned readers among the Jews, such as Solomon and Moses, at some corrupt and unclear spots, complain about their copyists who arranged holy scripture differently in some aspects from the way the prophets wrote it.)

Finally Bencini's *Tractatio Historica* is polemical against Spinoza's impostures, which deny divine inspiration of the Bible, discard the authority of

[11] Giacinto Gimma, *L'idea della storia dell'Italia letterata* two vols. (Naples: Mosca, 1723). On Gimma see D. Mauredonoja, *Breve ristretto della vita dell'abate sign. Giacinto Gimma* in *Raccolta d'opuscoli scientifici filosofici*, Vol. XVII (1738), pp. 338–427. See also Cesare Vasoli, "L'abate Gimma e la 'nova encyclopaedia' (cabalismo, lullismo, magia e 'nuova scienza,'" in *Studi in onore di Antonio Corsano* (Manduria: Lacaita, 1970), pp. 789–827.

[12] Biagio Garofalo, *Considerazioni intorno alla poesia degli Ebrei e dei Greci* (Rome: Gonzaga, 1707). Garofalo was a disciple of Domenico Aulisio and a friend of Giannone. See Pietro Giannone, *Vita scritta da lui medesimo*, ed. S. Bertelli (Milan: Feltrinelli, 1960), pp. 154–55. In general on this issue see Emilia Giancotti-Boscherini, "Note sulla diffusione della filosofia di Spinoza in Italia," in *Giornale critico della filosofia italiana*, 42 (1963), pp. 339–62. Of great usefulness on this point is Nicola Badaloni, *Introduzione a G. B. Vico*, cited in note 1.

Moses, and reduce the significance of prophecy to a merely natural form of knowledge.

There is no doubt that Vico alludes and responds to these debates in his *New Science*. Here the authority of St. Jerome is confirmed against his detractors. Equally confirmed is the belief in the divine inspiration of the Bible. At the time he wrote "Affetti di un disperato" (Affections of a Desperate Man) Vico had definite leanings toward the thought of Lucretius. Now in the *New Science* Spinoza's rational religion as well as his views of the republic are refuted because for Vico religion is not an abstract geometric calculus to be realized within the sphere of political economy.

Furthermore, the Book of Job, not the Pentateuch (on the authority of which philology has consistently cast doubts in order to demythologize it) is conceived as the founding text of the Bible. The myth of the fabulous antiquities of the pre-Adamites, which had been sketched by La Peyrère, is discarded. Finally, philology's assumed objectivity, which has as its inevitable and paradoxical outlet the dogmatism of facts which are certain but also partial, is rethought as the science of the probable. For Vico, the value of the probable is determined by philosophical presuppositions about what is true. More importantly, he absorbs the Bible's rejection of the tendency to reify the divinity as if the divinity could be an object of thought; and he questions the interpretation of the Bible as a self-enclosed text, and, indeed, questions the very principle of the separation of sacred and profane realities.

Vico's thought moves ceaselessly from one idea to the next; it ceaselessly shifts its ground, it resists a reduction within the rigid boundaries of any one system, and it refuses elevating one part to a totality. But it is not false to say that at the basis of his restless thinking in the *New Science* there is a religious core that shapes the work. The fragmentary references to the Bible, which call into question all totalizing claims and resist its assimilation to immanent totalities, are a symptom of Vico's religious vision. But the Bible cannot be viewed, as Finetti or Croce would have it, as absolutely outside of history. The idea of separation is thus replaced by the notion of liminality, the ambiguous dwelling place of a religious consciousness.

To be sure, Vico does not set out to prove the reality of God's existence, and he agrees with the formulation of Pascal, in the wake of St. Augustine, about the "dieu caché." This idea forces him to keep the Bible, indeed the figure of Christ, outside of his philosophical purview, exiled at the margin of history and of his thought. But they are outside not because they are separable from the concerns of history. Though God is hidden, as Vico's reading of the Bible shows him, he makes his own the principle set forth by Aquinas and Suarez, that, the autonomy of secular history notwithstanding, Providence is simultaneously transcendent and immanent in history. To grasp quickly Vico's sense of Providence we should view it side by side with Machiavelli's blindfolded, erratic Fortune: she wages war against and finally overpowers man's virtue. Vico radically reverses Machiavelli's classical myth by envisioning Providence as the manifestation of God, whose peculiarity is to work at odds with man's own destructive impulses and whose workings lie outside man's range of vision. More importantly for the religious focus of his thought, as politics becomes the stage of theology, the drastic separation established by interpreters of the Bible between religion and politics is questioned and abolished as untenable.

The yoking of theology and politics is rooted in Vico's sense of the human as the compound of reason and will. His rationale for positing the reality of religious consciousness and of human hunger for the divinity comes from man's consciousness of his finiteness when lightning strikes. It does not come merely from the recognition of the limits of knowledge, if the limit were to mean that belief in the divine emerges when knowledge founders against the bleak rocks of skepticism. Vico's sense of the divine comes to life from within the boundaries of knowledge and, indeed, it supplements knowledge. And yet it is not just in the mind, as happens with numbers or other abstractions contrived by the mind. It is an existential self-revelation. To present his rationale, Vico recuperates claims he has made about self, poetry, and knowledge. In the last two paragraphs of the *New Science*, after showing, as Chapter 8 has argued, how politically harmful are the atheistic philosophers, he also resorts to biblical language and to Augustinian theology:

> For religions alone can bring the peoples to do virtuous works by appeal to their feelings, which alone move men to perform them; and the reasoned maxims of the philosophers concerning virtue are of use only where employed by a good eloquence for kindling the feelings to do the duties of virtue. There is, however, an essential difference between our Christian religion, which is true, and all the others, which are false. In our religion, divine grace causes virtuous action for the sake of an eternal and infinite good. . . .
>
> But providence, through the order of civil institutions discussed in this work, makes itself palpable for us in these three feelings: the first, the marvel, the second, the veneration, hitherto felt by all the learned for the matchless wisdom of the ancients, and the third, the ardent desire with which they burned to seek and attain it. These are in fact three lights of the divine providence that aroused in them the aforesaid three beautiful and just sentiments; but these sentiments were later perverted by the conceit of scholars and by the conceit of nations—conceits we have sought throughout this work to discredit. The uncorrupted feelings are that all the learned should admire, venerate, and desire to unite themselves to the infinite wisdom of God.
>
> To sum up, from all that we have set forth in this work, it is to be finally concluded that this Science carries inseparably with the study of piety, and that he who is not pious cannot be truly wise. (NS/1111–12)

The pathos of this rhetoric leaves no doubt about the power of Vico's convictions. The *New Science*'s conclusion echoes the sapiential tradition about what it means to be wise, and it stresses the existential reality of "feelings" as the ingredient of knowledge. Both are essential to Vico's sense of the divine and of wisdom. In its turn, wisdom—which is the point of destination of science—cannot exist apart from piety: the two of them are "inseparable" from each other. By a repeated twist of the biblical insight into separation and division as the profound condition of religious life, piety and wisdom are again said to belong "indivisibilmente" (indivisibly) together. The link between piety and wisdom—an idea that goes back to Christian humanism wherein *sapientia est pietas* and the pride of knowledge is humbled—follows three stages: wonder, the veneration of the wisdom of the ancients, which is "innarrivabile" (out of reach), and the ardent desire to search for the infinite wisdom and achieve it. This triple concatenation of concepts—wonder, veneration, and infinite desire—describes the conditions necessary for the possibility of knowledge. It shows knowledge's limits as well as its necessarily infinite openness.

These qualities are bound up with man's total being. They make manifest the true, poetic origin of knowledge and its never-ending movement toward elusive rational perfection. Wonder, which is the other term for the *sublime* and is the beginning of every poetic and philosophical knowledge, opens up the world as an impenetrable, incomprehensible totality from which oneself is dissociated. Veneration (etymologically rooted in *Venus*) encompasses *devotio* or worship. It expresses an existential feeling of awe and admiration for the beauty of the virtues, and, in this sense, it reconciles man and world, esthetics and ethics. Desire for infinite wisdom has both biblical and Augustinian resonances. As happens in biblical poetics and the *Confessions*, this desire dramatizes man's mode of being as a spiritual quester, simultaneously in a radical, unending dislocation from and in steady pursuit of that infinite wisdom.

Man is caught, thus, in an alternating rhythm of spiritual openness and worldly closure or reconciliation. To say it differently, the infinite desire for the perfection of reason, which resides in the divine, is the other side of Vico's sense of history that is rooted in the contingency and finiteness of time. Yet, it shapes man's response to contingency. Desire belongs to the vocabulary of concrete, lived experience, and, as such, it alters our sense of the contingent and tells us that man's angle of vision is not only in the cogito. Moreover, it evokes man's interiority and brings the *New Science* back into the orbit of the subjectivity of Vico's *Autobiography*, though subjectivity is never only a private issue. But what unifies these three complementary stages in the open-ended journey to wisdom is *pietas*, a word for religion, which does not necessarily belong to any of them, but describes the mode of being of knowledge, the perception of the whole of life as a web of enigmatic meaningfulness, and the yoking of humbling knowledge to the stark realities of life. The joining together of wisdom and piety (or knowledge and belief or philosophy and theology) sheds light on Vico's whole project as a poetic, political, and religious conversation.

He has lucidly understood that the secularization of the world, indeed the iconoclasm and the rabid attacks against religion, brought in by seventeenth-century rationalists' myth of progress, promoted amnesia about the past and was a tragic misreading of the religious foundations of culture. It fomented powerful and self-deluded myths about fantastic new worlds to be made by forgetting the existing world, that is to say, by forgetting history itself. These misreadings of history endanger the very foundation of the human. They are the more dangerous in that they are presented to us as brilliant promises of scientific order, or with the innocent, alluring disguises of chiliastic fantasies, or even with the blandness of irresistibly reasonable plans. One such plan is by Locke, who, in the *Reasonableness of Christianity* (1695), as he distinguishes knowledge from belief, asserts the sovereignty of reason over revelation, and, in the name of tolerance, pushes religion out of the public square.[13] Malebranche's *Méditations chrétiennes et métaphysiques* (1683), which makes physics the path to God, is not exempt from these temptations.[14] Vico, who writes also from within the theological tradition, takes the longer, older view. He makes piety and wisdom the public way to take in order to restore the ruins of knowledge and to remake the world we have inherited. From this standpoint, religion and politics are intertwined experiences as well as exigencies of the public conversation.

In his view of religion as the underlying and unifying force of history, Vico is not blind to the reality of religion itself as a tragically divisive and divided force. He is also aware of the tradition of constructing systems where all oppositions are reconciled and a logical order reaffirmed. This tradition may possibly stem from the efforts of figures such as Bruno and Spinoza, who produce unitary systems that are, paradoxically, founded on the exclusion of individualities or even of divine transcendence. In his own days, the tradition is incarnated, above all, by both Grotius and Leibnitz, who, optimistically, dream of the religious pacification of the Christian sects

[13] Vico's *Autobiography* records Locke's debt to Epicurus (*Vita*, p. 19). For the role of Locke in Naples, see Paolo Mattia Doria, *Difesa della metafisica degli antichi filosofi contro il signor Giovanni Locke ed alcuni altri autori* (Venice, 1732).

[14] In the *Autobiography*, Vico points out Malebranche's failure to establish a Christian ethics (*Vita*, p. 22). But see Augusto Del Noce, *Il concetto di ateismo e la storia della filosofia come problema* (Bologna: Il Mulino, 1970), pp. 498–520, for the effect of Malebranche's ideas on Vico. For a study of the relationship between Descartes and Augustine (or science and belief) in Malebranche see Michael E. Hobart, *Science and Religion in the Thought of Nicolas Malebranche* (Chapel Hill: University of North Carolina Press, 1982).

by blunting the edge of their theological differences in order to achieve an impossible compromise of doctrines.

On his part, and with the authority of the teacher he has sought to be and has become, Vico conjures up a practical or poetic world, a world where there are no absolute panaceas, where evil is ambiguously confused with the good, and in which their mixture is better than the destruction and death inexorably engulfing every human project. Thus, he has envisioned a system that explains the chaos of human history and seeks to counter it. His *New Science* is such a fragile web of relations, a paradoxically unsystematic system, wherein the warring "religions" (as he calls them in the plural) are not repressed but find a common ground around the value of the work one produces. In his work, which shows how prudent politics depends on the interaction of rhetoric and theology, or *theologia rhetorica*, Vico proposes poetry as the mode of making whereby the discourse of particularities can be rethought as a project of totalizing relations. Forever aware of the role of the subject in philosophy, he opens up a public square, a *common place*, which is a political place for thought and discourse, where a civil conversation—a phrase that must be taken in its full humanistic and rhetorical sense of a turning toward civil wisdom—occurs.

In this dimension Vico finds his most disparate interlocutors: Socrates and Homer, Vergil and Dante, Bruno and Kircher, Suarez and Bodin, Hobbes and Gimma, Solomon and Seneca, Aquinas and Augustine, Bruno and Spinoza, Caloprese and Gravina, Scotus and Bossuet, Muratori and Descartes, Machiavelli, Campanella, and Doria, and, of course, Plato, Bacon, Tacitus, and Grotius—a vast *Kunstkammer* of the spheres of knowledge. For Grotius, the last of his four authors, the reflection on peace was a way of thinking about the unification of the Christian confessions. The "pious" Vico constructs a work in which unity recognizes differences. Of these differences he shows their provisional overlapping and he leaves them religiously, without exclusions, in the space of their irreducible heterogeneity.

In this heroic reconstitution of the sphere of public discourse he envisions a political order in which Christians are the vital "remnants" both inside and outside of history. And in his visionary realism he drafts a new map of the world wherein the diverse and mobile forms of knowledge, joined in a poetic, philosophical, and theological conversation, teach how to apprehend the unavoidable dangers and tragedies, and the true senses of history.

PRIMARY SOURCES

UNLESS otherwise stated, all citations are taken from these editions. References to Bacon's works indicate volume and page number. Citations from poems indicate canto number (or book) and lines. Citations from classical texts follow standard form of giving number and column.

Ammirato, Scipione. *Discorsi sopra C. Tacito*. Florence, 1594.

Aquinas, St. Thomas. *Summa Theologiae* (Latin text and English trans.) Blackfriars ed. New York: McGraw-Hill, 1964.

Aristotle, *Metaphysics*. Loeb Classical Library. Trans. Hugh Tredennick. Cambridge, Mass.: Harvard University Press, 1935–36.

———. *The Nichomachean Ethics*. Loeb Classical Library. Ed. and trans. H. Rackham. Cambridge, Mass.: Harvard University Press, 1982.

———. *Physics*. Loeb Classical Library. Trans. P. H. Wicksteed and F. Cornford. Cambridge. Mass.: Harvard University Press, 1963.

———. *Poetics*. Loeb Classical Library. Trans. Hamilton Fyfe. Cambridge, Mass.: Harvard University Press, 1973.

———. *Politics*. Loeb Classical Library. Trans. H. Rackham. Cambridge, Mass.: Harvard University Press, 1932.

———. *Rhetoric*. Loeb Classical Library. Trans. John H. Freese. Cambridge, Mass.: Harvard University Press, 1959.

Augustine, St. *The City of God*. Trans. Marcus Dods. New York: Modern Library, 1950.

———. *The Confessions of St. Augustine*. Trans. Rex Warner. New York: New American Library, 1963.

Bacon, Francis. *De sapientia veterum: The Wisedome of the Ancients*. Trans. A. G. Knight. London: John Bill, 1619.

———. *The Works of Francis Bacon*. Ed. James Spedding. 7 vol. London: Longman, 1858.

Boccaccio, Giovanni. *Genealogia deorum gentilium libri*. Ed. Vincenzo Romano. Bari: Laterza, 1951.

Boccalini, Traiano. *Ragguagli di Parnaso*. 3 vols. Ed. Giuseppe Rua. Scrittori d'Italia, nos. 6, 39, 199. Bari: Laterza, 1910–48.

Bodin, Jean. *The Six Bookes of a Commonweale*. Trans. Richard Knolles. London, 1606. Facsimile ed. Ed. and intr. Kenneth D. McRae. Cambridge, Mass.: Harvard University Press, 1962.

Boileau, Nicolas. *Art poetique*. In *Oeuvre de Boileau*. Paris: Bibliotheque Hachette, 1913.

Botero, Giovanni. *Della ragion di stato con tre libri delle cause della grandezza delle città, due aggiunte e un discorso sulla popolazione di Roma*. Ed. Luigi Firpo. Classici politici, no. 2. Turin: UTET, 1948.

———. *The Reason of State*. Trans. P. J. Waley and D. P. Waley. New Haven: Yale University Press, 1956.

Bruno, Giordano. *Dialoghi italiani*. In *Oeuvres completes de Giordano Bruno*. Eds. Yves Hersant and Nuccio Ordine. 6 vols. to date. Paris: Belles Lettres, 1992–.

———. *Opere latine conscripta*. 3 vols. in 8 parts. Eds. F. Fiorentino, F. Tocco, and V. Imbriani. Florence: Le Monnier, 1879–91.

Calderini, Apollinare de. *Discorsi sopra la ragion di stato del Signor Giovanni Botero*. Milan, 1609.

Campanella, Tommaso. *The Defense of Galileo*. Trans. Grant McColley. Merrick, N.Y.: Richwood Pub., 1976.

———. *Discorsi ai principi d'Italia e altri scritti filo-ispanici*. Ed. Luigi Firpo. Turin: Chiantore, 1945.

Cardano, Girolamo. *The Book of My Life*. Trans. J. Stoner. London: Dent, 1931.

———. *De vita propria liber* in *Opera Omnia*, Vol. 1. Ed. A. Buck. Stuttgart and Bad Cannstatt: Frommann, 1966.

Castelvetro, Lodovico. *Poetica d'Aristotele vulgarizzata et sposta* (1576). Ed. Werther Romani. Bari: Laterza, 1978.

Castiglione, Baldassarre. *Libro del cortegiano*. Ed. Bruno Maier. 2d ed. Turin: UTET, 1964.

Chiabrera, Gabriello. *Vita di Gabriello Chiabrera scritta da lui medesimo*. In *Canzonette, rime varie, dialoghi di Gabriello Chiabrera*. Ed. L. Negri. Turin: UTET, 1952.

Cicero. *De inventione: De optimo genere oratorum: Topica*. Loeb Classical Library. Trans. H. M. Hubbell. Cambridge, Mass.: Harvard University Press, 1976.

———. *De oratore*. Loeb Classical Library. Trans. E. W. Sutton and H. Rackham. Cambridge, Mass.: Harvard University Press, 1979.

———. *Tusculan Disputations*. Loeb Classical Library. Trans. J. E. King. Cambridge, Mass.: Harvard University Press, 1945.

Crescimbeni, Giovan Mario. *Le vite degli arcadi illustri*. Rome: Antonio de'Rossi, 1708.

Dante. *De vulgari eloquentia*. Ed. Pier Vincenzo Mengaldo. In *Opere minori*, Vol. 2. Milan-Naples: Ricciardi Editore, 1979.

———. *"La divina commedia" secondo l'antica vulgata*. Ed. Giorgio Petrocchi. 4 vols. Società dantesca italiana. Milan: Mondadori, 1966–67.

———. *The Divine Comedy: Inferno, Purgatorio, Paradiso*. Trans. with comm. by Charles Singleton. Bollingen Series 80. Princeton, N.J.: Princeton University Press, 1970–76.

———. *Vita Nuova*. Ed. Domenico De Robertis. In *Opere minori*, Vol. 1, pt. 1. Milan-Naples: Ricciardi Editore, 1979.

Descartes, Rene. *The Philosophical Writings of Descartes*. 2 vols. Trans. John Cottingham, Robert Stoothoff, and Dugald Murdoch. Cambridge: Cambridge University Press, 1985. (Volume 1: *Discourse on the Method*; *The Passions of the Soul*).

Doria, Paolo Mattia. *La vita civile con un trattato della educazione del Principe*. Naples, 1710.

Fajardo, Diego Saavedra. *Obras completas*. Ed. Angel Gonzalez Palencia. 2 vols. Madrid: Espasa-Calpe, 1955.

Ficino, Marsilio. *Three Books on Life*. Trans. and introd. by Carol V. Kaske and John R. Clark. Medieval and Renaissance Texts and Studies. Binghamton, N.Y.: Renaissance Society of America, 1989.

Galilei, Galileo. *Le opere di Galileo Galilei*. 20 vols. Edizione Nazionale. Ed. A. Favaro. Florence: Barbera, 1890–1909.

Gassendi, Pierre. *The Selected Works of Pierre Gassendi*. Ed. Craig B. Brush. New York: Johnson Reprint Corp., 1972.

Gentillet, Innocent. *Discours contre Machiavel*. Eds. A. D'Andrea and P. D. Stewart. Florence, 1974.

Giannone, Pietro. *The Civil History of the Kingdom of Naples*. Trans. James Ogilvie. London, 1729.

———. *Dell'istoria civile del regno di Napoli*. Naples: Naso, 1723.

Gravina, Gianvincenzo. *Della ragion poetica libri due*. In *Scritti critici e teorici*. Ed. A. Quondam. Bari: Laterza, 1973.

Grotius, Hugo. *De Veritate Religionis Christianae*. Lugduni: I. Maire, 1640.

———. *The Law of War and Peace*. (*De Jure Belli ac Pacis Libri Tres*.) Trans. Francis W. Kelsey. Oxford: Clarendon Press, 1925.

———. *Via ad Pacem Ecclesiasticam*. Paris, 1642.

Guicciardini, Francesco. *Scritti politici e ricordi*. Ed. R. Palmarocchi. Bari: Laterza, 1933.

———. *Storia d'Italia*. Ed. G. Panigata. 5 vols. Bari: Laterza, 1928.

———. *Hermes Trismegiste*. Ed. A.-J. Festugiere. 4th ed. 4 vols. Paris: Belles Lettres, 1983.

———. *Hermetica*. Ed. and trans. Brian P. Copenhaver. Cambridge: Cambridge University Press, 1992.

Hobbes, Thomas. *The English Works of Thomas Hobbes*. 11 vols. Ed. Sir W. Molesworth. London: John Bohn, 1839. Rep. Scientia Verlag Allen. Germany, 1966. (*Leviathan*, Vol. 3).

Homer. *The Odyssey*. Loeb Classical Library. Trans. A. T. Murray. Rev. G. E. Dimock. Cambridge, Mass.: Harvard University Press, 1925.

Iamblichus. *I misteri egiziani*. Ed. Angelo Sodano. Milan: Rusconi, 1984.

———. *On the Mysteries*. Trans. Thomas Taylor. San Diego: Wizards Bookshelf, 1984.

Isidore of Seville. *Etymologiarum Sive Originum Libri XX*. Ed. W. M. Lindsay. 2 vols. Oxford: Clarendon Press, 1911.

Kircher, Athanasius. *Musurgia Universalis*. 2 vols. Rome, 1650.

———. *Oedipus Aegyptiacus*. 3 vols. Rome, 1652–54.

———. *Polygraphia nova*. Rome, 1663.

———. *Turris Babel*. Amsterdam, 1679.

Le Clerc, Jean. *Ars critica, in qua ad studia linguarum latinae, graecae, et hebraicae via munitur*. Lugduni: Luchtmans, 1778.

Lipsius, Iustus. *Politicorum Sive Civilis Doctrinae Libri Sex*. Frankfurt, 1590.

———. *Sixe Bookes of Politikes or Civil Doctrine*. Trans. William Jones. London, 1594.

Locke, John. *An Essay Concerning Human Understanding*. Ed. P. H. Niddich. Oxford: Clarendon Press, 1975.

———. *Two Treatises of Government*. Ed. Peter Laslett. Cambridge: Cambridge University Press, 1963.

Lucretius. *De rerum natura*. Loeb Classical Library. Trans. W. H. D. Rouse. Cambridge, Mass.: Harvard University Press, 1966.

Machiavelli, Niccolò. *Tutte le opere.* Ed. Mario Martelli. Florence: Sansoni, 1971.

Malebranche, Nicolas. *Oeuvres completes.* 20 tomes and index. Ed. Andre Robinet. Paris: Librairie J. Vrin, 1958–70. (*De la recherche de la verite.* Ed. Genevieve Rodis-Lewis. In Vols. 1, 2, and 3.)

Muratori, Lodovico. *Della forza della fantasia umana.* Venice: Pasquali, 1745.

———. *Della perfetta poesia italiana.* Ed. Ada Ruschini. Milan: Marzorati, 1971–72.

Pascal, Blaise. *Pensées.* Paris: Garnier Freres, 1964.

Patrizi da Cherso, Francesco. *Della poetica.* Ed. Danilo Aguzzi Barbagli. 3 vols. Florence, 1969–71.

Petrarca, Francesco. *Posteritati.* In *Prose.* Ed. G. Martellotti. La letteratura italiana: Storia e testi. Milan-Naples: Ricciardi, 1955.

Pico della Mirandola, Giovanni. *Opera Omnia.* (*De Hominis Dignitate. Heptaplus. De Ente et Uno. Apologia.* Ed. E. Garin. 2 vols. Turin: Bottega d'Erasmo, 1971.

Plato. *The Collected Dialogues of Plato.* Eds. Edith Hamilton and Huntington Cairns. Bollingen Series 71. 1961. Reprint. Princeton, N.J.: Princeton University Press, 1971.

———. *Platonis Opera.* Ed. J. Burnett. 5 vols. Oxford: Clarendon Press, 1905.

Pliny. *Natural History.* Loeb Classical Library. Cambridge, Mass.: Harvard University Press, 1938.

Polybius. *The General History in Five Books.* Trans. Mr. Hampton. London: J. Hughs, 1756.

Possevino, Giovanni Battista. *Dialogo dell'honore di Giovanni Battista Possevino.* Venice: Gabriel Giolito de Ferrari, 1553.

Quintilian. *Institutio oratoria.* Loeb Classical Library. Trans. H. E. Butler. Cambridge, Mass.: Harvard University Press, 1969.

Ribadeneira, Pedro de. *Tratados de la religion y virtudes que debe tener el principe cristiano para gobernar y conservar sus estados, contra lo que Nicolas Maquiavelo y los politicos deste tiempo ensenan.* In *Obras escogidas del Padre Pedro de Rivadeneira.* Ed. Don Vicente de la Fuente, pp. 449–587. Madrid, 1868.

Scribani, Carlo. *Politico-Christianus.* Antwerp, 1624.

Seneca. *Naturales quaestiones.* Loeb Classical Library. Trans. Thomas H. Corcoran. Cambridge, Mass.: Harvard University Press, 1971.

Spinoza, Benedict de. *A Theologico-Political Treatise: A Political Treatise.* Trans. R. H. M. Elwes. New York: Dover, 1951.

Tacitus. *The Complete Works of Tacitus.* Trans. Alfred J. Church and William J. Brodribb. Ed. Moses Hadas. New York, 1942.

———. *Cornelii Taciti Annalium ab excessu divi Augusti libri.* Ed. C. D. Fischer. Scriptorum Classicorum Bibliotheca Oxoniensis. London, 1906.

Tasso, Torquato. *La Gerusalemme liberata.* Ed. Fredi Chiappelli. Florence: Salani, 1957.

Tesauro, Emanuele. *Il cannocchiale aristotelico.* Reprint of Turin 1670 ed. Ed. August Buck. Bad Homburg, 1968.

Varro, *On the Latin Language.* Loeb Classical Library. 2 vols. Trans. Roland G. Kent. Cambridge, Mass.: Harvard University Press, 1928.

Vitoria, Francisco de. *Obras de Francisco de Vitoria: Relecciones teologicas.* Biblioteca de autores cristianos. Ed. Teofilo Urdanoz. Madrid, 1960.

time, 21, 36–37, 124, 148
Toffanin, G., 20n
Torricelli, E., 60
Torrini, M., 189n
Torno, G., 234
Toulmin, S., 132n, 198n
tradition, 247
tragedy, 14, 174–76. *See also* law
tree of knowledge, 10
Trinkaus, C., 115n
tropes, 203
truth, 147–48, 158, 169, 225
Turner, F., 44n

Ulysses, 88–89, 99, 139
unity, 11. *See also* whole, the
universale fantastico, 8
university, 5, 31, 40–64; critique of, 54; curriculum, 49; marginal/liminal structure, 44, 46, 51, 63–64; and modernity, 58; of Naples, 48–49; and politics, 63–64
utopia, 47–49, 62, 87, 217–18

Valla, G., 97
Valla, L., 30, 37, 70, 148, 248 and n, 249–50
Varro, 238
Vasoli, C., 24n, 44n, 97n, 250n
Vaughan, F., 183n
Venturi, F., 183n, 236n
Verene, D. P., 21n, 23n, 108n, 122n
Verger, J., 45n
Vergerius, 47
Vergil, 30, 59, 135
Vico, G. B. (works by): "Affetti di un disperato," 17, 191; *Ancient Wisdom,* 119, 121; *Autobiography,* 11, 12, 16–39, 78, 121–22; *De antiquissima Italorum sapientia ex linguae latinae originibus eruenda (Ancient Wisdom),* 119, 121; *De Mente Heroica (On the Heroic Mind),* 10, 12, 44, 46, 59–63, 95–96, 132; *De nostri temporis studiorum ratione (On the*

Study Methods of Our Time), 4, 9, 12, 33, 37, 44–46, 52–57, 63–64, 132; *De Parthenopea coniuratione (The Neapolitan Conspiracy),* 4, 12, 66, 69–76, 192; *De rebus gestis Antonii Caraphei (The Life of Antonio Carafa),* 4, 12, 13, 17, 66, 69–70, 76–92; *De universi iuris uno principio, et fine Uno,* 8, 16, 33, 92–93, 95, 122, 164, 176; "In morte di Donn'Angela Cimmino," 17, 35; *Inaugural Orations,* 12, 33, 44–50, 52, 54, 70; *New Science (Scienza nuova prima),* 95; *New Science (Scienza nuova seconda),* 95–255; "Practic of the *New Science,*" 229
vita activa, 51, 102; *vita contemplativa,* 51
Vitoria, F. de, 167
Vives, L., 47
Vlastos, G., 224n
Vossius, G., 53, 102, 245

Walker, D. P., 115n
Weinberg, B., 109n, 140n
Weinberger, J., 189n, 213n
Whiston, W., 132n
White, H., 179n
Whitman, C. T., 151n
Whitney, C., 104n
whole, the, 5, 10–11, 53, 55
Wilcox, D. J., 238n
Wilde, O., 224n
Wind, E., 116n
wisdom, 9, 33, 44, 52, 62, 93, 214, 217; Egyptian, 117–19; poetic, 10, 98–99
Wittkower, R., 137n
Witz, H., 239
wonder, 108–9, 111, 231 and n, 253
work, 19, 227

Yates, F., 115n, 116n

Zabarella, G., 97
Zambelli, P., 183n
Zampaglione, G., 85n
Zeno, 182